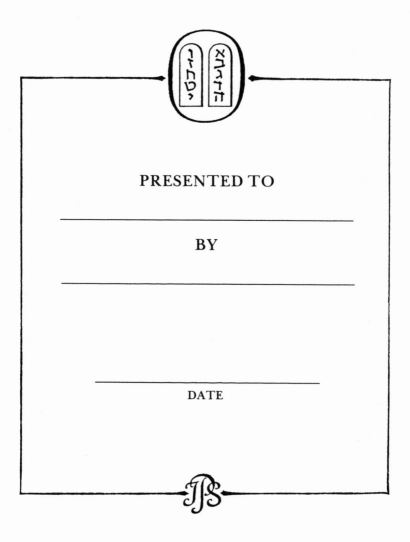

PRESENTED TO

_____

BY

_____




_____

DATE

# THE TORAH

# תורה

## THE FIVE BOOKS OF MOSES

# THE TORAH

# תורה

## THE FIVE BOOKS OF MOSES

*A new translation of*
# THE HOLY SCRIPTURES
*according to the Masoretic text*
FIRST SECTION

THE JEWISH PUBLICATION SOCIETY
*PHILADELPHIA / JERUSALEM*

Library of Congress Catalog Card Information
Bible. O.T. Pentateuch. English. Jewish Publication Society.
1963, 1992.
    The Torah: the five books of Moses. 3d ed.
    ISBN 0-8276-0015-1
    A new translation of the Holy Scriptures according to the
Masoritic text. First section.

BS1223 1963          222'.1'052          62-12948

This printing incorporates many revisions and additions
reflecting recent archaeological and scholarly research. The
text is consistent with the 1993 printing of the JPS TANAKH.

20  19  18  17  16  15  14  13  12  11  10  9  8  7  6  5  4

# PREFACE

The Jewish Publication Society of America produced its first translation of the Bible in 1917. It was quickly accepted by English-speaking Jews the world over; it is still in use and will no doubt continue to be widely favored. Nevertheless, the need for a new translation has been obvious for years.

For one thing, it is possible—and therefore necessary—to improve substantially on earlier versions in rendering both the shades of meaning of words and expressions and the force of grammatical forms and constructions. This can be done partly with the help of neglected insights of ancient and medieval Jewish scholarship, and partly by utilizing the new knowledge of the ancient, as well as of the more recent, Near East. For significant advances have been made during the past half century in biblical archaeology and in the recovery of the languages and civilizations of the peoples among whom the Israelites lived and whose modes of living and thinking they largely shared. In accuracy alone we believe this translation has vastly improved on the first JPS translation in literally hundreds of passages.

Secondly, because the Bible is an eternal book, it must be made intelligible to every generation. The King James Version, upon which almost all English translations of the Bible have hitherto been based, had an archaic flavor even for its readers in the year 1611, when it was first published. Moreover, it rendered the Hebrew to a considerable extent word for word rather than idiomatically, a procedure which nearly always results in quaintness or awkwardness and not infrequently in obscurity. A translation which is stilted where the original is natural, heavy where the original is graceful, or obscure where the original is perfectly intelligible, is the very opposite of faithful.

These were the primary reasons that the Trustees and the

Publication Committee of The Jewish Publication Society decided to have a new translation prepared. Dr. Harry M.
Orlinsky, Professor of Bible at the Hebrew Union College–
Jewish Institute of Religion, who had urged this undertaking
upon the Society, was asked to serve as editor-in-chief. To serve
with him as fellow editors, the Society invited two eminent
scholars: Dr. H. L. Ginsberg, Professor of Bible at the Jewish
Theological Seminary, and Dr. Ephraim A. Speiser, head of the
Department of Semitic and Oriental Languages at the Uni-
versity of Pennsylvania. The Society further associated with
them three learned rabbis familiar with the use of the Bible in
the synagogue and home: Rabbis Max Arzt, Bernard J.
Bamberger, and Harry Freedman, belonging to the three sections of organized Jewish religious life. Subsequently, Dr.
Freedman left the United States to assume a rabbinic post in
Australia; but, despite his inability to attend sessions, he has
participated actively in the committee's work. Dr. Solomon
Grayzel, editor of The Jewish Publication Society, served as sec-
retary of the committee.

Messrs. Louis E. Levinthal, Sol Satinsky, Edwin Wolf, 2nd,
and Lesser Zussman, by virtue of their positions in the Society,
participated in the solution of the committee's problems.

The committee carried on its work through meetings and
correspondence. Dr. Orlinsky prepared a draft translation
which was circulated among the seven working members, each
of whom made comments and suggested changes. These were in
turn circulated among the members who then, at periodic meetings, arrived at decisions by majority vote.

While the committee profited from the work of previous
translators, the present rendering is not a revision but essen-
tially a new translation. A few of its characteristics may be noted.
The committee undertook faithfully to follow the traditional
(Masoretic) text. There were certain points, however, at which
footnotes appeared necessary: 1) where the committee had to
admit that it did not understand a word or passage; 2) where an
alternative rendering was possible; 3) where an old rendering,
no longer retained, was so well known that it would very likely
be missed, in which case the traditional translation was given in

the name of "others," usually as found in the Society's version of 1917; 4) where the understanding of a passage could be facilitated by reference to another passage elsewhere in the Bible; 5) where textual variants are to be found in some of the ancient manuscripts or versions of the Bible.

Obsolete words and phrases were avoided; and Hebrew idioms were translated, in so far as possible, by means of their normal English equivalents. For the second person singular, the modern "you" was used, even when referring to the Deity ("You"), rather than the archaic "thou" ("Thou"). A further obvious difference between this translation and most of the older ones may be noted in the rendering of Hebrew particle *waw*, which is usually translated "and." The Hebrew Bible style demanded its frequent use. But in that style it had the force, not only of "and," but also of "however," "but," "yet," "when," and any number of such other words and particles, or of none at all that can be translated into English. Always to render it as "and" is to misrepresent the Hebrew rather than be faithful to it. Consequently, the committee translated the particle as the sense required, or left it untranslated.

The chapter and verse divisions found in the printed Bible are indispensable as a system of precise reference, but they do not always coincide with the organic divisions of the text. The chapter divisions, whose origin is neither ancient nor Jewish but medieval Christian, sometimes join or separate the wrong paragraphs, sentences, or even parts of sentences. The verse divisions, though considerably older and of Jewish origin, sometimes join together parts of different sentences or separate from each other parts of the same sentence. It is not surprising that Rav Saadia Gaon, the brilliant scholar who translated the Bible into Arabic in the tenth century, paid no attention to the chapter divisions, since they did not exist in his day. More noteworthy is the readiness with which he joined separate verses of the Masoretic text (whose authority he did not question) into single sentences when the sense required it. Thus, in joining Gen. 7.24 and 8.1 into a single sentence, the present translation is merely following the example of Saadia. The attentive reader will discover the other instances in which the translators have not hesitated to follow what they considered to be the logical conventional chapters and verses. These, however, are marked and numbered throughout.

Neither the trustees of the Society nor the translators suspected that the task was of such magnitude as quickly became apparent. It is, however, the hope of all those who have had a share in the work that the translation of the other two parts of the Holy Scriptures—the Prophets and the Writings—will be completed within a reasonable period of time and that the results of our labors will find favor with God and man.

The Jewish Publication Society
of America

ערב ראש השנה התשכ"ג

September 28, 1962


## PREFACE TO THE SECOND EDITION

The Trustees of The Jewish Publication Society and the Committee of Translators are grateful for the hundreds of suggestions and scores of reviews which this translation of the Torah evoked. The simpler improvements and the inevitable errors were corrected in the successive reprintings. The translators thought it necessary, however, for the sake of greater clarity and faithfulness to the Hebrew text, to subject their work to a thorough re-examination. They incorporated those substantive changes of whose need they had become convinced. Consequently, this second edition, while adhering to the same policies and principles of Bible translation that were followed in the first edition, occasionally differs from it in phrasing and sometimes in meaning.

One of those who took a leading part in the translation of the Torah did not participate in this revision. Ephraim A. Speiser departed this life in June of 1965. His memory will be for a blessing.

February 1, 1967                                                    JPS

# CONTENTS

## THE FIVE BOOKS OF THE TORAH

בראשית GENESIS 1–99

שמות EXODUS 101–183

ויקרא LEVITICUS 185–245

במדבר NUMBERS 247–330

דברים DEUTERONOMY 331–405

# TABLE OF SCRIPTURAL READINGS

**GENESIS**

| | |
|---|---|
| 1.1–6.8 בראשית | 3–12 |
| 6.9–11.32 נח | 12–20 |
| 12.1–17.27 לך לך | 21–29 |
| 18.1–22.24 וירא | 29–38 |
| 23.1–25.18 חיי שרה | 38–45 |
| 25.19–28.9 תולדת | 45–51 |
| 28.10–32.3 ויצא | 51–60 |
| 32.4–36.43 וישלח | 60–69 |
| 37.1–40.23 וישב | 69–76 |
| 41.1–44.17 מקץ | 76–86 |
| 44.18–47.27 ויגש | 86–93 |
| 47.28–50.26 ויחי | 93–99 |

**EXODUS**

| | |
|---|---|
| 1.1–6.1 שמות | 103–111 |
| 6.2–9.35 וארא | 111–119 |
| 10.1–13.16 בא | 119–126 |
| 13.17–17.16 בשלח | 127–135 |
| 18.1–20.23 יתרו | 136–141 |
| 21.1–24.18 משפטים | 141–148 |
| 25.1–27.19 תרומה | 148–154 |
| 27.20–30.10 תצוה | 154–161 |
| 30.11–34.35 כי תשא | 161–170 |
| 35.1–38.20 ויקהל | 170–177 |
| 38.21–40.38 פקודי | 178–183 |

LEVITICUS

| | |
|---|---|
| ויקרא 1.1–5.26 | 187–195 |
| צו 6.1–8.36 | 195–202 |
| שמיני 9.1–11.47 | 202–208 |
| תזריע 12.1–13.59 | 208–212 |
| מצרע 14.1–15.33 | 213–219 |
| אחרי מות 16.1–18.30 | 219–224 |
| קדשים 19.1–20.27 | 225–229 |
| אמר 21.1–24.23 | 229–237 |
| בהר 25.1–26.2 | 237–240 |
| בחקתי 26.3–27.34 | 240–245 |

NUMBERS

| | |
|---|---|
| במדבר 1.1–4.20 | 249–258 |
| נשא 4.21–7.89 | 258–269 |
| בהעלתך 8.1–12.16 | 269–278 |
| שלח לך 13.1–15.41 | 278–285 |
| קרח 16.1–18.32 | 285–292 |
| חקת 19.1–22.1 | 292–298 |
| בלק 22.2–25.9 | 298–306 |
| פינחס 25.10–30.1 | 307–316 |
| מטות 30.2–32.42 | 316–323 |
| מסעי 33.1–36.13 | 323–330 |

DEUTERONOMY

| | |
|---|---|
| דברים 1.1–3.22 | 333–340 |
| ואתחנן 3.23–7.11 | 340–349 |
| עקב 7.12–11.25 | 349–358 |
| ראה 11.26–16.17 | 358–367 |
| שפטים 16.18–21.9 | 367–374 |
| כי תצא 21.10–25.19 | 374–382 |
| כי תבוא 26.1–29.8 | 382–390 |
| נצבים 29.9–30.20 | 391–393 |
| וילך 31.1–30 | 394–396 |
| האזינו 32.1–52 | 396–401 |
| וזאת הברכה 33.1–34.12 | 401–405 |

# בראשית
# GENESIS

# בראשית
# GENESIS

1 When God began to create<sup>a</sup> heaven and earth—²the earth being unformed and void, with darkness over the surface of the deep and a wind from<sup>b</sup> God sweeping over the water—³God said, "Let there be light"; and there was light. ⁴God saw that the light was good, and God separated the light from the darkness. ⁵God called the light Day, and the darkness He called Night. And there was evening and there was morning, a first day.<sup>c</sup>

⁶God said, "Let there be an expanse in the midst of the water, that it may separate water from water." ⁷God made the expanse, and it separated the water which was below the expanse from the water which was above the expanse. And it was so. ⁸God called the expanse Sky. And there was evening and there was morning, a second day.

⁹God said, "Let the water below the sky be gathered into one area, that the dry land may appear." And it was so. ¹⁰God called the dry land Earth, and the gathering of waters He called Seas. And God saw that this was good. ¹¹And God said, "Let the earth sprout vegetation: seed-bearing plants, fruit trees of every kind on earth that bear fruit with the seed in it." And it was so. ¹²The earth brought forth vegetation: seed-bearing plants of every kind, and trees of every kind bearing fruit with the seed in it. And God saw that this was good. ¹³And there was evening and there was morning, a third day.

¹⁴God said, "Let there be lights in the expanse of the sky to separate day from night; they shall serve as signs for the set times—the days and the years; ¹⁵and they shall serve as lights in the expanse of the sky to shine upon the earth." And it was so.

<sup>a</sup> *Others "In the beginning God created"*
<sup>b</sup> *Others "the spirit of"*
<sup>c</sup> *Others "one day"*

3

[16]God made the two great lights, the greater light to dominate the day and the lesser light to dominate the night, and the stars. [17]And God set them in the expanse of the sky to shine upon the earth, [18]to dominate the day and the night, and to separate light from darkness. And God saw that this was good. [19]And there was evening and there was morning, a fourth day.

[20]God said, "Let the waters bring forth swarms of living creatures, and birds that fly above the earth across the expanse of the sky." [21]God created the great sea monsters, and all the living creatures of every kind that creep, which the waters brought forth in swarms, and all the winged birds of every kind. And God saw that this was good. [22]God blessed them, saying, "Be fertile and increase, fill the waters in the seas, and let the birds increase on the earth." [23]And there was evening and there was morning, a fifth day.

[24]God said, "Let the earth bring forth every kind of living creature: cattle, creeping things, and wild beasts of every kind." And it was so. [25]God made wild beasts of every kind and cattle of every kind, and all kinds of creeping things of the earth. And God saw that this was good. [26]And God said, "Let us make man in our image, after our likeness. They shall rule the fish of the sea, the birds of the sky, the cattle, the whole earth, and all the creeping things that creep on earth." [27]And God created man in His image, in the image of God He created him; male and female He created them. [28]God blessed them and God said to them, "Be fertile and increase, fill the earth and master it; and rule the fish of the sea, the birds of the sky, and all the living things that creep on earth."

[29]God said, "See, I give you every seed-bearing plant that is upon all the earth, and every tree that has seed-bearing fruit; they shall be yours for food. [30]And to all the animals on land, to all the birds of the sky, and to everything that creeps on earth, in which there is the breath of life, [I give] all the green plants for food." And it was so. [31]And God saw all that He had made, and

found it very good. And there was evening and there was morning, the sixth day.

# 2

The heaven and the earth were finished, and all their array. [2]On the seventh day God finished the work that He had been doing, and He ceased[a] on the seventh day from all the work that He had done. [3]And God blessed the seventh day and declared it holy, because on it God ceased from all the work of creation that He had done. [4]Such is the story of heaven and earth when they were created.

When the LORD God made earth and heaven—[5]when no shrub of the field was yet on earth and no grasses of the field had yet sprouted, because the LORD God had not sent rain upon the earth and there was no man to till the soil, [6]but a flow would well up from the ground and water the whole surface of the earth—[7]the LORD God formed man[b] from the dust of the earth.[c] He blew into his nostrils the breath of life, and man became a living being.

[8]The LORD God planted a garden in Eden, in the east, and placed there the man whom He had formed. [9]And from the ground the LORD God caused to grow every tree that was pleasing to the sight and good for food, with the tree of life in the middle of the garden, and the tree of knowledge of good and bad.

[10]A river issues from Eden to water the garden, and it then divides and becomes four branches. [11]The name of the first is Pishon, the one that winds through the whole land of Havilah, where the gold is. ([12]The gold of that land is good; bdellium is there, and lapis lazuli.[d]) [13]The name of the second river is Gihon, the one that winds through the whole land of Cush. [14]The name of the third river is Tigris, the one that flows east of Asshur. And the fourth river is the Euphrates.

[15]The LORD God took the man and placed him in the garden

---

[a] Or "rested"
[b] Heb 'adam
[c] Heb 'adamah
[d] Others "onyx"; meaning of Heb shoham uncertain

of Eden, to till it and tend it. ¹⁶And the LORD God commanded the man, saying, "Of every tree of the garden you are free to eat; ¹⁷but as for the tree of knowledge of good and bad, you must not eat of it; for as soon as you eat of it, you shall die."

¹⁸The LORD God said, "It is not good for man to be alone; I will make a fitting helper for him." ¹⁹And the LORD God formed out of the earth all the wild beasts and all the birds of the sky, and brought them to the man to see what he would call them; and whatever the man called each living creature, that would be its name. ²⁰And the man gave names to all the cattle and to the birds of the sky and to all the wild beasts; but for Adam no fitting helper was found. ²¹So the LORD God cast a deep sleep upon the man; and, while he slept, He took one of his ribs and closed up the flesh at that spot. ²²And the LORD God fashioned the rib that He had taken from the man into a woman; and He brought her to the man. ²³Then the man said,

"This one at last
Is bone of my bones
And flesh of my flesh.
This one shall be called Woman,ᵉ
For from manᶠ was she taken."

²⁴Hence a man leaves his father and mother and clings to his wife, so that they become one flesh.

**3** ²⁵The two of them were naked,ᵍ the man and his wife, yet they felt no shame. ¹Now the serpent was the shrewdest of all the wild beasts that the LORD God had made. He said to the woman, "Did God really say: You shall not eat of any tree of the garden?" ²The woman replied to the serpent, "We may eat of the fruit of the other trees of the garden. ³It is only about fruit of the tree in the middle of the garden that God said: 'You shall not eat of it or touch it, lest you die.'" ⁴And the serpent said to the woman, "You are not going to die, ⁵but God knows that as soon as you eat of it your eyes will be opened and you will be like ᵃ⁻divine

---

ᵉ *Heb* 'ishshah
ᶠ *Heb* 'ish
ᵍ *Heb* 'arummim, *play on* 'arum *"shrewd" in 3.1*
ᵃ⁻ᵃ *Others "God, who knows"*

beings who know-*a* good and bad." ⁶When the woman saw that the tree was good for eating and a delight to the eyes, and that the tree was desirable as a source of wisdom, she took of its fruit and ate. She also gave some to her husband, and he ate. ⁷Then the eyes of both of them were opened and they perceived that they were naked; and they sewed together fig leaves and made themselves loincloths.

⁸They heard the sound of the LORD God moving about in the garden at the breezy time of day; and the man and his wife hid from the LORD God among the trees of the garden. ⁹The LORD God called out to the man and said to him, "Where are you?" ¹⁰He replied, "I heard the sound of You in the garden, and I was afraid because I was naked, so I hid." ¹¹Then He asked, "Who told you that you were naked? Did you eat of the tree from which I had forbidden you to eat?" ¹²The man said, "The woman You put at my side—she gave me of the tree, and I ate." ¹³And the LORD God said to the woman, "What is this you have done!" The woman replied, "The serpent duped me, and I ate." ¹⁴Then the LORD God said to the serpent,

> "Because you did this,
> More cursed shall you be
> Than all cattle
> And all the wild beasts:
> On your belly shall you crawl
> And dirt shall you eat
> All the days of your life.
> ¹⁵I will put enmity
> Between you and the woman,
> And between your offspring and hers;
> They shall strike at your head,
> And you shall strike at their heel."

¹⁶And to the woman He said,

> "I will make most severe
> Your pangs in childbearing;

> In pain shall you bear children.
> Yet your urge shall be for your husband,
> And he shall rule over you."

¹⁷To Adam He said, "Because you did as your wife said and ate of the tree about which I commanded you, 'You shall not eat of it,'

> Cursed be the ground because of you;
> By toil shall you eat of it
> All the days of your life:
> ¹⁸Thorns and thistles shall it sprout for you.
> But your food shall be the grasses of the field;
> ¹⁹By the sweat of your brow
> Shall you get bread to eat,
> Until you return to the ground—
> For from it you were taken.
> For dust you are,
> And to dust you shall return."

²⁰The man named his wife Eve,ᵇ because she was the mother of all the living.ᶜ ²¹And the LORD God made garments of skins for Adam and his wife, and clothed them.

²²And the LORD God said, "Now that the man has become like one of us, knowing good and bad, what if he should stretch out his hand and take also from the tree of life and eat, and live forever!" ²³So the LORD God banished him from the garden of Eden, to till the soil from which he was taken. ²⁴He drove the man out, and stationed east of the garden of Eden the cherubim and the fiery ever-turning sword, to guard the way to the tree of life.

4 Now the man knew his wife Eve,ᵃ and she conceived and bore Cain, saying, "I have gainedᵇ a male child with the help of the LORD." ²She then bore his brother Abel. Abel became a keeper of sheep, and Cain became a tiller of the soil. ³In the

---

ᵇ *Heb* ḥawwah
ᶜ *Heb* ḥay

ᵃ *Heb* yadaʿ *often in a sexual sense*
ᵇ *Heb* qanithi, *connected with "Cain"*

course of time, Cain brought an offering to the LORD from the fruit of the soil; ⁴and Abel, for his part, brought the choicest of the firstlings of his flock. The LORD paid heed to Abel and his offering, ⁵but to Cain and his offering He paid no heed. Cain was much distressed and his face fell. ⁶And the Lord said to Cain,

"Why are you distressed,
And why is your face fallen?
⁷ᶜSurely, if you do right,
There is uplift.
But if you do not do right
Sin couches at the door;
Its urge is toward you,
Yet you can be its master."

⁸Cain said to his brother Abelᵈ ... and when they were in the field, Cain set upon his brother Abel and killed him. ⁹The LORD said to Cain, "Where is your brother Abel?" And he said, "I do not know. Am I my brother's keeper?" ¹⁰Then He said, "What have you done? Hark, your brother's blood cries out to Me from the ground! ¹¹Therefore, you shall be more cursed than the ground,ᵉ which opened its mouth to receive your brother's blood from your hand. ¹²If you till the soil, it shall no longer yield its strength to you. You shall become a ceaseless wanderer on earth."

¹³Cain said to the LORD, "My punishment is too great to bear! ¹⁴Since You have banished me this day from the soil, and I must avoid Your presence and become a restless wanderer on earth —anyone who meets me may kill me!" ¹⁵The LORD said to him, "I promise, if anyone kills Cain, sevenfold vengeance shall be taken on him." And the LORD put a mark on Cain, lest anyone who met him should kill him. ¹⁶Cain left the presence of the LORD and settled in the land of Nod, east of Eden.

¹⁷Cain knew his wife, and she conceived and bore Enoch. And he then founded a city, and named the city after his son Enoch.

---

ᶜ *Meaning of verse uncertain*
ᵈ *Ancient versions, including the Targum, read "Come, let us go out into the field"*
ᵉ *See 3.17*

¹⁸To Enoch was born Irad, and Irad begot Mehujael, and Mehujael*ᶠ* begot Methusael, and Methusael begot Lamech. ¹⁹Lamech took to himself two wives: the name of the one was Adah, and the name of the other was Zillah. ²⁰Adah bore Jabal; he was the ancestor of those who dwell in tents and amidst herds. ²¹And the name of his brother was Jubal; he was the ancestor of all who play the lyre and the pipe. ²²As for Zillah, she bore Tubal-cain, who forged all implements of copper and iron. And the sister of Tubal-cain was Naamah.

²³And Lamech said to his wives,

"Adah and Zillah, hear my voice;
O wives of Lamech, give ear to my speech.
I have slain a man for wounding me,
And a lad for bruising me.
²⁴If Cain is avenged sevenfold,
Then Lamech seventy-sevenfold."

²⁵Adam knew his wife again, and she bore a son and named him Seth, meaning, "God has *ᵍ⁻*provided me with*⁻ᵍ* another offspring in place of Abel," for Cain had killed him. ²⁶And to Seth, in turn, a son was born, and he named him Enosh. It was then that men began to invoke the LORD by name.

**5** This is the record of Adam's line.—When God created man, He made him in the likeness of God; ²male and female He created them. And when they were created, He blessed them and called them Man.—³When Adam had lived 130 years, he begot a son in his likeness after his image, and he named him Seth. ⁴After the birth of Seth, Adam lived 800 years and begot sons and daughters. ⁵All the days that Adam lived came to 930 years; then he died.

⁶When Seth had lived 105 years, he begot Enosh. ⁷After the birth of Enosh, Seth lived 807 years and begot sons and daughters. ⁸All the days of Seth came to 912 years; then he died.

⁹When Enosh had lived 90 years, he begot Kenan.¹⁰After the birth of Kenan, Enosh lived 815 years and begot sons and

ᶠ *Heb* Meḥijael
ᵍ⁻ᵍ *Or "established for me"; Heb* shath, *connected with "Seth"*

daughters. [11]All the days of Enosh came to 905 years; then he died.

[12]When Kenan had lived 70 years, he begot Mahalalel. [13]After the birth of Mahalalel, Kenan lived 840 years and begot sons and daughters. [14]All the days of Kenan came to 910 years; then he died.

[15]When Mahalalel had lived 65 years, he begot Jared. [16]After the birth of Jared, Mahalalel lived 830 years and begot sons and daughters. [17]All the days of Mahalalel came to 895 years; then he died.

[18]When Jared had lived 162 years, he begot Enoch. [19]After the birth of Enoch, Jared lived 800 years and begot sons and daughters. [20]All the days of Jared came to 962 years; then he died.

[21]When Enoch had lived 65 years, he begot Methuselah. [22]After the birth of Methuselah, Enoch walked with God 300 years; and he begot sons and daughters. [23]All the days of Enoch came to 365 years. [24]Enoch walked with God; then he was no more, for God took him.

[25]When Methuselah had lived 187 years, he begot Lamech. [26]After the birth of Lamech, Methuselah lived 782 years and begot sons and daughters. [27]All the days of Methuselah came to 969 years; then he died.

[28]When Lamech had lived 182 years, he begot a son. [29]And he named him Noah, saying, "This one will provide us relief[a] from our work and from the toil of our hands, out of the very soil which the LORD placed under a curse." [30]After the birth of Noah, Lamech lived 595 years and begot sons and daughters. [31]All the days of Lamech came to 777 years; then he died.

[32]When Noah had lived 500 years, Noah begot Shem, Ham, and Japheth.

6 When men began to increase on earth and daughters were born to them, [2]the divine beings[a] saw how beautiful the daughters of men were and took wives from among those that pleased

---

[a] *Connecting Noah with Heb* niḥam *"to comfort"; cf. 9.20 ff.*

[a] *Others "the sons of God"*

them.—³The Lᴏʀᴅ said, "My breath shall not abide*b* in man forever, since he too is flesh; let the days allowed him be one hundred and twenty years."—⁴It was then, and later too, that the Nephilim appeared on earth—when the divine beings cohabited with the daughters of men, who bore them offspring. They were the heroes of old, the men of renown.

⁵The Lᴏʀᴅ saw how great was man's wickedness on earth, and how every plan devised by his mind was nothing but evil all the time. ⁶And the Lᴏʀᴅ regretted that He had made man on earth, and His heart was saddened. ⁷The Lord said, "I will blot out from the earth the men whom I created—men together with beasts, creeping things, and birds of the sky; for I regret that I made them." ⁸But Noah found favor with the Lᴏʀᴅ.

נח

⁹This is the line of Noah.—Noah was a righteous man; he was blameless in his age; Noah walked with God.—¹⁰Noah begot three sons: Shem, Ham, and Japheth.

¹¹The earth became corrupt before God; the earth was filled with lawlessness. ¹²When God saw how corrupt the earth was, for all flesh had corrupted its ways on earth, ¹³God said to Noah, "I have decided to put an end to all flesh, for the earth is filled with lawlessness because of them: I am about to destroy them with the earth. ¹⁴Make yourself an ark of gopher wood; make it an ark with compartments, and cover it inside and out with pitch. ¹⁵This is how you shall make it: the length of the ark shall be three hundred cubits, its width fifty cubits, and its height thirty cubits. ¹⁶Make an opening for daylight in the ark, and *c*‑terminate it within a cubit of the top.*‑c* Put the entrance to the ark in its side; make it with bottom, second, and third decks.

¹⁷"For My part, I am about to bring the Flood—waters upon the earth—to destroy all flesh under the sky in which there is breath of life; everything on earth shall perish. ¹⁸But I will establish My covenant with you, and you shall enter the ark, with your sons, your wife, and your sons' wives. ¹⁹And of all that

b *Meaning of Heb uncertain*
c-c *Meaning of Hebrew uncertain*

lives, of all flesh, you shall take two of each into the ark to keep alive with you; they shall be male and female. [20]From birds of every kind, cattle of every kind, every kind of creeping thing on earth, two of each shall come to you to stay alive. [21]For your part, take of everything that is eaten and store it away, to serve as food for you and for them." [22]Noah did so; just as God commanded him, so he did.

**7** Then the Lord said to Noah, "Go into the ark, with all your household, for you alone have I found righteous before Me in this generation. [2]Of every clean animal you shall take seven pairs, males and their mates, and of every animal that is not clean, two, a male and its mate; [3]of the birds of the sky also, seven pairs, male and female, to keep seed alive upon all the earth. [4]For in seven days' time I will make it rain upon the earth, forty days and forty nights, and I will blot out from the earth all existence that I created." [5]And Noah did just as the Lord commanded him.

[6]Noah was six hundred years old when the Flood came, waters upon the earth. [7]Noah, with his sons, his wife, and his sons' wives, went into the ark because of the waters of the Flood. [8]Of the clean animals, of the animals that are not clean, of the birds, and of everything that creeps on the ground, [9]two of each, male and female, came to Noah into the ark, as God had commanded Noah. [10]And on the seventh day the waters of the Flood came upon the earth.

[11]In the six hundredth year of Noah's life, in the second month, on the seventeenth day of the month, on that day

All the fountains of the great deep burst apart,

And the floodgates of the sky broke open.

([12]The rain fell on the earth forty days and forty nights.) [13]That same day Noah and Noah's sons, Shem, Ham, and Japheth, went into the ark, with Noah's wife and the three wives of his sons—[14]they and all beasts of every kind, all cattle of every kind, all creatures of every kind that creep on the earth, and all birds of every kind, every bird, every winged thing. [15]They came to Noah into the ark, two each of all flesh in which there was breath of life. [16]Thus they that entered comprised male and female of all flesh, as God had commanded him. And the LORD shut him in.

[17]The Flood continued forty days on the earth, and the waters increased and raised the ark so that it rose above the earth. [18]The waters swelled and increased greatly upon the earth, and the ark drifted upon the waters. [19]When the waters had swelled much more upon the earth, all the highest mountains everywhere under the sky were covered. [20]Fifteen cubits higher did the waters swell, as the mountains were covered. [21]And all flesh that stirred on earth perished—birds, cattle, beasts, and all the things that swarmed upon the earth, and all mankind. [22]All in whose nostrils was the merest breath of life, all that was on dry land, died. [23]All existence on earth was blotted out—man, cattle, creeping things, and birds of the sky; they were blotted out from the earth. Only Noah was left, and those with him in the ark.

[24]And when the waters had swelled on the earth one hundred and fifty days, [1]God remembered Noah and all the beasts and all the cattle that were with him in the ark, and God caused a wind to blow across the earth, and the waters subsided. [2]The fountains of the deep and the floodgates of the sky were stopped up, and the rain from the sky was held back; [3]the waters then receded steadily from the earth. At the end of one hundred and fifty days the waters diminished, [4]so that in the seventh month, on the seventeenth day of the month, the ark came to rest on the mountains of Ararat. [5]The waters went on diminishing until the tenth month; in the tenth month, on the first of the month, the tops of the mountains became visible.

[6]At the end of forty days, Noah opened the window of the ark that he had made [7]and sent out the raven; it went to and fro until the waters had dried up from the earth. [8]Then he sent out

the dove to see whether the waters had decreased from the surface of the ground. ⁹But the dove could not find a resting place for its foot, and returned to him to the ark, for there was water over all the earth. So putting out his hand, he took it into the ark with him. ¹⁰He waited another seven days, and again sent out the dove from the ark. ¹¹The dove came back to him toward evening, and there in its bill was a plucked-off olive leaf! Then Noah knew that the waters had decreased on the earth. ¹²He waited still another seven days and sent the dove forth; and it did not return to him any more.

¹³In the six hundred and first year, in the first month, on the first of the month, the waters began to dry from the earth; and when Noah removed the covering of the ark, he saw that the surface of the ground was drying. ¹⁴And in the second month, on the twenty-seventh day of the month, the earth was dry.

¹⁵God spoke to Noah, saying, ¹⁶"Come out of the ark, together with your wife, your sons, and your sons' wives. ¹⁷Bring out with you every living thing of all flesh that is with you: birds, animals, and everything that creeps on earth; and let them swarm on the earth and be fertile and increase on earth." ¹⁸So Noah came out, together with his sons, his wife, and his sons' wives. ¹⁹Every animal, every creeping thing, and every bird, everything that stirs on earth came out of the ark by families.

²⁰Then Noah built an altar to the LORD and, taking of every clean animal and of every clean bird, he offered burnt offerings on the altar. ²¹The LORD smelled the pleasing odor, and the LORD said to Himself: "Never again will I doom the earth because of man, since the devisings of man's mind are evil from his youth; nor will I ever again destroy every living being, as I have done.

²²So long as the earth endures,
Seedtime and harvest,
Cold and heat,
Summer and winter,
Day and night
Shall not cease."

9 God blessed Noah and his sons, and said to them, "Be fertile and increase, and fill the earth. ²The fear and the dread of you shall be upon all the beasts of the earth and upon all the birds of the sky—everything with which the earth is astir—and upon all the fish of the sea; they are given into your hand. ³Every creature that lives shall be yours to eat; as with the green grasses, I give you all these. ⁴You must not, however, eat flesh with its life-blood in it. ⁵But for your own life-blood I will require a reckoning: I will require it of every beast; of man, too, will I require a reckoning for human life, of every man for that of his fellow man!

⁶Whoever sheds the blood of man,
By man shall his blood be shed;
For in His image
Did God make man.

⁷Be fertile, then, and increase; abound on the earth and increase on it."

⁸And God said to Noah and to his sons with him, ⁹"I now establish My covenant with you and your offspring to come, ¹⁰and with every living thing that is with you—birds, cattle, and every wild beast as well—all that have come out of the ark, every living thing on earth. ¹¹I will maintain My covenant with you: never again shall all flesh be cut off by the waters of a flood, and never again shall there be a flood to destroy the earth."

¹²God further said, "This is the sign that I set for the covenant between Me and you, and every living creature with you, for all ages to come. ¹³I have set My bow in the clouds, and it shall serve as a sign of the covenant between Me and the earth. ¹⁴When I bring clouds over the earth, and the bow appears in the clouds, ¹⁵I will remember My covenant between Me and you and every living creature among all flesh, so that the waters shall never again become a flood to destroy all flesh. ¹⁶When the bow is in the clouds, I will see it and remember the everlasting covenant between God and all living creatures, all flesh that is on earth.

¹⁷That," God said to Noah, "shall be the sign of the covenant that I have established between Me and all flesh that is on earth."

¹⁸The sons of Noah who came out of the ark were Shem, Ham, and Japheth—Ham being the father of Canaan. ¹⁹These three were the sons of Noah, and from these the whole world branched out.

²⁰Noah, the tiller of the soil, was the first to plant a vineyard. ²¹He drank of the wine and became drunk, and he uncovered himself within his tent. ²²Ham, the father of Canaan, saw his father's nakedness and told his two brothers outside. ²³But Shem and Japheth took a cloth, placed it against both their backs and, walking backward, they covered their father's nakedness; their faces were turned the other way, so that they did not see their father's nakedness. ²⁴When Noah woke up from his wine and learned what his youngest son had done to him, ²⁵he said,

"Cursed be Canaan;
The lowest of slaves
Shall he be to his brothers."
²⁶And he said,
"Blessed be the LORD,
The God of Shem;
Let Canaan be a slave to them.
²⁷May God enlarge*a* Japheth,
And let him dwell in the tents of Shem;
And let Canaan be a slave to them."
²⁸Noah lived after the Flood 350 years. ²⁹And all the days of Noah came to 950 years; then he died.

10 These are the lines of Shem, Ham, and Japheth, the sons of Noah: sons were born to them after the Flood.

²The descendants of Japheth: Gomer, Magog, Madai, Javan, Tubal, Meshech, and Tiras. ³The descendants of Gomer: Ashkenaz, Riphath, and Togarmah. ⁴The descendants of Javan:

a Heb yapht, *play on Heb* yepheth *"Japheth"*

17

Elishah and Tarshish, the Kittim and the Dodanim.*a* ⁵From these the maritime nations branched out. [These are the descendants of Japheth]*b* by their lands—each with its language—their clans and their nations.

⁶The descendants of Ham: Cush, Mizraim, Put, and Canaan. ⁷The descendants of Cush: Seba, Havilah, Sabtah, Raamah, and Sabteca. The descendants of Raamah: Sheba and Dedan.

⁸Cush also begot Nimrod, who was the first man of might on earth. ⁹He was a mighty hunter by the grace of the Lord; hence the saying, "Like Nimrod a mighty hunter by the grace of the Lord." ¹⁰The mainstays of his kingdom were Babylon, Erech, Accad, and Calneh*c* in the land of Shinar. ¹¹From that land Asshur went forth and built Nineveh, Rehoboth-ir, Calah, ¹²and Resen between Nineveh and Calah, that is the great city.

¹³And Mizraim begot the Ludim, the Anamim, the Lehabim, the Naphtuhim, ¹⁴the Pathrusim, the Casluhim, and the Caphtorim,*d* whence the Philistines came forth.

¹⁵Canaan begot Sidon, his first-born, and Heth; ¹⁶and the Jebusites, the Amorites, the Girgashites, ¹⁷the Hivites, the Arkites, the Sinites, ¹⁸the Arvadites, the Zemarites, and the Hamathites. Afterward the clans of the Canaanites spread out. (¹⁹The [original] Canaanite territory extended from Sidon as far as Gerar, near Gaza, and as far as Sodom, Gomorrah, Admah, and Zeboiim, near Lasha.) ²⁰These are the descendants of Ham, according to their clans and languages, by their lands and nations.

²¹Sons were also born to Shem, ancestor of all the descendants of Eber and older brother of Japheth. ²²The descendants of Shem: Elam, Asshur, Arpachshad, Lud, and Aram. ²³The descendants of Aram: Uz, Hul, Gether, and Mash. ²⁴Arpachshad begot Shelah, and Shelah begot Eber. ²⁵Two sons were born to Eber: the name of the first was Peleg, for in his days the earth was divided*e*; and the name of his brother was Joktan. ²⁶Joktan begot Almodad, Sheleph, Hazarmaveth, Jerah, ²⁷Hadoram,

---

a *Septuagint and I Chron. 1.7 "Rodanim"*
b *Cf. vv. 20 and 31*
c *Heb* we-khalneh, *better vocalized* we-khullanah *"all of them being"*
d *I.e. the Cretans; moved up for the sake of clarity; cf. Amos 9.7*
e *Heb* niphlegah, *play on "Peleg"*

Uzal, Diklah, [28]Obal, Abimael, Sheba, [29]Ophir, Havilah, and Jobab; all these were the descendants of Joktan. [30]Their settlements extended from Mesha as far as Sephar, the hill country to the east. [31]These are the descendants of Shem according to their clans and languages, by their lands, according to their nations.

[32]These are the groupings of Noah's descendants, according to their origins, by their nations; and from these the nations branched out over the earth after the Flood.

11 Everyone on earth had the same language and the same words. [2]And as they migrated from the east, they came upon a valley in the land of Shinar and settled there. [3]They said to one another, "Come, let us make bricks and burn them hard."— Brick served them as stone, and bitumen served them as mortar. —[4]And they said, "Come, let us build us a city, and a tower with its top in the sky, to make a name for ourselves; else we shall be scattered all over the world." [5]The LORD came down to look at the city and tower that man had built, [6]and the LORD said, "If, as one people with one language for all, this is how they have begun to act, then nothing that they may propose to do will be out of their reach. [7]Let us, then, go down and confound their speech there, so that they shall not understand one another's speech." [8]Thus the LORD scattered them from there over the face of the whole earth; and they stopped building the city. [9]That is why it was called Babel,[a] because there the LORD confounded[b] the speech of the whole earth; and from there the LORD scattered them over the face of the whole earth.

[10]This is the line of Shem. Shem was 100 years old when he begot Arpachshad, two years after the Flood. [11]After the birth of[c] Arpachshad, Shem lived 500 years and begot sons and daughters.

[a] *I.e. "Babylon"*
[b] *Heb* balal *"confound," play on "Babel"*
[c] *Lit. "After he begot," and so throughout*

¹²When Arpachshad had lived 35 years, he begot Shelah. ¹³After the birth of Shelah, Arpachshad lived 403 years and begot sons and daughters.

¹⁴When Shelah had lived 30 years, he begot Eber.¹⁵After the birth of Eber, Shelah lived 403 years and begot sons and daughters.

¹⁶When Eber had lived 34 years, he begot Peleg.¹⁷After the birth of Peleg, Eber lived 430 years and begot sons and daughters.

¹⁸When Peleg had lived 30 years, he begot Reu. ¹⁹After the birth of Reu, Peleg lived 209 years and begot sons and daughters.

²⁰When Reu had lived 32 years, he begot Serug. ²¹After the birth of Serug, Reu lived 207 years and begot sons and daughters.

²²When Serug had lived 30 years, he begot Nahor.²³After the birth of Nahor, Serug lived 200 years and begot sons and daughters.

²⁴When Nahor had lived 29 years, he begot Terah.²⁵After the birth of Terah, Nahor lived 119 years and begot sons and daughters.

²⁶When Terah had lived 70 years, he begot Abram, Nahor, and Haran. ²⁷Now this is the line of Terah: Terah begot Abram, Nahor, and Haran; and Haran begot Lot. ²⁸Haran died in the lifetime of his father Terah, in his native land, Ur of the Chaldeans. ²⁹Abram and Nahor took to themselves wives, the name of Abram's wife being Sarai and that of Nahor's wife Milcah, the daughter of Haran, the father of Milcah and Iscah. ³⁰Now Sarai was barren, she had no child.

³¹Terah took his son Abram, his grandson Lot the son of Haran, and his daughter-in-law Sarai, the wife of his son Abram, and they set out together from Ur of the Chaldeans for the land of Canaan; but when they had come as far as Haran, they settled there. ³²The days of Terah came to 205 years; and Terah died in Haran.

לך לך

**12** The Lord said to Abram, "Go forth from your native land and from your father's house to the land that I will show you.

²I will make of you a great nation,
And I will bless you;
I will make your name great,
And you shall be a blessing.*ᵃ*
³I will bless those who bless you
And curse him that curses you;
And all the families of the earth
Shall bless themselves by you."

⁴Abram went forth as the Lord had commanded him, and Lot went with him. Abram was seventy-five years old when he left Haran. ⁵Abram took his wife Sarai and his brother's son Lot, and all the wealth that they had amassed, and the persons that they had acquired in Haran; and they set out for the land of Canaan. When they arrived in the land of Canaan, ⁶Abram passed through the land as far as the site of Shechem, at the terebinth of Moreh. The Canaanites were then in the land.

⁷The Lord appeared to Abram and said, "I will assign this land to your heirs." And he built an altar there to the Lord who had appeared to him. ⁸From there he moved on to the hill country east of Bethel and pitched his tent, with Bethel on the west and Ai on the east; and he built there an altar to the Lord and invoked the Lord by name. ⁹Then Abram journeyed by stages toward the Negeb.

¹⁰There was a famine in the land, and Abram went down to Egypt to sojourn there, for the famine was severe in the land. ¹¹As he was about to enter Egypt, he said to his wife Sarai, "I*ᵇ* know what a beautiful woman you are. ¹²If the Egyptians see you, and think, 'She is his wife,' they will kill me and let you live. ¹³Please say that you are my sister, that it may go well with me because of you, and that I may remain alive thanks to you."

---

ᵃ *I.e. a standard by which blessing is invoked; cf. v. 3 end*
ᵇ *Or "You"; cf. the second person feminine form -ti in Judges 5.7; Jer. 2.20; Mic. 4.13, etc.*

21

¹⁴When Abram entered Egypt, the Egyptians saw how very beautiful the woman was. ¹⁵Pharaoh's courtiers saw her and praised her to Pharaoh, and the woman was taken into Pharaoh's palace. ¹⁶And because of her, it went well with Abram; he acquired sheep, oxen, asses, male and female slaves, she-asses, and camels.

¹⁷But the LORD afflicted Pharaoh and his household with mighty plagues on account of Sarai, the wife of Abram. ¹⁸Pharaoh sent for Abram and said, "What is this you have done to me! Why did you not tell me that she was your wife? ¹⁹Why did you say, 'She is my sister,' so that I took her as my wife? Now, here is your wife; take her and begone!" ²⁰And Pharaoh put men in charge of him, and they sent him off with his wife and all that he possessed.

13 From Egypt, Abram went up into the Negeb, with his wife and all that he possessed, together with Lot. ²Now Abram was very rich in cattle, silver, and gold. ³And he proceeded by stages from the Negeb as far as Bethel, to the place where his tent had been formerly, between Bethel and Ai, ⁴the site of the altar that he had built there at first; and there Abram invoked the LORD by name.

⁵Lot, who went with Abram, also had flocks and herds and tents, ⁶so that the land could not support them staying together; for their possessions were so great that they could not remain together. ⁷And there was quarreling between the herdsmen of Abram's cattle and those of Lot's cattle.—The Canaanites and Perizzites were then dwelling in the land.—⁸Abram said to Lot, "Let there be no strife between you and me, between my herdsmen and yours, for we are kinsmen. ⁹Is not the whole land before you? Let us separate*a*: if you go north, I will go south; and if you go south, I will go north." ¹⁰Lot looked about him and saw how well watered was the whole plain of the Jordan, all of it—

---

a *Lit. "Please separate from me"*

this was before the Lord had destroyed Sodom and Gomorrah —all the way to Zoar, like the garden of the Lord, like the land of Egypt. ¹¹So Lot chose for himself the whole plain of the Jordan, and Lot journeyed eastward. Thus they parted from each other; ¹²Abram remained in the land of Canaan, while Lot settled in the cities of the Plain, pitching his tents near Sodom. ¹³Now the inhabitants of Sodom were very wicked sinners against the Lord.

¹⁴And the Lord said to Abram, after Lot had parted from him, "Raise your eyes and look out from where you are, to the north and south, to the east and west, ¹⁵for I give all the land that you see to you and your offspring forever. ¹⁶I will make your offspring as the dust of the earth, so that if one can count the dust of the earth, then your offspring too can be counted. ¹⁷Up, walk about the land, through its length and its breadth, for I give it to you." ¹⁸And Abram moved his tent, and came to dwell at the terebinths of Mamre, which are in Hebron; and he built an altar there to the Lord.

14 Now, when King Amraphel of Shinar, King Arioch of Ellasar, King Chedorlaomer of Elam, and King Tidal of Goiim ²made war on King Bera of Sodom, King Birsha of Gomorrah, King Shinab of Admah, King Shemeber of Zeboiim, and the king of Bela, which is Zoar, ³all the latter joined forces at the Valley of Siddim, now the Dead Sea.ᵃ ⁴Twelve years they served Chedorlaomer, and in the thirteenth year they rebelled. ⁵In the fourteenth year Chedorlaomer and the kings who were with him came and defeated the Rephaim at Ashteroth-karnaim, the Zuzim at Ham, the Emim at Shaveh-kiriathaim, ⁶and the Horites in their hill country of Seir as far as El-paran, which is by the wilderness. ⁷On their way back they came to En-mishpat, which is Kadesh, and subdued all the territory of the Amalekites, and also the Amorites who dwelt in Hazazon-tamar. ⁸Then the king of Sodom, the king of Gomorrah, the king of Admah, the king of Zeboiim, and the king of Bela, which is Zoar, went forth and

ᵃ *Heb "Salt Sea"*

engaged them in battle in the Valley of Siddim: ⁹King Chedor-laomer of Elam, King Tidal of Goiim, King Amraphel of Shinar, and King Arioch of Ellasar—four kings against those five.

¹⁰Now the Valley of Siddim was dotted with bitumen pits; and the kings of Sodom and Gomorrah, in their flight, threw themselves into them, while the rest escaped to the hill country. ¹¹[The invaders] seized all the wealth of Sodom and Gomorrah and all their provisions, and went their way. ¹²They also took Lot, the son of Abram's brother, and his possessions, and departed; for he had settled in Sodom.

¹³A fugitive brought the news to Abram the Hebrew, who was dwelling at the terebinths of Mamre the Amorite, kinsman of Eshkol and Aner, these being Abram's allies. ¹⁴When Abram heard that his kinsman had been taken captive, he mustered his retainers,ᵇ born into his household, numbering three hundred and eighteen, and went in pursuit as far as Dan. ¹⁵At night, he and his servants deployed against them and defeated them; and he pursued them as far as Hobah, which is north of Damascus. ¹⁶He brought back all the possessions; he also brought back his kinsman Lot and his possessions, and the women and the rest of the people.

¹⁷When he returned from defeating Chedorlaomer and the kings with him, the king of Sodom came out to meet him in the Valley of Shaveh, which is the Valley of the King. ¹⁸And King Melchizedek of Salem brought out bread and wine; he was a priest of God Most High.ᶜ ¹⁹He blessed him, saying,

"Blessed be Abram of God Most High,
Creator of heaven and earth.
²⁰And blessed be God Most High,
Who has delivered your foes into your hand."

And [Abram] gave him a tenth of everything.

²¹Then the king of Sodom said to Abram, "Give me the persons, and take the possessions for yourself." ²²But Abram said to the king of Sodom, "I swearᵈ to the LORD, God Most

---

ᵇ *Meaning of Heb* ḥanikh *uncertain*
ᶜ *Heb* El ʿElyon
ᵈ *Lit. "lift up my hand"*

High, Creator of heaven and earth: ²³I will not take so much as a thread or a sandal strap of what is yours; you shall not say, 'It is I who made Abram rich.' ²⁴For me, nothing but what my servants have used up; as for the share of the men who went with me— Aner, Eshkol, and Mamre—let them take their share."

**15** Some time later, the word of the LORD came to Abram in a vision. He said,

"Fear not, Abram,
I am a shield to you;
Your reward shall be very great."

²But Abram said, "O Lord God, what can You give me, seeing that I shall die childless ᵃ˙and the one in charge of my household is Dammesek Eliezer!"⁻ᵃ ³Abram said further, "Since You have granted me no offspring, my steward will be my heir." ⁴The word of the LORD came to him in reply, "That one shall not be your heir; none but your very own issue shall be your heir." ⁵He took him outside and said, "Look toward heaven and count the stars, if you are able to count them." And He added, "So shall your offspring be." ⁶And because he put his trust in the LORD, He reckoned it to his merit.

⁷Then He said to him, "I am the LORD who brought you out from Ur of the Chaldeans to assign this land to you as a possession." ⁸And he said, "O Lord GOD, how shall I know that I am to possess it?" ⁹He answered, "Bring Me a three-year-old heifer, a three-year-old she-goat, a three-year-old ram, a turtledove, and a young bird." ¹⁰He brought Him all these and cut them in two, placing each half opposite the other; but he did not cut up the bird. ¹¹Birds of prey came down upon the carcasses, and Abram drove them away. ¹²As the sun was about to set, a deep sleep fell upon Abram, and a great dark dread descended upon him. ¹³And He said to Abram, "Know well that your offspring shall be strangers in a land not theirs, and they shall be enslaved and op-

---

ᵃ⁻ᵃ *Meaning of Heb uncertain*

pressed four hundred years; [14]but I will execute judgment on the nation they shall serve, and in the end they shall go free with great wealth. [15]As for you,

> You shall go to your fathers in peace;
> You shall be buried at a ripe old age.

[16]And they shall return here in the fourth generation, for the iniquity of the Amorites is not yet complete."

[17]When the sun set and it was very dark, there appeared a smoking oven, and a flaming torch which passed between those pieces. [18]On that day the LORD made a covenant with Abram, saying, "To your offspring I assign this land, from the river of Egypt to the great river, the river Euphrates: [19]the Kenites, the Kenizzites, the Kadmonites, [20]the Hittites, the Perizzites, the Rephaim, [21]the Amorites, the Canaanites, the Girgashites, and the Jebusites."

# 16

Sarai, Abram's wife, had borne him no children. She had an Egyptian maidservant whose name was Hagar. [2]And Sarai said to Abram, "Look, the LORD has kept me from bearing. Consort with my maid; perhaps I shall have a son[a] through her." And Abram heeded Sarai's request. [3]So Sarai, Abram's wife, took her maid, Hagar the Egyptian—after Abram had dwelt in the land of Canaan ten years—and gave her to her husband Abram as concubine. [4]He cohabited with Hagar and she conceived; and when she saw that she had conceived, her mistress was lowered in her esteem. [5]And Sarai said to Abram, "The wrong done me is your fault! I myself put my maid in your bosom; now that she sees that she is pregnant, I am lowered in her esteem. The LORD decide between you and me!" [6]Abram said to Sarai, "Your maid is in your hands. Deal with her as you think right." Then Sarai treated her harshly, and she ran away from her.

[7]An angel of the LORD found her by a spring of water in the wilderness, the spring on the road to Shur, [8]and said, "Hagar,

---

[a] Lit. "be built up," play on ben "son" and banah "build up"

slave of Sarai, where have you come from, and where are you going?" And she said, "I am running away from my mistress Sarai."

⁹And the angel of the LORD said to her, "Go back to your mistress, and submit to her harsh treatment." ¹⁰And the angel of the LORD said to her,

"I will greatly increase your offspring,
And they shall be too many to count."

¹¹The angel of the LORD said to her further,

"Behold, you are with child
And shall bear a son;
You shall call him Ishmael,ᵇ
For the LORD has paid heed to your suffering.
¹²He shall be a wild ass of a man;
His hand against everyone,
And everyone's hand against him;
He shall dwell alongside of all his kinsmen."

¹³And she called the LORD who spoke to her, "You are El-roi,"ᶜ by which she meant, ᵈ-"Have I not gone on seeing after He saw me!"⁻ᵈ ¹⁴Therefore the well was called Beer-lahai-roi;ᵉ it is between Kadesh and Bered.—¹⁵Hagar bore a son to Abram, and Abram gave the son that Hagar bore him the name Ishmael. ¹⁶Abram was eighty-six years old when Hagar bore Ishmael to Abram.

17 When Abram was ninety-nine years old, the LORD appeared to Abram and said to him, "I am El Shaddai.ᵃ Walk in My ways and be blameless. ²I will establish My covenant between Me and you, and I will make you exceedingly numerous."

³Abram threw himself on his face; and God spoke to him further, ⁴"As for Me, this is My covenant with you: You shall be the father of a multitude of nations. ⁵And you shall no longer be called Abram, but your name shall be Abraham,ᵇ for I make you the father of a multitude of nations. ⁶I will make you exceed-

---

ᵇ *I.e. "God heeds"*   ᶜ *Apparently "God of Seeing"*
ᵈ⁻ᵈ *Meaning of Heb uncertain*
ᵉ *Apparently "the Well of the Living One Who sees me"*
ᵃ *Traditionally rendered "God Almighty"*   ᵇ *Understood as "father of a multitude"*

ingly fertile, and make nations of you; and kings shall come forth from you. ⁷I will maintain My covenant between Me and you, and your offspring to come, as an everlasting covenant throughout the ages, to be God to you and to your offspring to come. ⁸I assign the land you sojourn in to you and your offspring to come, all the land of Canaan, as an everlasting holding. I will be their God."

⁹God further said to Abraham, "As for you, you and your offspring to come throughout the ages shall keep My covenant. ¹⁰Such shall be the covenant between Me and you and your offspring to follow which you shall keep: every male among you shall be circumcised. ¹¹You shall circumcise the flesh of your foreskin, and that shall be the sign of the covenant between Me and you. ¹²And throughout the generations, every male among you shall be circumcised at the age of eight days. As for the homeborn slave and the one bought from an outsider who is not of your offspring, ¹³they must be circumcised, homeborn and purchased alike. Thus shall My covenant be marked in your flesh as an everlasting pact. ¹⁴And if any male who is uncircumcised fails to circumcise the flesh of his foreskin, that person shall be cut off from his kin; he has broken My covenant."

¹⁵And God said to Abraham, "As for your wife Sarai, you shall not call her Sarai, but her name shall be Sarah.ᶜ ¹⁶I will bless her; indeed, I will give you a son by her. I will bless her so that she shall give rise to nations; rulers of peoples shall issue from her." ¹⁷Abraham threw himself on his face and laughed, as he said to himself, "Can a child be born to a man a hundred years old, or can Sarah bear a child at ninety?" ¹⁸And Abraham said to God, "O that Ishmael might live by Your favor!" ¹⁹God said, "Nevertheless, Sarah your wife shall bear you a son, and you shall name him Isaacᵈ; and I will maintain My covenant with him as an everlasting covenant for his offspring to come. ²⁰As for Ishmael, I have heeded you.ᵉ I hereby bless him. I will make him fertile and exceedingly numerous. He shall be the father of twelve chieftains, and I will make of him a great nation. ²¹But My

ᶜ *I.e. "princess"*

ᵈ *Heb* Yiṣḥaq, *from* ṣaḥaq, *"laugh"*

ᵉ *Heb* shemaʿtikha, *play on "Ishmael"*

covenant I will maintain with Isaac, whom Sarah shall bear to you at this season next year." <sup>22</sup>And when He was done speaking with him, God was gone from Abraham.

<sup>23</sup>Then Abraham took his son Ishmael, and all his homeborn slaves and all those he had bought, every male in Abraham's household, and he circumcised the flesh of their foreskins on that very day, as God had spoken to him. <sup>24</sup>Abraham was ninety-nine years old when he circumcised the flesh of his foreskin, <sup>25</sup>and his son Ishmael was thirteen years old when he was circumcised in the flesh of his foreskin. <sup>26</sup>Thus Abraham and his son Ishmael were circumcised on that very day; <sup>27</sup>and all his household, his homeborn slaves and those that had been bought from outsiders, were circumcised with him.

וירא

18 The LORD appeared to him by the terebinths of Mamre; he was sitting at the entrance of the tent as the day grew hot. <sup>2</sup>Looking up, he saw three men standing near him. As soon as he saw them, he ran from the entrance of the tent to greet them and, bowing to the ground, <sup>3</sup>he said, "My lords,<sup>a</sup> if it please you, do not go on past your servant. <sup>4</sup>Let a little water be brought; bathe your feet and recline under the tree. <sup>5</sup>And let me fetch a morsel of bread that you may refresh yourselves; then go on— seeing that you have come your servant's way." They replied, "Do as you have said."

Abraham hastened into the tent to Sarah, and said, "Quick, three *seah*s of choice flour! Knead and make cakes!" <sup>7</sup>Then Abraham ran to the herd, took a calf, tender and choice, and gave it to a servant-boy, who hastened to prepare it. <sup>8</sup>He took curds and milk and the calf that had been prepared and set these before them; and he waited on them under the tree as they ate.

<sup>9</sup>They said to him, "Where is your wife Sarah?" And he replied, "There, in the tent." <sup>10</sup>Then one said, "I will return to you next year,<sup>b</sup> and your wife Sarah shall have a son!" Sarah was listening at the entrance of the tent, which was behind him.

<sup>a</sup> Or "My Lord"
<sup>b</sup> Cf. Gen 17.21; II Kings 4.16–17

¹¹Now Abraham and Sarah were old, advanced in years; Sarah had stopped having the periods of women. ¹²And Sarah laughed to herself, saying, "Now that I am withered, am I to have enjoyment—with my husband so old?" ¹³Then the LORD said to Abraham, "Why did Sarah laugh, saying, 'Shall I in truth bear a child, old as I am?' ¹⁴Is anything too wondrous for the LORD? I will return to you at the same season next year, and Sarah shall have a son." ¹⁵Sarah lied, saying, "I did not laugh," for she was frightened. But He replied, "You did laugh."

¹⁶The men set out from there and looked down toward Sodom, Abraham walking with them to see them off. ¹⁷Now the LORD had said, "Shall I hide from Abraham what I am about to do, ¹⁸since Abraham is to become a great and populous nation and all the nations of the earth are to bless themselves by him? ¹⁹For I have singled him out, that he may instruct his children and his posterity to keep the way of the LORD by doing what is just and right, in order that the LORD may bring about for Abraham what He has promised him." ²⁰Then the LORD said, "The outrage of Sodom and Gomorrah is so great, and their sin so grave! ²¹I will go down to see whether they have acted altogether according to the outcry that has reached Me; if not, I will take note."

²²The men went on from there to Sodom, while Abraham remained standing before the LORD. ²³Abraham came forward and said, "Will You sweep away the innocent along with the guilty? ²⁴What if there should be fifty innocent within the city; will You then wipe out the place and not forgive it for the sake of the innocent fifty who are in it? ²⁵Far be it from You to do such a thing, to bring death upon the innocent as well as the guilty, so that innocent and guilty fare alike. Far be it from You! Shall not the Judge of all the earth deal justly?" ²⁶And the LORD answered, "If I find within the city of Sodom fifty innocent ones, I will forgive the whole place for their sake." ²⁷Abraham spoke up, saying, "Here I venture to speak to my Lord, I who am but dust and ashes: ²⁸What if the fifty innocent should lack five? Will You

destroy the whole city for want of the five?" And He answered, "I will not destroy if I find forty-five there." [29]But he spoke to Him again, and said, "What if forty should be found there?" And He answered, "I will not do it, for the sake of the forty." [30]And he said, "Let not my Lord be angry if I go on: What if thirty should be found there?" And He answered, "I will not do it if I find thirty there." [31]And he said, "I venture again to speak to my Lord: What if twenty should be found there?" And He answered, "I will not destroy, for the sake of the twenty." [32]And he said, "Let not my Lord be angry if I speak but this last time: What if ten should be found there?" And He answered, "I will not destroy, for the sake of the ten."

[33]When the LORD had finished speaking to Abraham, He departed; and Abraham returned to his place.

19 The two angels arrived in Sodom in the evening, as Lot was sitting in the gate of Sodom. When Lot saw them, he rose to greet them and, bowing low with his face to the ground, [2]he said, "Please, my lords, turn aside to your servant's house to spend the night, and bathe your feet; then you may be on your way early." But they said, "No, we will spend the night in the square." [3]But he urged them strongly, so they turned his way and entered his house. He prepared a feast for them and baked unleavened bread, and they ate.

[4]They had not yet lain down, when the townspeople, the men of Sodom, young and old—all the people to the last man—gathered about the house. [5]And they shouted to Lot and said to him, "Where are the men who came to you tonight? Bring them out to us, that we may be intimate with them." [6]So Lot went out to them to the entrance, shut the door behind him, [7]and said, "I beg you, my friends, do not commit such a wrong. [8]Look, I have two daughters who have not known a man. Let me bring them out to you, and you may do to them as you please; but do not do anything to these men, since they have come under the shelter of my roof." [9]But they said, "Stand back! The fellow," they said,

"came here as an alien, and already he acts the ruler! Now we will deal worse with you than with them." And they pressed hard against the person of Lot, and moved forward to break the door. ¹⁰But the men stretched out their hands and pulled Lot into the house with them, and shut the door. ¹¹And the people who were at the entrance of the house, young and old, were struck with blinding light, so that they were helpless to find the entrance.

¹²Then the men said to Lot, "Whom else have you here? Sons-in-law, your sons and daughters, or anyone else that you have in the city—bring them out of the place. ¹³For we are about to destroy this place; because the outcry against them before the LORD has become so great that the LORD has sent us to destroy it." ¹⁴So Lot went out and spoke to his sons-in-law, who had married his daughters, and said, "Up, get out of this place, for the LORD is about to destroy the city." But he seemed to his sons-in-law as one who jests.

¹⁵As dawn broke, the angels urged Lot on, saying, "Up, take your wife and your two remaining daughters, lest you be swept away because of the iniquity of the city." ¹⁶Still he delayed. So the men seized his hand, and the hands of his wife and his two daughters—in the LORD's mercy on him—and brought him out and left him outside the city. ¹⁷When they had brought them outside, one said, "Flee for your life! Do not look behind you, nor stop anywhere in the Plain; flee to the hills, lest you be swept away." ¹⁸But Lot said to them, "Oh no, my lord! ¹⁹You have been so gracious to your servant, and have already shown me so much kindness in order to save my life; but I cannot flee to the hills, lest the disaster overtake me and I die. ²⁰Look, that town there is near enough to flee to; it is such a little place! Let me flee there—it is such a little place—and let my life be saved." ²¹He replied, "Very well, I will grant you this favor too, and I will not annihilate the town of which you have spoken. ²²Hurry, flee there, for I cannot do anything until you arrive there." Hence the town came to be called Zoar.ᵃ

---

ᵃ Connected with miṣʿar "a little place," v. 20

²³As the sun rose upon the earth and Lot entered Zoar, ²⁴the LORD rained upon Sodom and Gomorrah sulfurous fire from the LORD out of heaven. ²⁵He annihilated those cities and the entire Plain, and all the inhabitants of the cities and the vegetation of the ground. ²⁶Lot's*b* wife looked back,*c* and she thereupon turned into a pillar of salt.

²⁷Next morning, Abraham hurried to the place where he had stood before the LORD, ²⁸and, looking down toward Sodom and Gomorrah and all the land of the Plain, he saw the smoke of the land rising like the smoke of a kiln.

²⁹Thus it was that, when God destroyed the cities of the Plain and annihilated the cities where Lot dwelt, God was mindful of Abraham and removed Lot from the midst of the upheaval.

³⁰Lot went up from Zoar and settled in the hill country with his two daughters, for he was afraid to dwell in Zoar; and he and his two daughters lived in a cave. ³¹And the older one said to the younger, "Our father is old, and there is not a man on earth to consort with us in the way of all the world. ³²Come, let us make our father drink wine, and let us lie with him, that we may maintain life through our father." ³³That night they made their father drink wine, and the older one went in and lay with her father; he did not know when she lay down or when she rose. ³⁴The next day the older one said to the younger, "See, I lay with Father last night; let us make him drink wine tonight also, and you go and lie with him, that we may maintain life through our father." ³⁵That night also they made their father drink wine, and the younger one went and lay with him; he did not know when she lay down or when she rose.

³⁶Thus the two daughters of Lot came to be with child by their father. ³⁷The older one bore a son and named him Moab*d*; he is the father of the Moabites of today. ³⁸And the younger also bore a son, and she called him Ben-ammi*e*; he is the father of the Ammonites of today.

---

b *Lit. "His"*
c *Lit. "behind him."*
d *As though* me-'ab *"from (my) father"*
e *As though "son of my (paternal) kindred"*

20 Abraham journeyed from there to the region of the Negeb and settled between Kadesh and Shur. While he was sojourning in Gerar, ²Abraham said of Sarah his wife, "She is my sister." So King Abimelech of Gerar had Sarah brought to him. ³But God came to Abimelech in a dream by night and said to him, "You are to die because of the woman that you have taken, for she is a married woman." ⁴Now Abimelech had not approached her. He said, "O Lord, will You slay people even though innocent? ⁵He himself said to me, 'She is my sister!' And she also said, 'He is my brother.' When I did this, my heart was blameless and my hands were clean." ⁶And God said to him in the dream, "I knew that you did this with a blameless heart, and so I kept you from sinning against Me. That was why I did not let you touch her. ⁷Therefore, restore the man's wife—since he is a prophet, he will intercede for you—to save your life. If you fail to restore her, know that you shall die, you and all that are yours."

⁸Early next morning, Abimelech called his servants and told them all that had happened; and the men were greatly frightened. ⁹Then Abimelech summoned Abraham and said to him, "What have you done to us? What wrong have I done that you should bring so great a guilt upon me and my kingdom? You have done to me things that ought not to be done. ¹⁰What, then," Abimelech demanded of Abraham, "was your purpose in doing this thing?" ¹¹"I thought," said Abraham, "surely there is no fear of God in this place, and they will kill me because of my wife. ¹²And besides, she is in truth my sister, my father's daughter though not my mother's; and she became my wife. ¹³So when God made me wander from my father's house, I said to her, 'Let this be the kindness that you shall do me: whatever place we come to, say there of me: He is my brother.'"

¹⁴Abimelech took sheep and oxen, and male and female slaves, and gave them to Abraham; and he restored his wife Sarah to him. ¹⁵And Abimelech said, "Here, my land is before

you; settle wherever you please." [16]And to Sarah he said, "I herewith give your brother a thousand pieces of silver; this will serve you as vindication[a] before all who are with you, and you are cleared before everyone." [17]Abraham then prayed to God, and God healed Abimelech and his wife and his slave girls, so that they bore children; [18]for the LORD had closed fast every womb of the household of Abimelech because of Sarah, the wife of Abraham.

# 21

The LORD took note of Sarah as He had promised, and the LORD did for Sarah as He had spoken. [2]Sarah conceived and bore a son to Abraham in his old age, at the set time of which God had spoken. [3]Abraham gave his newborn son, whom Sarah had borne him, the name of Isaac. [4]And when his son Isaac was eight days old, Abraham circumcised him, as God had commanded him. [5]Now Abraham was a hundred years old when his son Isaac was born to him. [6]Sarah said, "God has brought me laughter; everyone who hears will laugh with[a] me." [7]And she added,

> "Who would have said to Abraham
> That Sarah would suckle children!
> Yet I have borne a son in his old age."

[8]The child grew up and was weaned, and Abraham held a great feast on the day that Isaac was weaned.

[9]Sarah saw the son whom Hagar the Egyptian had borne to Abraham playing. [10]She said to Abraham, "Cast out that slave-woman and her son, for the son of that slave shall not share in the inheritance with my son Isaac." [11]The matter distressed Abraham greatly, for it concerned a son of his. [12]But God said to Abraham, "Do not be distressed over the boy or your slave; whatever Sarah tells you, do as she says, for it is through Isaac that offspring shall be continued[b] for you. [13]As for the son of the slave-woman, I will make a nation of him, too, for he is your seed."

---

a Lit. "a covering of the eyes"; meaning of latter half of verse uncertain

a Lit. "for"

b Lit. "called"

¹⁴Early next morning Abraham took some bread and a skin of water, and gave them to Hagar. He placed them over her shoulder, together with the child, and sent her away. And she wandered about in the wilderness of Beersheba. ¹⁵When the water was gone from the skin, she left the child under one of the bushes, ¹⁶and went and sat down at a distance, a bowshot away; for she thought, "Let me not look on as the child dies." And sitting thus afar, she burst into tears.

¹⁷God heard the cry of the boy, and an angel of God called to Hagar from heaven and said to her, "What troubles you, Hagar? Fear not, for God has heeded the cry of the boy where he is. ¹⁸Come, lift up the boy and hold him by the hand, for I will make a great nation of him." ¹⁹Then God opened her eyes and she saw a well of water. She went and filled the skin with water, and let the boy drink. ²⁰God was with the boy and he grew up; he dwelt in the wilderness and became a bowman. ²¹He lived in the wilderness of Paran; and his mother got a wife for him from the land of Egypt.

²²At that time Abimelech and Phicol, chief of his troops, said to Abraham, "God is with you in everything that you do. ²³Therefore swear to me here by God that you will not deal falsely with me or with my kith and kin, but will deal with me and with the land in which you have sojourned as loyally as I have dealt with you." ²⁴And Abraham said, "I swear it."

²⁵Then Abraham reproached Abimelech for the well of water which the servants of Abimelech had seized. ²⁶But Abimelech said, "I do not know who did this; you did not tell me, nor have I heard of it until today." ²⁷Abraham took sheep and oxen and gave them to Abimelech, and the two of them made a pact. ²⁸Abraham then set seven ewes of the flock by themselves, ²⁹and Abimelech said to Abraham, "What mean these seven ewes which you have set apart?" ³⁰He replied, "You are to accept these seven ewes from me as proof that I dug this well." ³¹Hence that place was called Beer-sheba,ᶜ for there the two of them

---

ᶜ *I.e. "well of seven" or "well of oath"*

swore an oath. ³²When they had concluded the pact at Beer-sheba, Abimelech and Phicol, chief of his troops, departed and returned to the land of the Philistines. ³³[Abraham] planted a tamarisk at Beer-sheba, and invoked there the name of the LORD, the Everlasting God. ³⁴And Abraham resided in the land of the Philistines a long time.

22 Some time afterward, God put Abraham to the test. He said to him, "Abraham," and he answered, "Here I am." ²And He said, "Take your son, your favored one, Isaac, whom you love, and go to the land of Moriah, and offer him there as a burnt offering on one of the heights that I will point out to you." ³So early next morning, Abraham saddled his ass and took with him two of his servants and his son Isaac. He split the wood for the burnt offering, and he set out for the place of which God had told him. ⁴On the third day Abraham looked up and saw the place from afar. ⁵Then Abraham said to his servants, "You stay here with the ass. The boy and I will go up there; we will worship and we will return to you."

⁶Abraham took the wood for the burnt offering and put it on his son Isaac. He himself took the firestone*ᵃ* and the knife; and the two walked off together. ⁷Then Isaac said to his father Abraham, "Father!" And he answered, "Yes, my son." And he said, "Here are the firestone and the wood; but where is the sheep for the burnt offering?" ⁸And Abraham said, "God will see to the sheep for His burnt offering, my son." And the two of them walked on together.

⁹They arrived at the place of which God had told him. Abraham built an altar there; he laid out the wood; he bound his son Isaac; he laid him on the altar, on top of the wood. ¹⁰And Abraham picked up the knife to slay his son. ¹¹Then an angel of the LORD called to him from heaven: "Abraham! Abraham!" And he answered, "Here I am." ¹²And he said, "Do not raise your hand against the boy, or do anything to him. For now I

ᵃ *Lit. "fire"*

know that you fear God, since you have not withheld your son, your favored one, from Me." [13]When Abraham looked up, his eye fell upon a[b] ram, caught in the thicket by its horns. So Abraham went and took the ram and offered it up as a burnt offering in place of his son. [14]And Abraham named that site Adonai-yireh,[c] whence the present saying, "On the mount of the LORD there is vision."[d]

[15]The angel of the LORD called to Abraham a second time from heaven, [16]and said, "By Myself I swear, the LORD declares: Because you have done this and have not withheld your son, your favored one, [17]I will bestow My blessing upon you and make your descendants as numerous as the stars of heaven and the sands on the seashore; and your descendants shall seize the gates of their foes. [18]All the nations of the earth shall bless themselves by your descendants, because you have obeyed My command." [19]Abraham then returned to his servants, and they departed together for Beer-sheba; and Abraham stayed in Beer-sheba.

[20]Some time later, Abraham was told, "Milcah too has borne children to your brother Nahor: [21]Uz the first-born, and Buz his brother, and Kemuel the father of Aram; [22]and Chesed, Hazo, Pildash, Jidlaph, and Bethuel"—[23]Bethuel being the father of Rebekah. These eight Milcah bore to Nahor, Abraham's brother. [24]And his concubine, whose name was Reumah, also bore children: Tebah, Gaham, Tahash, and Maacah.

חיי שרה

**23** Sarah's lifetime—the span of Sarah's life—came to one hundred and twenty-seven years. [2]Sarah died in Kiriath-arba—now Hebron—in the land of Canaan; and Abraham proceeded to mourn for Sarah and to bewail her. [3]Then Abraham rose from beside his dead, and spoke to the Hittites, saying, [4]"I am a resident alien among you; sell me a burial site among you, that I may remove my dead for burial." [5]And the Hittites replied to Abraham, saying to him, [6]"Hear us, my lord: you are the elect of

b  *Reading* 'eḥad *with many Heb mss. and ancient versions; text* 'aḥar *"after"*
c  *I.e. "the Lord will see"; cf. v. 8*
d  *Heb* Behar Adonai yera'eh

God among us. Bury your dead in the choicest of our burial places; none of us will withhold his burial place from you for burying your dead." [7]Thereupon Abraham bowed low to the people of the land, the Hittites, [8]and he said to them, "If it is your wish that I remove my dead for burial, you must agree to intercede for me with Ephron son of Zohar. [9]Let him sell me the cave of Machpelah that he owns, which is at the edge of his land. Let him sell it to me, at the full price, for a burial site in your midst."

[10]Ephron was present among the Hittites; so Ephron the Hittite answered Abraham in the hearing of the Hittites, all who entered the gate of his town,[a] saying, [11]"No, my lord, hear me: I give you the field and I give you the cave that is in it; I give it to you in the presence of my people. Bury your dead." [12]Then Abraham bowed low before the people of the land, [13]and spoke to Ephron in the hearing of the people of the land, saying, "If only you would hear me out! Let me pay the price of the land; accept it from me, that I may bury my dead there." [14]And Ephron replied to Abraham, saying to him, [15]"My lord, do hear me! A piece of land worth four hundred shekels of silver—what is that between you and me? Go and bury your dead." [16]Abraham accepted Ephron's terms. Abraham paid out to Ephron the money that he had named in the hearing of the Hittites—four hundred shekels of silver at the going merchants' rate.

[17]So Ephron's land in Machpelah, near Mamre—the field with its cave and all the trees anywhere within the confines of that field—passed [18]to Abraham as his possession, in the presence of the Hittites, of all who entered the gate of his town.[a] [19]And then Abraham buried his wife Sarah in the cave of the field of Machpelah, facing Mamre—now Hebron—in the land of Canaan. [20]Thus the field with its cave passed from the Hittites to Abraham, as a burial site.

# 24

Abraham was now old, advanced in years, and the LORD had blessed Abraham in all things. [2]And Abraham said to the

---

[a] *I.e. all his fellow townsmen*

senior servant of his household, who had charge of all that he owned, "Put your hand under my thigh ³and I will make you swear by the LORD, the God of heaven and the God of the earth, that you will not take a wife for my son from the daughters of the Canaanites among whom I dwell, ⁴but will go to the land of my birth and get a wife for my son Isaac." ⁵And the servant said to him, "What if the woman does not consent to follow me to this land, shall I then take your son back to the land from which you came?" ⁶Abraham answered him, "On no account must you take my son back there! ⁷The LORD, the God of heaven, who took me from my father's house and from my native land, who promised me on oath, saying, 'I will assign this land to your offspring'— He will send His angel before you, and you will get a wife for my son from there. ⁸And if the woman does not consent to follow you, you shall then be clear of this oath to me; but do not take my son back there." ⁹So the servant put his hand under the thigh of his master Abraham and swore to him as bidden.ᵃ

¹⁰Then the servant took ten of his master's camels and set out, taking with him all the bounty of his master; and he made his way to Aram-naharaim, to the city of Nahor. ¹¹He made the camels kneel down by the well outside the city, at evening time, the time when women come out to draw water. ¹²And he said, "O LORD, God of my master Abraham, grant me good fortune this day, and deal graciously with my master Abraham: ¹³Here I stand by the spring as the daughters of the townsmen come out to draw water; ¹⁴let the maiden to whom I say, 'Please, lower your jar that I may drink,' and who replies, 'Drink, and I will also water your camels'—let her be the one whom You have decreed for Your servant Isaac. Thereby shall I know that You have dealt graciously with my master."

¹⁵He had scarcely finished speaking, when Rebekah, who was born to Bethuel, the son of Milcah the wife of Abraham's brother Nahor, came out with her jar on her shoulder. ¹⁶The maiden was very beautiful, a virgin whom no man had known. She went down to the spring, filled her jar, and came up. ¹⁷The servant ran toward her and said, "Please, let me sip a little water

ᵃ Lit. "about this matter"

from your jar." ¹⁸"Drink, my lord," she said, and she quickly lowered her jar upon her hand and let him drink. ¹⁹When she had let him drink his fill, she said, "I will also draw for your camels, until they finish drinking." ²⁰Quickly emptying her jar into the trough, she ran back to the well to draw, and she drew for all his camels.

²¹The man, meanwhile, stood gazing at her, silently wondering whether the LORD had made his errand successful or not. ²²When the camels had finished drinking, the man took a gold nose-ring weighing a half-shekel,ᵇ and two gold bands for her arms, ten shekels in weight. ²³"Pray tell me," he said, "whose daughter are you? Is there room in your father's house for us to spend the night?" ²⁴She replied, "I am the daughter of Bethuel the son of Milcah, whom she bore to Nahor." ²⁵And she went on, "There is plenty of strawᶜ and feed at home, and also room to spend the night." ²⁶The man bowed low in homage to the LORD ²⁷and said, "Blessed be the LORD, the God of my master Abraham, who has not withheld His steadfast faithfulness from my master. For I have been guided on my errand by the LORD, to the house of my master's kinsmen."

²⁸The maiden ran and told all this to her mother's household. ²⁹Now Rebekah had a brother whose name was Laban. Laban ran out to the man at the spring—³⁰when he saw the nose-ring and the bands on his sister's arms, and when he heard his sister Rebekah say, "Thus the man spoke to me." He went up to the man, who was still standing beside the camels at the spring. ³¹"Come in, O blessed of the LORD," he said, "why do you remain outside, when I have made ready the house and a place for the camels?" ³²So the man entered the house, and the camels were unloaded. The camels were given straw and feed, and water was brought to bathe his feet and the feet of the men with him. ³³But when food was set before him, he said, "I will not eat until I have told my tale." He said, "Speak, then."

³⁴"I am Abraham's servant," he began. ³⁵"The LORD has greatly blessed my master, and he has become rich: He has given him sheep and cattle, silver and gold, male and female slaves,

---

ᵇ *Heb* beqaʿ
ᶜ *Heb* teben, *shredded straw, which in the East is mixed with feed; cf. v. 32*

camels and asses. ³⁶And Sarah, my master's wife, bore my master a son in her old age, and he has assigned to him everything he owns. ³⁷Now my master made me swear, saying, 'You shall not get a wife for my son from the daughters of the Canaanites in whose land I dwell; ³⁸but you shall go to my father's house, to my kindred, and get a wife for my son.' ³⁹And I said to my master, 'What if the woman does not follow me?' ⁴⁰He replied to me, 'The LORD, whose ways I have followed, will send His angel with you and make your errand successful; and you will get a wife for my son from my kindred, from my father's house. ⁴¹Thus only shall you be freed from my adjuration: if, when you come to my kindred, they refuse you—only then shall you be freed from my adjuration.'

⁴²"I came today to the spring, and I said: O LORD, God of my master Abraham, if You would indeed grant success to the errand on which I am engaged! ⁴³As I stand by the spring of water, let the young woman who comes out to draw and to whom I say, 'Please, let me drink a little water from your jar,' ⁴⁴and who answers, 'You may drink, and I will also draw for your camels'—let her be the wife whom the LORD has decreed for my master's son.' ⁴⁵I had scarcely finished praying in my heart, when Rebekah came out with her jar on her shoulder, and went down to the spring and drew. And I said to her, 'Please give me a drink.' ⁴⁶She quickly lowered her jar and said, 'Drink, and I will also water your camels.' So I drank, and she also watered the camels. ⁴⁷I inquired of her, 'Whose daughter are you?' And she said, 'The daughter of Bethuel, son of Nahor, whom Milcah bore to him.' And I put the ring on her nose and the bands on her arms. ⁴⁸Then I bowed low in homage to the LORD and blessed the LORD, the God of my master Abraham, who led me on the right way to get the daughter of my master's brother for his son. ⁴⁹And now, if you mean to treat my master with true kindness, tell me; and if not, tell me also, that I may turn right or left."

⁵⁰Then Laban and Bethuel answered, "The matter was de-

creed by the LORD; we cannot speak to you bad or good. <sup>51</sup>Here
is Rebekah before you; take her and go, and let her be a wife to
your master's son, as the LORD has spoken." <sup>52</sup>When Abraham's
servant heard their words, he bowed low to the ground before
the LORD. <sup>53</sup>The servant brought out objects of silver and gold,
and garments, and gave them to Rebekah; and he gave presents
to her brother and her mother. <sup>54</sup>Then he and the men with him
ate and drank, and they spent the night. When they arose next
morning, he said, "Give me leave to go to my master." <sup>55</sup>But her
brother and her mother said, "Let the maiden remain with us
<sup>d-</sup>some ten days;<sup>-d</sup> then you may go." <sup>56</sup>He said to them, "Do not
delay me, now that the LORD has made my errand successful.
Give me leave that I may go to my master." <sup>57</sup>And they said, "Let
us call the girl and ask for her reply." <sup>58</sup>They called Rebekah and
said to her, "Will you go with this man?" And she said, "I will."
<sup>59</sup>So they sent off their sister Rebekah and her nurse along with
Abraham's servant and his men. <sup>60</sup>And they blessed Rebekah
and said to her,

"O sister!
May you grow
Into thousands of myriads;
May your offspring seize
The gates of their foes."

<sup>61</sup>Then Rebekah and her maids arose, mounted the camels, and
followed the man. So the servant took Rebekah and went his
way.

<sup>62</sup>Isaac had just come back from the vicinity of Beer-lahai-roi,
for he was settled in the region of the Negeb. <sup>63</sup>And Isaac went
out walking<sup>e</sup> in the field toward evening and, looking up, he saw
camels approaching. <sup>64</sup>Raising her eyes, Rebekah saw Isaac. She
alighted from the camel <sup>65</sup>and said to the servant, "Who is that
man walking in the field toward us?" And the servant said, "That
is my master." So she took her veil and covered herself. <sup>66</sup>The
servant told Isaac all the things that he had done. <sup>67</sup>Isaac then
brought her into the tent of his mother Sarah, and he took

<sup>d-d</sup> Lit. "days or ten"
<sup>e</sup> Others "to meditate"; meaning of Heb uncertain

Rebekah as his wife. Isaac loved her, and thus found comfort after his mother's death.

# 25

Abraham took another wife, whose name was Keturah. ²She bore him Zimran, Jokshan, Medan, Midian, Ishbak, and Shuah. ³Jokshan begot Sheba and Dedan. The descendants of Dedan were the Asshurim, the Letushim, and the Leummim. ⁴The descendants of Midian were Ephah, Epher, Enoch,ᵃ Abida, and Eldaah. All these were descendants of Keturah. ⁵Abraham willed all that he owned to Isaac; ⁶but to Abraham's sons by concubines Abraham gave gifts while he was still living, and he sent them away from his son Isaac eastward, to the land of the East.

⁷This was the total span of Abraham's life: one hundred and seventy-five years. ⁸And Abraham breathed his last, dying at a good ripe age, old and contented; and he was gathered to his kin. ⁹His sons Isaac and Ishmael buried him in the cave of Machpelah, in the field of Ephron son of Zohar the Hittite, facing Mamre, ¹⁰the field that Abraham had bought from the Hittites; there Abraham was buried, and Sarah his wife. ¹¹After the death of Abraham, God blessed his son Isaac. And Isaac settled near Beer-lahai-roi.

¹²This is the line of Ishmael, Abraham's son, whom Hagar the Egyptian, Sarah's slave, bore to Abraham. ¹³These are the names of the sons of Ishmael, by their names, in the order of their birth: Nebaioth, the first-born of Ishmael, Kedar, Adbeel, Mibsam, ¹⁴Mishma, Dumah, Massa, ¹⁵Hadad, Tema, Jetur, Naphish, and Kedmah. ¹⁶These are the sons of Ishmael and these are their names by their villages and by their encampments: twelve chieftains of as many tribes.—¹⁷These were the years of the life of Ishmael: one hundred and thirty-seven years; then he breathed his last and died, and was gathered to his kin.—¹⁸They dwelt from Havilah, by Shur, which is close to

ᵃ Or "Hanoch"

Egypt, all the way to Asshur; they camped alongside all their kinsmen.

תולדת

[19]This is the story of Isaac, son of Abraham. Abraham begot Isaac. [20]Isaac was forty years old when he took to wife Rebekah, daughter of Bethuel the Aramean of Paddan-aram, sister of Laban the Aramean. [21]Isaac pleaded with the LORD on behalf of his wife, because she was barren; and the LORD responded to his plea, and his wife Rebekah conceived. [22]But the children struggled in her womb, and she said, "If so, why do I exist?"[b] She went to inquire of the LORD, [23]and the LORD answered her,

"Two nations are in your womb,
Two separate peoples shall issue from your body;
One people shall be mightier than the other,
And the older shall serve the younger."

[24]When her time to give birth was at hand, there were twins in her womb. [25]The first one emerged red, like a hairy mantle all over; so they named him Esau.[c] [26]Then his brother emerged, holding on to the heel of Esau; so they named him Jacob.[d] Isaac was sixty years old when they were born.

[27]When the boys grew up, Esau became a skillful hunter, a man of the outdoors; but Jacob was a mild man who stayed in camp. [28]Isaac favored Esau because [e]he had a taste for game[e]; but Rebekah favored Jacob. [29]Once when Jacob was cooking a stew, Esau came in from the open, famished. [30]And Esau said to Jacob, "Give me some of that red stuff to gulp down, for I am famished"—which is why he was named Edom.[f] [31]Jacob said, "First sell me your birthright." [32]And Esau said, "I am at the point of death, so of what use is my birthright to me?" [33]But Jacob said, "Swear to me first." So he swore to him, and sold his birthright to Jacob. [34]Jacob then gave Esau bread and lentil stew; he ate and drank, and he rose and went away. Thus did Esau spurn the birthright.

---

[b] Meaning of Heb uncertain
[c] Synonym of "Seir," play on Heb se'ar "hair"
[d] Play on Heb 'aqeb "heel"
[e-e] Lit. "game was in his mouth"
[f] Play on Heb 'adom "red"

26 There was a famine in the land—aside from the previous famine that had occurred in the days of Abraham—and Isaac went to Abimelech, king of the Philistines, in Gerar. ²The LORD had appeared to him and said, "Do not go down to Egypt; stay in the land which I point out to you. ³Reside in this land, and I will be with you and bless you; I will assign all these lands to you and to your heirs, fulfilling the oath that I swore to your father Abraham. ⁴I will make your heirs as numerous as the stars of heaven, and assign to your heirs all these lands, so that all the nations of the earth shall bless themselves by your heirs— ⁵inasmuch as Abraham obeyed Me and kept My charge: My commandments, My laws, and My teachings."

⁶So Isaac stayed in Gerar. ⁷When the men of the place asked him about his wife, he said, "She is my sister," for he was afraid to say "my wife," thinking, "The men of the place might kill me on account of Rebekah, for she is beautiful." ⁸When some time had passed, Abimelech king of the Philistines, looking out of the window, saw Isaac fondling his wife Rebekah. ⁹Abimelech sent for Isaac and said, "So she is your wife! Why then did you say: 'She is my sister?'" Isaac said to him, "Because I thought I might lose my life on account of her." ¹⁰Abimelech said, "What have you done to us! One of the people might have lain with your wife, and you would have brought guilt upon us." ¹¹Abimelech then charged all the people, saying, "Anyone who molests this man or his wife shall be put to death."

¹²Isaac sowed in that land and reaped a hundredfold the same year. The LORD blessed him, ¹³and the man grew richer and richer until he was very wealthy: ¹⁴he acquired flocks and herds, and a large household, so that the Philistines envied him. ¹⁵And the Philistines stopped up all the wells which his father's servants had dug in the days of his father Abraham, filling them with earth. ¹⁶And Abimelech said to Isaac, "Go away from us, for you have become far too big for us."

¹⁷So Isaac departed from there and encamped in the wadi of

Gerar, where he settled. [18]Isaac dug anew the wells which had been dug in the days of his father Abraham and which the Philistines had stopped up after Abraham's death; and he gave them the same names that his father had given them. [19]But when Isaac's servants, digging in the wadi, found there a well of spring water, [20]the herdsmen of Gerar quarreled with Isaac's herdsmen, saying, "The water is ours." He named that well Esek,[a] because they contended with him. [21]And when they dug another well, they disputed over that one also; so he named it Sitnah.[b] [22]He moved from there and dug yet another well, and they did not quarrel over it; so he called it Rehoboth, saying, "Now at last the LORD has granted us ample space[c] to increase in the land."

[23]From there he went up to Beer-sheba. [24]That night the LORD appeared to him and said, "I am the God of your father Abraham. Fear not, for I am with you, and I will bless you and increase your offspring for the sake of My servant Abraham." [25]So he built an altar there and invoked the LORD by name. Isaac pitched his tent there and his servants started digging a well. [26]And Abimelech came to him from Gerar, with Ahuzzath his councilor and Phicol chief of his troops. [27]Isaac said to them, "Why have you come to me, seeing that you have been hostile to me and have driven me away from you?" [28]And they said, "We now see plainly that the LORD has been with you, and we thought: Let there be a sworn treaty between our two parties, between you and us. Let us make a pact with you [29]that you will not do us harm, just as we have not molested you but have always dealt kindly with you and sent you away in peace. From now on, be you blessed of the LORD!" [30]Then he made for them a feast, and they ate and drank.

[31]Early in the morning, they exchanged oaths. Isaac then bade them farewell, and they departed from him in peace. [32]That same day Isaac's servants came and told him about the well they had dug, and said to him, "We have found water!" [33]He named it Shibah[d]; therefore the name of the city is Beer-sheba to this day.

---

[a] *I.e. "contention"*
[b] *I.e. "harassment"*
[c] *Heb hirhib, connected with "Rehoboth"*
[d] *As though "oath"*

³⁴When Esau was forty years old, he took to wife Judith daughter of Beeri the Hittite, and Basemath daughter of Elon the Hittite; ³⁵and they were a source of bitterness to Isaac and Rebekah.

27 When Isaac was old and his eyes were too dim to see, he called his older son Esau and said to him, "My son." He answered, "Here I am." ²And he said, "I am old now, and I do not know how soon I may die. ³Take your gear, your quiver and bow, and go out into the open and hunt me some game. ⁴Then prepare a dish for me such as I like, and bring it to me to eat, so that I may give you my innermost blessing before I die."

⁵Rebekah had been listening as Isaac spoke to his son Esau. When Esau had gone out into the open to hunt game to bring home, ⁶Rebekah said to her son Jacob, "I overheard your father speaking to your brother Esau, saying, ⁷'Bring me some game and prepare a dish for me to eat, that I may bless you, with the LORD's approval, before I die.' ⁸Now, my son, listen carefully as I instruct you. ⁹Go to the flock and fetch me two choice kids, and I will make of them a dish for your father, such as he likes. ¹⁰Then take it to your father to eat, in order that he may bless you before he dies." ¹¹Jacob answered his mother Rebekah, "But my brother Esau is a hairy man and I am smooth-skinned. ¹²If my father touches me, I shall appear to him as a trickster and bring upon myself a curse, not a blessing." ¹³But his mother said to him, "Your curse, my son, be upon me! Just do as I say and go fetch them for me."

¹⁴He got them and brought them to his mother, and his mother prepared a dish such as his father liked. ¹⁵Rebekah then took the best clothes of her older son Esau, which were there in the house, and had her younger son Jacob put them on; ¹⁶and she covered his hands and the hairless part of his neck with the skins of the kids. ¹⁷Then she put in the hands of her son Jacob the dish and the bread that she had prepared.

¹⁸He went to his father and said, "Father." And he said, "Yes,

which of my sons are you?" ¹⁹Jacob said to his father, "I am Esau, your first-born; I have done as you told me. Pray sit up and eat of my game, that you may give me your innermost blessing." ²⁰Isaac said to his son, "How did you succeed so quickly, my son?" And he said, "Because the LORD your God granted me good fortune." ²¹Isaac said to Jacob, "Come closer that I may feel you, my son—whether you are really my son Esau or not." ²²So Jacob drew close to his father Isaac, who felt him and wondered. "The voice is the voice of Jacob, yet the hands are the hands of Esau." ²³He did not recognize him, because his hands were hairy like those of his brother Esau; and so he blessed him.

²⁴He asked, "Are you really my son Esau?" And when he said, "I am," ²⁵he said, "Serve me and let me eat of my son's game that I may give you my innermost blessing." So he served him and he ate, and he brought him wine and he drank. ²⁶Then his father Isaac said to him, "Come close and kiss me, my son"; ²⁷and he went up and kissed him. And he smelled his clothes and he blessed him, saying, "Ah, the smell of my son is like the smell of the fields that the LORD has blessed.

²⁸"May God give you
Of the dew of heaven and the fat of the earth,
Abundance of new grain and wine.
²⁹Let peoples serve you,
And nations bow to you;
Be master over your brothers,
And let your mother's sons bow to you.
Cursed be they who curse you,
Blessed they who bless you."

³⁰No sooner had Jacob left the presence of his father Isaac—after Isaac had finished blessing Jacob—than his brother Esau came back from his hunt. ³¹He too prepared a dish and brought it to his father. And he said to his father, "Let my father sit up and eat of his son's game, so that you may give me your innermost blessing." ³²His father Isaac said to him, "Who are you?" And he said, "I am your son, Esau, your first-born!" ³³Isaac was seized with very violent trembling. "Who was it then," he de-

manded, "that hunted game and brought it to me? Moreover, I ate of it before you came, and I blessed him; now he must remain blessed!" ³⁴When Esau heard his father's words, he burst into wild and bitter sobbing, and said to his father, "Bless me too, Father!" ³⁵But he answered, "Your brother came with guile and took away your blessing." ³⁶[Esau] said, "Was he, then, named Jacob that he might supplant me^a these two times? First he took away my birthright and now he has taken away my blessing!" And he added, "Have you not reserved a blessing for me?" ³⁷Isaac answered, saying to Esau, "But I have made him master over you: I have given him all his brothers for servants, and sustained him with grain and wine. What, then, can I still do for you, my son?" ³⁸And Esau said to his father, "Have you but one blessing, Father? Bless me too, Father!" And Esau wept aloud. ³⁹And his father Isaac answered, saying to him,

"See, your abode shall ^b-enjoy the fat of the earth
And^-b the dew of heaven above.
⁴⁰Yet by your sword you shall live,
And you shall serve your brother;
But when you grow restive,
You shall break his yoke from your neck."

⁴¹Now Esau harbored a grudge against Jacob because of the blessing which his father had given him, and Esau said to himself, "Let but the mourning period of my father come, and I will kill my brother Jacob." ⁴²When the words of her older son Esau were reported to Rebekah, she sent for her younger son Jacob and said to him, "Your brother Esau is consoling himself by planning to kill you. ⁴³Now, my son, listen to me. Flee at once to Haran, to my brother Laban. ⁴⁴Stay with him a while, until your brother's fury subsides—⁴⁵until your brother's anger against you subsides—and he forgets what you have done to him. Then I will fetch you from there. Let me not lose you both in one day!"

⁴⁶Rebekah said to Isaac, "I am disgusted with my life because of the Hittite women. If Jacob marries a Hittite woman like these, from among the native women, what good will life be to

a *Heb* ʿaqab, *connected with "Jacob"*
b-b *Others "be away from the fat of the earth and from"*

**28** me?" ¹So Isaac sent for Jacob and blessed him. He instructed him, saying, "You shall not take a wife from among the Canaanite women. ²Up, go to Paddan-aram, to the house of Bethuel, your mother's father, and take a wife there from among the daughters of Laban, your mother's brother. ³May El Shaddai*ᵃ* bless you, make you fertile and numerous, so that you become an assembly of peoples. ⁴May He grant the blessing of Abraham to you and your offspring, that you may possess the land where you are sojourning, which God assigned to Abraham."

⁵Then Isaac sent Jacob off, and he went to Paddan-aram, to Laban the son of Bethuel the Aramean, the brother of Rebekah, mother of Jacob and Esau.

⁶When Esau saw that Isaac had blessed Jacob and sent him off to Paddan-aram to take a wife from there, charging him, as he blessed him, "You shall not take a wife from among the Canaanite women," ⁷and that Jacob had obeyed his father and mother and gone to Paddan-aram, ⁸Esau realized that the Canaanite women displeased his father Isaac. ⁹So Esau went to Ishmael and took to wife, in addition to the wives he had, Mahalath the daughter of Ishmael son of Abraham, sister of Nebaioth.

ויצא

¹⁰Jacob left Beer-sheba, and set out for Haran. ¹¹He came upon a certain place and stopped there for the night, for the sun had set. Taking one of the stones of that place, he put it under his head and lay down in that place. ¹²He had a dream; a stairway*ᵇ* was set on the ground and its top reached to the sky, and angels of God were going up and down on it. ¹³And the LORD was standing beside him and He said, "I am the LORD, the God of your father Abraham and the God of Isaac: the ground on which you are lying I will assign to you and to your offspring. ¹⁴Your descendants shall be as the dust of the earth; you shall

---

ᵃ *See note at 17.1*
ᵇ *Or "ramp"; others "ladder"*

spread out to the west and to the east, to the north and to the south. All the families of the earth shall bless themselves by you and your descendants. [15]Remember, I am with you: I will protect you wherever you go and will bring you back to this land. I will not leave you until I have done what I have promised you."

[16]Jacob awoke from his sleep and said, "Surely the LORD is present in this place, and I did not know it!" [17]Shaken, he said, "How awesome is this place! This is none other than the abode of God, and that is the gateway to heaven." [18]Early in the morning, Jacob took the stone that he had put under his head and set it up as a pillar and poured oil on the top of it. [19]He named that site Bethel;[c] but previously the name of the city had been Luz.

[20]Jacob then made a vow, saying, "If God remains with me, if He protects me on this journey that I am making, and gives me bread to eat and clothing to wear, [21]and if I return safe to my father's house—the LORD shall be my God. [22]And this stone, which I have set up as a pillar, shall be God's abode; and of all that You give me, I will set aside a tithe for You."

# 29

Jacob [a]resumed his journey[a] and came to the land of the Easterners. [2]There before his eyes was a well in the open. Three flocks of sheep were lying there beside it, for the flocks were watered from that well. The stone on the mouth of the well was large. [3]When all the flocks were gathered there, the stone would be rolled from the mouth of the well and the sheep watered; then the stone would be put back in its place on the mouth of the well.

[4]Jacob said to them, "My friends, where are you from?" And they said, "We are from Haran." [5]He said to them, "Do you know Laban the son of Nahor?" And they said, "Yes, we do." [6]He continued, "Is he well?" They answered, "Yes, he is; and there is his daughter Rachel, coming with the flock." [7]He said, "It is still broad daylight, too early to round up the animals; water the flock and take them to pasture." [8]But they said, "We

c *I.e. "house of God"*

a-a *Lit. "lifted up his feet"*

cannot, until all the flocks are rounded up; then the stone is rolled off the mouth of the well and we water the sheep."

⁹While he was still speaking with them, Rachel came with her father's flock; for she was a shepherdess. ¹⁰And when Jacob saw Rachel, the daughter of his uncle*ᵇ* Laban, and the flock of his uncle Laban, Jacob went up and rolled the stone off the mouth of the well, and watered the flock of his uncle Laban. ¹¹Then Jacob kissed Rachel, and broke into tears. ¹²Jacob told Rachel that he was her father's kinsman, that he was Rebekah's son; and she ran and told her father. ¹³On hearing the news of his sister's son Jacob, Laban ran to greet him; he embraced him and kissed him, and took him into his house. He told Laban all that had happened, ¹⁴and Laban said to him, "You are truly my bone and flesh."

When he had stayed with him a month's time, ¹⁵Laban said to Jacob, "Just because you are a kinsman, should you serve me for nothing? Tell me, what shall your wages be?" ¹⁶Now Laban had two daughters; the name of the older one was Leah, and the name of the younger was Rachel. ¹⁷Leah had weak eyes; Rachel was shapely and beautiful. ¹⁸Jacob loved Rachel; so he answered, "I will serve you seven years for your younger daughter Rachel." ¹⁹Laban said, "Better that I give her to you than that I should give her to an outsider. Stay with me." ²⁰So Jacob served seven years for Rachel and they seemed to him but a few days because of his love for her.

²¹Then Jacob said to Laban, "Give me my wife, for my time is fulfilled, that I may cohabit with her." ²²And Laban gathered all the people of the place and made a feast. ²³When evening came, he took his daughter Leah and brought her to him; and he cohabited with her.—²⁴Laban had given his maidservant Zilpah to his daughter Leah as her maid.—²⁵When morning came, there was Leah! So he said to Laban, "What is this you have done to me? I was in your service for Rachel! Why did you deceive me?" ²⁶Laban said, "It is not the practice in our place to marry off the younger before the older. ²⁷Wait until the bridal week of

___

ᵇ Lit. "his mother's brother"

this one is over and we will give you that one too, provided you serve me another seven years." [28]Jacob did so; he waited out the bridal week of the one, and then he gave him his daughter Rachel as wife.—[29]Laban had given his maid-servant Bilhah to his daughter Rachel as her maid.—[30]And Jacob cohabited with Rachel also; indeed, he loved Rachel more than Leah. And he served him another seven years.

[31]The LORD saw that Leah was unloved and he opened her womb; but Rachel was barren. [32]Leah conceived and bore a son, and named him Reuben[c]; for she declared, "It means: 'The LORD has seen[d] my affliction'; it also means: 'Now my husband will love me.[e]'" [33]She conceived again and bore a son, and declared, "This is because the LORD heard[f] that I was unloved and has given me this one also"; so she named him Simeon. [34]Again she conceived and bore a son and declared, "This time my husband will become attached[g] to me, for I have borne him three sons." Therefore he was named Levi. [35]She conceived again and bore a son, and declared, "This time I will praise[h] the LORD." Therefore she named him Judah. Then she stopped bearing.

30 When Rachel saw that she had borne Jacob no children, she became envious of her sister; and Rachel said to Jacob, "Give me children, or I shall die." [2]Jacob was incensed at Rachel, and said, "Can I take the place of God, who has denied you fruit of the womb?" [3]She said, "Here is my maid Bilhah. Consort with her, that she may bear on my knees and that through her I too may have children." [4]So she gave him her maid Bilhah as concubine, and Jacob cohabited with her. [5]Bilhah conceived and bore Jacob a son. [6]And Rachel said, "God has vindicated me[a]; indeed, He has heeded my plea and given me a son." Therefore she named him Dan. [7]Rachel's maid Bilhah conceived again and bore Jacob a second son. [8]And Rachel said, "[b-]A fateful contest I

---

[c] *Understood as "See a son"*    [d] *Heb* ra'ah, *connected with the first part of "Reuben"*
[e] *Heb* ye'ehabani, *connected with the last part of "Reuben"*
[f] *Heb* shama', *connected with "Simeon"*    [g] *Heb* yillaweh, *connected with "Levi"*
[h] *Heb* 'odeh, *connected with "Judah"*

[a] *Heb* dananni, *connected with "Dan"*

waged[b] with my sister; yes, and I have prevailed." So she named him Naphtali.

[9]When Leah saw that she had stopped bearing, she took her maid Zilpah and gave her to Jacob as concubine. [10]And when Leah's maid Zilpah bore Jacob a son, [11]Leah said, "What luck!"[c] So she named him Gad. [12]When Leah's maid Zilpah bore Jacob a second son, [13]Leah declared, "What fortune!"[d] meaning, "Women will deem me fortunate." So she named him Asher.

[14]Once, at the time of the wheat harvest, Reuben came upon some mandrakes in the field and brought them to his mother Leah. Rachel said to Leah, "Please give me some of your son's mandrakes." [15]But she said to her, "Was it not enough for you to take away my husband, that you would also take my son's mandrakes?" Rachel replied, "I promise, he shall lie with you tonight, in return for your son's mandrakes." [16]When Jacob came home from the field in the evening, Leah went out to meet him and said, "You are to sleep with me, for I have hired you with my son's mandrakes." And he lay with her that night. [17]God heeded Leah, and she conceived and bore him a fifth son. [18]And Leah said, "God has given me my reward[e] for having given my maid to my husband." So she named him Issachar. [19]When Leah conceived again and bore Jacob a sixth son, [20]Leah said, "God has given me a choice gift[f]; this time my husband will exalt me,[g] for I have borne him six sons." So she named him Zebulun. [21]Last, she bore him a daughter, and named her Dinah.

[22]Now God remembered Rachel; God heeded her and opened her womb. [23]She conceived and bore a son, and said, "God has taken away[h] my disgrace." [24]So she named him Joseph, which is to say, "May the LORD add[i] another son for me."

[25]After Rachel had borne Joseph, Jacob said to Laban, "Give me leave to go back to my own homeland. [26]Give me my wives and my children, for whom I have served you, that I may go; for well you know what services I have rendered you." [27]But Laban

---

b-b *Heb* naphtule...naphtalti, *connected with "Naphtali." Lit. "A contest of God..."*
c *Kethib* begad; *the* qere *reads* ba gad *"luck has come"; connected with "Gad"*
d *Heb* be-'oshri, *connected with "Asher"*    e *Heb* sekhari, *connected with "Issachar"*
f *Heb* zebadani . . . zebed    g *Heb* yizbeleni; *others "will dwell with me"*
h *Heb* 'asaph    i *Heb* yoseph

said to him, "If you will indulge me,$^j$ I have learned by divination that the LORD has blessed me on your account." $^{28}$And he continued, "Name the wages due from me, and I will pay you." $^{29}$But he said, "You know well how I have served you and how your livestock has fared with me. $^{30}$For the little you had before I came has grown to much, since the LORD has blessed you wherever I turned. And now, when shall I make provision for my own household?" $^{31}$He said, "What shall I pay you?" And Jacob said, "Pay me nothing! If you will do this thing for me, I will again pasture and keep your flocks: $^{32}$let me pass through your whole flock today, removing from there every speckled and spotted animal—every dark-colored sheep and every spotted and speckled goat. Such shall be my wages. $^{33}$In the future when you go over my wages, let my honesty toward you testify for me: if there are among my goats any that are not speckled or spotted or any sheep that are not dark-colored, they got there by theft." $^{34}$And Laban said, "Very well, let it be as you say."

$^{35}$But that same day he removed the streaked and spotted he-goats and all the speckled and spotted she-goats—every one that had white on it—and all the dark-colored sheep, and left them in the charge of his sons. $^{36}$And he put a distance of three days' journey between himself and Jacob, while Jacob was pasturing the rest of Laban's flock.

$^{37}$Jacob then got fresh shoots of poplar, and of almond and plane, and peeled white stripes in them, laying bare the white of the shoots. $^{38}$The rods that he had peeled he set up in front of the goats$^k$ in the troughs, the water receptacles, that the goats came to drink from. Their mating occurred when they came to drink, $^{39}$and since the goats mated by the rods, the goats brought forth streaked, speckled, and spotted young. $^{40}$But Jacob dealt separately with the sheep; he made these animals face the streaked or wholly dark-colored animals in Laban's flock. And so he produced special flocks for himself, which he did not put with Laban's flocks. $^{41}$Moreover, when the sturdier$^l$ animals were mating, Jacob would place the rods in the troughs,

j  *Lit. "If I have found favor in your eyes"*
k  *Lit. "flocks"*
l  *Or "early-breeding"*

in full view of the animals, so that they mated by the rods; <sup>42</sup>but with the feebler<sup>m</sup> animals he would not place them there. Thus the feeble ones went to Laban and the sturdy to Jacob. <sup>43</sup>So the man grew exceedingly prosperous, and came to own large flocks, maidservants and menservants, camels and asses.

31 Now he heard the things that Laban's sons were saying: "Jacob has taken all that was our father's, and from that which was our father's he has built up all this wealth." <sup>2</sup>Jacob also saw that Laban's manner toward him was not as it had been in the past. <sup>3</sup>Then the LORD said to Jacob, "Return to the land of your fathers where you were born, and I will be with you." <sup>4</sup>Jacob had Rachel and Leah called to the field, where his flock was, <sup>5</sup>and said to them, "I see that your father's manner toward me is not as it has been in the past. But the God of my father has been with me. <sup>6</sup>As you know, I have served your father with all my might; <sup>7</sup>but your father has cheated me, changing my wages time and again.<sup>a</sup> God, however, would not let him do me harm. <sup>8</sup>If he said thus, 'The speckled shall be your wages,' then all the flocks would drop speckled young; and if he said thus, 'The streaked shall be your wages,' then all the flocks would drop streaked young. <sup>9</sup>God has taken away your father's livestock and given it to me.

<sup>10</sup>"Once, at the mating time of the flocks, <sup>b-</sup>I had a dream in which I saw<sup>-b</sup> that the he-goats mating with the flock were streaked, speckled, and mottled. <sup>11</sup>And in the dream an angel of God said to me, 'Jacob!' 'Here,' I answered. <sup>12</sup>And he said, 'Note well that all the he-goats which are mating with the flock are streaked, speckled, and mottled; for I have noted all that Laban has been doing to you. <sup>13</sup>I am the God of Beth-el, where you anointed a pillar and where you made a vow to Me. Now, arise and leave this land and return to your native land.'"

<sup>14</sup>Then Rachel and Leah answered him, saying, "Have we still a share in the inheritance of our father's house? <sup>15</sup>Surely, he

<sup>m</sup> Or *"late-breeding"*

<sup>a</sup> Lit. *"ten times"*

<sup>b-b</sup> Lit. *"I raised my eyes and saw in a dream, behold"*

regards us as outsiders, now that he has sold us and has used up our purchase price. ¹⁶Truly, all the wealth that God has taken away from our father belongs to us and to our children. Now then, do just as God has told you."

¹⁷Thereupon Jacob put his children and wives on camels; ¹⁸and he drove off all his livestock and all the wealth that he had amassed, the livestock in his possession that he had acquired in Paddan-aram, to go to his father Isaac in the land of Canaan.

¹⁹Meanwhile Laban had gone to shear his sheep, and Rachel stole her father's household idols. ²⁰Jacob ᶜ⁻kept Laban the Aramean in the dark,⁻ᶜ not telling him that he was fleeing, ²¹and fled with all that he had. Soon he was across the Euphrates and heading toward the hill country of Gilead.

²²On the third day, Laban was told that Jacob had fled. ²³So he took his kinsmen with him and pursued him a distance of seven days, catching up with him in the hill country of Gilead. ²⁴But God appeared to Laban the Aramean in a dream by night and said to him, "Beware of attempting anything with Jacob, good or bad."

²⁵Laban overtook Jacob. Jacob had pitched his tent on the Height, and Laban with his kinsmen encamped in the hill country of Gilead. ²⁶And Laban said to Jacob, "What did you mean by keeping me in the dark and carrying off my daughters like captives of the sword? ²⁷Why did you flee in secrecy and mislead me and not tell me? I would have sent you off with festive music, with timbrel and lyre. ²⁸You did not even let me kiss my sons and daughters good-by! It was a foolish thing for you to do. ²⁹I have it in my power to do you harm; but the God of your father said to me last night, 'Beware of attempting anything with Jacob, good or bad.' ³⁰Very well, you had to leave because you were longing for your father's house; but why did you steal my gods?"

³¹Jacob answered Laban, saying, "I was afraid because I thought you would take your daughters from me by force. ³²But anyone with whom you find your gods shall not remain alive! In the presence of our kinsmen, point out what I have of yours and

ᶜ⁻ᶜ *Lit. "stole the mind of Laban the Aramean"; similarly in v. 26* take it." Jacob, of course, did not know that Rachel had stolen them.

³³So Laban went into Jacob's tent and Leah's tent and the tents of the two maidservants; but he did not find them. Leaving Leah's tent, he entered Rachel's tent. ³⁴Rachel, meanwhile, had taken the idols and placed them in the camel cushion and sat on them; and Laban rummaged through the tent without finding them. ³⁵For she said to her father, "Let not my lord take it amiss that I cannot rise before you, for the period of women is upon me." Thus he searched, but could not find the household idols.

³⁶Now Jacob became incensed and took up his grievance with Laban. Jacob spoke up and said to Laban, "What is my crime, what is my guilt that you should pursue me? ³⁷You rummaged through all my things; what have you found of all your household objects? Set it here, before my kinsmen and yours, and let them decide between us two.

³⁸"These twenty years I have spent in your service, your ewes and she-goats never miscarried, nor did I feast on rams from your flock. ³⁹That which was torn by beasts I never brought to you; I myself made good the loss; you exacted it of me, whether snatched by day or snatched by night. ⁴⁰Often,ᵈ scorching heat ravaged me by day and frost by night; and sleep fled from my eyes. ⁴¹Of the twenty years that I spent in your household, I served you fourteen years for your two daughters, and six years for your flocks; and you changed my wages time and again.ᵉ ⁴²Had not the God of my father, the God of Abraham and the Fearᶠ of Isaac, been with me, you would have sent me away empty-handed. But God took notice of my plight and the toil of my hands, and He gave judgment last night."

⁴³Then Laban spoke up and said to Jacob, "The daughters are my daughters, the children are my children, and the flocks are my flocks; all that you see is mine. Yet what can I do now about my daughters or the children they have borne? ⁴⁴Come, then, let us make a pact, you and I, that there may be a witness between you and me." ⁴⁵Thereupon Jacob took a stone and set it up as a

ᵈ *Lit. "I was"*
ᵉ *Lit. "ten times"*
ᶠ *Meaning of Heb* paḥad *uncertain*

pillar. ⁴⁶And Jacob said to his kinsmen, "Gather stones." So they took stones and made a mound; and they partook of a meal there by the mound. ⁴⁷Laban named it Yegar-sahadutha,ᵍ but Jacob named it Gal-ed.ʰ And Laban declared, "This mound is a witness between you and me this day." That is why it was named Gal-ed; ⁴⁹And [it was called] Mizpah, because he said, "May the LORD watchⁱ between you and me, when we are out of sight of each other. ⁵⁰If you ill-treat my daughters or take other wives besides my daughters—though no one else be about, remember, God Himself will be witness between you and me."

⁵¹And Laban said to Jacob, "Here is this mound and here the pillar which I have set up between you and me: ⁵²this mound shall be witness and this pillar shall be witness that I am not to cross to you past this mound, and that you are not to cross to me past this mound and this pillar, with hostile intent. ⁵³May the God of Abraham and the god of Nahor"—their ancestral deities —"judge between us." And Jacob swore by the Fearᶠ of his father Isaac. ⁵⁴Jacob then offered up a sacrifice on the Height, and invited his kinsmen to partake of the meal. After the meal, they spent the night on the Height.

32 Early in the morning, Laban kissed his sons and daughters and bade them good-by; then Laban left on his journey homeward. ²Jacob went on his way, and angels of God encountered him. ³When he saw them, Jacob said, "This is God's camp." So he named that place Mahanaim.ᵃ

וישלח

⁴Jacob sent messengers ahead to his brother Esau in the land of Seir, the country of Edom, ⁵and instructed them as follows, ᵇ⁻"Thus shall you say, 'To my lord Esau, thus says your servant Jacob:⁻ᵇ I stayed with Laban and remained until now; ⁶I have acquired cattle, asses, sheep, and male and female slaves; and I send this message to my lord in the hope of gaining your favor.'"

---

ᵍ Aramaic for "the mound (or, stone-heap) of witness"    ʰ Heb for "the mound (or, stone-heap) of witness," reflecting the name Gilead, v. 23    ⁱ Heb yiseph, associated with "Mizpah"    ᶠ Meaning of Heb paḥad; meaning uncertain

ᵃ Connected with Heb maḥaneh "camp"
ᵇ⁻ᵇ Or "Thus you shall say to my lord Esau, 'Thus says your servant Jacob,' . . ."

7The messengers returned to Jacob, saying, "We came to your brother Esau; he himself is coming to meet you, and there are four hundred men with him." 8Jacob was greatly frightened; in his anxiety, he divided the people with him, and the flocks and herds and camels, into two camps, 9thinking, "If Esau comes to the one camp and attacks it, the other camp may yet escape."

10Then Jacob said, "O God of my father Abraham and God of my father Isaac, O LORD, who said to me, 'Return to your native land and I will deal bountifully with you'! 11I am unworthy of all the kindness that You have so steadfastly shown Your servant: with my staff alone I crossed this Jordan, and now I have become two camps. 12Deliver me, I pray, from the hand of my brother, from the hand of Esau; else, I fear, he may come and strike me down, mothers and children alike. 13Yet You have said, 'I will deal bountifully with you and make your offspring as the sands of the sea, which are too numerous to count.'"

14After spending the night there, he selected from what was at hand these presents for his brother Esau: 15200 she-goats and 20 he-goats; 200 ewes and 20 rams; 1630 milch camels with their colts; 40 cows and 10 bulls; 20 she-asses and 10 he-asses. 17These he put in the charge of his servants, drove by drove, and he told his servants, "Go on ahead, and keep a distance between droves." 18He instructed the one in front as follows, "When my brother Esau meets you and asks you, 'Whose man are you? Where are you going? And whose [animals] are these ahead of you?' 19you shall answer, 'Your servant Jacob's; they are a gift sent to my lord Esau; and [Jacob] himself is right behind us.'" 20He gave similar instructions to the second one, and the third, and all the others who followed the droves, namely, "Thus and so shall you say to Esau when you reach him. 21And you shall add, 'And your servant Jacob himself is right behind us.'" For he reasoned, "If I propitiate him with presents in advance, and then face him, perhaps he will show me favor." 22And so the gift went on ahead, while he remained in camp that night.

23That same night he arose, and taking his two wives, his two

61

maidservants, and his eleven children, he crossed the ford of the Jabbok. <sup>24</sup>After taking them across the stream, he sent across all his possessions. <sup>25</sup>Jacob was left alone. And a man wrestled with him until the break of dawn. <sup>26</sup>When he saw that he had not prevailed against him, he wrenched Jacob's hip at its socket, so that the socket of his hip was strained as he wrestled with him. <sup>27</sup>Then he said, "Let me go, for dawn is breaking." But he answered, "I will not let you go, unless you bless me." <sup>28</sup>Said the other, "What is your name?" He replied, "Jacob." <sup>29</sup>Said he, "Your name shall no longer be Jacob, but Israel, for you have striven<sup>c</sup> with <sup>d-</sup>beings divine and human,<sup>-d</sup> and have prevailed." <sup>30</sup>Jacob asked, "Pray tell me your name." But he said, "You must not ask my name!" And he took leave of him there. <sup>31</sup>So Jacob named the place Peniel,<sup>e</sup> meaning, "I have seen a divine being face to face, yet my life has been preserved." <sup>32</sup>The sun rose upon him as he passed Penuel, limping on his hip. <sup>33</sup>That is why the children of Israel to this day do not eat the thigh muscle that is on the socket of the hip, since Jacob's hip socket was wrenched at the thigh muscle.

**33** Looking up, Jacob saw Esau coming, accompanied by four hundred men. He divided the children among Leah, Rachel, and the two maids, <sup>2</sup>putting the maids and their children first, Leah and her children next, and Rachel and Joseph last. <sup>3</sup>He himself went on ahead and bowed low to the ground seven times until he was near his brother. <sup>4</sup>Esau ran to greet him. He embraced him and, falling on his neck, he kissed him; and they wept. <sup>5</sup>Looking about, he saw the women and the children. "Who," he asked, "are these with you?" He answered, "The children with whom God has favored your servant." <sup>6</sup>Then the maids, with their children, came forward and bowed low; <sup>7</sup>next Leah, with her children, came forward and bowed low; and last, Joseph and Rachel came forward and bowed low; <sup>8</sup>And he asked, "What do you mean by all this company which I have met?" He answered, "To gain my lord's favor." <sup>9</sup>Esau said, "I

---

c *Heb* saritha, *connected with first part of "Israel"*
d-d *Or* "God (Elohim, *connected with second part of 'Israel') and men"*
e *Understood as "face of God"*

have enough, my brother; let what you have remain yours." [10]But Jacob said, "No, I pray you; if you would do me this favor, accept from me this gift; for to see your face is like seeing the face of God, and you have received me favorably. [11]Please accept my present which has been brought to you, for God has favored me and I have plenty." And when he urged him, he accepted.

[12]And [Esau] said, "Let us start on our journey, and I will proceed at your pace." [13]But he said to him, "My lord knows that the children are frail and that the flocks and herds, which are nursing, are a care to me; if they are driven hard a single day, all the flocks will die. [14]Let my lord go on ahead of his servant, while I travel slowly, at the pace of the cattle before me and at the pace of the children, until I come to my lord in Seir."

[15]Then Esau said, "Let me assign to you some of the men who are with me." But he said, "Oh no, my lord is too kind to me!" [16]So Esau started back that day on his way to Seir. [17]But Jacob journeyed on to Succoth, and built a house for himself and made stalls for his cattle; that is why the place was called Succoth.[a]

[18]Jacob arrived safe in the city of Shechem which is in the land of Canaan—having come thus from Paddan-aram—and he encamped before the city. [19]The parcel of land where he pitched his tent he purchased from the children of Hamor, Shechem's father, for a hundred kesitahs.[b] [20]He set up an altar there, and called it El-elohe-yisrael.[c]

# 34

Now Dinah, the daughter whom Leah had borne to Jacob, went out to visit the daughters of the land. [2]Shechem son of Hamor the Hivite, chief of the country, saw her, and took her and lay with her by force. [3]Being strongly drawn to Dinah daughter of Jacob, and in love with the maiden, he spoke to the maiden tenderly. [4]So Shechem said to his father Hamor, "Get me this girl as a wife."

[a] Meaning "stalls," "huts," "booths"
[b] Heb qesiṭah, a unit of unknown value
[c] "El, God of Israel"

⁵Jacob heard that he had defiled his daughter Dinah; but since his sons were in the field with his cattle, Jacob kept silent until they came home. ⁶Then Shechem's father Hamor came out to Jacob to speak to him. ⁷Meanwhile Jacob's sons, having heard the news, came in from the field. The men were distressed and very angry, because he had committed an outrage in Israel by lying with Jacob's daughter—a thing not to be done.

⁸And Hamor spoke with them, saying, "My son Shechem longs for your daughter. Please give her to him in marriage. ⁹Intermarry with us: give your daughters to us, and take our daughters for yourselves: ¹⁰You will dwell among us, and the land will be open before you; settle, move about, and acquire holdings in it." ¹¹Then Shechem said to her father and brothers, "Do me this favor, and I will pay whatever you tell me. ¹²Ask of me a bride-price ever so high, as well as gifts, and I will pay what you tell me; only give me the maiden for a wife."

¹³Jacob's sons answered Shechem and his father Hamor—speaking with guile because he had defiled their sister Dinah—¹⁴and said to them, "We cannot do this thing, to give our sister to a man who is uncircumcised, for that is a disgrace among us. ¹⁵Only on this condition will we agree with you; that you will become like us in that every male among you is circumcised. ¹⁶Then we will give our daughters to you and take your daughters to ourselves; and we will dwell among you and become as one kindred. ¹⁷But if you will not listen to us and become circumcised, we will take our daughter and go."

¹⁸Their words pleased Hamor and Hamor's son Shechem. ¹⁹And the youth lost no time in doing the thing, for he wanted Jacob's daughter. Now he was the most respected in his father's house. ²⁰So Hamor and his son Shechem went to the ᵃ-public placeᵃ of their town and spoke to their fellow townsmen, saying, ²¹"These people are our friends; let them settle in the land and move about in it, for the land is large enough for them; we will take their daughters to ourselves as wives and give our daughters to them. ²²But only on this condition will the men agree

a-a Lit. "gate"

with us to dwell among us and be as one kindred: that all our males become circumcised as they are circumcised. ²³Their cattle and substance and all their beasts will be ours, if we only agree to their terms, so that they will settle among us." ²⁴All ᵇ-who went out of the gate of his town-ᵇ heeded Hamor and his son Shechem, and all males, ᵇ-all those who went out of the gate of his town,-ᵇ were circumcised.

²⁵On the third day, when they were in pain, Simeon and Levi, two of Jacob's sons, brothers of Dinah, took each his sword, came upon the city unmolested, and slew all the males. ²⁶They put Hamor and his son Shechem to the sword, took Dinah out of Shechem's house, and went away. ²⁷The other sons of Jacob came upon the slain and plundered the town, because their sister had been defiled. ²⁸They seized their flocks and herds and asses, all that was inside the town and outside; ²⁹all their wealth, all their children, and their wives, all that was in the houses, they took as captives and booty.

³⁰Jacob said to Simeon and Levi, "You have brought trouble on me, making me odious among the inhabitants of the land, the Canaanites and the Perizzites; my men are few in number, so that if they unite against me and attack me, I and my house will be destroyed." ³¹But they answered, "Should our sister be treated like a whore?"

3 5 God said to Jacob, "Arise, go up to Bethel and remain there; and build an altar there to the God who appeared to you when you were fleeing from your brother Esau." ²So Jacob said to his household and to all who were with him, "Rid yourselves of the alien gods in your midst, purify yourselves, and change your clothes. ³Come, let us go up to Bethel, and I will build an altar there to the God who answered me when I was in distress and who has been with me wherever I have gone." ⁴They gave to Jacob all the alien gods that they had, and the rings that were in their ears, and Jacob buried them under the terebinth that

---

b-b *I.e. all his fellow townsmen*

was near Shechem. [5]As they set out, a terror from God fell on the cities round about, so that they did not pursue the sons of Jacob.

[6]Thus Jacob came to Luz—that is, Bethel—in the land of Canaan, he and all the people who were with him. [7]There he built an altar and named the site El-bethel,[a] for it was there that God had revealed Himself to him when he was fleeing from his brother.

[8]Deborah, Rebekah's nurse, died, and was buried under the oak below Bethel; so it was named Allon-bacuth.[b]

[9]God appeared again to Jacob on his arrival from Paddan-aram, and He blessed him. [10]God said to him,

"You whose name is Jacob,
You shall be called Jacob no more,
But Israel shall be your name."

Thus He named him Israel.

[11]And God said to him,

"I am El Shaddai.[c]
Be fertile and increase;
A nation, yea an assembly of nations,
Shall descend from you.
Kings shall issue from your loins.
[12]The land that I assigned to Abraham and Isaac
I assign to you;
And to your offspring to come
Will I assign the land."

[13]God parted from him at the spot where He had spoken to him; [14]and Jacob set up a pillar at the site where He had spoken to him, a pillar of stone, and he offered a libation on it and poured oil upon it. [15]Jacob gave the site, where God had spoken to him, the name of Bethel.

[16]They set out from Bethel; but when they were still some distance short of Ephrath, Rachel was in childbirth, and she had hard labor. [17]When her labor was at its hardest, the midwife said

a *"The God of Bethel"*
b *Understood as "the oak of the weeping"*
c *Cf. 17.1*

to her, "Have no fear, for it is another boy for you." ¹⁸But as she breathed her last—for she was dying—she named him Ben-oni*ᵈ*; but his father called him Benjamin.*ᵉ* Thus Rachel died. She was buried on the road to Ephrath—now Bethlehem. ²⁰Over her grave Jacob set up a pillar; it is the pillar at Rachel's grave to this day. ²¹Israel journeyed on, and pitched his tent beyond Migdal-eder.

²²While Israel stayed in that land, Reuben went and lay with Bilhah, his father's concubine; and Israel found out.

Now the sons of Jacob were twelve in number. ²³The sons of Leah: Reuben—Jacob's first-born—Simeon, Levi, Judah, Issachar, and Zebulun. ²⁴The sons of Rachel: Joseph and Benjamin. ²⁵The sons of Bilhah, Rachel's maid: Dan and Naphtali. ²⁶And the sons of Zilpah, Leah's maid: Gad and Asher. These are the sons of Jacob who were born to him in Paddan-aram.

²⁷And Jacob came to his father Isaac at Mamre, at Kiriath-arba—now Hebron—where Abraham and Isaac had sojourned. ²⁸Isaac was a hundred and eighty years old ²⁹when he breathed his last and died. He*ᶠ* was gathered to his kin in ripe old age; and he was buried by his sons Esau and Jacob.

# 36 This is the line of Esau—that is, Edom.

²Esau took his wives from among the Canaanite women—Adah daughter of Elon the Hittite, and Oholibamah daughter of Anah daughter of Zibeon the Hivite*ᵃ*—³and also Basemath daughter of Ishmael and sister of Nebaioth. ⁴Adah bore to Esau Eliphaz; Basemath bore Reuel; ⁵and Oholibamah bore Jeush, Jalam, and Korah. Those were the sons of Esau, who were born to him in the land of Canaan.

⁶Esau took his wives, his sons and daughters, and all the members of his household, his cattle and all his livestock, and all the property that he had acquired in the land of Canaan, and went to

ᵈ *Understood as "son of my suffering (or, strength)"*
ᵉ *I.e. "son of the right hand," or "son of the south"*
ᶠ *Lit. "Isaac"*

ᵃ *Cf. v. 20, "Horite"*

another land because of his brother Jacob. [7]For their possessions were too many for them to dwell together, and the land where they sojourned could not support them because of their livestock. [8]So Esau settled in the hill country of Seir—Esau being Edom.

[9]This, then, is the line of Esau, the ancestor of the Edomites, in the hill country of Seir.

[10]These are the names of Esau's sons: Eliphaz, the son of Esau's wife Adah; Reuel, the son of Esau's wife Basemath. [11]The sons of Eliphaz were Teman, Omar, Zepho, Gatam, and Kenaz. [12]Timna was a concubine of Esau's son Eliphaz; she bore Amalek to Eliphaz. Those were the descendants of Esau's wife Adah. [13]And these were the sons of Reuel: Nahath, Zerah, Shammah, and Mizzah. Those were the descendants of Esau's wife Basemath. [14]And these were the sons of Esau's wife Oholibamah, daughter of Anah daughter of Zibeon: she bore to Esau Jeush, Jalam, and Korah.

[15]These are the clans of the children of Esau. The descendants of Esau's first-born Eliphaz: the clans Teman, Omar, Zepho, Kenaz, [16]Korah, Gatam, and Amalek; these are the clans of Eliphaz in the land of Edom. Those are the descendants of Adah. [17]And these are the descendants of Esau's son Reuel: the clans Nahath, Zerah, Shammah, and Mizzah; these are the clans of Reuel in the land of Edom. Those are the descendants of Esau's wife Basemath. [18]And these are the descendants of Esau's wife Oholibamah: the clans Jeush, Jalam, and Korah; these are the clans of Esau's wife Oholibamah, the daughter of Anah. [19]Those were the sons of Esau—that is, Edom—and those are their clans.

[20]These were the sons of Seir the Horite, who were settled in the land: Lotan, Shobal, Zibeon, Anah, [21]Dishon, Ezer, and Dishan. Those are the clans of the Horites, the descendants of Seir, in the land of Edom.

[22]The sons of Lotan were Hori and Hemam; and Lotan's sister was Timna. [23]The sons of Shobal were these: Alvan, Manahath, Ebal, Shepho, and Onam. [24]The sons of Zibeon were these: Aiah[b] and Anah—that was the Anah who discovered the hot springs[c] in

b *Heb "and Aiah"*
c *Meaning of Heb* yemim *uncertain*

the wilderness while pasturing the asses of his father Zibeon. ²⁵The children of Anah were these: Dishon and Anah's daughter Oholibamah. ²⁶The sons of Dishon*ᵈ* were these: Hemdan, Eshban, Ithran, and Cheran. ²⁷The sons of Ezer were these: Bilhan, Zaavan, and Akan. ²⁸And the sons of Dishan were these: Uz and Aran.

²⁹These are the clans of the Horites: the clans Lotan, Shobal, Zibeon, Anah, ³⁰Dishon, Ezer, and Dishan. Those are the clans of the Horites, clan by clan, in the land of Seir.

³¹These are the kings who reigned in the land of Edom before any king reigned over the Israelites. ³²Bela son of Beor reigned in Edom, and the name of his city was Dinhabah. ³³When Bela died, Jobab son of Zerah, from Bozrah, succeeded him as king. ³⁴When Jobab died, Husham of the land of the Temanites succeeded him as king. ³⁵When Husham died, Hadad son of Bedad, who defeated the Midianites in the country of Moab, succeeded him as king; the name of his city was Avith. ³⁶When Hadad died, Samlah of Masrekah succeeded him as king. ³⁷When Samlah died, Saul*ᵉ* of Rehoboth-on-the-river succeeded him as king. ³⁸When Saul died, Baal-hanan son of Achbor succeeded him as king. ³⁹And when Baal-hanan son of Achbor died, Hadar succeeded him as king; the name of his city was Pau, and his wife's name was Mehetabel daughter of Matred daughter of Me-zahab.

⁴⁰These are the names of the clans of Esau, each with its families and locality, name by name: the clans Timna, Alvah, Jetheth, ⁴¹Oholibamah, Elah, Pinon, ⁴²Kenaz, Teman, Mibzar, ⁴³Magdiel, and Iram. Those are the clans of Edom—that is, of Esau, father of the Edomites—by their settlements in the land which they hold.

וישב

**37** Now Jacob was settled in the land where his father had sojourned, the land of Canaan. ²This, then, is the line of Jacob:

At seventeen years of age, Joseph tended the flocks with his brothers, as a helper to the sons of his father's wives Bilhah and

---

ᵈ *Heb* Dishan; *but cf. vv. 21, 25, 28, and 30, and I Chron 1.41*
ᵉ *Or "Shaul"*

Zilpah. And Joseph brought bad reports of them to their father. ³Now Israel loved Joseph best of all his sons, for he was the child of his old age; and he had made him an ornamented tunic.ᵃ ⁴And when his brothers saw that their father loved him more than any of his brothers, they hated him so that they could not speak a friendly word to him.

⁵Once Joseph had a dream which he told to his brothers; and they hated him even more. ⁶He said to them, "Hear this dream which I have dreamed: ⁷There we were binding sheaves in the field, when suddenly my sheaf stood up and remained upright; then your sheaves gathered around and bowed low to my sheaf." ⁸His brothers answered, "Do you mean to reign over us? Do you mean to rule over us?" And they hated him even more for his talk about his dreams.

⁹He dreamed another dream and told it to his brothers, saying, "Look, I have had another dream: And this time, the sun, the moon, and eleven stars were bowing down to me." ¹⁰And when he told it to his father and brothers, his father berated him. "What," he said to him, "is this dream you have dreamed? Are we to come, I and your mother and your brothers, and bow low to you to the ground?" ¹¹So his brothers were wrought up at him, and his father kept the matter in mind.

¹²One time, when his brothers had gone to pasture their father's flock at Shechem, ¹³Israel said to Joseph, "Your brothers are pasturing at Shechem. Come, I will send you to them." He answered, "I am ready." ¹⁴And he said to him, "Go and see how your brothers are and how the flocks are faring, and bring me back word." So he sent him from the valley of Hebron.

When he reached Shechem, ¹⁵a man came upon him wandering in the fields. The man asked him, "What are you looking for?" ¹⁶He answered, "I am looking for my brothers. Could you tell me where they are pasturing?" ¹⁷The man said, "They have gone from here, for I heard them say: Let us go to Dothan." So Joseph followed his brothers and found them at Dothan.

¹⁸They saw him from afar, and before he came close to them they conspired to kill him. ¹⁹They said to one another, "Here

ᵃ Or "a coat of many colors"; meaning of Heb uncertain

comes that dreamer! [20]Come now, let us kill him and throw him into one of the pits; and we can say, 'A savage beast devoured him.' We shall see what comes of his dreams!" [21]But when Reuben heard it, he tried to save him from them. He said, "Let us not take his life." [22]And Reuben went on, "Shed no blood! Cast him into that pit out in the wilderness, but do not touch him yourselves"— intending to save him from them and restore him to his father. [23]When Joseph came up to his brothers, they stripped Joseph of his tunic, the ornamented tunic that he was wearing, [24]and took him and cast him into the pit. The pit was empty; there was no water in it.

[25]Then they sat down to a meal. Looking up, they saw a caravan of Ishmaelites coming from Gilead, their camels bearing gum, balm, and ladanum to be taken to Egypt. [26]Then Judah said to his brothers, "What do we gain by killing our brother and covering up his blood? [27]Come, let us sell him to the Ishmaelites, but let us not do away with him ourselves. After all, he is our brother, our own flesh." His brothers agreed. [28]When Midianite traders passed by, they pulled Joseph up out of the pit. They sold Joseph for twenty pieces of silver to the Ishmaelites, who brought Joseph to Egypt.

[29]When Reuben returned to the pit and saw that Joseph was not in the pit, he rent his clothes. [30]Returning to his brothers, he said, "The boy is gone! Now, what am I to do?" [31]Then they took Joseph's tunic, slaughtered a kid, and dipped the tunic in the blood. [32]They had the ornamented tunic taken to their father, and they said, "We found this. Please examine it; is it your son's tunic or not?" [33]He recognized it, and said, "My son's tunic! A savage beast devoured him! Joseph was torn by a beast!" [34]Jacob rent his clothes, put sackcloth on his loins, and observed mourning for his son many days. [35]All his sons and daughters sought to comfort him; but he refused to be comforted, saying, "No, I will go down mourning to my son in Sheol." Thus his father bewailed him.

[36]The Midianites,[b] meanwhile, sold him in Egypt to Potiphar, a courtier of Pharaoh and his chief steward.

b *Heb "Medanites"*

38 About that time Judah left his brothers and camped near a certain Adullamite whose name was Hirah. [2]There Judah saw the daughter of a certain Canaanite whose name was Shua, and he married her and cohabited with her. [3]She conceived and bore a son, and he named him Er. [4]She conceived again and bore a son, and named him Onan. [5]Once again she bore a son, and named him Shelah; he was at Chezib when she bore him.

[6]Judah got a wife for Er his first-born; her name was Tamar. [7]But Er, Judah's first-born, was displeasing to the LORD, and the LORD took his life. [8]Then Judah said to Onan, "Join with your brother's wife and do your duty by her as a brother-in-law,[a] and provide offspring for your brother." [9]But Onan, knowing that the seed would not count as his, let it go to waste[b] whenever he joined with his brother's wife, so as not to provide offspring for his brother. [10]What he did was displeasing to the LORD, and He took his life also. [11]Then Judah said to his daughter-in-law Tamar, "Stay as a widow in your father's house until my son Shelah grows up"—for he thought, "He too might die like his brothers." So Tamar went to live in her father's house.

[12]A long time afterward, Shua's daughter, the wife of Judah, died. When [c-]his period of mourning was over,[-c] Judah went up to Timnah to his sheepshearers, together with his friend Hirah the Adullamite. [13]And Tamar was told, "Your father-in-law is coming up to Timnah for the sheepshearing." [14]So she took off her widow's garb, covered her face with a veil, and, wrapping herself up, sat down at the entrance to Enaim,[d] which is on the road to Timnah; for she saw that Shelah was grown up, yet she had not been given to him as wife. [15]When Judah saw her, he took her for a harlot; for she had covered her face. [16]So he turned aside to her by the road and said, "Here, let me sleep with you"—for he did not know that she was his daughter-in-law. "What," she asked, "will you pay for sleeping with me?" [17]He replied, "I will send a kid from my flock." But she said, "You must leave a pledge until you have sent it." [18]And he said, "What pledge shall I give you?" She

a Cf. Deut. 25.5
b Lit. "spoil on the ground"
c-c Lit. "he was comforted"
d Cf. Enam, Josh. 15.34 Others "in an open place" or "at the crossroad"

replied, "Your seal and cord, and the staff which you carry." So he gave them to her and slept with her, and she conceived by him. ¹⁹Then she went on her way. She took off her veil and again put on her widow's garb.

²⁰Judah sent the kid by his friend the Adullamite, to redeem the pledge from the woman; but he could not find her. ²¹He inquired of the people of that town, "Where is the cult prostitute, the one at Enaim, by the road?" But they said, "There has been no prostitute here." ²²So he returned to Judah and said, "I could not find her; moreover, the townspeople said: There has been no prostitute here." ²³Judah said, "Let her keep them, lest we become a laughingstock. I did send her this kid, but you did not find her."

²⁴About three months later, Judah was told, "Your daughter-in-law Tamar has played the harlot; in fact, she is with child by harlotry." "Bring her out," said Judah, "and let her be burned." ²⁵As she was being brought out, she sent this message to her father-in-law, "I am with child by the man to whom these belong." And she added, "Examine these: whose seal and cord and staff are these?" ²⁶Judah recognized them, and said, "She is more in the right than I, inasmuch as I did not give her to my son Shelah." And he was not intimate with her again.

²⁷When the time came for her to give birth, there were twins in her womb! ²⁸While she was in labor, one of them put out his hand, and the midwife tied a crimson thread on that hand, to signify: This one came out first. ²⁹But just then he drew back his hand, and out came his brother; and she said, "What a breach* you have made for yourself!" So he was named Perez. ³⁰Afterward his brother came out, on whose hand was the crimson thread; he was named Zerah.ᶠ

# 39

When Joseph was taken down to Egypt, a certain Egyptian, Potiphar, a courtier of Pharaoh and his chief steward, bought him from the Ishmaelites who had brought him there. ²The

---

ᵉ *Heb* pereṣ
ᶠ *I.e. "brightness," perhaps alluding to the crimson thread*

LORD was with Joseph, and he was a successful man; and he stayed in the house of his Egyptian master. ³And when his master saw that the LORD was with him and that the LORD lent success to everything he undertook, ⁴he took a liking to Joseph. He made him his personal attendant and put him in charge of his household, placing in his hands all that he owned. ⁵And from the time that the Egyptian put him in charge of his household and of all that he owned, the LORD blessed his house for Joseph's sake, so that the blessing of the LORD was upon everything that he owned, in the house and outside. ⁶He left all that he had in Joseph's hands and, with him there, he paid attention to nothing save the food that he ate. Now Joseph was well built and handsome.

⁷After a time, his master's wife cast her eyes upon Joseph and said, "Lie with me." ⁸But he refused. He said to his master's wife, "Look, with me here, my master gives no thought to anything in this house, and all that he owns he has placed in my hands. ⁹He wields no more authority in this house than I, and he has withheld nothing from me except yourself, since you are his wife. How then could I do this most wicked thing, and sin before God?" ¹⁰And much as she coaxed Joseph day after day, he did not yield to her request to lie beside her, to be with her.

¹¹One such day, he came into the house to do his work. None of the household being there inside, ¹²she caught hold of him by his garment and said, "Lie with me!" But he left his garment in her hand and got away and fled outside. ¹³When she saw that he had left it in her hand and had fled outside, ¹⁴she called out to her servants and said to them, "Look, he had to bring us a Hebrew to dally with us! This one came to lie with me; but I screamed loud. ¹⁵And when he heard me screaming at the top of my voice, he left his garment with me and got away and fled outside." ¹⁶She kept his garment beside her, until his master came home. ¹⁷Then she told him the same story, saying, "The Hebrew slave whom you brought into our house came to me to dally with me; ¹⁸but when I screamed at the top of my voice, he left his garment with me and fled outside."

[19]When his master heard the story that his wife told him, namely, "Thus and so your slave did to me," he was furious. [20]So Joseph's master had him put in prison, where the king's prisoners were confined. But even while he was there in prison, [21]the LORD was with Joseph: He extended kindness to him and disposed the chief jailer favorably toward him. [22]The chief jailer put in Joseph's charge all the prisoners who were in that prison, and he was the one to carry out everything that was done there. [23]The chief jailer did not supervise anything that was in Joseph's[a] charge, because the LORD was with him, and whatever he did the LORD made successful.

# 40

Some time later, the cupbearer and the baker of the king of Egypt gave offense to their lord the king of Egypt. [2]Pharaoh was angry with his two courtiers, the chief cupbearer and the chief baker, [3]and put them in custody, in the house of the chief steward, in the same prison house where Joseph was confined. [4]The chief steward assigned Joseph to them, and he attended them.

When they had been in custody for some time, [5]both of them—the cupbearer and the baker of the king of Egypt, who were confined in the prison—dreamed in the same night, each his own dream and each dream with its own meaning. [6]When Joseph came to them in the morning, he saw that they were distraught. [7]He asked Pharaoh's courtiers, who were with him in custody in his master's house, saying, "Why do you appear downcast today?" [8]And they said to him, "We had dreams, and there is no one to interpret them." So Joseph said to them, "Surely God can interpret! Tell me [your dreams]."

[9]Then the chief cupbearer told his dream to Joseph. He said to him, "In my dream, there was a vine in front of me. [10]On the vine were three branches. It had barely budded, when out came its blossoms and its clusters ripened into grapes. [11]Pharaoh's cup was in my hand, and I took the grapes, pressed them into Pharaoh's

---

[a] *Lit. "his"*

cup, and placed the cup in Pharaoh's hand." [12]Joseph said to him, "This is its interpretation: The three branches are three days. [13]In three days Pharaoh will pardon you[a] and restore you to your post; you will place Pharaoh's cup in his hand, as was your custom formerly when you were his cupbearer. [14]But think of me when all is well with you again, and do me the kindness of mentioning me to Pharaoh, so as to free me from this place. [15]For in truth, I was kidnapped from the land of the Hebrews; nor have I done anything here that they should have put me in the dungeon."

[16]When the chief baker saw how favorably he had interpreted, he said to Joseph, "In my dream, similarly, there were three openwork baskets[b] on my head. [17]In the uppermost basket were all kinds of food for Pharaoh that a baker prepares; and the birds were eating it out of the basket above my head." [18]Joseph answered, "This is its interpretation: The three baskets are three days. [19]In three days Pharaoh will lift off your head and impale you upon a pole; and the birds will pick off your flesh."

[20]On the third day—his birthday—Pharaoh made a banquet for all his officials, and he singled out[c] his chief cupbearer and his chief baker from among his officials. [21]He restored the chief cupbearer to his cupbearing, and he placed the cup in Pharaoh's hand; [22]but the chief baker he impaled—just as Joseph had interpreted to them.

[23]Yet the chief cupbearer did not think of Joseph; he forgot him.

מקץ

**41** After two years' time, Pharaoh dreamed that he was standing by the Nile, [2]when out of the Nile there came up seven cows, handsome and sturdy, and they grazed in the reed grass. [3]But presently, seven other cows came up from the Nile close behind them, ugly and gaunt, and stood beside the cows on the bank of the Nile; [4]and the ugly gaunt cows ate up the seven handsome sturdy cows. And Pharaoh awoke.

---

[a] Lit. "lift up your head"
[b] Others "baskets with white bread" or "white baskets"; meaning of Heb hori uncertain
[c] Lit. "lifted the head of"

⁵He fell asleep and dreamed a second time: Seven ears of grain, solid and healthy, grew on a single stalk. ⁶But close behind them sprouted seven ears, thin and scorched by the east wind. ⁷And the thin ears swallowed up the seven solid and full ears. Then Pharaoh awoke: it was a dream!

⁸Next morning, his spirit was agitated, and he sent for all the magicians of Egypt, and all its wise men; and Pharaoh told them his dreams, but none could interpret them for Pharaoh.

⁹The chief cupbearer then spoke up and said to Pharaoh, "I must make mention today of my offenses. ¹⁰Once Pharaoh was angry with his servants, and placed me in custody in the house of the chief steward, together with the chief baker. ¹¹We had dreams the same night, he and I, each of us a dream with a meaning of its own. ¹²A Hebrew youth was there with us, a servant of the chief steward; and when we told him our dreams, he interpreted them for us, telling each of the meaning of his dream. ¹³And as he interpreted for us, so it came to pass: I was restored to my post, and the other was impaled."

¹⁴Thereupon Pharaoh sent for Joseph, and he was rushed from the dungeon. He had his hair cut and changed his clothes, and he appeared before Pharaoh. ¹⁵And Pharaoh said to Joseph, "I have had a dream, but no one can interpret it. Now I have heard it said of you that for you to hear a dream is to tell its meaning." ¹⁶Joseph answered Pharaoh, saying, "Not I! God will see to Pharaoh's welfare."

¹⁷Then Pharaoh said to Joseph, "In my dream, I was standing on the bank of the Nile, ¹⁸when out of the Nile came up seven sturdy and well-formed cows and grazed in the reed grass. ¹⁹Presently there followed them seven other cows, scrawny, ill-formed, and emaciated—never had I seen their likes for ugliness in all the land of Egypt! ²⁰And the seven lean and ugly cows ate up the first seven cows, the sturdy ones; ²¹but when they had consumed them, one could not tell that they had consumed them, for they looked just as bad as before. And I awoke. ²²In my other dream, I

saw seven ears of grain, full and healthy, growing on a single stalk; 23but right behind them sprouted seven ears, shriveled, thin, and scorched by the east wind. 24And the thin ears swallowed the seven healthy ears. I have told my magicians, but none has an explanation for me."

25And Joseph said to Pharaoh, "Pharaoh's dreams are one and the same: God has told Pharaoh what He is about to do. 26The seven healthy cows are seven years, and the seven healthy ears are seven years; it is the same dream. 27The seven lean and ugly cows that followed are seven years, as are also the seven empty ears scorched by the east wind; they are seven years of famine. 28It is just as I have told Pharaoh: God has revealed to Pharaoh what He is about to do. 29Immediately ahead are seven years of great abundance in all the land of Egypt. 30After them will come seven years of famine, and all the abundance in the land of Egypt will be forgotten. As the land is ravaged by famine, 31no trace of the abundance will be left in the land because of the famine thereafter, for it will be very severe. 32As for Pharaoh having had the same dream twice, it means that the matter has been determined by God, and that God will soon carry it out.

33"Accordingly, let Pharaoh find a man of discernment and wisdom, and set him over the land of Egypt. 34And let Pharaoh take steps to appoint overseers over the land, and organize*a* the land of Egypt in the seven years of plenty. 35Let all the food of these good years that are coming be gathered, and let the grain be collected under Pharaoh's authority as food to be stored in the cities. 36Let that food be a reserve for the land for the seven years of famine which will come upon the land of Egypt, so that the land may not perish in the famine."

37The plan pleased Pharaoh and all his courtiers. 38And Pharaoh said to his courtiers, "Could we find another like him, a man in whom is the spirit of God?" 39So Pharaoh said to Joseph, "Since God has made all this known to you, there is none so discerning and wise as you. 40You shall be in charge of my court, and by your

---

a Others "take a fifth part of"; meaning of Heb uncertain

command shall all my people be directed[b]; only with respect to the throne shall I be superior to you." 41Pharaoh further said to Joseph, "See, I put you in charge of all the land of Egypt." 42And removing his signet ring from his hand, Pharaoh put it on Joseph's hand; and he had him dressed in robes of fine linen, and put a gold chain about his neck. 43He had him ride in the chariot of his second-in-command, and they cried before him, "Abrek!"[c] Thus he placed him over all the land of Egypt.

44Pharaoh said to Joseph, "I am Pharaoh; yet without you, no one shall lift up hand or foot in all the land of Egypt." 45Pharaoh then gave Joseph the name Zaphenath-paneah[d]; and he gave him for a wife Asenath daughter of Poti-phera, priest of On. Thus Joseph emerged in charge of the land of Egypt.—46Joseph was thirty years old when he entered the service of Pharaoh king of Egypt.—Leaving Pharaoh's presence, Joseph traveled through all the land of Egypt.

47During the seven years of plenty, the land produced in abundance. 48And he gathered all the grain of [e-the seven years that the land of Egypt was enjoying,-e] and stored the grain in the cities; he put in each city the grain of the fields around it. 49So Joseph collected produce in very large quantity, like the sands of the sea, until he ceased to measure it, for it could not be measured.

50Before the years of famine came, Joseph became the father of two sons, whom Asenath daughter of Poti-phera, priest of On, bore to him. 51Joseph named the first-born Manasseh, meaning, "God has made me forget[f] completely my hardship and my parental home." 52And the second he named Ephraim, meaning, "God has made me fertile[g] in the land of my affliction."

53The seven years of abundance that the land of Egypt enjoyed came to an end, 54and the seven years of famine set in, just as Joseph had foretold. There was famine in all lands, but throughout the land of Egypt there was bread. 55And when all the land of Egypt felt the hunger, the people cried out to Pharaoh for bread; and Pharaoh said to all the Egyptians, "Go to Joseph; whatever he

---

b Others "order themselves" or "pay homage"; meaning of Heb yishshaq uncertain
c Others "Bow the knee," as though from Heb barakh "to kneel"; perhaps from an Egyptian word of unknown meaning    d Egyptian for "God speaks; he lives," or "creator of life"    e-e Lit. "the seven years that were in the land of Egypt"    f Heb nashshani, connected with Manasseh (Menashsheh)
g Heb hiphrani, connected with "Ephraim"

tells you, you shall do."—⁵⁶Accordingly, when the famine became severe in the land of Egypt, Joseph laid open all that was within, and rationed out grain to the Egyptians. The famine, however, spread over the whole world. ⁵⁷So all the world came to Joseph in Egypt to procure rations, for the famine had become severe throughout the world.

**42** When Jacob saw that there were food rations to be had in Egypt, he*ᵃ* said to his sons, "Why do you keep looking at one another? ²Now I hear," he went on, "that there are rations to be had in Egypt. Go down and procure rations for us there, that we may live and not die." ³So ten of Joseph's brothers went down to get grain rations in Egypt; ⁴for Jacob did not send Joseph's brother Benjamin with his brothers, since he feared that he might meet with disaster. ⁵Thus the sons of Israel were among those who came to procure rations, for the famine extended to the land of Canaan.

⁶Now Joseph was the vizier of the land; it was he who dispensed rations to all the people of the land. And Joseph's brothers came and bowed low to him, with their faces to the ground. ⁷When Joseph saw his brothers, he recognized them; but he acted like a stranger toward them and spoke harshly to them. He asked them, "Where do you come from?" And they said, "From the land of Canaan, to procure food." ⁸For though Joseph recognized his brothers, they did not recognize him. ⁹Recalling the dreams that he had dreamed about them, Joseph said to them, "You are spies, you have come to see the land in its nakedness." ¹⁰But they said to him, "No, my lord! Truly, your servants have come to procure food. ¹¹We are all of us sons of the same man; we are honest men; your servants have never been spies!" ¹²And he said to them, "No, you have come to see the land in its nakedness!" ¹³And they replied, "We your servants were twelve brothers, sons of a certain man in the land of Canaan; the youngest, however, is now with

ᵃ *Lit. "Jacob"*

80

our father, and one is no more." ¹⁴But Joseph said to them, "It is just as I have told you: You are spies! ¹⁵By this you shall be put to the test: unless your youngest brother comes here, by Pharaoh, you shall not depart from this place! ¹⁶Let one of you go and bring your brother, while the rest of you remain confined, that your words may be put to the test whether there is truth in you. Else, by Pharaoh, you are nothing but spies!" ¹⁷And he confined them in the guardhouse for three days.

¹⁸On the third day Joseph said to them, "Do this and you shall live, for I am a God-fearing man. ¹⁹If you are honest men, let one of you brothers be held in your place of detention, while the rest of you go and take home rations for your starving households; ²⁰but you must bring me your youngest brother, that your words may be verified and that you may not die." And they did accordingly. ²¹They said to one another, "Alas, we are being punished on account of our brother, because we looked on at his anguish, yet paid no heed as he pleaded with us. That is why this distress has come upon us." ²²Then Reuben spoke up and said to them, "Did I not tell you, 'Do no wrong to the boy'? But you paid no heed. Now comes the reckoning for his blood." ²³They did not know that Joseph understood, for there was an interpreter between him and them. ²⁴He turned away from them and wept. But he came back to them and spoke to them; and he took Simeon from among them and had him bound before their eyes. ²⁵Then Joseph gave orders to fill their bags with grain, return each one's money to his sack, and give them provisions for the journey; and this was done for them. ²⁶So they loaded their asses with the rations and departed from there.

²⁷As one of them was opening his sack to give feed to his ass at the night encampment, he saw his money right there at the mouth of his bag. ²⁸And he said to his brothers, "My money has been returned! It is here in my bag!" Their hearts sank; and, trembling, they turned to one another, saying, "What is this that God has done to us?"

²⁹When they came to their father Jacob in the land of Canaan, they told him all that had befallen them, saying, ³⁰"The man who is lord of the land spoke harshly to us and accused us of spying on the land. ³¹We said to him, 'We are honest men; we have never been spies! ³²There were twelve of us brothers, sons by the same father; but one is no more, and the youngest is now with our father in the land of Canaan.' ³³But the man who is lord of the land said to us, 'By this I shall know that you are honest men: leave one of your brothers with me, and take something for your starving households and be off. ³⁴And bring your youngest brother to me, that I may know that you are not spies but honest men. I will then restore your brother to you, and you shall be free to move about in the land.'"

³⁵As they were emptying their sacks, there, in each one's sack, was his money-bag! When they and their father saw their money-bags, they were dismayed. ³⁶Their father Jacob said to them, "It is always me that you bereave: Joseph is no more and Simeon is no more, and now you would take away Benjamin. These things always happen to me!" ³⁷Then Reuben said to his father, "You may kill my two sons if I do not bring him back to you. Put him in my care, and I will return him to you." ³⁸But he said, "My son must not go down with you, for his brother is dead and he alone is left. If he meets with disaster on the journey you are taking, you will send my white head down to Sheol in grief."

43 But the famine in the land was severe. ²And when they had eaten up the rations which they had brought from Egypt, their father said to them, "Go again and procure some food for us." ³But Judah said to him, "The man warned us, 'Do not let me see your faces unless your brother is with you.' ⁴If you will let our brother go with us, we will go down and procure food for you; ⁵but if you will not let him go, we will not go down, for the man said to us, '*ᵃ*Do not let me see your faces*ᵃ* unless your brother is with you.'" ⁶And Israel said, "Why did you serve me so ill as to tell

a-a *Lit. "Do not see my face"*

82

the man that you had another brother?" ⁷They replied, "But the man kept asking about us and our family, saying, 'Is your father still living? Have you another brother?' And we answered him accordingly. How were we to know that he would say, 'Bring your brother here'?"

⁸Then Judah said to his father Israel, "Send the boy in my care, and let us be on our way, that we may live and not die—you and we and our children. ⁹I myself will be surety for him; you may hold me responsible: if I do not bring him back to you and set him before you, I shall stand guilty before you forever. ¹⁰For we could have been there and back twice if we had not dawdled."

¹¹Then their father Israel said to them, "If it must be so, do this: take some of the choice products of the land in your baggage, and carry them down as a gift for the man—some balm and some honey, gum, ladanum, pistachio nuts, and almonds. ¹²And take with you double the money, carrying back with you the money that was replaced in the mouths of your bags; perhaps it was a mistake. ¹³Take your brother too; and go back at once to the man. ¹⁴And may El Shaddai dispose the man to mercy toward you, that he may release to you your other brother, as well as Benjamin. As for me, if I am to be bereaved, I shall be bereaved."

¹⁵So the men took that gift, and they took with them double the money, as well as Benjamin. They made their way down to Egypt, where they presented themselves to Joseph. ¹⁶When Joseph saw Benjamin with them, he said to his house steward, "Take the men into the house; slaughter and prepare an animal, for the men will dine with me at noon." ¹⁷The man did as Joseph said, and he brought the men into Joseph's house. ¹⁸But the men were frightened at being brought into Joseph's house. "It must be," they thought, "because of the money replaced in our bags the first time that we have been brought inside, as a pretext to attack us and seize us as slaves, with our pack animals." ¹⁹So they went up to Joseph's house steward and spoke to him at the entrance of the house. ²⁰"If you please, my lord," they said, "we came down once before to procure food. ²¹But when we arrived at the night

encampment and opened our bags, there was each one's money in the mouth of his bag, our money in full.[b] So we have brought it back with us. [22]And we have brought down with us other money to procure food. We do not know who put the money in our bags." [23]He replied, "All is well with you; do not be afraid. Your God, the God of your father, must have put treasure in your bags for you. I got your payment." And he brought out Simeon to them.

[24]Then the man brought the men into Joseph's house; he gave them water to bathe their feet, and he provided feed for their asses. [25]They laid out their gifts to await Joseph's arrival at noon, for they had heard that they were to dine there.

[26]When Joseph came home, they presented to him the gifts that they had brought with them into the house, bowing low before him to the ground. [27]He greeted them, and he said, "How is your aged father of whom you spoke? Is he still in good health?" [28]They replied, "It is well with your servant our father; he is still in good health." And they bowed and made obeisance.

[29]Looking about, he saw his brother Benjamin, his mother's son, and asked, "Is this your youngest brother of whom you spoke to me?" And he went on, "May God be gracious to you, my boy." [30]With that, Joseph hurried out, for he was overcome with feeling toward his brother and was on the verge of tears; he went into a room and wept there. [31]Then he washed his face, reappeared, and—now in control of himself—gave the order, "Serve the meal." [32]They served him by himself, and them by themselves, and the Egyptians who ate with him by themselves; for the Egyptians could not dine with the Hebrews, since that would be abhorrent to the Egyptians. [33]As they were seated by his direction, from the oldest in the order of his seniority to the youngest in the order of his youth, the men looked at one another in astonishment. [34]Portions were served them from his table; but Benjamin's portion was several[c] times that of anyone else. And they drank their fill with him.

---

b  *Lit. "by its weight"*
c  *Lit. "five"*

44 Then he instructed his house steward as follows, "Fill the men's bags with food, as much as they can carry, and put each one's money in the mouth of his bag. ²Put my silver goblet in the mouth of the bag of the youngest one, together with his money for the rations." And he did as Joseph told him.

³With the first light of morning, the men were sent off with their pack animals. ⁴They had just left the city and had not gone far, when Joseph said to his steward, "Up, go after the men! And when you overtake them, say to them, 'Why did you repay good with evil? ⁵It is the very one from which my master drinks and which he uses for divination. It was a wicked thing for you to do!'"

⁶He overtook them and spoke those words to them. ⁷And they said to him, "Why does my lord say such things? Far be it from your servants to do anything of the kind! ⁸Here we brought back to you from the land of Canaan the money that we found in the mouths of our bags. How then could we have stolen any silver or gold from your master's house! ⁹Whichever of your servants it is found with shall die; the rest of us, moreover, shall become slaves to my lord." ¹⁰He replied, "Although what you are proposing is right, only the one with whom it is found shall be my slave; but the rest of you shall go free."

¹¹So each one hastened to lower his bag to the ground, and each one opened his bag. ¹²He searched, beginning with the oldest and ending with the youngest; and the goblet turned up in Benjamin's bag. ¹³At this they rent their clothes. Each reloaded his pack animal, and they returned to the city.

¹⁴When Judah and his brothers reentered the house of Joseph, who was still there, they threw themselves on the ground before him. ¹⁵Joseph said to them, "What is this deed that you have done? Do you not know that a man like me practices divination?" ¹⁶Judah replied, "What can we say to my lord? How can we plead, how can we prove our innocence? God has uncovered the crime of your servants. Here we are, then, slaves of my lord, the rest of

us as much as he in whose possession the goblet was found." ¹⁷But he replied, "Far be it from me to act thus! Only he in whose possession the goblet was found shall be my slave; the rest of you go back in peace to your father."

ויגש

¹⁸Then Judah went up to him and said, "Please, my lord, let your servant appeal to my lord, and do not be impatient with your servant, you who are the equal of Pharaoh. ¹⁹My lord asked his servants, 'Have you a father or another brother?' ²⁰We told my lord, 'We have an old father, and there is a child of his old age, the youngest; his full brother is dead, so that he alone is left of his mother, and his father dotes on him.' ²¹Then you said to your servants, 'Bring him down to me, that I may set eyes on him.' ²²We said to my lord, 'The boy cannot leave his father; if he were to leave him, his father would die.' ²³But you said to your servants, 'Unless your youngest brother comes down with you, do not let me see your faces.' ²⁴When we came back to your servant my father, we reported my lord's words to him.

²⁵"Later our father said, 'Go back and procure some food for us.' ²⁶We answered, 'We cannot go down; only if our youngest brother is with us can we go down, for we may not ᵃ⁻show our faces to the manᵃ unless our youngest brother is with us.' ²⁷Your servant my father said to us, 'As you know, my wife bore me two sons. ²⁸But one is gone from me, and I said: Alas, he was torn by a beast! And I have not seen him since. ²⁹If you take this one from me, too, and he meets with disaster, you will send my white head down to Sheol in sorrow.'

³⁰"Now, if I come to your servant my father and the boy is not with us—since his own life is so bound up with his—³¹when he sees that the boy is not with us, he will die, and your servants will send the white head of your servant our father down to Sheol in grief. ³²Now your servant has pledged himself for the boy to my father, saying, 'If I do not bring him back to you, I shall stand

---

ᵃ⁻ᵃ *Lit. "see the man's face"*

guilty before my father forever.' ³³Therefore, please let your servant remain as a slave to my lord instead of the boy, and let the boy go back with his brothers. ³⁴For how can I go back to my father unless the boy is with me? Let me not be witness to the woe that would overtake my father!"

45 Joseph could no longer control himself before all his attendants, and he cried out, "Have everyone withdraw from me!" So there was no one else about when Joseph made himself known to his brothers. ²His sobs were so loud that the Egyptians could hear, and so the news reached Pharaoh's palace.

³Joseph said to his brothers, "I am Joseph. Is my father still well?" But his brothers could not answer him, so dumfounded were they on account of him.

⁴Then Joseph said to his brothers, "Come forward to me." And when they came forward, he said, "I am your brother Joseph, he whom you sold into Egypt. ⁵Now, do not be distressed or reproach yourselves because you sold me hither; it was to save life that God sent me ahead of you. ⁶It is now two years that there has been famine in the land, and there are still five years to come in which there shall be no yield from tilling. ⁷God has sent me ahead of you to ensure your survival on earth, and to save your lives in an extraordinary deliverance. ⁸So, it was not you who sent me here, but God; and He has made me a father to Pharaoh, lord of all his household, and ruler over the whole land of Egypt.

⁹"Now, hurry back to my father and say to him: Thus says your son Joseph, 'God has made me lord of all Egypt; come down to me without delay. ¹⁰You will dwell in the region of Goshen, where you will be near me—you and your children and your grandchildren, your flocks and herds, and all that is yours. ¹¹There I will provide for you—for there are yet five years of famine to come—that you and your household and all that is yours may not suffer want.' ¹²You can see for yourselves, and my brother Ben-

jamin for himself, that it is indeed I who am speaking to you.
[13]And you must tell my father everything about my high station
in Egypt and all that you have seen; and bring my father here with
all speed."

[14]With that he embraced[a] his brother Benjamin around the
neck and wept, and Benjamin wept on his neck. [15]He kissed all his
brothers and wept upon them; only then were his brothers able to
talk to him.

[16]The news reached Pharaoh's palace: "Joseph's brothers have
come." Pharaoh and his courtiers were pleased. [17]And Pharaoh
said to Joseph, "Say to your brothers, 'Do as follows: load up your
beasts and go at once to the land of Canaan. [18]Take your father
and your households and come to me; I will give you the best of
the land of Egypt and you shall live off the fat of the land.' [19]And
you are bidden [to add] , 'Do as follows: take from the land of
Egypt wagons for your children and your wives, and bring your
father here. [20]And never mind your belongings, for the best of all
the land of Egypt shall be yours.' "

[21]The sons of Israel did so; Joseph gave them wagons as Pharaoh had commanded, and he supplied them with provisions for
the journey. [22]To each of them, moreover, he gave a change of
clothing; but to Benjamin he gave three hundred pieces of silver
and several[b] changes of clothing. [23]And to his father he sent the
following: ten he-asses laden with the best things of Egypt, and
ten she-asses laden with grain, bread, and provisions for his
father on the journey. [24]As he sent his brothers off on their way,
he told them, "Do not be quarrelsome on the way."

[25]They went up from Egypt and came to their father Jacob in
the land of Canaan. [26]And they told him, "Joseph is still alive; yes,
he is ruler over the whole land of Egypt." His heart went numb,
for he did not believe them. [27]But when they recounted all that
Joseph had said to them, and when he saw the wagons that Joseph
had sent to transport him, the spirit of their father Jacob revived.
[28]"Enough!" said Israel. "My son Joseph is still alive! I must go and
see him before I die."

---

a  *Lit. "fell on"*
b  *Lit. "five"; cf. 43.34*

46 So Israel set out with all that was his, and he came to Beer-sheba, where he offered sacrifices to the God of his father Isaac. [2]God called to Israel in a vision by night: "Jacob! Jacob!" He answered, "Here." [3]And He said, "I am God, the God of your father. Fear not to go down to Egypt, for I will make you there into a great nation. [4]I Myself will go down with you to Egypt, and I Myself will also bring you back; and Joseph's hand shall close your eyes."

[5]So Jacob set out from Beer-sheba. The sons of Israel put their father Jacob and their children and their wives in the wagons that Pharaoh had sent to transport him; [6]and they took along their livestock and the wealth that they had amassed in the land of Canaan. Thus Jacob and all his offspring with him came to Egypt: [7]he brought with him to Egypt his sons and grandsons, his daughters and granddaughters—all his offspring.

[8]These are the names of the Israelites, Jacob and his descendants, who came to Egypt.

Jacob's first-born Reuben; [9]Reuben's sons: Enoch,[a] Pallu, Hezron, and Carmi. [10]Simeon's sons: Jemuel, Jamin, Ohad, Jachin, Zohar, and Saul[b] the son of a Canaanite woman. [11]Levi's sons: Gershon, Kohath, and Merari. [12]Judah's sons: Er, Onan, Shelah, Perez, and Zerah—but Er and Onan had died in the land of Canaan; and Perez's sons were Hezron and Hamul. [13]Issachar's sons: Tola, Puvah, Iob, and Shimron. [14]Zebulun's sons: Sered, Elon, and Jahleel. [15]Those were the sons whom Leah bore to Jacob in Paddan-aram, in addition to his daughter Dinah. Persons in all, male and female: 33.[c]

[16]Gad's sons: Ziphion, Haggi, Shuni, Ezbon, Eri, Arodi, and Areli. [17]Asher's sons: Imnah, Ishvah, Ishvi, and Beriah, and their sister Serah. Beriah's sons: Heber and Malchiel. [18]These were the descendants of Zilpah, whom Laban had given to his daughter Leah. These she bore to Jacob—16 persons.

[19]The sons of Jacob's wife Rachel were Joseph and Benjamin. [20]To Joseph were born in the land of Egypt Manasseh and

a *Or "Hanoch"*
b *Or "Shaul"*
c *Including Jacob*

Ephraim, whom Asenath daughter of Poti-phera priest of On bore to him. ²¹Benjamin's sons: Bela, Becher, Ashbel, Gera, Naaman, Ehi, Rosh, Muppim, Huppim, and Ard. ²²These were the descendants of Rachel who were born to Jacob—14 persons in all.

²³Dan's son*d*: Hushim. ²⁴Naphtali's sons: Jahzeel, Guni, Jezer, and Shillem. ²⁵These were the descendants of Bilhah, whom Laban had given to his daughter Rachel. These she bore to Jacob—7 persons in all.

²⁶All the persons belonging to Jacob who came to Egypt*e*—his own issue, aside from the wives of Jacob's sons—all these persons numbered 66. ²⁷And Joseph's sons who were born to him in Egypt were two in number. Thus the total of Jacob's household who came to Egypt was seventy persons.*f*

²⁸He had sent Judah ahead of him to Joseph, to point the way before him to Goshen. So when they came to the region of Goshen, ²⁹Joseph ordered*g* his chariot and went to Goshen to meet his father Israel; he presented himself to him and, embracing him around the neck, he wept on his neck a good while. ³⁰Then Israel said to Joseph, "Now I can die, having seen for myself that you are still alive."

³¹Then Joseph said to his brothers and to his father's household, "I will go up and tell the news to Pharaoh, and say to him, 'My brothers and my father's household, who were in the land of Canaan, have come to me. ³²The men are shepherds; they have always been breeders of livestock, and they have brought with them their flocks and herds and all that is theirs.' ³³So when Pharaoh summons you and asks, 'What is your occupation?' ³⁴you shall answer, 'Your servants have been breeders of livestock from the start until now, both we and our fathers'—so that you may stay in the region of Goshen. For all shepherds are abhorrent to Egyptians."

---

d *Heb "sons"*
e *Not including Joseph and Joseph's two sons*
f *Including Jacob and Joseph*
g *Lit. "hitched"*

47 Then Joseph came and reported to Pharaoh, saying, "My father and my brothers, with their flocks and herds and all that is theirs, have come from the land of Canaan and are now in the region of Goshen." ²And selecting a few*a* of his brothers, he presented them to Pharaoh. ³Pharaoh said to his brothers, "What is your occupation?" They answered Pharaoh, "We your servants are shepherds, as were also our fathers. ⁴We have come," they told Pharaoh, "to sojourn in this land, for there is no pasture for your servants' flocks, the famine being severe in the land of Canaan. Pray, then, let your servants stay in the region of Goshen." ⁵Then Pharaoh said to Joseph, "As regards your father and your brothers who have come to you, ⁶the land of Egypt is open before you: settle your father and your brothers in the best part of the land; let them stay in the region of Goshen. And if you know any capable men among them, put them in charge of my livestock."

⁷Joseph then brought his father Jacob and presented him to Pharaoh; and Jacob greeted Pharaoh. ⁸Pharaoh asked Jacob, "How many are the years of your life?" ⁹And Jacob answered Pharaoh, "The years of my sojourn [on earth] are one hundred and thirty. Few and hard have been the years of my life, nor do they come up to the life spans of my fathers during their sojourns." ¹⁰Then Jacob bade Pharaoh farewell, and left Pharaoh's presence.

¹¹So Joseph settled his father and his brothers, giving them holdings in the choicest part of the land of Egypt, in the region of Rameses, as Pharaoh had commanded. ¹²Joseph sustained his father, and his brothers, and all his father's household with bread, down to the little ones.

¹³Now there was no bread in all the world, for the famine was very severe; both the land of Egypt and the land of Canaan

---

a *Lit. "five"*

languished because of the famine. ¹⁴Joseph gathered in all the money that was to be found in the land of Egypt and in the land of Canaan, as payment for the rations that were being procured, and Joseph brought the money into Pharaoh's palace. ¹⁵And when the money gave out in the land of Egypt and in the land of Canaan, all the Egyptians came to Joseph and said, "Give us bread, lest we die before your very eyes; for the money is gone!" ¹⁶And Joseph said, "Bring your livestock, and I will sell to you against your livestock, if the money is gone." ¹⁷So they brought their livestock to Joseph, and Joseph gave them bread in exchange for the horses, for the stocks of sheep and cattle, and the asses; thus he provided them with bread that year in exchange for all their livestock. ¹⁸And when that year was ended, they came to him the next year and said to him, "We cannot hide from my lord that, with all the money and animal stocks consigned to my lord, nothing is left at my lord's disposal save our persons and our farmland. ¹⁹Let us not perish before your eyes, both we and our land. Take us and our land in exchange for bread, and we with our land will be serfs to Pharaoh; provide the seed, that we may live and not die, and that the land may not become a waste."

²⁰So Joseph gained possession of all the farm land of Egypt for Pharaoh, every Egyptian having sold his field because the famine was too much for them; thus the land passed over to Pharaoh. ²¹And he removed the population town by town,ᵇ from one end of Egypt's border to the other. ²²Only the land of the priests he did not take over, for the priests had an allotment from Pharaoh, and they lived off the allotment which Pharaoh had made to them; therefore they did not sell their land.

²³Then Joseph said to the people, "Whereas I have this day acquired you and your land for Pharaoh, here is seed for you to sow the land. ²⁴And when harvest comes, you shall give one-fifth to Pharaoh, and four-fifths shall be yours as seed for the fields and as food for you and those in your households, and as nourishment for your children." ²⁵And they said, "You have saved our lives!

ᵇ *Meaning of Heb uncertain*

We are grateful to my lord, and we shall be serfs to Pharaoh."
²⁶And Joseph made it into a land law in Egypt, which is still valid,
that a fifth should be Pharaoh's; only the land of the priests did
not become Pharaoh's.

²⁷Thus Israel settled in the country of Egypt, in the region of
Goshen; they acquired holdings in it, and were fertile and increased greatly.

ויחי

²⁸Jacob lived seventeen years in the land of Egypt, so that the
span of Jacob's life came to one hundred and forty-seven years.
²⁹And when the time approached for Israel to die, he summoned
his son Joseph and said to him, "Do me this favor, place your hand
under my thigh as a pledge of your steadfast loyalty: please do not
bury me in Egypt. ³⁰When I lie down with my fathers, take me up
from Egypt and bury me in their burial-place." He replied, "I will
do as you have spoken." ³¹And he said, "Swear to me." And he
swore to him. Then Israel bowed at the head of the bed.

**48** Some time afterward, Joseph was told, "Your father is ill."
So he took with him his two sons, Manasseh and Ephraim. ²When
Jacob was told, "Your son Joseph has come to see you," Israel
summoned his strength and sat up in bed.

³And Jacob said to Joseph, "El Shaddai appeared to me at Luz
in the land of Canaan, and He blessed me, ⁴and said to me, 'I will
make you fertile and numerous, making of you a community of
peoples; and I will assign this land to your offspring to come for an
everlasting possession.' ⁵Now, your two sons, who were born to
you in the land of Egypt before I came to you in Egypt, shall be
mine; Ephraim and Manasseh shall be mine no less than Reuben
and Simeon. ⁶But progeny born to you after them shall be yours;
they shall be recorded instead*ᵃ* of their brothers in their inheritance. ⁷I [do this because], when I was returning from Paddan,

---

ᵃ *Lit. "under the name"*

Rachel died, to my sorrow, while I was journeying in the land of Canaan, when still some distance short of Ephrath; and I buried her there on the road to Ephrath"—now Bethlehem.

8Noticing Joseph's sons, Israel asked, "Who are these?" 9And Joseph said to his father, "They are my sons, whom God has given me here." "Bring them up to me," he said, "that I may bless them." 10Now Israel's eyes were dim with age; he could not see. So [Joseph] brought them close to him, and he kissed them and embraced them. 11And Israel said to Joseph, "I never expected to see you again, and here God has let me see your children as well."

12Joseph then removed them from his knees, and bowed low with his face to the ground. 13Joseph took the two of them, Ephraim with his right hand—to Israel's left—and Manasseh with his left hand—to Israel's right—and brought them close to him. 14But Israel stretched out his right hand and laid it on Ephraim's head, though he was the younger, and his left hand on Manasseh's head—thus crossing his hands—although Manasseh was the first-born. 15And he blessed Joseph, saying,

"The God in whose ways my fathers Abraham and
Isaac walked,
The God who has been my shepherd from my birth to
this day—
16The Angel who has redeemed me from all harm—
Bless the lads.
In them may my name be recalled,
And the names of my fathers Abraham and Isaac,
And may they be teeming multitudes upon the earth."

17When Joseph saw that his father was placing his right hand on Ephraim's head, he thought it wrong; so he took hold of his father's hand to move it from Ephraim's head to Manasseh's. 18"Not so, Father," Joseph said to his father, "for the other is the first-born; place your right hand on his head." 19But his father objected, saying, "I know, my son, I know. He too shall become a people, and he too shall be great. Yet his younger brother shall be greater than he, and his offspring shall be plentiful enough for nations." <sup>20</sup>So he blessed them that day, saying, "By you shall Israel invoke blessings, saying: God make you like Ephraim and Manasseh." Thus he put Ephraim before Manasseh.

<sup>21</sup>Then Israel said to Joseph, "I am about to die; but God will be with you and bring you back to the land of your fathers. <sup>22</sup>And now, I assign to you one portion<sup>b</sup> more than to your brothers, which I wrested from the Amorites with my sword and bow."

**49** And Jacob called his sons and said, "Come together that I may tell you what is to befall you in days to come.

<sup>2</sup>Assemble and hearken, O sons of Jacob;
Hearken to Israel your father:

<sup>3</sup>Reuben, you are my first-born,
My might and first fruit of my vigor,
Exceeding in rank
And exceeding in honor.
<sup>4</sup>Unstable as water, you shall excel no longer;
For when you mounted your father's bed,
You brought disgrace—my couch he mounted!

<sup>5</sup>Simeon and Levi are a pair;
Their weapons are tools of lawlessness.
<sup>6</sup>Let not my person be included in their council,
Let not my being be counted in their assembly.
For when angry they slay men,
And when pleased they maim oxen.
<sup>7</sup>Cursed be their anger so fierce,
And their wrath so relentless.
I will divide them in Jacob,
Scatter them in Israel.

<sup>8</sup>You, O Judah, your brothers shall praise;
Your hand shall be on the nape of your foes;
Your father's sons shall bow low to you.

---

<sup>b</sup> *Meaning of Heb* shekhem *uncertain; others "mountain slope"*

⁹Judah is a lion's whelp;
On prey, my son, have you grown.
He crouches, lies down like a lion,
Like the *ᵃ-king of beasts*ᵃ—who dare rouse him?
¹⁰The scepter shall not depart from Judah,
Nor the ruler's staff from between his feet;
So that tribute shall come to him*ᵇ*
And the homage of peoples be his.

¹¹He tethers his ass to a vine,
His ass's foal to a choice vine;
He washes his garment in wine,
His robe in blood of grapes.
¹²*ᶜ-His eyes are darker than wine;
His teeth are whiter than milk.*ᶜ

¹³Zebulun shall dwell by the seashore;
He shall be a haven for ships,
And his flank shall rest on Sidon.

¹⁴Issachar is a strong-boned ass,
Crouching among the sheepfolds.
¹⁵When he saw how good was security,
And how pleasant was the country,
He bent his shoulder to the burden,
And became a toiling serf.

¹⁶Dan shall govern his people,
As one of the tribes of Israel.
¹⁷Dan shall be a serpent by the road,
A viper by the path,
That bites the horse's heels
So that his rider is thrown backward.

¹⁸I wait for Your deliverance, O LORD!

¹⁹Gad shall be raided by raiders,
But he shall raid at their heels.

---

ᵃ⁻ᵃ *Heb* labi, *another word for "lion"*
ᵇ *Shiloh, understood as* shai loh *"tribute to him," following Midrash; cf. Isa. 18.7.*
  *Meaning of Heb uncertain; lit. "Until he comes to Shiloh"*
ᶜ⁻ᶜ *Or "His eyes are dark from wine,*
    *And his teeth are white from milk"*

²⁰Asher's bread shall be rich,
And he shall yield royal dainties.

²¹Naphtali is a hind let loose,
Which yields lovely fawns.

²²ᵈ⁻Joseph is a wild ass,
A wild ass by a spring
—Wild colts on a hillside.⁻ᵈ

²³Archers bitterly assailed him;
They shot at him and harried him.
²⁴Yet his bow stayed taut,
And his armsᵉ were made firm
By the hands of the Mighty One of Jacob—
There, the Shepherd, the Rock of Israel—
²⁵The God of your father who helps you,
And Shaddai who blesses you
With blessings of heaven above,
Blessings of the deep that couches below,
Blessings of the breast and womb.
²⁶ᶠ⁻The blessings of your father
Surpass the blessings of my ancestors,
To the utmost bounds of the eternal hills.⁻ᶠ
May they rest on the head of Joseph,
On the brow of the elect of his brothers.

²⁷Benjamin is a ravenous wolf;
In the morning he consumes the foe,ᵍ
And in the evening he divides the spoil."

²⁸All these were the tribes of Israel, twelve in number, and this is what their father said to them as he bade them farewell, addressing to each a parting word appropriate to him.

²⁹Then he instructed them, saying to them, "I am about to be gathered to my kin. Bury me with my fathers in the cave which is in the field of Ephron the Hittite, ³⁰the cave which is in the field of Machpelah, facing Mamre, in the land of Canaan, the field that

---

ᵈ⁻ᵈ Others "Joseph is a fruitful bough,
  A fruitful bough by a spring,
  Its branches run over a wall"
ᵉ Heb "the arms of his hands"   ᶠ⁻ᶠ Meaning of Heb uncertain
ᵍ Meaning of Heb uncertain; others "booty"

Abraham bought from Ephron the Hittite for a burial site— ³¹there Abraham and his wife Sarah were buried; there Isaac and his wife Rebekah were buried; and there I buried Leah—³²the field and the cave in it, bought from the Hittites." ³³When Jacob finished his instructions to his sons, he drew his feet into the bed and, breathing his last, he was gathered to his people.

50 Joseph flung himself upon his father's face and wept over him and kissed him. ²Then Joseph ordered the physicians in his service to embalm his father, and the physicians embalmed Israel. ³It required forty days, for such is the full period of embalming. The Egyptians bewailed him seventy days; ⁴and when the wailing period was over, Joseph spoke to Pharaoh's court, saying, "Do me this favor, and lay this appeal before Pharaoh: ⁵'My father made me swear, saying, "I am about to die. Be sure to bury me in the grave which I made ready for myself in the land of Canaan." Now, therefore, let me go up and bury my father; then I shall return.'" ⁶And Pharaoh said, "Go up and bury your father, as he made you promise on oath."

⁷So Joseph went up to bury his father; and with him went up all the officials of Pharaoh, the senior members of his court, and all of Egypt's dignitaries, ⁸together with all of Joseph's household, his brothers, and his father's household; only their children, their flocks, and their herds were left in the region of Goshen. ⁹Chariots, too, and horsemen went up with him; it was a very large troop.

¹⁰When they came to Goren*ᵃ* ha-Atad, which is beyond the Jordan, they held there a very great and solemn lamentation; and he observed a mourning period of seven days for his father. ¹¹And when the Canaanite inhabitants of the land saw the mourning at Goren ha-Atad, they said, "This is a solemn mourning on the part of the Egyptians." That is why it was named Abel-mizraim,ᵇ which is beyond the Jordan. ¹²Thus his sons did for him as he had instructed them. ¹³His sons carried him to the land of

ᵃ Or "the threshing floor of"
ᵇ Interpreted as "the mourning of the Egyptians"

Canaan, and buried him in the cave of the field of Machpelah, the field near Mamre, which Abraham had bought for a burial site from Ephron the Hittite. [14]After burying his father, Joseph returned to Egypt, he and his brothers and all who had gone up with him to bury his father.

[15]When Joseph's brothers saw that their father was dead, they said, "What if Joseph still bears a grudge against us and pays us back for all the wrong that we did him!" [16]So they sent this message to Joseph, "Before his death your father left this instruction: [17]So shall you say to Joseph, 'Forgive, I urge you, the offense and guilt of your brothers who treated you so harshly.' Therefore, please forgive the offense of the servants of the God of your father." And Joseph was in tears as they spoke to him.

[18]His brothers went to him themselves, flung themselves before him, and said, "We are prepared to be your slaves." [19]But Joseph said to them, "Have no fear! Am I a substitute for God? [20]Besides, although you intended me harm, God intended it for good, so as to bring about the present result—the survival of many people. [21]And so, fear not. I will sustain you and your children." Thus he reassured them, speaking kindly to them.

[22]So Joseph and his father's household remained in Egypt. Joseph lived one hundred and ten years. [23]Joseph lived to see children of the third generation of Ephraim; the children of Machir son of Manasseh were likewise born upon Joseph's knees. [24]At length, Joseph said to his brothers, "I am about to die. God will surely take notice of you and bring you up from this land to the land that He promised on oath to Abraham, to Isaac, and to Jacob." [25]So Joseph made the sons of Israel swear, saying, "When God has taken notice of you, you shall carry up my bones from here."

[26]Joseph died at the age of one hundred and ten years; and he was embalmed and placed in a coffin in Egypt.

חזק

# שמות
## EXODUS

# שמות
# EXODUS

1 These are the names of the sons of Israel who came to Egypt with Jacob, each coming with his household: ²Reuben, Simeon, Levi, and Judah; ³Issachar, Zebulun, and Benjamin; ⁴Dan and Naphtali, Gad and Asher. ⁵The total number of persons that were of Jacob's issue came to seventy, Joseph being already in Egypt. ⁶Joseph died, and all his brothers, and all that generation. ⁷But the Israelites were fertile and prolific; they multiplied and increased very greatly, so that the land was filled with them.

⁸A new king arose over Egypt who did not know Joseph. ⁹And he said to his people, "Look, the Israelite people are much too numerous for us. ¹⁰Let us deal shrewdly with them, so that they may not increase; otherwise in the event of war they may join our enemies in fighting against us and ᵃ⁻rise from the ground.⁻ᵃ" ¹¹So they set taskmasters over them to oppress them with forced labor; and they built garrison citiesᵇ for Pharaoh: Pithom and Raamses. ¹²But the more they were oppressed, the more they increased and spread out, so that the [Egyptians] came to dread the Israelites.

¹³The Egyptians ruthlessly imposed upon the Israelites ¹⁴ᶜ⁻the various labors that they made them perform. Ruthlessly⁻ᶜ they made life bitter for them with harsh labor at mortar and bricks and with all sorts of tasks in the field.

¹⁵The king of Egypt spoke to the Hebrew midwives, one of whom was named Shiphrah and the other Puah, ¹⁶saying, "When you deliver the Hebrew women, look at the birthstool:ᵈ

---

ᵃ⁻ᵃ *Meaning perhaps from their wretched condition, cf. Hos. 2.2; or "gain ascendancy over the country." Others "get them up out of the land"*
ᵇ *Others "store cities"*
ᶜ⁻ᶜ *Brought up from the end of the verse for clarity*
ᵈ *More exactly, the brick or stone supports used by Egyptian women during childbirth*

if it is a boy, kill him; if it is a girl, let her live." [17]The midwives, fearing God, did not do as the king of Egypt had told them; they let the boys live. [18]So the king of Egypt summoned the midwives and said to them, "Why have you done this thing, letting the boys live?" [19]The midwives said to Pharaoh, "Because the Hebrew women are not like the Egyptian women: they are vigorous. Before the midwife can come to them, they have given birth." [20]And God dealt well with the midwives; and the people multiplied and increased greatly. [21]And because the midwives feared God, He established households[e] for them. [22]Then Pharaoh charged all his people, saying, "Every boy that is born you shall throw into the Nile, but let every girl live."

2 A certain man of the house of Levi went and married a Levite woman. [2]The woman conceived and bore a son; and when she saw how beautiful he was, she hid him for three months. [3]When she could hide him no longer, she got a wicker basket for him and caulked it with bitumen and pitch. She put the child into it and placed it among the reeds by the bank of the Nile. [4]And his sister stationed herself at a distance, to learn what would befall him.

[5]The daughter of Pharaoh came down to bathe in the Nile, while her maidens walked along the Nile. She spied the basket among the reeds and sent her slave girl to fetch it. [6]When she opened it, she saw that it was a child, a boy crying. She took pity on it and said, "This must be a Hebrew child." [7]Then his sister said to Pharaoh's daughter, "Shall I go and get you a Hebrew nurse to suckle the child for you?" [8]And Pharaoh's daughter answered, "Yes." So the girl went and called the child's mother. [9]And Pharaoh's daughter said to her, "Take this child and nurse it for me, and I will pay your wages." So the woman took the child and nursed it. [10]When the child grew up, she brought him to Pharaoh's daughter, who made him her son. She named him Moses,[a] explaining, "I drew him out of the water."

---

[e] *Meaning of Heb* batim *uncertain*

[a] *Heb* Mosheh *from Egyptian for "born of"; here associated with* mashah *"draw out"*

¹¹Some time after that, when Moses had grown up, he went out to his kinsfolk and witnessed their labors. He saw an Egyptian beating a Hebrew, one of his kinsmen. ¹²He turned this way and that and, seeing no one about, he struck down the Egyptian and hid him in the sand. ¹³When he went out the next day, he found two Hebrews fighting; so he said to the offender, "Why do you strike your fellow?" ¹⁴He retorted, "Who made you chief and ruler over us? Do you mean to kill me as you killed the Egyptian?" Moses was frightened, and thought: Then the matter is known! ¹⁵When Pharaoh learned of the matter, he sought to kill Moses; but Moses fled from Pharaoh. He arrived*b* in the land of Midian, and sat down beside a well.

¹⁶Now the priest of Midian had seven daughters. They came to draw water, and filled the troughs to water their father's flock; ¹⁷but shepherds came and drove them off. Moses rose to their defense, and he watered their flock. ¹⁸When they returned to their father Reuel, he said, "How is it that you have come back so soon today?" ¹⁹They answered, "An Egyptian rescued us from the shepherds; he even drew water for us and watered the flock." ²⁰He said to his daughters, "Where is he then? Why did you leave the man? Ask him in to break bread." ²¹Moses consented to stay with the man, and he gave Moses his daughter Zipporah as wife. ²²She bore a son whom he named Gershom,*c* for he said, "I have been a stranger in a foreign land."

²³A long time after that, the king of Egypt died. The Israelites were groaning under the bondage and cried out; and their cry for help from the bondage rose up to God. ²⁴God heard their moaning, and God remembered His covenant with Abraham and Isaac and Jacob. ²⁵God looked upon the Israelites, and God took notice of them.

3 Now Moses, tending the flock of his father-in-law Jethro, the priest of Midian, drove the flock into the wilderness, and came

---

b *Lit. "sat" or "settled"*
c *Associated with* ger sham *"a stranger there"*

to Horeb, the mountain of God. [2]An angel of the LORD appeared to him in a blazing fire out of a bush. He gazed, and there was a bush all aflame, yet the bush was not consumed. [3]Moses said, "I must turn aside to look at this marvelous sight; why doesn't the bush burn up?" [4]When the LORD saw that he had turned aside to look, God called to him out of the bush: "Moses! Moses!" He answered, "Here I am." [5]And He said, "Do not come closer. Remove your sandals from your feet, for the place on which you stand is holy ground. [6]I am," He said, "the God of your father, the God of Abraham, the God of Isaac, and the God of Jacob." And Moses hid his face, for he was afraid to look at God.

[7]And the LORD continued, "I have marked well the plight of My people in Egypt and have heeded their outcry because of their taskmasters; yes, I am mindful of their sufferings. [8]I have come down to rescue them from the Egyptians and to bring them out of that land to a good and spacious land, a land flowing with milk and honey, the region of the Canaanites, the Hittites, the Amorites, the Perizzites, the Hivites, and the Jebusites. [9]Now the cry of the Israelites has reached Me; moreover, I have seen how the Egyptians oppress them. [10]Come, therefore, I will send you to Pharaoh, and you shall free My people, the Israelites, from Egypt."

[11]But Moses said to God, "Who am I that I should go to Pharaoh and free the Israelites from Egypt?" [12]And He said, "I will be with you; that shall be your sign that it was I who sent you. And when you have freed the people from Egypt, you shall worship God at this mountain."

[13]Moses said to God, "When I come to the Israelites and say to them 'The God of your fathers has sent me to you,' and they ask me, 'What is His name?' what shall I say to them?" [14]And God said to Moses, "Ehyeh-Asher-Ehyeh.[a]" He continued, "Thus shall you say to the Israelites, 'Ehyeh[b] sent me to you.'" [15]And God said further to Moses, "Thus shall you speak to the Israelites: The LORD,[c] the God of your fathers, the God of Abraham, the God of Isaac, and the God of Jacob, has sent me to you:

[a] *Meaning of Heb uncertain; variously translated: "I Am That I Am"; "I Am Who I Am"; "I Will Be What I Will Be"; etc.* [b] *Others "I Am" or "I Will Be"*
[c] *The name* YHWH *(traditionally read* Adonai *"the* LORD*") is here associated with the root* hayah *"to be"*

This shall be My name forever,
This My appellation for all eternity.

¹⁶"Go and assemble the elders of Israel and say to them: the LORD, the God of your fathers, the God of Abraham, Isaac, and Jacob, has appeared to me and said, 'I have taken note of you and of what is being done to you in Egypt, ¹⁷and I have declared: I will take you out of the misery of Egypt to the land of the Canaanites, the Hittites, the Amorites, the Perizzites, the Hivites, and the Jebusites, to a land flowing with milk and honey.' ¹⁸They will listen to you; then you shall go with the elders of Israel to the king of Egypt and you shall say to him, 'The LORD, the God of the Hebrews, manifested Himself to us. Now therefore, let us go a distance of three days into the wilderness to sacrifice to the LORD our God.' ¹⁹Yet I know that the king of Egypt will let you go only because of a greater might. ²⁰So I will stretch out My hand and smite Egypt with various wonders which I will work upon them; after that he shall let you go. ²¹And I will dispose the Egyptians favorably toward this people, so that when you go, you will not go away empty-handed. ²²Each woman shall borrow from her neighbor and the lodger in her house objects of silver and gold, and clothing, and you shall put these on your sons and daughters, thus stripping the Egyptians."

4 But Moses spoke up and said, "What if they do not believe me and do not listen to me, but say: The LORD did not appear to you?" ²The LORD said to him, "What is that in your hand?" And he replied, "A rod." ³He said, "Cast it on the ground." He cast it on the ground and it became a snake; and Moses recoiled from it. ⁴Then the LORD said to Moses, "Put out your hand and grasp it by the tail"—he put out his hand and seized it, and it became a rod in his hand—⁵"that they may believe that the LORD, the God of their fathers, the God of Abraham, the God of Isaac, and the God of Jacob, did appear to you."

⁶The LORD said to him further, "Put your hand into your bosom." He put his hand into his bosom; and when he took it

out, his hand was encrusted with snowy scales[a]! [7]And He said, "Put your hand back into your bosom."—He put his hand back into his bosom; and when he took it out of his bosom, there it was again like the rest of his body.—[8]"And if they do not believe you or pay heed to the first sign, they will believe the second. [9]And if they are not convinced by both these signs and still do not heed you, take some water from the Nile and pour it on the dry ground, and it—the water that you take from the Nile—will turn to blood on the dry ground."

[10]But Moses said to the LORD, "Please, O Lord, I have never been a man of words, either in times past or now that You have spoken to Your servant; I am slow of speech and slow of tongue." [11]And the LORD said to him, "Who gives man speech? Who makes him dumb or deaf, seeing or blind? Is it not I, the LORD? [12]Now go, and I will be with you as you speak and will instruct you what to say." [13]But he said, "Please, O Lord, make someone else Your agent.[b]" [14]The LORD became angry with Moses, and He said, "There is your brother Aaron the Levite. He, I know, speaks readily. Even now he is setting out to meet you, and he will be happy to see you. [15]You shall speak to him and put the words in his mouth—I will be with you and with him as you speak, and tell both of you what to do—[16]and he shall speak for you to the people. Thus he shall serve as your spokesman, with you playing the role of God[c] to him, [17]And take with you this rod, with which you shall perform the signs."

[18]Moses went back to his father-in-law Jether[d] and said to him, "Let me go back to my kinsmen in Egypt and see how they are faring."[e] And Jethro said to Moses, "Go in peace."

[19]The LORD said to Moses in Midian, "Go back to Egypt, for all the men who sought to kill you are dead." [20]So Moses took his wife and sons, mounted them on an ass, and went back to the land of Egypt; and Moses took the rod of God with him.

[21]And the LORD said to Moses, "When you return to Egypt, see that you perform before Pharaoh all the marvels that I have put within your power. I, however, will stiffen his heart so that

---

[a] *Cf. Lev. 13.2–3*

[b] *Lit. "send through whomever You will send"*

[c] *Cf. 7.1*

[d] *I.e. Jethro*

[e] *Lit. "whether they are still alive"*

he will not let the people go. [22]Then you shall say to Pharaoh, 'Thus says the LORD: Israel is My first-born son. [23]I have said to you, "Let My son go, that he may worship Me," yet you refuse to let him go. Now I will slay your first-born son.'"

[24]At a night encampment on the way, the LORD encountered him and sought to kill him. [25]*f*So Zipporah took a flint and cut off her son's foreskin, and touched his legs with it, saying, "You are truly a bridegroom of blood to me!" [26]And when He let him alone, she added, "A bridegroom of blood because of the circumcision."

[27]The LORD said to Aaron, "Go to meet Moses in the wilderness." He went and met him at the mountain of God, and he kissed him. [28]Moses told Aaron about all the things that the LORD had committed to him and all the signs about which He had instructed him. [29]Then Moses and Aaron went and assembled all the elders of the Israelites. [30]Aaron repeated all the words that the LORD had spoken to Moses, and he performed the signs in the sight of the people, [31]and the people were convinced. When they heard that the LORD had taken note of the Israelites and that He had seen their plight, they bowed low in homage.

5 Afterward Moses and Aaron went and said to Pharaoh, "Thus says the LORD, the God of Israel: Let My people go that they may celebrate a festival for Me in the wilderness." [2]But Pharaoh said, "Who is the LORD that I should heed Him and let Israel go? I do not know the LORD, nor will I let Israel go." [3]They answered, "The God of the Hebrews has manifested Himself to us. Let us go, we pray, a distance of three days into the wilderness to sacrifice to the LORD our God, lest He strike us with pestilence or sword." [4]But the king of Egypt said to them, "Moses and Aaron, why do you distract the people from their

[f] *Meaning of vv. 25–26 uncertain*

tasks? Get to your labors!" ⁵And Pharaoh continued, "ᵃ⁻The people of the land are already so numerous,⁻ᵃ and you would have them cease from their labors!"ᵇ

⁶That same day Pharaoh charged the taskmasters and foremen of the people, saying, ⁷"You shall no longer provide the people with straw for making bricks as heretofore; let them go and gather straw for themselves. ⁸But impose upon them the same quota of bricks as they have been making heretofore; do not reduce it, for they are shirkers; that is why they cry, 'Let us go and sacrifice to our God!' ⁹Let heavier work be laid upon the men; let them keep at it and not pay attention to deceitful promises."

¹⁰So the taskmasters and foremen of the people went out and said to the people, "Thus says Pharaoh: I will not give you any straw. ¹¹You must go and get the straw yourselves wherever you can find it; but there shall be no decrease whatever in your work." ¹²Then the people scattered throughout the land of Egypt to gather stubble for straw. ¹³And the taskmasters pressed them, saying, "You must complete the same work assignment each day as when you had straw." ¹⁴And the foremen of the Israelites, whom Pharaoh's taskmasters had set over them, were beaten. "Why," they were asked, "did you not complete the prescribed amount of bricks, either yesterday or today, as you did before?"

¹⁵Then the foremen of the Israelites came to Pharaoh and cried: "Why do you deal thus with your servants? ¹⁶No straw is issued to your servants, yet they demand of us: Make bricks! Thus your servants are being beaten, when the fault is with your own people." ¹⁷He replied, "You are shirkers, shirkers! That is why you say, 'Let us go and sacrifice to the LORD.' ¹⁸Be off now to your work! No straw shall be issued to you, but you must produce your quota of bricks!"

¹⁹Now the foremen of the Israelites found themselves in trouble because of the order, "You must not reduce your daily quantity of bricks." ²⁰As they left Pharaoh's presence, they came

---

ᵃ⁻ᵃ Samaritan "Even now they are more numerous than the people of the land," i.e., than the native population (cf. Gen. 23.7)
ᵇ See 1.5–11

upon Moses and Aaron standing in their path, <sup>21</sup>and they said to them, "May the LORD look upon you and punish you for making us loathsome to Pharaoh and his courtiers—putting a sword in their hands to slay us." <sup>22</sup>Then Moses returned to the LORD and said, "O Lord, why did You bring harm upon this people? Why did You send me? <sup>23</sup>Ever since I came to Pharaoh to speak in Your name, he has dealt worse with this people; and still You have not delivered Your people."

6 Then the LORD said to Moses, "You shall soon see what I will do to Pharaoh: he shall let them go because of a greater might; indeed, because of a greater might he shall drive them from his land."

וארא

<sup>2</sup>God spoke to Moses and said to him, "I am the LORD. <sup>3</sup>I appeared to Abraham, Isaac, and Jacob as El Shaddai, but I did not make myself known to them by My name יהוה.<sup>a</sup> <sup>4</sup>I also established My covenant with them, to give them the land of Canaan, the land in which they lived as sojourners. <sup>5</sup>I have now heard the moaning of the Israelites because the Egyptians are holding them in bondage, and I have remembered My covenant. <sup>6</sup>Say, therefore, to the Israelite people: I am the LORD. I will free you from the labors of the Egyptians and deliver you from their bondage. I will redeem you with an outstretched arm and through extraordinary chastisements. <sup>7</sup>And I will take you to be My people, and I will be your God. And you shall know that I, the LORD, am your God who freed you from the labors of the Egyptians. <sup>8</sup>I will bring you into the land which I swore<sup>b</sup> to give to Abraham, Isaac, and Jacob, and I will give it to you for a possession, I the LORD." <sup>9</sup>But when Moses told this to the Israelites, they would not listen to Moses, their spirits crushed by cruel bondage.

<sup>10</sup>The LORD spoke to Moses, saying, <sup>11</sup>"Go and tell Pharaoh

<sup>a</sup> *This divine name is traditionally not pronounced; instead,* Adonai, *"(the)* LORD*," is regularly substituted for it.*
<sup>b</sup> *Lit. "raised My hand"*

king of Egypt to let the Israelites depart from his land." ¹²But Moses appealed to the LORD, saying, "The Israelites would not listen to me; how then should Pharaoh heed me, a man of impeded speech!" ¹³So the LORD spoke to both Moses and Aaron in regard to the Israelites and Pharaoh king of Egypt, instructing them to deliver the Israelites from the land of Egypt.

¹⁴The following are the heads of their respective clans.

The sons of Reuben, Israel's first-born: Enoch^c and Pallu, Hezron and Carmi; those are the families of Reuben. ¹⁵The sons of Simeon: Jemuel, Jamin, Ohad, Jachin, Zohar, and Saul^d the son of a Canaanite woman; those are the families of Simeon. ¹⁶These are the names of Levi's sons by their lineage: Gershon, Kohath, and Merari; and the span of Levi's life was 137 years. ¹⁷The sons of Gershon: Libni and Shimei, by their families. ¹⁸The sons of Kohath: Amram, Izhar, Hebron, and Uzziel; and the span of Kohath's life was 133 years. ¹⁹The sons of Merari: Mahli and Mushi. These are the families of the Levites by their lineage.

²⁰Amram took to wife his father's sister Jochebed, and she bore him Aaron and Moses; and the span of Amram's life was 137 years. ²¹The sons of Izhar: Korah, Nepheg, and Zichri. ²²The sons of Uzziel: Mishael, Elzaphan, and Sithri. ²³Aaron took to wife Elisheba, daughter of Amminadab and sister of Nahshon, and she bore him Nadab and Abihu, Eleazar and Ithamar. ²⁴The sons of Korah: Assir, Elkanah, and Abiasaph. Those are the families of the Korahites. ²⁵And Aaron's son Eleazar took to wife one of Putiel's daughters, and she bore him Phinehas. Those are the heads of the fathers' houses of the Levites by their families.

²⁶It is the same Aaron and Moses to whom the LORD said, "Bring forth the Israelites from the land of Egypt, troop by troop." ²⁷It was they who spoke to Pharaoh king of Egypt to free the Israelites from the Egyptians; these are the same Moses and Aaron. ²⁸For when the LORD spoke to Moses in the land of

c *Or "Hanoch"; cf. on Gen. 46.9*
d *Or "Shaul"; cf. on Gen. 46.10*

Egypt [29]and the LORD said to Moses, "I am the LORD; speak to Pharaoh king of Egypt all that I will tell you," [30]Moses appealed to the LORD, saying, "See, I am of impeded speech; how then should Pharaoh heed me!"

7 The LORD replied to Moses, "See, I place you in the role of God to Pharaoh, with your brother Aaron as your prophet.[a] [2]You shall repeat all that I command you, and your brother Aaron shall speak to Pharaoh to let the Israelites depart from his land. [3]But I will harden Pharaoh's heart, that I may multiply My signs and marvels in the land of Egypt. [4]When Pharaoh does not heed you, I will lay My hand upon Egypt and deliver My ranks, My people the Israelites, from the land of Egypt with extraordinary chastisements. [5]And the Egyptians shall know that I am the LORD, when I stretch out My hand over Egypt and bring out the Israelites from their midst." [6]This Moses and Aaron did; as the LORD commanded them, so they did. [7]Moses was eighty years old and Aaron eighty-three, when they made their demand on Pharaoh.

[8]The LORD said to Moses and Aaron, [9]"When Pharaoh speaks to you and says, 'Produce your marvel,' you shall say to Aaron, 'Take your rod and cast it down before Pharaoh.' It shall turn into a serpent." [10]So Moses and Aaron came before Pharaoh and did just as the LORD had commanded: Aaron cast down his rod in the presence of Pharaoh and his courtiers, and it turned into a serpent. [11]Then Pharaoh, for his part, summoned the wise men and the sorcerers; and the Egyptian magicians, in turn, did the same with their spells; [12]each cast down his rod, and they turned into serpents. But Aaron's rod swallowed their rods. [13]Yet Pharaoh's heart stiffened and he did not heed them, as the LORD had said.

[14]And the LORD said to Moses, "Pharaoh is stubborn; he refuses to let the people go. [15]Go to Pharaoh in the morning, as he is coming out to the water, and station yourself before him at

[a] *Cf. 4.16*

the edge of the Nile, taking with you the rod that turned into a snake. <sup>16</sup>And say to him, 'The LORD, the God of the Hebrews, sent me to you to say, "Let My people go that they may worship Me in the wilderness." But you have paid no heed until now. <sup>17</sup>Thus says the LORD, "By this you shall know that I am the LORD." See, I shall strike the water in the Nile with the rod that is in my hand, and it will be turned into blood; <sup>18</sup>and the fish in the Nile will die. The Nile will stink so that the Egyptians will find it impossible to drink the water of the Nile.' "

<sup>19</sup>And the LORD said to Moses, "Say to Aaron: Take your rod and hold out your arm over the waters of Egypt—its rivers, its canals, its ponds, all its bodies of water—that they may turn to blood; there shall be blood throughout the land of Egypt, even in [vessels of] wood and stone." <sup>20</sup>Moses and Aaron did just as the LORD commanded: he lifted up the rod and struck the water in the Nile in the sight of Pharaoh and his courtiers, and all the water in the Nile was turned into blood <sup>21</sup>and the fish in the Nile died. The Nile stank so that the Egyptians could not drink water from the Nile; and there was blood throughout the land of Egypt. <sup>22</sup>But when the Egyptian magicians did the same with their spells, Pharaoh's heart stiffened and he did not heed them—as the LORD had spoken. <sup>23</sup>Pharaoh turned and went into his palace, paying no regard even to this. <sup>24</sup>And all the Egyptians had to dig round about the Nile for drinking water, because they could not drink the water of the Nile.

<sup>25</sup>When seven days had passed after the LORD struck the Nile, <sup>26</sup>the LORD said to Moses, "Go to Pharaoh and say to him, 'Thus says the LORD: Let My people go that they may worship Me. <sup>27</sup>If you refuse to let them go, then I will plague your whole country with frogs. <sup>28</sup>The Nile shall swarm with frogs, and they shall come up and enter your palace, your bedchamber and your bed, the houses of your courtiers and your people, and your ovens and your kneading bowls. <sup>29</sup>The frogs shall come up on you and on your people and on all your courtiers.' "

8 And the LORD said to Moses, "Say to Aaron: Hold out your arm with the rod over the rivers, the canals, and the ponds, and bring up the frogs on the land of Egypt." ²Aaron held out his arm over the waters of Egypt, and the frogs came up and covered the land of Egypt. ³But the magicians did the same with their spells, and brought frogs upon the land of Egypt.

⁴Then Pharaoh summoned Moses and Aaron and said, "Plead with the LORD to remove the frogs from me and my people, and I will let the people go to sacrifice to the LORD." ⁵And Moses said to Pharaoh, "You may have this triumph over me: for what time shall I plead in behalf of you and your courtiers and your people, that the frogs be cut off from you and your houses, to remain only in the Nile?" ⁶"For tomorrow," he replied. And [Moses] said, "As you say—that you may know that there is none like the LORD our God; ⁷the frogs shall retreat from you and your courtiers and your people; they shall remain only in the Nile." ⁸Then Moses and Aaron left Pharaoh's presence, and Moses cried out to the LORD in the matter of the frogs which He had inflicted upon Pharaoh. ⁹And the LORD did as Moses asked; the frogs died out in the houses, the courtyards, and the fields. ¹⁰And they piled them up in heaps, till the land stank. ¹¹But when Pharaoh saw that there was relief, he became stubborn and would not heed them, as the LORD had spoken.

¹²Then the LORD said to Moses, "Say to Aaron: Hold out your rod and strike the dust of the earth, and it shall turn to lice throughout the land of Egypt." ¹³And they did so. Aaron held out his arm with the rod and struck the dust of the earth, and vermin came upon man and beast; all the dust of the earth turned to lice throughout the land of Egypt. ¹⁴The magicians did the like with their spells to produce lice, but they could not. The vermin remained upon man and beast; ¹⁵and the magicians said to Pharaoh, "This is the finger of God!" But Pharaoh's heart stiffened and he would not heed them, as the LORD had spoken.

¹⁶And the LORD said to Moses, "Early in the morning present yourself to Pharaoh, as he is coming out to the water, and say to him, 'Thus says the LORD: Let My people go that they may worship Me. ¹⁷For if you do not let My people go, I will let loose *⁻swarms of insects⁻ᵃ* against you and your courtiers and your people and your houses; the houses of the Egyptians, and the very ground they stand on, shall be filled with swarms of insects. ¹⁸But on that day I will set apart the region of Goshen, where My people dwell, so that no swarms of insects shall be there, that you may know that I the LORD am in the midst of the land. ¹⁹And I will make a distinction*ᵇ* between My people and your people. Tomorrow this sign shall come to pass.'" ²⁰And the LORD did so. Heavy swarms of insects invaded Pharaoh's palace and the houses of his courtiers; throughout the country of Egypt the land was ruined because of the swarms of insects.

²¹Then Pharaoh summoned Moses and Aaron and said, "Go and sacrifice to your God within the land." ²²But Moses replied, "It would not be right to do this, for what we sacrifice to the LORD our God is untouchable to the Egyptians. If we sacrifice that which is untouchable to the Egyptians before their very eyes, will they not stone us! ²³So we must go a distance of three days into the wilderness and sacrifice to the LORD our God as He may command us." ²⁴Pharaoh said, "I will let you go to sacrifice to the LORD your God in the wilderness; but do not go very far. Plead, then, for me." ²⁵And Moses said, "When I leave your presence, I will plead with the LORD that the swarms of insects depart tomorrow from Pharaoh and his courtiers and his people; but let not Pharaoh again act deceitfully, not letting the people go to sacrifice to the LORD."

²⁶So Moses left Pharaoh's presence and pleaded with the LORD. ²⁷And the LORD did as Moses asked: He removed the swarms of insects from Pharaoh, from his courtiers, and from his people; not one remained. ²⁸But Pharaoh became stubborn this time also, and would not let the people go.

---

ᵃ⁻ᵃ *Others "wild beasts"*
ᵇ *Meaning of* peduth *uncertain*

9 The LORD said to Moses, "Go to Pharaoh and say to him, 'Thus says the LORD, the God of the Hebrews: Let My people go to worship Me. ²For if you refuse to let them go, and continue to hold them, ³then the hand of the LORD will strike your livestock in the fields—the horses, the asses, the camels, the cattle, and the sheep—with a very severe pestilence. ⁴But the LORD will make a distinction between the livestock of Israel and the livestock of the Egyptians, so that nothing shall die of all that belongs to the Israelites. ⁵The LORD has fixed the time: tomorrow the LORD will do this thing in the land.'" ⁶And the LORD did so the next day: all the livestock of the Egyptians died, but of the livestock of the Israelites not a beast died. ⁷When Pharaoh inquired, he found that not a head of the livestock of Israel had died; yet Pharaoh remained stubborn, and he would not let the people go.

⁸Then the LORD said to Moses and Aaron, "Each of you take handfuls of soot from the kiln, and let Moses throw it toward the sky in the sight of Pharaoh. ⁹It shall become a fine dust all over the land of Egypt, and cause an inflammation breaking out in boils on man and beast throughout the land of Egypt." ¹⁰So they took soot of the kiln and appeared before Pharaoh; Moses threw it toward the sky, and it caused an inflammation breaking out in boils on man and beast. ¹¹The magicians were unable to confront Moses because of the inflammation, for the inflammation afflicted the magicians as well as all the other Egyptians. ¹²But the LORD stiffened the heart of Pharaoh, and he would not heed them, just as the LORD had told Moses.

¹³The LORD said to Moses, "Early in the morning present yourself to Pharaoh and say to him, 'Thus says the LORD, the God of the Hebrews: Let My people go to worship Me. ¹⁴For this time I will send all My plagues upon your person, and your courtiers, and your people, in order that you may know that there is none like Me in all the world. ¹⁵I could have stretched

forth My hand and stricken you and your people with pestilence, and you would have been effaced from the earth. [16]Nevertheless I have spared you for this purpose: in order to show you My power, and in order that My fame may resound throughout the world. [17]Yet you continue to thwart[a] My people, and do not let them go! [18]This time tomorrow I will rain down a very heavy hail, such as has not been in Egypt from the day it was founded until now. [19]Therefore, order your livestock and everything you have in the open brought under shelter; every man and beast that is found outside, not having been brought indoors, shall perish when the hail comes down upon them!'" [20]Those among Pharaoh's courtiers who feared the LORD's word brought their slaves and livestock indoors to safety; [21]but those who paid no regard to the word of the LORD left their slaves and livestock in the open.

[22]The LORD said to Moses, "Hold out your arm toward the sky that hail may fall on all the land of Egypt, upon man and beast and all the grasses of the field in the land of Egypt." [23]So Moses held out his rod toward the sky, and the LORD sent thunder and hail, and fire streamed down to the ground, as the LORD rained down hail upon the land of Egypt. [24]The hail was very heavy—fire flashing in the midst of the hail—such as had not fallen on the land of Egypt since it had become a nation. [25]Throughout the land of Egypt the hail struck down all that were in the open, both man and beast; the hail also struck down all the grasses of the field and shattered all the trees of the field. [26]Only in the region of Goshen, where the Israelites were, there was no hail.

[27]Thereupon Pharaoh sent for Moses and Aaron and said to them, "I stand guilty this time. The LORD is in the right, and I and my people are in the wrong. [28]Plead with the LORD that there may be an end of God's thunder and of hail. I will let you go; you need stay no longer." [29]Moses said to him, "As I go out of the city, I shall spread out my hands to the LORD; the thunder will cease and the hail will fall no more, so that you may know that the earth is the LORD's. [30]But I know that you and your

a *Others "exalt yourself over"*

118

courtiers do not yet fear the LORD God."—³¹Now the flax and barley were ruined, for the barley was in the ear and the flax was in bud; ³²but the wheat and the emmer*ᵇ* were not hurt, for they ripen late.—³³Leaving Pharaoh, Moses went outside the city and spread out his hands to the LORD: the thunder and the hail ceased, and no rain came pouring down upon the earth. ³⁴But when Pharaoh saw that the rain and the hail and the thunder had ceased, he became stubborn and reverted to his guilty ways, as did his courtiers. ³⁵So Pharaoh's heart stiffened and he would not let the Israelites go, just as the LORD had foretold through Moses.

בא

10 Then the LORD said to Moses, "Go to Pharaoh. For I have hardened his heart and the hearts of his courtiers, in order that I may display these My signs among them, ²and that you may recount in the hearing of your sons and of your sons' sons how I made a mockery of the Egyptians and how I displayed My signs among them—in order that you may know that I am the LORD." ³So Moses and Aaron went to Pharaoh and said to him, "Thus says the LORD, the God of the Hebrews, 'How long will you refuse to humble yourself before Me? Let My people go that they may worship Me. ⁴For if you refuse to let My people go, tomorrow I will bring locusts on your territory. ⁵They shall cover the surface of the land, so that no one will be able to see the land. They shall devour the surviving remnant that was left to you after the hail; and they shall eat away all your trees that grow in the field. ⁶Moreover, they shall fill your palaces and the houses of all your courtiers and of all the Egyptians—something that neither your fathers nor fathers' fathers have seen from the day they appeared on earth to this day.'" With that he turned and left Pharaoh's presence.

⁷Pharaoh's courtiers said to him, "How long shall this one be a snare to us? Let the men go to worship the LORD their God! Are you not yet aware that Egypt is lost?" ⁸So Moses and Aaron were

ᵇ *A kind of wheat*

brought back to Pharaoh and he said to them, "Go, worship the LORD your God! Who are the ones to go?" [9]Moses replied, "We will all go, young and old: we will go with our sons and daughters, our flocks and herds; for we must observe the LORD'S festival." [10]But he said to them, "The LORD be with you the same as I mean to let your children go with you! Clearly, you are bent on mischief. [11]No! You menfolk go and worship the LORD, since that is what you want." And they were expelled from Pharaoh's presence.

[12]Then the LORD said to Moses, "Hold out your arm over the land of Egypt for the locusts, that they may come upon the land of Egypt and eat up all the grasses in the land, whatever the hail has left." [13]So Moses held out his rod over the land of Egypt, and the LORD drove an east wind over the land all that day and all night; and when morning came, the east wind had brought the locusts. [14]Locusts invaded all the land of Egypt and settled within all the territory of Egypt in a thick mass; never before had there been so many, nor will there ever be so many again. [15]They hid all the land from view, and the land was darkened; and they ate up all the grasses of the field and all the fruit of the trees which the hail had left, so that nothing green was left, of tree or grass of the field, in all the land of Egypt.

[16]Pharaoh hurriedly summoned Moses and Aaron and said, "I stand guilty before the LORD your God and before you. [17]Forgive my offense just this once, and plead with the LORD your God that He but remove this death from me." [18]So he left Pharaoh's presence and pleaded with the LORD. [19]The LORD caused a shift to a very strong west wind, which lifted the locusts and hurled them into the Sea of Reeds[a]; not a single locust remained in all the territory of Egypt. [20]But the LORD stiffened Pharaoh's heart, and he would not let the Israelites go.

[21]Then the LORD said to Moses, "Hold out your arm toward the sky that there may be darkness upon the land of Egypt, a darkness that can be touched." [22]Moses held out his arm toward the sky and thick darkness descended upon all the land of Egypt

---

[a] *Traditionally, but incorrectly, "Red Sea"*

for three days. <sup>23</sup>People could not see one another, and for three days no one could get up from where he was; but all the Israelites enjoyed light in their dwellings.

<sup>24</sup>Pharaoh then summoned Moses and said, "Go, worship the LORD! Only your flocks and your herds shall be left behind; even your children may go with you." <sup>25</sup>But Moses said, "You yourself must provide us with sacrifices and burnt offerings to offer up to the LORD our God; <sup>26</sup>our own livestock, too, shall go along with us—not a hoof shall remain behind: for we must select from it for the worship of the LORD our God; and we shall not know with what we are to worship the LORD until we arrive there." <sup>27</sup>But the LORD stiffened Pharaoh's heart and he would not agree to let them go. <sup>28</sup>Pharaoh said to him, "Be gone from me! Take care not to see me again, for the moment you look upon my face you shall die." <sup>29</sup>And Moses replied, "You have spoken rightly. I shall not see your face again!"

11 And the LORD said to Moses, "I will bring but one more plague upon Pharaoh and upon Egypt; after that he shall let you go from here; indeed, when he lets you go, he will drive you out of here one and all. <sup>2</sup>Tell the people to borrow, each man from his neighbor and each woman from hers, objects of silver and gold." <sup>3</sup>The LORD disposed the Egyptians favorably toward the people. Moreover, Moses himself was much esteemed in the land of Egypt, among Pharaoh's courtiers and among the people.

<sup>4</sup>Moses said, "Thus says the LORD: Toward midnight I will go forth among the Egyptians, <sup>5</sup>and every first-born in the land of Egypt shall die, from the first-born of Pharaoh who sits on his throne to the first-born of the slave girl who is behind the millstones; and all the first-born of the cattle. <sup>6</sup>And there shall be a loud cry in all the land of Egypt, such as has never been or will ever be again; <sup>7</sup>but not a dog shall snarl[a] at any of the Israelites, at man or beast—in order that you may know that the LORD

---

[a] *Others "move (or whet) his tongue"*

makes a distinction between Egypt and Israel. ⁸Then all these courtiers of yours shall come down to me and bow low to me, saying, 'Depart, you and all the people who follow you!' After that I will depart." And he left Pharaoh's presence in hot anger.

⁹Now the LORD had said to Moses, "Pharaoh will not heed you, in order that My marvels may be multiplied in the land of Egypt." ¹⁰Moses and Aaron had performed all these marvels before Pharaoh, but the LORD had stiffened the heart of Pharaoh so that he would not let the Israelites go from his land.

**12** The LORD said to Moses and Aaron in the land of Egypt: ²This month shall mark for you the beginning of the months; it shall be the first of the months of the year for you. ³Speak to the whole community of Israel and say that on the tenth of this month each of them shall take a lamb*ᵃ* to a family, a lamb to a household. ⁴But if the household is too small for a lamb, let him share one with a neighbor who dwells nearby, in proportion to the number of persons; you shall contribute for the lamb according to what each household will eat. ⁵Your lamb shall be without blemish, a yearling male; you may take it from the sheep or from the goats. ⁶You shall keep watch over it until the fourteenth day of this month; and all the assembled congregation of the Israelites shall slaughter it at twilight. ⁷They shall take some of the blood and put it on the two doorposts and the lintel of the houses in which they are to eat it. ⁸They shall eat the flesh that same night; they shall eat it roasted over the fire, with unleavened bread and with bitter herbs. ⁹Do not eat any of it raw, or cooked in any way with water, but roasted—head, legs, and entrails—over the fire. ¹⁰You shall not leave any of it over until morning; if any of it is left until morning, you shall burn it.

¹¹This is how you shall eat it: your loins girded, your sandals on your feet, and your staff in your hand; and you shall eat it hurriedly: it is a passover offering*ᵇ* to the LORD. ¹²For that night I will go through the land of Egypt and strike down every first-

ᵃ *Or "kid." Heb* seh *means either "sheep" or "goat." Cf. v. 5*
ᵇ *Or "protective offering"; Heb* pesaḥ

born in the land of Egypt, both man and beast; and I will mete out punishments to all the gods of Egypt, I the LORD. [13]And the blood on the houses where you are staying shall be a sign for you: when I see the blood I will pass over you, so that no plague will destroy you when I strike the land of Egypt.

[14]This day shall be to you one of remembrance: you shall celebrate it as a festival to the LORD throughout the ages; you shall celebrate it as an institution for all time. [15]Seven days you shall eat unleavened bread; on the very first day you shall remove leaven from your houses, for whoever eats leavened bread from the first day to the seventh day, that person shall be cut off from Israel.

[16]You shall celebrate a sacred occasion on the first day, and a sacred occasion on the seventh day; no work at all shall be done on them; only what every person is to eat, that alone may be prepared for you. [17]You shall observe the [Feast of] Unleavened Bread, for on this very day I brought your ranks out of the land of Egypt; you shall observe this day throughout the ages as an institution for all time. [18]In the first month, from the fourteenth day of the month at evening, you shall eat unleavened bread until the twenty-first day of the month at evening. [19]No leaven shall be found in your houses for seven days. For whoever eats what is leavened, that person shall be cut off from the community of Israel, whether he is a stranger or a citizen of the country. [20]You shall eat nothing leavened; in all your settlements you shall eat unleavened bread.

[21]Moses then summoned all the elders of Israel and said to them, "Go, pick out lambs for your families, and slaughter the passover offering. [22]Take a bunch of hyssop, dip it in the blood that is in the basin, and apply some of the blood that is in the basin to the lintel and to the two doorposts. None of you shall go outside the door of his house until morning. [23]For when the LORD goes through to smite the Egyptians, He will see the blood on the lintel and the two doorposts, and the LORD will pass over[c] the door and not let the Destroyer enter and smite your home.

---

[c] Or "protect"; cf. v. 11, note b

24"You shall observe this as an institution for all time, for you and for your descendants. 25And when you enter the land that the LORD will give you, as He has promised, you shall observe this rite. 26And when your children ask you, 'What do you mean by this rite?' 27you shall say, 'It is the passover sacrifice to the LORD, because He passed over the houses of the Israelites in Egypt when He smote the Egyptians, but saved our houses.'"

The people then bowed low in homage. 28And the Israelites went and did so; just as the LORD had commanded Moses and Aaron, so they did.

29In the middle of the night the LORD struck down all the first-born in the land of Egypt, from the first-born of Pharaoh who sat on the throne to the first-born of the captive who was in the dungeon, and all the first-born of the cattle. 30And Pharaoh arose in the night, with all his courtiers and all the Egyptians— because there was a loud cry in Egypt; for there was no house where there was not someone dead. 31He summoned Moses and Aaron in the night and said, "Up, depart from among my people, you and the Israelites with you! Go, worship the LORD as you said! 32Take also your flocks and your herds, as you said, and begone! And may you bring a blessing upon me also!"

33The Egyptians urged the people on, impatient to have them leave the country, for they said, "We shall all be dead." 34So the people took their dough before it was leavened, their kneading bowls wrapped in their cloaks upon their shoulders. 35The Israelites had done Moses' bidding and borrowed from the Egyptians objects of silver and gold, and clothing. 36And the LORD had disposed the Egyptians favorably toward the people, and they let them have their request; thus they stripped the Egyptians.

37The Israelites journeyed from Rameses to Succoth, about six hundred thousand men on foot, aside from children. 38Moreover, a mixed multitude went up with them, and very much livestock, both flocks and herds. 39And they baked un-leavened cakes of the dough that they had taken out of Egypt, for it was not leavened, since they had been driven out of Egypt and could not delay; nor had they prepared any provisions for themselves.

⁴⁰The length of time that the Israelites lived in Egypt was four hundred and thirty years; ⁴¹at the end of the four hundred and thirtieth year, to the very day, all the ranks of the LORD departed from the land of Egypt. ⁴²That was for the LORD a night of vigil to bring them out of the land of Egypt; that same night is the LORD'S, one of vigil for all the children of Israel throughout the ages.

⁴³The LORD said to Moses and Aaron: This is the law of the passover offering: No foreigner shall eat of it. ⁴⁴But any slave a man has bought may eat of it once he has been circumcised. ⁴⁵No bound or hired laborer shall eat of it. ⁴⁶It shall be eaten in one house: you shall not take any of the flesh outside the house; nor shall you break a bone of it. ⁴⁷The whole community of Israel shall offer it. ⁴⁸If a stranger who dwells with you would offer the passover to the LORD, all his males must be circumcised; then he shall be admitted to offer it; he shall then be as a citizen of the country. But no uncircumcised person may eat of it. ⁴⁹There shall be one law for the citizen and for the stranger who dwells among you.

⁵⁰And all the Israelites did so; as the LORD had commanded Moses and Aaron, so they did.

⁵¹That very day the LORD freed the Israelites from the land of Egypt, troop by troop.

**13** The LORD spoke further to Moses, saying, ²"Consecrate to Me every first-born; man and beast, the first issue of every womb among the Israelites is Mine."

³And Moses said to the people,

"Remember this day, on which you went free from Egypt, the house of bondage, how the LORD freed you from it with a mighty hand: no leavened bread shall be eaten. [4]You go free on this day, in the month[a] of Abib. [5]So, when the LORD has brought you into the land of the Canaanites, the Hittites, the Amorites, the Hivites, and the Jebusites, which He swore to your fathers to give you, a land flowing with milk and honey, you shall observe in this month the following practice:

[6]"Seven days you shall eat unleavened bread, and on the seventh day there shall be a festival of the LORD. [7]Throughout the seven days unleavened bread shall be eaten; no leavened bread shall be found with you, and no leaven shall be found in all your territory. [8]And you shall explain to your son on that day, 'It is because of what the LORD did for me when I went free from Egypt.'

[9]"And this shall serve you as a sign on your hand and as a reminder on your forehead[b]—in order that the Teaching of the LORD may be in your mouth—that with a mighty hand the LORD freed you from Egypt. [10]You shall keep this institution at its set time from year to year.

[11]"And when the LORD has brought you into the land of the Canaanites, as He swore to you and to your fathers, and has given it to you, [12]you shall set apart for the LORD every first issue of the womb: every male firstling that your cattle drop shall be the LORD's. [13]But every firstling ass you shall redeem with a sheep; if you do not redeem it, you must break its neck. And you must redeem every first-born male among your children. [14]And when, in time to come, your son asks you, saying, 'What does this mean?' you shall say to him, 'It was with a mighty hand that the LORD brought us out from Egypt, the house of bondage. [15]When Pharaoh stubbornly refused to let us go, the LORD slew every first-born in the land of Egypt, the first-born of both man and beast. Therefore I sacrifice to the LORD every first male issue of the womb, but redeem every first-born among my sons.'

[16]"And so it shall be as a sign upon your hand and as a symbol[c] on your forehead that with a mighty hand the LORD freed us from Egypt."

---

[a] Or "on the new moon"
[b] Lit. "between your eyes"
[c] Others "frontlet"

בשלח

<sup>17</sup>Now when Pharaoh let the people go, God did not lead them by way of the land of the Philistines, although it was nearer; for God said, "The people may have a change of heart when they see war, and return to Egypt." <sup>18</sup>So God led the people roundabout, by way of the wilderness at the Sea of Reeds.

Now the Israelites went up armed<sup>d</sup> out of the land of Egypt. <sup>19</sup>And Moses took with him the bones of Joseph, who had exacted an oath from the children of Israel, saying, "God will be sure to take notice of you: then you shall carry up my bones from here with you."

<sup>20</sup>They set out from Succoth, and encamped at Etham, at the edge of the wilderness. <sup>21</sup>The LORD went before them in a pillar of cloud by day, to guide them along the way, and in a pillar of fire by night, to give them light, that they might travel day and night. <sup>22</sup>The pillar of cloud by day and the pillar of fire by night did not depart from before the people.

**14** The LORD said to Moses: <sup>2</sup>Tell the Israelites to turn back and encamp before Pi-hahiroth, between Migdol and the sea, before Baal-zephon; you shall encamp facing it, by the sea. <sup>3</sup>Pharaoh will say of the Israelites, "They are astray in the land; the wilderness has closed in on them." <sup>4</sup>Then I will stiffen Pharaoh's heart and he will pursue them, that I may gain glory through Pharaoh and all his host; and the Egyptians shall know that I am the LORD.

And they did so.

<sup>5</sup>When the king of Egypt was told that the people had fled, Pharaoh and his courtiers had a change of heart about the people and said, "What is this we have done, releasing Israel from our service?" <sup>6</sup>He ordered<sup>a</sup> his chariot and took his men with him; <sup>7</sup>he took six hundred of his picked chariots, and the rest of the chariots of Egypt, with officers<sup>b</sup> in all of them. <sup>8</sup>The

<sup>d</sup> *Meaning of Heb* ḥamushim *uncertain*

<sup>a</sup> *See on Gen.* 46.29

<sup>b</sup> *Heb* shalish; *originally* "third man on royal chariot"; *hence* "adjutant," "officer"

LORD stiffened the heart of Pharaoh king of Egypt, and he gave chase to the Israelites. As the Israelites were departing defiantly,[c] [9]the Egyptians gave chase to them, and all the chariot horses of Pharaoh, his horsemen, and his warriors overtook them encamped by the sea, near Pi-hahiroth, before Baal-zephon.

[10]As Pharaoh drew near, the Israelites caught sight of the Egyptians advancing upon them. Greatly frightened, the Israelites cried out to the LORD. [11]And they said to Moses, "Was it for want of graves in Egypt that you brought us to die in the wilderness? What have you done to us, taking us out of Egypt? [12]Is this not the very thing we told you in Egypt, saying, 'Let us be, and we will serve the Egyptians, for it is better for us to serve the Egyptians than to die in the wilderness'?" [13]But Moses said to the people, "Have no fear! Stand by, and witness the deliverance which the LORD will work for you today; for the Egyptians whom you see today you will never see again. [14]The LORD will battle for you; you hold your peace!"

[15]Then the LORD said to Moses, "Why do you cry out to Me? Tell the Israelites to go forward. [16]And you lift up your rod and hold out your arm over the sea and split it, so that the Israelites may march into the sea on dry ground. [17]And I will stiffen the hearts of the Egyptians so that they go in after them; and I will gain glory through Pharaoh and all his warriors, his chariots and his horsemen. [18]Let the Egyptians know that I am LORD, when I gain glory through Pharaoh, his chariots, and his horsemen."

[19]The angel of God, who had been going ahead of the Israelite army, now moved and followed behind them; and the pillar of cloud shifted from in front of them and took up a place behind them, [20]and it came between the army of the Egyptians and the army of Israel. Thus there was the cloud with the darkness, and it cast a spell[d] upon the night, so that the one could not come near the other all through the night.

[21]Then Moses held out his arm over the sea and the LORD drove back the sea with a strong east wind all that night, and

---

[c] Lit. "with upraised hand"
[d] From root 'rr, "cast a spell" or "curse." Others "and it lit up"

turned the sea into dry ground. The waters were split, [22]and the Israelites went into the sea on dry ground, the waters forming a wall for them on their right and on their left. [23]The Egyptians came in pursuit after them into the sea, all of Pharaoh's horses, chariots, and horsemen. [24]At the morning watch, the LORD looked down upon the Egyptian army from a pillar of fire and cloud, and threw the Egyptian army into panic. [25]He locked [e] the wheels of their chariots so that they moved forward with difficulty. And the Egyptians said, "Let us flee from the Israelites, for the LORD is fighting for them against Egypt."

[26]Then the LORD said to Moses, "Hold out your arm over the sea, that the waters may come back upon the Egyptians and upon their chariots and upon their horsemen." [27]Moses held out his arm over the sea, and at daybreak the sea returned to its normal state, and the Egyptians fled at its approach. But the LORD hurled the Egyptians into the sea. [28]The waters turned back and covered the chariots and the horsemen—Pharaoh's entire army that followed them into the sea; not one of them remained. [29]But the Israelites had marched through the sea on dry ground, the waters forming a wall for them on their right and on their left.

[30]Thus the LORD delivered Israel that day from the Egyptians. Israel saw the Egyptians dead on the shore of the sea. [31]And when Israel saw the wondrous power which the LORD had wielded against the Egyptians, the people feared the LORD; they had faith in the LORD and His servant Moses.

15 Then Moses and the Israelites sang this song to the LORD. They said:

> I will sing to the LORD, for He has triumphed
>   gloriously;
> Horse and driver He has hurled into the sea.
> [2]The LORD[a] is my strength and might[b];
> He is become my deliverance.

---

[e] *From root* 'sr, *with several ancient versions. Others "took off"*

[a] *Heb* Yah
[b] *Others "song"*

This is my God and I will enshrine[c] Him;
The God of my father, and I will exalt Him.
³The LORD, the Warrior—
LORD is His name!
⁴Pharaoh's chariots and his army
He has cast into the sea;
And the pick of his officers
Are drowned in the Sea of Reeds.
⁵The deeps covered them;
They went down into the depths like a stone.
⁶Your right hand, O LORD, glorious in power,
Your right hand, O LORD, shatters the foe!
⁷In Your great triumph You break Your
    opponents;
You send forth Your fury, it consumes them
    like straw.
⁸At the blast of Your nostrils the waters piled up,
The floods stood straight like a wall;
The deeps froze in the heart of the sea.
⁹The foe said,
"I will pursue, I will overtake,
I will divide the spoil;
My desire shall have its fill of them.
I will bare my sword—
My hand shall subdue them."
¹⁰You made Your wind blow, the sea covered them;
They sank like lead in the majestic waters.

¹¹Who is like You, O LORD, among the celestials[d];
Who is like You, majestic in holiness,
Awesome in splendor, working wonders!
¹²You put out Your right hand,
The earth swallowed them.
¹³In Your love You lead the people You redeemed;
In Your strength You guide them to Your holy abode.

c  *Others "glorify"*
d  *Others "mighty"*

130

¹⁴The peoples hear, they tremble;
Agony grips the dwellers in Philistia.
¹⁵Now are the clans of Edom dismayed;
The tribes of Moab—trembling grips them;
All the dwellers in Canaan are aghast.
¹⁶Terror and dread descend upon them;
Through the might of Your arm they are still as
stone—
Till Your people cross over, O Lord,
Till Your people cross whom You have ransomed.

¹⁷You will bring them and plant them in
Your own mountain,
The place You made to dwell in, O Lord,
The sanctuary, O Lord, which Your hands
established.
¹⁸The Lord will reign for ever and ever!

¹⁹For the horses of Pharaoh, with his chariots and horsemen, went into the sea; and the Lord turned back on them the waters of the sea; but the Israelites marched on dry ground in the midst of the sea.

²⁰Then Miriam the prophetess, Aaron's sister, took a timbrel in her hand, and all the women went out after her in dance with timbrels. ²¹And Miriam chanted for them:

Sing to the Lord, for He has triumphed gloriously;
Horse and driver He has hurled into the sea.

²²Then Moses caused Israel to set out from the Sea of Reeds. They went on into the wilderness of Shur; they traveled three days in the wilderness and found no water. ²³They came to Marah, but they could not drink the water of Marah because it was bitter; that is why it was named Marah.ᵉ ²⁴And the people

---

ᵉ I.e. "bitter"

grumbled against Moses, saying, "What shall we drink?" ²⁵So he cried out to the LORD, and the LORD showed him a piece of wood; he threw it into the water and the water became sweet.

There He made for them a fixed rule, and there He put them to the test. ²⁶He said, "If you will heed the LORD your God diligently, doing what is upright in His sight, giving ear to His commandments and keeping all His laws, then I will not bring upon you any of the diseases that I brought upon the Egyptians, for I the LORD am your healer."

²⁷And they came to Elim, where there were twelve springs of water and seventy palm trees; and they encamped there beside the water.

**16** Setting out from Elim, the whole Israelite community came to the wilderness of Sin, which is between Elim and Sinai, on the fifteenth day of the second month after their departure from the land of Egypt. ²In the wilderness, the whole Israelite community grumbled against Moses and Aaron. ³The Israelites said to them, "If only we had died by the hand of the LORD in the land of Egypt, when we sat by the fleshpots, when we ate our fill of bread! For you have brought us out into this wilderness to starve this whole congregation to death."

⁴And the LORD said to Moses, "I will rain down bread for you from the sky, and the people shall go out and gather each day that day's portion—that I may thus test them, to see whether they will follow My instructions or not. ⁵But on the sixth day, when they apportion what they have brought in, it shall prove to be double the amount they gather each day." ⁶So Moses and Aaron said to all the Israelites, "By evening you shall know it was the LORD who brought you out from the land of Egypt; ⁷and in the morning you shall behold the Presence*ᵃ* of the LORD, because He has heard your grumblings against the LORD. For who are we that you should grumble against us? ⁸Since it is the LORD," Moses continued, "who will give you flesh to eat in the

ᵃ *Others "glory"*

132

evening and bread in the morning to the full, because the LORD has heard the grumblings you utter against Him, what is our part? Your grumbling is not against us, but against the LORD!"

⁹Then Moses said to Aaron, "Say to the whole Israelite community: Advance toward the LORD, for He has heard your grumbling." ¹⁰And as Aaron spoke to the whole Israelite community, they turned toward the wilderness, and there, in a cloud, appeared the Presence of the LORD.

¹¹The LORD spoke to Moses: ¹²"I have heard the grumbling of the Israelites. Speak to them and say: By evening you shall eat flesh, and in the morning you shall have your fill of bread; and you shall know that I the LORD am your God."

¹³In the evening quail appeared and covered the camp; in the morning there was a fall of dew about the camp. ¹⁴When the fall of dew lifted, there, over the surface of the wilderness, lay a fine and flaky substance, as fine as frost on the ground. ¹⁵When the Israelites saw it, they said to one another, "What is it?ᵇ"—for they did not know what it was. And Moses said to them, "That is the bread which the LORD has given you to eat. This is what the LORD has commanded: Gather as much of it as each of you requires to eat, an *omer* to a person for as many of you as there are; each of you shall fetch for those in his tent."

¹⁷The Israelites did so, some gathering much, some little. ¹⁸But when they measured it by the *omer*, he who had gathered much had no excess, and he who had gathered little had no deficiency: they had gathered as much as they needed to eat. ¹⁹And Moses said to them, "Let no one leave any of it over until morning." ²⁰But they paid no attention to Moses; some of them left of it until morning, and it became infested with maggots and stank. And Moses was angry with them.

²¹So they gathered it every morning, each as much as he needed to eat; for when the sun grew hot, it would melt. ²²On the sixth day they gathered double the amount of food, two *omers* for each; and when all the chieftains of the community came and told Moses, ²³he said to them, "This is what the LORD

ᵇ *Heb* man hu; *others "It is manna"*

meant: Tomorrow is a day of rest, a holy sabbath of the LORD. Bake what you would bake and boil what you would boil; and all that is left put aside to be kept until morning." [24]So they put it aside until morning, as Moses had ordered; and it did not turn foul, and there were no maggots in it. [25]Then Moses said, "Eat it today, for today is a sabbath of the LORD; you will not find it today on the plain. [26]Six days you shall gather it; on the seventh day, the sabbath, there will be none."

[27]Yet some of the people went out on the seventh day to gather, but they found nothing. [28]And the LORD said to Moses, "How long will you people refuse to obey My commandments and My teachings? [29]Mark that the LORD has given you the sabbath; therefore He gives you two days' food on the sixth day. Let everyone remain where he is: let no one leave his place on the seventh day." [30]So the people remained inactive on the seventh day.

[31]The house of Israel named it manna[c]; it was like coriander seed, white, and it tasted like wafers[d] in honey. [32]Moses said, "This is what the LORD has commanded: Let one *omer* of it be kept throughout the ages, in order that they may see the bread that I fed you in the wilderness when I brought you out from the land of Egypt." [33]And Moses said to Aaron, "Take a jar, put one *omer* of manna in it, and place it before the LORD, to be kept throughout the ages." [34]As the LORD had commanded Moses, Aaron placed it before the Pact,[e] to be kept. [35]And the Israelites ate manna forty years, until they came to a settled land; they ate the manna until they came to the border of the land of Canaan. [36]The *omer* is a tenth of an *ephah*.

**17** From the wilderness of Sin the whole Israelite community continued by stages as the LORD would command. They encamped at Rephidim, and there was no water for the people to drink. [2]The people quarreled with Moses. "Give us water to

---

[c] *Heb* man
[d] *Meaning of Heb* ṣappiḥith *uncertain*
[e] *Others "Testimony"*

drink," they said; and Moses replied to them, "Why do you quarrel with me? Why do you try the LORD?" ³But the people thirsted there for water; and the people grumbled against Moses and said, "Why did you bring us up from Egypt, to kill us and our children and livestock with thirst?" ⁴Moses cried out to the LORD, saying, "What shall I do with this people? Before long they will be stoning me!" ⁵Then the LORD said to Moses, "Pass before the people; take with you some of the elders of Israel, and take along the rod with which you struck the Nile, and set out. ⁶I will be standing there before you on the rock at Horeb. Strike the rock and water will issue from it, and the people will drink." And Moses did so in the sight of the elders of Israel. ⁷The place was named Massah*a* and Meribah,*b* because the Israelites quarreled and because they tried the LORD, saying, "Is the LORD present among us or not?"

⁸Amalek came and fought with Israel at Rephidim. ⁹Moses said to Joshua, "Pick some men for us, and go out and do battle with Amalek. Tomorrow I will station myself on the top of the hill, with the rod of God in my hand." ¹⁰Joshua did as Moses told him and fought with Amalek, while Moses, Aaron, and Hur went up to the top of the hill. ¹¹Then, whenever Moses held up his hand, Israel prevailed; but whenever he let down his hand, Amalek prevailed. ¹²But Moses' hands grew heavy; so they took a stone and put it under him and he sat on it, while Aaron and Hur, one on each side, supported his hands; thus his hands remained steady until the sun set. ¹³And Joshua overwhelmed the people of Amalek*c* with the sword.

¹⁴Then the LORD said to Moses, "Inscribe this in a document as a reminder, and read it aloud to Joshua: I will utterly blot out the memory of Amalek from under heaven!" ¹⁵And Moses built an altar and named it Adonai-nissi.*d* ¹⁶He said, "It means, 'Hand upon the throne*e* of the LORD!' The LORD will be at war with Amalek throughout the ages."

---

a *I.e. "Trial"*
b *I.e. "Quarrel"*
c *Lit. "Amalek and his people"*
d *I.e. "The LORD is my banner"*
e *Meaning of Heb* kes *uncertain*

**18** Jethro priest of Midian, Moses' father-in-law, heard all that God had done for Moses and for Israel His people, how the LORD had brought Israel out from Egypt. ²So Jethro, Moses' father-in-law, took Zipporah, Moses' wife, after she had been sent home, ³and her two sons—of whom one was named Gershom, that is to say, "I have been a stranger*a* in a foreign land"; ⁴and the other was named Eliezer,*b* meaning, "The God of my father was my help, and He delivered me from the sword of Pharaoh." ⁵Jethro, Moses' father-in-law, brought Moses' sons and wife to him in the wilderness, where he was encamped at the mountain of God. ⁶He sent word to Moses, "I, your father-in-law Jethro, am coming to you, with your wife and her two sons." ⁷Moses went out to meet his father-in-law; he bowed low and kissed him; each asked after the other's welfare, and they went into the tent.

⁸Moses then recounted to his father-in-law everything that the LORD had done to Pharaoh and to the Egyptians for Israel's sake, all the hardships that had befallen them on the way, and how the LORD had delivered them. ⁹And Jethro rejoiced over all the kindness that the LORD had shown Israel when He delivered them from the Egyptians. ¹⁰"Blessed be the LORD," Jethro said, "who delivered you from the Egyptians and from Pharaoh, and who delivered the people from under the hand of the Egyptians. ¹¹Now I know that the LORD is greater than all gods, *ᶜyes, by the result of their very schemes against [the people]."ᶜ* ¹²And Jethro, Moses' father-in-law, brought a burnt offering and sacrifices for God; and Aaron came with all the elders of Israel to partake of the meal before God with Moses' father-in-law.

¹³Next day, Moses sat as magistrate among the people, while the people stood about Moses from morning until evening. ¹⁴But when Moses' father-in-law saw how much he had to do for the people, he said, "What is this thing that you are doing to the

---

a *Heb* ger
b *Lit. "(My) God is help"*
c-c *Meaning of Heb uncertain*

136

people? Why do you act[d] alone, while all the people stand about you from morning until evening?" [15]Moses replied to his father-in-law, "It is because the people come to me to inquire of God. [16]When they have a dispute, it comes before me, and I decide between one person and another, and I make known the laws and teachings of God."

[17]But Moses' father-in-law said to him, "The thing you are doing is not right; [18]you will surely wear yourself out, and these people as well. For the task is too heavy for you; you cannot do it alone. [19]Now listen to me. I will give you counsel, and God be with you! You represent the people before God: you bring the disputes before God, [20]and enjoin upon them the laws and the teachings, and make known to them the way they are to go and the practices they are to follow. [21]You shall also seek out from among all the people capable men who fear God, trustworthy men who spurn ill-gotten gain. Set these over them as chiefs of thousands, hundreds, fifties, and tens, and [22]let them judge the people at all times. Have them bring every major dispute to you, but let them decide every minor dispute themselves. Make it easier for yourself by letting them share the burden with you. [23]If you do this—and God so commands you—you will be able to bear up; and all these people too will go home unwearied."

[24]Moses heeded his father-in-law and did just as he had said. [25]Moses chose capable men out of all Israel, and appointed them heads over the people—chiefs of thousands, hundreds, fifties, and tens; [26]and they judged the people at all times: the difficult matters they would bring to Moses, and all the minor matters they would decide themselves. [27]Then Moses bade his father-in-law farewell, and he went his way to his own land.

# 19

On the third new moon after the Israelites had gone forth from the land of Egypt, on that very day, they entered the wilderness of Sinai. [2]Having journeyed from Rephidim, they entered the wilderness of Sinai and encamped in the wilderness.

---

d Lit. "sit" as magistrate; cf. v. 13

Israel encamped there in front of the mountain, [3]and Moses went up to God. The LORD called to him from the mountain, saying, "Thus shall you say to the house of Jacob and declare to the children of Israel: [4]'You have seen what I did to the Egyptians, how I bore you on eagles' wings and brought you to Me. [5]Now then, if you will obey Me faithfully and keep My covenant, you shall be My treasured possession among all the peoples. Indeed, all the earth is Mine, [6]but you shall be to Me a kingdom of priests and a holy nation.' These are the words that you shall speak to the children of Israel."

[7]Moses came and summoned the elders of the people and put before them all that the LORD had commanded him. [8]All the people answered as one, saying, "All that the LORD has spoken we will do!" And Moses brought back the people's words to the LORD. [9]And the LORD said to Moses, "I will come to you in a thick cloud, in order that the people may hear when I speak with you and so trust you ever after." Then Moses reported the people's words to the LORD, [10]and the LORD said to Moses, "Go to the people and warn them to stay pure[a] today and tomorrow. Let them wash their clothes. [11]Let them be ready for the third day; for on the third day the LORD will come down, in the sight of all the people, on Mount Sinai. [12]You shall set bounds for the people round about, saying, 'Beware of going up the mountain or touching the border of it. Whoever touches the mountain shall be put to death: [13]no hand shall touch him, but he shall be either stoned or shot; beast or man, he shall not live.' When the ram's horn [b]sounds a long blast,[b] they may go up on the mountain."

[14]Moses came down from the mountain to the people and warned the people to stay pure, and they washed their clothes. [15]And he said to the people, "Be ready for the third day; do not go near a woman."

---

[a] *Cf. v. 15*
[b-b] *Meaning of Heb uncertain*

¹⁶On the third day, as morning dawned, there was thunder, and lightning, and a dense cloud upon the mountain, and a very loud blast of the horn; and all the people who were in the camp trembled. ¹⁷Moses led the people out of the camp toward God, and they took their places at the foot of the mountain.

¹⁸Now Mount Sinai was all in smoke, for the LORD had come down upon it in fire; the smoke rose like the smoke of a kiln, and the whole mountainᶜ trembled violently. ¹⁹The blare of the horn grew louder and louder. As Moses spoke, God answered him in thunder. ²⁰The LORD came down upon Mount Sinai, on the top of the mountain, and the LORD called Moses to the top of the mountain and Moses went up. ²¹The LORD said to Moses, "Go down, warn the people not to break through to the LORD to gaze, lest many of them perish. ²²The priests also, who come near the LORD, must stay pure, lest the LORD break out against them." ²³But Moses said to the LORD, "The people cannot come up to Mount Sinai, for You warned us saying, 'Set bounds about the mountain and sanctify it.'" ²⁴So the LORD said to him, "Go down, and come back together with Aaron; but let not the priests or the people break through to come up to the LORD, lest He break out against them." ²⁵And Moses went down to the people and spoke to them.

# 20

God spoke all these words,ᵃ saying:

²I the LORD am your God who brought you out of the land of Egypt, the house of bondage: ³You shall have no other gods besides Me.

⁴You shall not make for yourself a sculptured image, or any likeness of what is in the heavens above, or on the earth below, or in the waters under the earth. ⁵You shall not bow down to them or serve them. For I the LORD your God am an impassioned God, visiting the guilt of the parents upon the children,

ᶜ *Some Hebrew manuscripts and the Greek read, "all the people"; cf. v. 16*

ᵃ *Tradition varies as to the division of the Commandments in vv. 2–14, and as to the numbering of the verses from 13 on* upon the third and upon the fourth generations of those who reject Me, [6]but showing kindness to the thousandth generation of those who love Me and keep My commandments.

[7]You shall not [b-]swear falsely by[-b] the name of the LORD your God; for the LORD will not clear one who swears falsely by His name.

[8]Remember the sabbath day and keep it holy. [9]Six days you shall labor and do all your work, [10]but the seventh day is a sabbath of the LORD your God: you shall not do any work—you, your son or daughter, your male or female slave, or your cattle, or the stranger who is within your settlements. [11]For in six days the LORD made heaven and earth and sea, and all that is in them, and He rested on the seventh day; therefore the LORD blessed the sabbath day and hallowed it.

[12]Honor your father and your mother, that you may long endure on the land that the LORD your God is assigning to you.

[13]You shall not murder.

You shall not commit adultery.

You shall not steal.

You shall not bear false witness against your neighbor.

[14]You shall not covet your neighbor's house: you shall not covet your neighbor's wife, or his male or female slave, or his ox or his ass, or anything that is your neighbor's.

[15]All the people witnessed the thunder and lightning, the blare of the horn and the mountain smoking; and when the people saw it, they fell back and stood at a distance. [16]"You speak to us," they said to Moses, "and we will obey; but let not God speak to us, lest we die." [17]Moses answered the people, "Be not afraid; for God has come only in order to test you, and in order that the fear of Him may be ever with you, so that you do not go astray." [18]So the people remained at a distance, while Moses approached the thick cloud where God was.

b-b *Others "take in vain"*

[19]The LORD said to Moses:

Thus shall you say to the Israelites: You yourselves saw that I spoke to you from the very heavens: [20]With Me, therefore, you shall not make any gods of silver, nor shall you make for yourselves any gods of gold. [21]Make for Me an altar of earth and sacrifice on it your burnt offerings and your sacrifices of well-being,[c] your sheep and your oxen; in every place where I cause My name to be mentioned I will come to you and bless you. [22]And if you make for Me an altar of stones, do not build it of hewn stones; for by wielding your tool upon them you have profaned them. [23]Do not ascend My altar by steps, that your nakedness may not be exposed upon it.

מִשְׁפָּטִים

# 21 These are the rules that you shall set before them:

[2]When you acquire a Hebrew slave, he shall serve six years; in the seventh year he shall go free, without payment. [3]If he came single, he shall leave single; if he had a wife, his wife shall leave with him. [4]If his master gave him a wife, and she has borne him children, the wife and her children shall belong to the master, and he shall leave alone. [5]But if the slave declares, "I love my master, and my wife and children: I do not wish to go free," [6]his master shall take him before God.[a] He shall be brought to the door or the doorpost, and his master shall pierce his ear with an awl; and he shall then remain his slave for life.

[7]When a man sells his daughter as a slave, she shall not be freed as male slaves are. [8]If she proves to be displeasing to her master, who designated her for himself, he must let her be redeemed; he shall not have the right to sell her to outsiders, since he broke faith with her. [9]And if he designated her for his son, he shall deal with her as is the practice with free maidens. [10]If he marries another, he must not withhold from this one her food, her clothing, or her conjugal rights.[b] [11]If he fails her in these three ways, she shall go free, without payment.

---

[c] *Others "peace-offering." Meaning of* shelamim *uncertain*

[a] *Others "to the judges"*

[b] *Or "ointments"*

¹²He who fatally strikes a man shall be put to death. ¹³If he did not do it by design, but it came about by an act of God, I will assign you a place to which he can flee.

¹⁴When a man schemes against another and kills him treacherously, you shall take him from My very altar to be put to death.

¹⁵He who strikes his father or his mother shall be put to death.

¹⁶He who kidnaps a man—whether he has sold him or is still holding him—shall be put to death.

¹⁷He who insults⁣ᶜ his father or his mother shall be put to death.

¹⁸When men quarrel and one strikes the other with stone or fist, and he does not die but has to take to his bed—¹⁹if he then gets up and walks outdoors upon his staff, the assailant shall go unpunished, except that he must pay for his idleness and his cure.

²⁰When a man strikes his slave, male or female, with a rod, and he dies there and then,ᵈ he must be avenged. ²¹But if he survives a day or two, he is not to be avenged, since he is the other's property.

²²When men fight, and one of them pushes a pregnant woman and a miscarriage results, but no other damage ensues, the one responsibleᵉ shall be fined according as the woman's husband may exact from him, the payment to be based on reckoning.ᶠ ²³But if other damage ensues, the penalty shall be life for life, ²⁴eye for eye, tooth for tooth, hand for hand, foot for foot, ²⁵burn for burn, wound for wound, bruise for bruise.

²⁶When a man strikes the eye of his slave, male or female, and destroys it, he shall let him go free on account of his eye. ²⁷If he knocks out the tooth of his slave, male or female, he shall let him go free on account of his tooth.

²⁸When an ox gores a man or a woman to death, the ox shall be stoned and its flesh shall not be eaten, but the owner of the ox is not to be punished. ²⁹If, however, that ox has been in the habit of goring, and its owner, although warned, has failed to guard it,

---

ᶜ Or "reviles"
ᵈ Lit. "under his hand"
ᵉ Heb "he"
ᶠ Others "as the judges determine"

and it kills a man or a woman—the ox shall be stoned and its owner, too, shall be put to death. <sup>30</sup>If ransom is laid upon him, he must pay whatever is laid upon him to redeem his life. <sup>31</sup>So, too, if it gores a minor, male or female, [the owner] shall be dealt with according to the same rule. <sup>32</sup>But if the ox gores a slave, male or female, he shall pay thirty shekels of silver to the master, and the ox shall be stoned.

<sup>33</sup>When a man opens a pit, or digs a pit and does not cover it, and an ox or an ass falls into it, <sup>34</sup>the one responsible for the pit must make restitution; he shall pay the price to the owner, but shall keep the dead animal.

<sup>35</sup>When a man's ox injures his neighbor's ox and it dies, they shall sell the live ox and divide its price; they shall also divide the dead animal. <sup>36</sup>If, however, it is known that the ox was in the habit of goring, and its owner has failed to guard it, he must restore ox for ox, but shall keep the dead animal.

<sup>37g</sup>When a man steals an ox or a sheep, and slaughters it or

**22** sells it, he shall pay five oxen for the ox, and four sheep for the sheep.—<sup>1</sup>If the thief is seized while tunneling,<sup>a</sup> and he is beaten to death, there is no bloodguilt in his case. <sup>2</sup>If the sun has risen on him, there is bloodguilt in that case.—He<sup>b</sup> must make restitution; if he lacks the means, he shall be sold for his theft. <sup>3</sup>But if what he stole—whether ox or ass or sheep—is found alive in his possession, he shall pay double.

<sup>4</sup>When a man lets his livestock loose to graze in another's land, and so allows a field or a vineyard to be grazed bare, he must make restitution for the impairment<sup>c</sup> of that field or vineyard.

<sup>5</sup>When a fire is started and spreads to thorns, so that stacked, standing, or growing<sup>d</sup> grain is consumed, he who started the fire must make restitution.

<sup>6</sup>When a man gives money or goods to another for safe-keeping, and they are stolen from the man's house—if the thief is caught, he shall pay double; <sup>7</sup>if the thief is not caught, the owner of the house shall depose before God<sup>e</sup> that he has not laid hands on the other's property. <sup>8</sup>In all charges of misappropria-

---

<sup>g</sup> *This constitutes Chap. 22.1 in some editions*

<sup>a</sup> *I.e. under a wall for housebreaking*    <sup>b</sup> *I.e. the thief of 21.37*

<sup>c</sup> *Lit. "excellence"*    <sup>d</sup> *Lit. "field"*    <sup>e</sup> *See note on 21.6*

tion—pertaining to an ox, an ass, a sheep, a garment, or any other loss, whereof one party alleges, "This is it"—the case of both parties shall come before God: he whom God declares guilty shall pay double to the other.

⁹When a man gives to another an ass, an ox, a sheep or any other animal to guard, and it dies or is injured or is carried off, with no witness about, ¹⁰an oath before the LORD shall decide between the two of them that the one has not laid hands on the property of the other; the owner must acquiesce, and no restitution shall be made. ¹¹But if [the animal] was stolen from him, he shall make restitution to its owner. ¹²If it was torn by beasts, he shall bring it as evidence; he need not replace what has been torn by beasts.

¹³When a man borrows [an animal] from another and it dies or is injured, its owner not being with it, he must make restitution. ¹⁴If its owner was with it, no restitution need be made; but if it was hired, he is entitled to the hire.

¹⁵If a man seduces a virgin for whom the bride-price has not been paid,ᶠ and lies with her, he must make her his wife by payment of a bride-price. ¹⁶If her father refuses to give her to him, he must still weigh out silver in accordance with the bride-price for virgins.

¹⁷You shall not tolerateᵍ a sorceress.

¹⁸Whoever lies with a beast shall be put to death.

¹⁹Whoever sacrifices to a god other than the LORD alone shall be proscribed.ʰ

²⁰You shall not wrong a stranger or oppress him, for you were strangers in the land of Egypt.

²¹You shall not ill-treat any widow or orphan. ²²If you do mistreat them, I will heed their outcry as soon as they cry out to Me, ²³and My anger shall blaze forth and I will put you to the sword, and your own wives shall become widows and your children orphans.

²⁴If you lend money to My people, to the poor among you, do not act toward them as a creditor: exact no interest from them.

---

ᶠ *So that she is unmarried; cf. Deut. 20.7; 22.23ff.*     ᵍ *Lit. "let live"*
ʰ *See Lev. 27.29*

[25]If you take your neighbor's garment in pledge, you must return it to him before the sun sets; [26]it is his only clothing, the sole covering for his skin. In what else shall he sleep? Therefore, if he cries out to Me, I will pay heed, for I am compassionate.

[27]You shall not revile God, nor put a curse upon a chieftain among your people.

[28]You shall not [i]put off the skimming of the first yield of your vats.[i] You shall give Me the first-born among your sons. [29]You shall do the same with your cattle and your flocks: seven days it[j] shall remain with its mother; on the eighth day you shall give it to Me.

[30]You shall be holy people to Me: you must not eat flesh torn by beasts in the field; you shall cast it to the dogs.

# 23

You must not carry false rumors; you shall not join hands with the guilty to act as a malicious witness: [2]You shall neither side with the mighty[a] to do wrong—you shall not give perverse testimony in a dispute so as to pervert it in favor of the mighty[a]—[3]nor shall you show deference to a poor man in his dispute.

[4]When you encounter your enemy's ox or ass wandering, you must take it back to him.

[5]When you see the ass of your enemy lying under its burden and would refrain from raising[b] it, you must nevertheless raise it with him.

[6]You shall not subvert the rights of your needy in their disputes. [7]Keep far from a false charge; do not bring death on those who are innocent and in the right, for I will not acquit the wrongdoer. [8]Do not take bribes, for bribes blind the clear-sighted and upset the pleas of those who are in the right.

[9]You shall not oppress a stranger, for you know the feelings of the stranger, having yourselves been strangers in the land of Egypt.

[10]Six years you shall sow your land and gather in its yield;

---

[i-i] *Meaning of Heb uncertain*
[j] *I.e. the male first-born*

[a] *Others "multitude"*
[b] *For this use of the verb 'zb cf. Neh. 3.8, 34. For the whole verse see Deut. 22.4*

[11]but in the seventh you shall let it rest and lie fallow. Let the needy among your people eat of it, and what they leave let the wild beasts eat. You shall do the same with your vineyards and your olive groves.

[12]Six days you shall do your work, but on the seventh day you shall cease from labor, in order that your ox and your ass may rest, and that your bondman and the stranger may be refreshed.

[13]Be on guard concerning all that I have told you. Make no mention of the names of other gods; they shall not be heard on your lips.

[14]Three times a year you shall hold a festival for Me: [15]You shall observe the Feast of Unleavened Bread—eating unleavened bread for seven days as I have commanded you—at the set time in the month[c] of Abib, for in it you went forth from Egypt; and none shall appear before Me empty-handed; [16]and the Feast of the Harvest, of the first fruits of your work, of what you sow in the field; and the Feast of Ingathering at the end of the year, when you gather in the results of your work from the field. [17]Three times a year all your males shall appear before the Sovereign, the LORD.

[18]You shall not offer the blood of My sacrifice with anything leavened; and the fat of My festal offering shall not be left lying until morning.

[19]The choice first fruits of your soil you shall bring to the house of the LORD your God.

You shall not boil a kid in its mother's milk.

[20]I am sending an angel before you to guard you on the way and to bring you to the place that I have made ready. [21]Pay heed to him and obey him. Do not defy him, for he will not pardon your offenses, since My Name is in him; [22]but if you obey him and do all that I say, I will be an enemy to your enemies and a foe to your foes.

[23]When My angel goes before you and brings you to the Amorites, the Hittites, the Perizzites, the Canaanites, the Hivites, and the Jebusites, and I annihilate them, [24]you shall not bow

[c] See note at 13.4

down to their gods in worship or follow their practices, but shall tear them down and smash their pillars to bits. ²⁵You shall serve the LORD your God, and He will bless your bread and your water. And I will remove sickness from your midst. ²⁶No woman in your land shall miscarry or be barren. I will let you enjoy the full count of your days.

²⁷I will send forth My terror before you, and I will throw into panic all the people among whom you come, and I will make all your enemies turn tail*ᵈ* before you. ²⁸I will send a plague*ᵉ* ahead of you, and it shall drive out before you the Hivites, the Canaanites, and the Hittites. ²⁹I will not drive them out before you in a single year, lest the land become desolate and the wild beasts multiply to your hurt. ³⁰I will drive them out before you little by little, until you have increased and possess the land. ³¹I will set your borders from the Sea of Reeds to the Sea of Philistia, and from the wilderness to the Euphrates; for I will deliver the inhabitants of the land into your hands, and you will drive them out before you. ³²You shall make no covenant with them and their gods. ³³They shall not remain in your land, lest they cause you to sin against Me; for you will serve their gods—and it will prove a snare to you.

**24** Then He said to Moses, "Come up to the LORD, with Aaron, Nadab and Abihu, and seventy elders of Israel, and bow low from afar. ²Moses alone shall come near the LORD; but the others shall not come near, nor shall the people come up with him."

³Moses went and repeated to the people all the commands of the LORD and all the rules; and all the people answered with one voice, saying, "All the things that the LORD has commanded we will do!" ⁴Moses then wrote down all the commands of the LORD.

Early in the morning, he set up an altar at the foot of the mountain, with twelve pillars for the twelve tribes of Israel. ⁵He designated some young men among the Israelites, and they

---

ᵈ *Lit. "back"*
ᵉ *Others "hornet"; meaning of Heb uncertain*

offered burnt offerings and sacrificed bulls as offerings of well-being to the LORD. <sup>6</sup>Moses took one part of the blood and put it in basins, and the other part of the blood he dashed against the altar. <sup>7</sup>Then he took the record of the covenant and read it aloud to the people. And they said, "All that the LORD has spoken <sup>a-</sup>we will faithfully do!"<sup>-a</sup> <sup>8</sup>Moses took the blood and dashed it on the people and said, "This is the blood of the covenant that the LORD now makes with you concerning all these commands."

<sup>9</sup>Then Moses and Aaron, Nadab and Abihu, and seventy elders of Israel ascended; <sup>10</sup>and they saw the God of Israel: under His feet there was the likeness of a pavement of sapphire, like the very sky for purity. <sup>11</sup>Yet He did not raise His hand against the leaders<sup>b</sup> of the Israelites; they beheld God, and they ate and drank.

<sup>12</sup>The LORD said to Moses, "Come up to Me on the mountain and wait there, and I will give you the stone tablets with the teachings and commandments which I have inscribed to instruct them." <sup>13</sup>So Moses and his attendant Joshua arose, and Moses ascended the mountain of God. <sup>14</sup>To the elders he had said, "Wait here for us until we return to you. You have Aaron and Hur with you; let anyone who has a legal matter approach them."

<sup>15</sup>When Moses had ascended the mountain, the cloud covered the mountain. <sup>16</sup>The Presence of the LORD abode on Mount Sinai, and the cloud hid it for six days. On the seventh day He called to Moses from the midst of the cloud. <sup>17</sup>Now the Presence of the LORD appeared in the sight of the Israelites as a consuming fire on the top of the mountain. <sup>18</sup>Moses went inside the cloud and ascended the mountain; and Moses remained on the mountain forty days and forty nights.

תרומה

**25** The LORD spoke to Moses, saying: <sup>2</sup>Tell the Israelite

---

<sup>a-a</sup> *Lit. "we will do and obey"*
<sup>b</sup> *Meaning of Heb* 'aṣilim *uncertain*

people to bring Me gifts; you shall accept gifts for Me from every person whose heart so moves him. ³And these are the gifts that you shall accept from them: gold, silver, and copper; ⁴blue, purple, and crimson yarns, fine linen, goats' hair; ⁵tanned ram skins,ᵃ dolphin skins,ᵇ and acacia wood; ⁶oil for lighting, spices for the anointing oil and for the aromatic incense; ⁷lapis lazuliᶜ and other stones for setting, for the ephod and for the breastpiece. ⁸And let them make Me a sanctuary that I may dwell among them. ⁹Exactly as I show you—the pattern of the Tabernacle and the pattern of all its furnishings—so shall you make it.

¹⁰They shall make an ark of acacia wood, two and a half cubits long, a cubit and a half wide, and a cubit and a half high. ¹¹Overlay it with pure gold—overlay it inside and out—and make upon it a gold molding round about. ¹²Cast four gold rings for it, to be attached to its four feet, two rings on one of its side walls and two on the other. ¹³Make poles of acacia wood and overlay them with gold; ¹⁴then insert the poles into the rings on the side walls of the ark, for carrying the ark. ¹⁵The poles shall remain in the rings of the ark: they shall not be removed from it. ¹⁶And deposit in the Ark [the tablets of] the Pact which I will give you.

¹⁷You shall make a cover of pure gold, two and a half cubits long and a cubit and a half wide. ¹⁸Make two cherubim of gold—make them of hammered work—at the two ends of the cover. ¹⁹Make one cherub at one end and the other cherub at the other end; of one piece with the cover shall you make the cherubim at its two ends. ²⁰The cherubim shall have their wings spread out above, shielding the cover with their wings. They shall confront each other, the faces of the cherubim being turned toward the cover. ²¹Place the cover on top of the Ark, after depositing inside the Ark the Pact that I will give you. ²²There I will meet with you, and I will impart to you—from above the cover, from between the two cherubim that are on top

---

ᵃ Others "rams' skins dyed red"
ᵇ Or "dugong"; meaning of Heb taḥash uncertain
ᶜ Cf. Gen. 2.12 and note

of the Ark of the Pact—all that I will command you concerning the Israelite people.

23You shall make a table of acacia wood, two cubits long, one cubit wide, and a cubit and a half high. 24Overlay it with pure gold, and make a gold molding around it. 25Make a rim of a hand's breadth around it, and make a gold molding for its rim round about. 26Make four gold rings for it, and attach the rings to the four corners at its four legs. 27The rings shall be next to the rim, as holders for poles to carry the table. 28Make the poles of acacia wood, and overlay them with gold; by these the table shall be carried. 29Make its bowls, ladles, jars and jugs with which to offer libations; make them of pure gold. 30And on the table you shall set the bread of display, to be before Me always.

31You shall make a lampstand of pure gold; the lampstand shall be made of hammered work; its base and its shaft, its cups, calyxes, and petals shall be of one piece. 32Six branches shall issue from its sides; three branches from one side of the lampstand and three branches from the other side of the lampstand. 33On one branch there shall be three cups shaped like almond-blossoms, each with calyx and petals, and on the next branch there shall be three cups shaped like almond-blossoms, each with calyx and petals; so for all six branches issuing from the lampstand. 34And on the lampstand itself there shall be four cups shaped like almond-blossoms, each with calyx and petals: 35a calyx, of one piece with it, under a pair of branches; and a calyx, of one piece with it, under the second pair of branches, and a calyx, of one piece with it, under the last pair of branches; so for all six branches issuing from the lampstand. 36Their calyxes and their stems shall be of one piece with it, the whole of it a single hammered piece of pure gold. 37Make its seven lamps —the lamps shall be so mounted as to give the light on its front side—38and its tongs and fire pans of pure gold. 39It shall be made, with all these furnishings, out of a talent of pure gold. 40Note well, and follow the patterns for them that are being shown you on the mountain.

26 As for the Tabernacle,[a] make it of ten strips of cloth; make these of fine twisted linen, of blue, purple, and crimson yarns, with a design of cherubim worked into them. [2]The length of each cloth shall be twenty-eight cubits, and the width of each cloth shall be four cubits, all the cloths to have the same measurements. [3]Five of the cloths shall be joined to one another, and the other five cloths shall be joined to one another. [4]Make loops of blue wool on the edge of the outermost cloth of the one set; and do likewise on the edge of the outermost cloth of the other set: [5]make fifty loops on the one cloth, and fifty loops on the edge of the end cloth of the other set, the loops to be opposite one another. [6]And make fifty gold clasps, and couple the cloths to one another with the clasps, so that the Tabernacle becomes one whole.

[7]You shall then make cloths of goats' hair for a tent over the Tabernacle; make the cloths eleven in number. [8]The length of each cloth shall be thirty cubits, and the width of each cloth shall be four cubits, the eleven cloths to have the same measurements. [9]Join five of the cloths by themselves, and the other six cloths by themselves; and fold over the sixth cloth at the front of the tent. [10]Make fifty loops on the edge of the outermost cloth of the one set, and fifty loops on the edge of the cloth of the other set. [11]Make fifty copper clasps, and fit the clasps into the loops, and couple the tent together so that it becomes one whole. [12]As for the overlapping excess of the cloths of the tent, the extra half-cloth shall overlap the back of the Tabernacle, [13]while the extra cubit at either end of each length of tent cloth shall hang down to the bottom of the two sides of the Tabernacle and cover it. [14]And make for the tent a covering of tanned ram skins, and a covering of dolphin skins above.

[15]You shall make the planks for the Tabernacle of acacia wood, upright. [16]The length of each plank shall be ten cubits and the width of each plank a cubit and a half. [17]Each plank shall have two tenons, parallel[b] to each other; do the same with all the

---

a  *Here the lowest of the covers of the Tabernacle*
b  *Meaning of Heb* meshullaboth *uncertain*

planks of the Tabernacle. <sup>18</sup>Of the planks of the Tabernacle, make twenty planks on the south<sup>c</sup> side: <sup>19</sup>making forty silver sockets under the twenty planks, two sockets under the one plank for its two tenons and two sockets under each following plank for its two tenons; <sup>20</sup>and for the other side wall of the Tabernacle, on the north side, twenty planks, <sup>21</sup>with their forty silver sockets, two sockets under the one plank and two sockets under each following plank. <sup>22</sup>And for the rear of the Tabernacle, to the west, make six planks; <sup>23</sup>and make two planks for the corners of the Tabernacle at the rear. <sup>24d-</sup>They shall match at the bottom, and terminate alike at the top inside one ring;<sup>-d</sup> thus shall it be with both of them: they shall form the two corners. <sup>25</sup>Thus there shall be eight planks with their sockets of silver: sixteen sockets, two sockets under the first plank, and two sockets under each of the other planks.

<sup>26</sup>You shall make bars of acacia wood: five for the planks of the one side wall of the Tabernacle, <sup>27</sup>five bars for the planks of the other side wall of the Tabernacle, and five bars for the planks of the wall of the Tabernacle at the rear to the west. <sup>28</sup>The center bar halfway up the planks shall run from end to end. <sup>29</sup>Overlay the planks with gold, and make their rings of gold, as holders for the bars; and overlay the bars with gold. <sup>30</sup>Then set up the Tabernacle according to the manner of it that you were shown on the mountain.

<sup>31</sup>You shall make a curtain of blue, purple, and crimson yarns, and fine twisted linen; it shall have a design of cherubim worked into it. <sup>32</sup>Hang it upon four posts of acacia wood overlaid with gold and having hooks of gold, [set] in four sockets of silver. <sup>33</sup>Hang the curtain under the clasps, and carry the Ark of the Pact there, behind the curtain, so that the curtain shall serve you as a partition between the Holy and the Holy of Holies. <sup>34</sup>Place the cover upon the Ark of the Pact in the Holy of Holies. <sup>35</sup>Place the table outside the curtain, and the lampstand by the south wall of the Tabernacle opposite the table, which is to be placed by the north wall.

<sup>c</sup> *Heb uses two terms for "south"*
<sup>d-d</sup> *Meaning of Heb uncertain*

<sup>36</sup>You shall make a screen for the entrance of the Tent, of blue, purple, and crimson yarns, and fine twisted linen, done in embroidery. <sup>37</sup>Make five posts of acacia wood for the screen and overlay them with gold—their hooks being of gold—and cast for them five sockets of copper.

# 27

You shall make the altar of acacia wood, five cubits long and five cubits wide—the altar is to be square—and three cubits high. <sup>2</sup>Make its horns on the four corners, the horns to be of one piece with it; and overlay it with copper. <sup>3</sup>Make the pails for removing its ashes, as well as its scrapers, basins, flesh hooks, and fire pans—make all its utensils of copper. <sup>4</sup>Make for it a grating of meshwork in copper; and on the mesh make four copper rings at its four corners. <sup>5</sup>Set the mesh below, under the ledge of the altar, so that it extends to the middle of the altar. <sup>6</sup>And make poles for the altar, poles of acacia wood, and overlay them with copper. <sup>7</sup>The poles shall be inserted into the rings, so that the poles remain on the two sides of the altar when it is carried. <sup>8</sup>Make it hollow, of boards. As you were shown on the mountain, so shall they be made.

<sup>9</sup>You shall make the enclosure of the Tabernacle:
On the south side,<sup>a</sup> a hundred cubits of hangings of fine twisted linen for the length of the enclosure on that side— <sup>10</sup>with its twenty posts and their twenty sockets of copper, the hooks and bands of the posts to be of silver.

<sup>11</sup>Again a hundred cubits of hangings for its length along the north side—with its twenty posts and their twenty sockets of copper, the hooks and bands of the posts to be of silver.

<sup>12</sup>For the width of the enclosure, on the west side, fifty cubits of hangings, with their ten posts and their ten sockets.

<sup>13</sup>For the width of the enclosure on the front, or east side, fifty cubits: <sup>14</sup>fifteen cubits of hangings on the one flank, with their three posts and their three sockets; <sup>15</sup>fifteen cubits of hangings on the other flank, with their three posts and their three sockets;

<sup>a</sup> *Cf. note at 26.18*

¹⁶and for the gate of the enclosure, a screen of twenty cubits, of blue, purple, and crimson yarns, and fine twisted linen, done in embroidery, with their four posts and their four sockets. ¹⁷All the posts round the enclosure shall be banded with silver and their hooks shall be of silver; their sockets shall be of copper. ¹⁸The length of the enclosure shall be a hundred cubits, and the width fifty throughout; and the height five cubits—[with hangings] of fine twisted linen. The sockets shall be of copper: ¹⁹all the utensils of the Tabernacle,$^b$ for all its service, as well as all its pegs and all the pegs of the court, shall be of copper.

תצוה

²⁰You shall further instruct the Israelites to bring you clear oil of beaten olives for lighting, for kindling lamps regularly. ²¹Aaron and his sons shall set them up in the Tent of Meeting, outside the curtain which is over [the Ark of] the Pact, [to burn] from evening to morning before the LORD. It shall be a due from the Israelites for all time, throughout the ages.

28 You shall bring forward your brother Aaron, with his sons, from among the Israelites, to serve Me as priests: Aaron, Nadab and Abihu, Eleazar and Ithamar, the sons of Aaron. ²Make sacral vestments for your brother Aaron, for dignity and adornment. ³Next you shall instruct all who are $^a$ skillful, whom I have endowed with the gift of skill,$^{-a}$ to make Aaron's vestments, for consecrating him to serve Me as priest. ⁴These are the vestments they are to make: a breastpiece, an ephod, a robe, a fringed$^b$ tunic, a headdress, and a sash. They shall make those sacral vestments for your brother Aaron and his sons, for priestly service to Me; ⁵they, therefore, shall receive the gold, the blue, purple, and crimson yarns, and the fine linen.

⁶They shall make the ephod of gold, of blue, purple, and crimson yarns, and of fine twisted linen, worked into designs. ⁷It

---

$^b$ *I.e. of the Tabernacle enclosure; the furnishings inside were of gold*

$^{a-a}$ *Lit. "wise of heart, whom I have filled with a spirit of wisdom"*

$^b$ *Others "checkered"*

shall have two shoulder-pieces attached; they shall be attached at its two ends. [8]And the decorated band that is upon it shall be made like it, of one piece with it: of gold, of blue, purple, and crimson yarns, and of fine twisted linen. [9]Then take two lazuli stones and engrave on them the names of the sons of Israel: [10]six of their names on the one stone, and the names of the remaining six on the other stone, in the order of their birth. [11]On the two stones you shall make seal engravings—the work of a lapidary—of the names of the sons of Israel. Having bordered them with frames of gold, [12]attach the two stones to the shoulder-pieces of the ephod, as stones for remembrance of the Israelite people, whose names Aaron shall carry upon his two shoulder-pieces for remembrance before the LORD.

[13]Then make frames of gold [14]and two chains of pure gold; braid these like corded work, and fasten the corded chains to the frames.

[15]You shall make a breastpiece of decision,[c] worked into a design; make it in the style of the ephod: make it of gold, of blue, purple, and crimson yarns, and of fine twisted linen. [16]It shall be square and doubled, a span in length and a span in width. [17]Set in it mounted stones, in four rows of stones. The first row shall be a row of [d]carnelian, chrysolite, and emerald; [18]the second row: a turquoise, a sapphire, and an amethyst; [19]the third row: a jacinth, an agate, and a crystal; [20]and the fourth row: a beryl, a lapis lazuli, and a jasper. They shall be framed with gold in their mountings. [21]The stones shall correspond [in number] to the names of the sons of Israel: twelve, corresponding to their names. They shall be engraved like seals, each with its name, for the twelve tribes.

[22]On the breastpiece make braided chains of corded work in pure gold. [23]Make two rings of gold on the breastpiece, and fasten the two rings at the two ends of the breastpiece, [24]attaching the two golden cords to the two rings at the ends of the breastpiece. [25]Then fasten the two ends of the cords to the two frames, which you shall attach to the shoulder-pieces of the

---

[c] See v. 30 below; others "judgment"

[d] The identity of several of these twelve stones is uncertain

ephod, at the front. ²⁶Make two rings of gold and attach them to the two ends of the breastpiece, at its inner edge, which faces the ephod. ²⁷And make two other rings of gold and fasten them on the front of the ephod, low on the two shoulder-pieces, close to its seam above the decorated band. ²⁸The breastpiece shall be held in place by a cord of blue from its rings to the rings of the ephod, so that the breastpiece rests on the decorated band and does not come loose from the ephod. ²⁹Aaron shall carry the names of the sons of Israel on the breastpiece of decision over his heart, when he enters the sanctuary, for remembrance before the LORD at all times. ³⁰Inside the breastpiece of decision you shall place the Urim and Thummim,ᵉ so that they are over Aaron's heart when he comes before the LORD. Thus Aaron shall carry the instrument of decision for the Israelites over his heart before the LORD at all times.

³¹You shall make the robe of the ephod of pure blue.ᶠ ³²The opening for the head shall be in the middle of it; the opening shall have a binding of woven work round about—it shall be like the opening of a coat of mail—so that it does not tear. ³³On its hem make pomegranates of blue, purple, and crimson yarns, all around the hem, with bells of gold between them all around: ³⁴a golden bell and a pomegranate, a golden bell and a pomegranate, all around the hem of the robe. ³⁵Aaron shall wear it while officiating, so that the sound of it is heard when he comes into the sanctuary before the LORD and when he goes out—that he may not die.

³⁶You shall make a frontlet of pure gold and engrave on it the seal inscription: "Holy to the LORD." ³⁷Suspend it on a cord of blue, so that it may remain on the headdress; it shall remain on the front of the headdress. ³⁸It shall be on Aaron's forehead, that Aaron may take away any sin arising from the holy things that the Israelites consecrate, from any of their sacred donations; it shall be on his forehead at all times, to win acceptance for them before the LORD.

---

ᵉ *Meaning of these two words uncertain. They designate a kind of oracle; cf. Num. 27.21*
ᶠ *Others "all of blue"*

[39]You shall make the fringed tunic of fine linen.

You shall make the headdress of fine linen.

You shall make the sash of embroidered work.

[40]And for Aaron's sons also you shall make tunics, and make sashes for them, and make turbans for them, for dignity and adornment. [41]Put these on your brother Aaron and on his sons as well; anoint them, and ordain them[g] and consecrate them to serve Me as priests.

[42]You shall also make for them linen breeches to cover their nakedness; they shall extend from the hips to the thighs. [43]They shall be worn by Aaron and his sons when they enter the Tent of Meeting or when they approach the altar to officiate in the sanctuary, so that they do not incur punishment and die. It shall be a law for all time for him and for his offspring to come.

# 29

This is what you shall do to them in consecrating them to serve Me as priests: Take a young bull of the herd and two rams without blemish; [2]also unleavened bread, unleavened cakes with oil mixed in, and unleavened wafers spread with oil—make these of choice wheat flour. [3]Place these in one basket and present them in the basket, along with the bull and the two rams. [4]Lead Aaron and his sons up to the entrance of the Tent of Meeting, and wash them with water. [5]Then take the vestments, and clothe Aaron with the tunic, the robe of the ephod, the ephod, and the breastpiece, and gird him with the decorated band of the ephod. [6]Put the headdress on his head, and place the holy diadem upon the headdress. [7]Take the anointing oil and pour it on his head and anoint him. [8]Then bring his sons forward; clothe them with tunics [9]and wind turbans upon them. And gird both Aaron and his sons with sashes. And so they shall have priesthood as their right for all time.

You shall then ordain Aaron and his sons. [10]Lead the bull up to the front of the Tent of Meeting, and let Aaron and his sons

g  Lit. "and fill their hands"

lay their hands upon the head of the bull. ¹¹Slaughter the bull before the LORD, at the entrance of the Tent of Meeting, ¹²and take some of the bull's blood and put it on the horns of the altar with your finger; then pour out the rest of the blood at the base of the altar. ¹³Take all the fat that covers the entrails, the protuberance on the liver, and the two kidneys with the fat on them, and turn them into smoke upon the altar. ¹⁴The rest of the flesh of the bull, its hide, and its dung shall be put to the fire outside the camp; it is a sin offering.

¹⁵Next take the one ram, and let Aaron and his sons lay their hands upon the ram's head. ¹⁶Slaughter the ram, and take its blood and dash it against all sides of the altar. ¹⁷Cut up the ram into sections, wash its entrails and legs, and put them with its quarters and its head. ¹⁸Turn all of the ram into smoke upon the altar. It is a burnt offering to the LORD, a pleasing odor, an offering by fire to the LORD.

¹⁹Then take the other ram, and let Aaron and his sons lay their hands upon the ram's head. ²⁰Slaughter the ram, and take some of its blood and put it on the ridge*ᵃ* of Aaron's right ear and on the ridges of his sons' right ears, and on the thumbs of their right hands, and on the big toes of their right feet; and dash the rest of the blood against every side of the altar round about. ²¹Take some of the blood that is on the altar and some of the anointing oil and sprinkle upon Aaron and his vestments, and also upon his sons and his sons' vestments. Thus shall he and his vestments be holy, as well as his sons and his sons' vestments.

²²You shall take from the ram the fat parts—the broad tail, the fat that covers the entrails, the protuberance on the liver, the two kidneys with the fat on them—and the right thigh; for this is a ram of ordination. ²³Add one flat loaf of bread, one cake of oil bread, and one wafer, from the basket of unleavened bread that is before the LORD. ²⁴Place all these on the palms of Aaron and his sons, and offer them as an elevation offering before the LORD. ²⁵Take them from their hands and turn them into smoke upon the altar with the burnt offering, as a pleasing odor before the LORD; it is an offering by fire to the LORD.

ᵃ Or *"lobe"*

[26]Then take the breast of Aaron's ram of ordination and offer it as an elevation offering before the LORD; it shall be your portion. [27]You shall consecrate the breast that was offered as an elevation offering and the thigh that was offered as a gift offering from the ram of ordination—from that which was Aaron's and from that which was his sons'—[28]and those parts shall be a due for all time from the Israelites to Aaron and his descendants. For they are a gift; and so shall they be a gift from the Israelites, their gift to the LORD out of their sacrifices of well-being.

[29]The sacral vestments of Aaron shall pass on to his sons after him, for them to be anointed and ordained in. [30]He among his sons who becomes priest in his stead, who enters the Tent of Meeting to officiate within the sanctuary, shall wear them seven days.

[31]You shall take the ram of ordination and boil its flesh in the sacred precinct; [32]and Aaron and his sons shall eat the flesh of the ram, and the bread that is in the basket, at the entrance of the Tent of Meeting. [33]These things shall be eaten only by those for whom expiation was made with them when they were ordained and consecrated; they may not be eaten by a layman, for they are holy. [34]And if any of the flesh of ordination, or any of the bread, is left until morning, you shall put what is left to the fire; it shall not be eaten, for it is holy.

[35]Thus you shall do to Aaron and his sons, just as I have commanded you. You shall ordain them through seven days, [36]and each day you shall prepare a bull as a sin offering for expiation; you shall purge the altar by performing purification upon it, and you shall anoint it to consecrate it. [37]Seven days you shall perform purification for the altar to consecrate it, and the altar shall become most holy; whatever touches the altar shall become consecrated.

[38]Now this is what you shall offer upon the altar: two yearling lambs each day, regularly. [39]You shall offer the one lamb in the morning, and you shall offer the other lamb at twilight. [40]There shall be a tenth of a measure of choice flour with a quarter of a

*hin* of beaten oil mixed in, and a libation of a quarter *hin* of wine for one lamb; ⁴¹and you shall offer the other lamb at twilight, repeating with it the meal offering of the morning with its libation—an offering by fire for a pleasing odor to the LORD, ⁴²a regular burnt offering throughout the generations, at the entrance of the Tent of Meeting before the LORD.

For there I will meet with you, and there I will speak with you, ⁴³and there I will meet with the Israelites, and it shall be sanctified by My Presence. ⁴⁴I will sanctify the Tent of Meeting and the altar, and I will consecrate Aaron and his sons to serve Me as priests. ⁴⁵I will abide among the Israelites, and I will be their God. ⁴⁶And they shall know that I the LORD am their God, who brought them out from the land of Egypt that I might abide among them, I the LORD their God.

30 You shall make an altar for burning incense; make it of acacia wood. ²It shall be a cubit long and a cubit wide—it shall be square—and two cubits high, its horns of one piece with it. ³Overlay it with pure gold: its top, its sides round about, and its horns; and make a gold molding for it round about. ⁴And make two gold rings for it under its molding; make them on its two side walls, on opposite*ᵃ* sides. They shall serve as holders for poles with which to carry it. ⁵Make the poles of acacia wood, and overlay them with gold.

⁶Place it in front of the curtain that is over the Ark of the Pact—in front of the cover that is over the Pact—where I will meet with you. ⁷On it Aaron shall burn aromatic incense: he shall burn it every morning when he tends the lamps, ⁸and Aaron shall burn it at twilight when he lights the lamps—a regular incense offering before the LORD throughout the ages. ⁹You shall not offer alien incense on it, or a burnt offering or a meal offering; neither shall you pour a libation on it. ¹⁰Once a year Aaron shall perform purification upon its horns with blood of the sin offering of purification; purification shall be per-

ᵃ *Lit. "its two"*

formed upon it once a year throughout the ages. It is most holy to the LORD.

כי תשא

<sup>11</sup>The LORD spoke to Moses, saying: <sup>12</sup>When you take a census of the Israelite people according to their enrollment, each shall pay the LORD a ransom for himself on being enrolled, that no plague may come upon them through their being enrolled. <sup>13</sup>This is what everyone who is entered in the records shall pay: a half-shekel by the sanctuary weight—twenty *gerahs* to the shekel —a half-shekel as an offering to the LORD. <sup>14</sup>Everyone who is entered in the records, from the age of twenty years up, shall give the LORD's offering: <sup>15</sup>the rich shall not pay more and the poor shall not pay less than half a shekel when giving the LORD's offering as expiation for your persons. <sup>16</sup>You shall take the expiation money from the Israelites and assign it to the service of the Tent of Meeting; it shall serve the Israelites as a reminder before the LORD, as expiation for your persons.

<sup>17</sup>The LORD spoke to Moses, saying: <sup>18</sup>Make a laver of copper and a stand of copper for it, for washing; and place it between the Tent of Meeting and the altar. Put water in it, <sup>19</sup>and let Aaron and his sons wash their hands and feet [in water drawn] from it. <sup>20</sup>When they enter the Tent of Meeting they shall wash with water, that they may not die; or when they approach the altar to serve, to turn into smoke an offering by fire to the LORD, <sup>21</sup>they shall wash their hands and feet, that they may not die. It shall be a law for all time for them—for him and his offspring— throughout the ages.

<sup>22</sup>The LORD spoke to Moses, saying: <sup>23</sup>Next take choice spices: five hundred weight of solidified<sup>b</sup> myrrh, half as much—two hundred and fifty—of fragrant cinnamon, two hundred and fifty of aromatic cane, <sup>24</sup>five hundred—by the sanctuary weight —of cassia, and a *hin* of olive oil. <sup>25</sup>Make of this a sacred

---

<sup>b</sup> Others *"flowing"*

anointing oil, a compound of ingredients expertly blended, to serve as sacred anointing oil. ²⁶With it anoint the Tent of Meeting, the Ark of the Pact, ²⁷the table and all its utensils, the lampstand and all its fittings, the altar of incense, ²⁸the altar of burnt offering and all its utensils, and the laver and its stand. ²⁹Thus you shall consecrate them so that they may be most holy; whatever touches them shall be consecrated. ³⁰You shall also anoint Aaron and his sons, consecrating them to serve Me as priests.

³¹And speak to the Israelite people, as follows: This shall be an anointing oil sacred to Me throughout the ages. ³²It must not be rubbed on any person's body, and you must not make anything like it in the same proportions; it is sacred, to be held sacred by you. ³³Whoever compounds its like, or puts any of it on a layman, shall be cut off from his kin.

³⁴And the LORD said to Moses: Take the herbs stacte, onycha, and galbanum—these herbs together with pure frankincense; let there be an equal part of each. ³⁵Make them into incense, a compound expertly blended, refined, pure, sacred. ³⁶Beat some of it into powder, and put some before the Pact in the Tent of Meeting, where I will meet with you; it shall be most holy to you. ³⁷But when you make this incense, you must not make any in the same proportions for yourselves; it shall be held by you sacred to the LORD. Whoever makes any like it, to smell of it, shall be cut off from his kin.

31 The LORD spoke to Moses: ²See, I have singled out by name Bezalel son of Uri son of Hur, of the tribe of Judah. ³I have endowed him with a divine spirit of skill, ability, and knowledge in every kind of craft; ⁴to make designs for work in gold, silver, and copper, ⁵to cut stones for setting and to carve wood—to work in every kind of craft. ⁶Moreover, I have assigned to him Oholiab son of Ahisamach, of the tribe of Dan;

and I have also granted skill to all who are skillful, that they may make everything that I have commanded you: [7]the Tent of Meeting, the Ark for the Pact and the cover upon it, and all the furnishings of the Tent; [8]the table and its utensils, the pure lampstand[a] and all its fittings, and the altar of incense; [9]the altar of burnt offering and all its utensils, and the laver and its stand; [10]the service[b] vestments, the sacral vestments of Aaron the priest and the vestments of his sons, for their service as priests; [11]as well as the anointing oil and the aromatic incense for the sanctuary. Just as I have commanded you, they shall do.

[12]And the LORD said to Moses: [13]Speak to the Israelite people and say: Nevertheless, you must keep My sabbaths, for this is a sign between Me and you throughout the ages, that you may know that I the LORD have consecrated you. [14]You shall keep the sabbath, for it is holy for you. He who profanes it shall be put to death: whoever does work on it, that person shall be cut off from among his kin. [15]Six days may work be done, but on the seventh day there shall be a sabbath of complete rest, holy to the LORD; whoever does work on the sabbath day shall be put to death. [16]The Israelite people shall keep the sabbath, observing the sabbath throughout the ages as a covenant for all time: [17]it shall be a sign for all time between Me and the people of Israel. For in six days the LORD made heaven and earth, and on the seventh day He ceased from work and was refreshed.

[18]When He finished speaking with him on Mount Sinai, He gave Moses the two tablets of the Pact, stone tablets inscribed with the finger of God.

**32** When the people saw that Moses was so long in coming down from the mountain, the people gathered against Aaron and said to him, "Come, make us a god who shall go before us, for that man Moses, who brought us from the land of Egypt—

---

[a] Or "lampstand of pure gold"
[b] Others "plaited"

we do not know what has happened to him." ²Aaron said to them, "Take off the gold rings that are on the ears of your wives, your sons, and your daughters, and bring them to me." ³And all the people took off the gold rings that were in their ears and brought them to Aaron. ⁴This he took from them and *ᵃ*cast in a mold,*ᵃ* and made it into a molten calf. And they exclaimed, *ᵇ*"This is your god,*ᵇ* O Israel, who brought you out of the land of Egypt!" ⁵When Aaron saw this, he built an altar before it; and Aaron announced: "Tomorrow shall be a festival of the LORD!" ⁶Early next day, the people offered up burnt offerings and brought sacrifices of well-being; they sat down to eat and drink, and then rose to dance.

⁷The LORD spoke to Moses, "Hurry down, for your people, whom you brought out of the land of Egypt, have acted basely. ⁸They have been quick to turn aside from the way that I enjoined upon them. They have made themselves a molten calf and bowed low to it and sacrificed to it, saying: 'This is your god, O Israel, who brought you out of the land of Egypt!'"

⁹The LORD further said to Moses, "I see that this is a stiff-necked people. ¹⁰Now, let Me be, that My anger may blaze forth against them and that I may destroy them, and make of you a great nation." ¹¹But Moses implored the LORD his God, saying, "Let not Your anger, O LORD, blaze forth against Your people, whom You delivered from the land of Egypt with great power and with a mighty hand. ¹²Let not the Egyptians say, 'It was with evil intent that He delivered them, only to kill them off in the mountains and annihilate them from the face of the earth.' Turn from Your blazing anger, and renounce the plan to punish Your people. ¹³Remember Your servants, Abraham, Isaac, and Jacob, how You swore to them by Your Self and said to them: I will make your offspring as numerous as the stars of heaven, and I will give to your offspring this whole land of which I spoke, to possess forever." ¹⁴And the LORD renounced the punishment He had planned to bring upon His people.

¹⁵Thereupon Moses turned and went down from the moun-

---

ᵃ⁻ᵃ *Cf. Zech. 11.13 (beth* hayyoṣer, *"foundry"); others "fashioned it with a graving tool"*

ᵇ⁻ᵇ *Others "These are your gods"*

tain bearing the two tablets of the Pact, tablets inscribed on both their surfaces: they were inscribed on the one side and on the other. ¹⁶The tablets were God's work, and the writing was God's writing, incised upon the tablets. ¹⁷When Joshua heard the sound of the people in its boisterousness, he said to Moses, "There is a cry of war in the camp." ¹⁸But he answered,

"It is not the sound of the tune of triumph,
Or the sound of the tune of defeat;
It is the sound of song that I hear!"

¹⁹As soon as Moses came near the camp and saw the calf and the dancing, he became enraged; and he hurled the tablets from his hands and shattered them at the foot of the mountain. ²⁰He took the calf that they had made and burned it; he ground it to powder and strewed it upon the water and so made the Israelites drink it.

²¹Moses said to Aaron, "What did this people do to you that you have brought such great sin upon them?" ²²Aaron said, "Let not my lord be enraged. You know that this people is bent on evil. ²³They said to me, 'Make us a god to lead us; for that man Moses, who brought us from the land of Egypt—we do not know what has happened to him.' ²⁴So I said to them, 'Whoever has gold, take it off!' They gave it to me and I hurled it into the fire and out came this calf!"

²⁵Moses saw that the people were out of control—since Aaron had let them get out of control—so that they were a menaceᶜ to any who might oppose them. ²⁶Moses stood up in the gate of the camp and said, "Whoever is for the LORD, come here!" And all the Levites rallied to him. ²⁷He said to them, "Thus says the LORD, the God of Israel: Each of you put sword on thigh, go back and forth from gate to gate throughout the camp, and slay brother, neighbor, and kin." ²⁸The Levites did as Moses had bidden; and some three thousand of the people fell that day. ²⁹And Moses said, "Dedicate yourselvesᵈ to the LORD this day—for each of you has been against son and brother—that He may bestow a blessing upon you today."

---

ᶜ Others "an object of derision"
ᵈ Lit. "fill your hands"

³⁰The next day Moses said to the people, "You have been guilty of a great sin. Yet I will now go up to the LORD; perhaps I may win forgiveness for your sin." ³¹Moses went back to the LORD and said, "Alas, this people is guilty of a great sin in making for themselves a god of gold. ³²Now, if You will forgive their sin [well and good]; but if not, erase me from the record which You have written!" ³³But the LORD said to Moses, "He who has sinned against Me, him only will I erase from My record. ³⁴Go now, lead the people where I told you. See, My angel shall go before you. But when I make an accounting, I will bring them to account for their sins."

³⁵Then the LORD sent a plague upon the people, ᵉ⁻for what they did with the calf that Aaron made.⁻ᵉ

**33** Then the LORD said to Moses, "Set out from here, you and the people that you have brought up from the land of Egypt, to the land of which I swore to Abraham, Isaac, and Jacob, saying, 'To your offspring will I give it'—²I will send an angel before you, and I will drive out the Canaanites, the Amorites, the Hittites, the Perizzites, the Hivites, and the Jebusites—³a land flowing with milk and honey. But I will not go in your midst, since you are a stiffnecked people, lest I destroy you on the way."

⁴When the people heard this harsh word, they went into mourning, and none put on his finery.

⁵The LORD said to Moses, "Say to the Israelite people, 'You are a stiffnecked people. If I were to go in your midst for one moment, I would destroy you. Now, then, leave off your finery, and I will consider what to do to you.'" ⁶So the Israelites remained stripped of the finery from Mount Horeb on.

⁷Now Moses would take the Tent and pitch it outside the camp, at some distance from the camp. It was called the Tent of Meeting, and whoever sought the LORD would go out to the Tent of Meeting that was outside the camp. ⁸Whenever Moses went out to the Tent, all the people would rise and stand, each at

ᵉ⁻ᵉ *Meaning of Heb uncertain*

the entrance of his tent, and gaze after Moses until he had entered the Tent. ⁹And when Moses entered the Tent, the pillar of cloud would descend and stand at the entrance of the Tent, while He spoke with Moses. ¹⁰When all the people saw the pillar of cloud poised at the entrance of the Tent, all the people would rise and bow low, each at the entrance of his tent. ¹¹The LORD would speak to Moses face to face, as one man speaks to another. And he would then return to the camp; but his attendant, Joshua son of Nun, a youth, would not stir out of the Tent.

¹²Moses said to the LORD, "See, You say to me, 'Lead this people forward,' but You have not made known to me whom You will send with me. Further, You have said, 'I have singled you out by name, and you have, indeed, gained My favor.' ¹³Now, if I have truly gained Your favor, pray let me know Your ways, that I may know You and continue in Your favor. Consider, too, that this nation is Your people." ¹⁴And He said, *ᵃ⁻*"I will go in the lead and will⁻ᵃ lighten your burden." ¹⁵And he said to Him, "Unless You go in the lead, do not make us leave this place. ¹⁶For how shall it be known that Your people have gained Your favor unless You go with us, so that we may be distinguished, Your people and I, from every people on the face of the earth?"

¹⁷And the LORD said to Moses, "I will also do this thing that you have asked; for you have truly gained My favor and I have singled you out by name." ¹⁸He said, "Oh, let me behold Your Presence!" ¹⁹And He answered, "I will make all My goodness pass before you, and I will proclaim before you the name LORD, *ᵇ⁻*and the grace that I grant and the compassion that I show.⁻ᵇ ²⁰But," He said, "you cannot see My face, for man may not see Me and live." ²¹And the LORD said, "See, there is a place near Me. Station yourself on the rock ²²and, as My Presence passes by, I will put you in a cleft of the rock and shield you with My hand until I have passed by. ²³Then I will take My hand away and you will see My back; but My face must not be seen."

---

ᵃ⁻ᵃ *Lit. "My face will go and I will"*
ᵇ⁻ᵇ *Lit. "and I will grant the grace that I will grant and show the compassion that I will show"*

**34** The Lord said to Moses: "Carve two tablets of stone like the first, and I will inscribe upon the tablets the words that were on the first tablets, which you shattered. ²Be ready by morning, and in the morning come up to Mount Sinai and present yourself there to Me, on the top of the mountain. ³No one else shall come up with you, and no one else shall be seen anywhere on the mountain; neither shall the flocks and the herds graze at the foot of this mountain."

⁴So Moses carved two tablets of stone, like the first, and early in the morning he went up on Mount Sinai, as the Lord had commanded him, taking the two stone tablets with him. ⁵The Lord came down in a cloud; He stood with him there, and proclaimed the name Lord. ⁶The Lord passed before him ᵃ⁻and proclaimed: "The Lord! the Lord!⁻ᵃ a God compassionate and gracious, slow to anger, abounding in kindness and faithfulness, ⁷extending kindness to the thousandth generation, forgiving iniquity, transgression, and sin; yet He does not remit all punishment, but visits the iniquity of parents upon children and children's children, upon the third and fourth generations."

⁸Moses hastened to bow low to the ground in homage, ⁹and said, "If I have gained Your favor, O Lord, pray, let the Lord go in our midst, even though this is a stiffnecked people. Pardon our iniquity and our sin, and take us for Your own!"

¹⁰He said: I hereby make a covenant. Before all your people I will work such wonders as have not been wrought on all the earth or in any nation; and all the people ᵇ⁻who are with you⁻ᵇ shall see how awesome are the Lord's deeds which I will perform for you. ¹¹Mark well what I command you this day. I will drive out before you the Amorites, the Canaanites, the Hittites, the Perizzites, the Hivites, and the Jebusites. ¹²Beware of making a covenant with the inhabitants of the land against which you are advancing, lest they be a snare in your midst. ¹³No, you must tear down their altars, smash their pillars, and cut down their sacred posts; ¹⁴for you must not worship any other god, because

---

a-a *Or "and the Lord proclaimed: The Lord! a God compassionate," etc. Cf. Num. 14.17–18*
b-b *Lit. "in whose midst you are"*

the LORD, whose name is Impassioned, is an impassioned God. [15]You must not make a covenant with the inhabitants of the land, for they will lust after their gods and sacrifice to their gods and invite you, and you will eat of their sacrifices. [16]And when you take wives from among their daughters for your sons, their daughters will lust after their gods and will cause your sons to lust after their gods.

[17]You shall not make molten gods for yourselves.

[18]You shall observe the Feast of Unleavened Bread—eating unleavened bread for seven days, as I have commanded you—at the set time of the month[c] of Abib, for in the month of Abib you went forth from Egypt.

[19]Every first issue of the womb is Mine, from all your livestock that drop a male[d] as firstling, whether cattle or sheep. [20]But the firstling of an ass you shall redeem with a sheep; if you do not redeem it, you must break its neck. And you must redeem every first-born among your sons.

None shall appear before Me empty-handed.

[21]Six days you shall work, but on the seventh day you shall cease from labor; you shall cease from labor even at plowing time and harvest time.

[22]You shall observe the Feast of Weeks, of the first fruits of the wheat harvest; and the Feast of Ingathering at the turn of the year. [23]Three times a year all your males shall appear before the Sovereign LORD, the God of Israel. [24]I will drive out nations from your path and enlarge your territory; no one will covet your land when you go up to appear before the LORD your God three times a year.

[25]You shall not offer the blood of My sacrifice with anything leavened; and the sacrifice of the Feast of Passover shall not be left lying until morning.

[26]The choice first fruits of your soil you shall bring to the house of the LORD your God.

You shall not boil a kid in its mother's milk.

[27]And the LORD said to Moses: Write down these command-

___

c *See note at 13.4*
d *Heb* tizzakhar, *form uncertain*

ments, for in accordance with these commandments I make a covenant with you and with Israel.

²⁸And he was there with the LORD forty days and forty nights; he ate no bread and drank no water; and he wrote down on the tablets the terms of the covenant, the Ten Commandments.

²⁹So Moses came down from Mount Sinai. And as Moses came down from the mountain bearing the two tablets of the Pact, Moses was not aware that the skin of his face was radiant, since he had spoken with Him. ³⁰Aaron and all the Israelites saw that the skin of Moses' face was radiant; and they shrank from coming near him. ³¹But Moses called to them, and Aaron and all the chieftains in the assembly returned to him, and Moses spoke to them. ³²Afterward all the Israelites came near, and he instructed them concerning all that the LORD had imparted to him on Mount Sinai. ³³And when Moses had finished speaking with them, he put a veil over his face.

³⁴Whenever Moses went in before the LORD to speak with Him, he would leave the veil off until he came out; and when he came out and told the Israelites what he had been commanded, ³⁵the Israelites would see how radiant the skin of Moses' face was. Moses would then put the veil back over his face until he went in to speak with Him.

ויקהל

35 Moses then convoked the whole Israelite community and said to them:

These are the things that the LORD has commanded you to do: ²On six days work may be done, but on the seventh day you shall have a sabbath of complete rest, holy to the LORD; whoever does any work on it shall be put to death. ³You shall kindle no fire throughout your settlements on the sabbath day.

⁴Moses said further to the whole community of Israelites:

This is what the LORD has commanded: ⁵Take from among you gifts to the LORD; everyone whose heart so moves him shall bring them—gifts for the LORD: gold, silver, and copper; [6a]blue, purple, and crimson yarns, fine linen, and goats' hair; [7]tanned ram skins, dolphin skins, and acacia wood; [8]oil for lighting, spices for the anointing oil and for the aromatic incense; [9]lapis lazuli and other stones for setting, for the ephod and the breastpiece.

[10]And let all among you who are skilled come and make all that the LORD has commanded: [11]the Tabernacle, its tent and its covering, its clasps and its planks, its bars, its posts, and its sockets; [12]the ark and its poles, the cover, and the curtain for the screen; [13]the table, and its poles and all its utensils; and the bread of display; [14]the lampstand for lighting, its furnishings and its lamps, and the oil for lighting; [15]the altar of incense and its poles; the anointing oil and the aromatic incense; and the entrance screen for the entrance of the Tabernacle; [16]the altar of burnt offering, its copper grating, its poles, and all its furnishings; the laver and its stand; [17]the hangings of the enclosure, its posts and its sockets, and the screen for the gate of the court; [18]the pegs for the Tabernacle, the pegs for the enclosure, and their cords; [19]the service vestments for officiating in the sanctuary, the sacral vestments of Aaron the priest and the vestments of his sons for priestly service.

[20]So the whole community of the Israelites left Moses' presence. [21]And everyone who excelled in ability and everyone whose spirit moved him came, bringing to the LORD his offering for the work of the Tent of Meeting and for all its service and for the sacral vestments. [22]Men and women, all whose hearts moved them, all who would make an elevation offering of gold to the LORD, came bringing brooches, earrings, rings, and pendants[b]—gold objects of all kinds. [23]And everyone who had in his possession blue, purple, and crimson yarns, fine linen, goats' hair, tanned ram skins, and dolphin skins, brought them; [24]everyone who would make gifts of silver or copper brought them as gifts for the LORD; and everyone who had in his possession acacia wood for any work of the service brought that.

---

[a] *See 25.4 ff. and the notes there*
[b] *Meaning of Heb* kumaz *uncertain*

<sup>25</sup>And all the skilled women spun with their own hands, and brought what they had spun, in blue, purple, and crimson yarns, and in fine linen. <sup>26</sup>And all the women who excelled in that skill spun the goats' hair. <sup>27</sup>And the chieftains brought lapis lazuli and other stones for setting, for the ephod and for the breast-piece; <sup>28</sup>and spices and oil for lighting, for the anointing oil, and for the aromatic incense. <sup>29</sup>Thus the Israelites, all the men and women whose hearts moved them to bring anything for the work that the Lord, through Moses, had commanded to be done, brought it as a freewill offering to the Lord.

<sup>30</sup>And Moses said to the Israelites: See, the Lord has singled out by name Bezalel, son of Uri son of Hur, of the tribe of Judah. <sup>31</sup>He has endowed him with a divine spirit of skill, ability, and knowledge in every kind of craft <sup>32</sup>and <sup>c-</sup>has inspired him<sup>-c</sup> to make designs for work in gold, silver, and copper, <sup>33</sup>to cut stones for setting and to carve wood—to work in every kind of designer's craft—<sup>34</sup>and to give directions. He and Oholiab son of Ahisamach of the tribe of Dan <sup>35</sup>have been endowed with the skill to do any work—of the carver, the designer, the embroiderer in blue, purple crimson yarns, and in fine linen, and of the weaver—as workers in all crafts and as makers of designs. <sup>1</sup>Let then, Bezalel and Oholiab and all the skilled persons whom the Lord has endowed with skill and ability to perform expertly all the tasks connected with the service of the sanctuary carry out all that the Lord has commanded.

<sup>2</sup>Moses then called Bezalel and Oholiab, and every skilled person whom the Lord had endowed with skill, everyone who excelled in ability, to undertake the task and carry it out. <sup>3</sup>They took over from Moses all the gifts that the Israelites had brought, to carry out the tasks connected with the service of the sanctuary. But when these continued to bring freewill offerings to him morning after morning, <sup>4</sup>all the artisans who were engaged in the tasks of the sanctuary came, each from the task upon which he was engaged, <sup>5</sup>and said to Moses, "The people

---

<sup>c-c</sup> *Moved up from v. 34 for clarity*

172

are bringing more than is needed for the tasks entailed in the work that the LORD has commanded to be done." ⁶Moses thereupon had this proclamation made throughout the camp: "Let no man or woman make further effort toward gifts for the sanctuary!" So the people stopped bringing: ⁷their efforts had been more than enough for all the tasks to be done.

⁸Then all the skilled among those engaged in the work made the Tabernacle of ten strips of cloth, which they made of fine twisted linen, blue, purple, and crimson yarns; into these they worked a design of cherubim. ⁹The length of each cloth was twenty-eight cubits, and the width of each cloth was four cubits, all cloths having the same measurements. ¹⁰They joined five of the cloths to one another, and they joined the other five cloths to one another. ¹¹They made loops of blue wool on the edge of the outermost cloth of the one set, and did the same on the edge of the outermost cloth of the other set: ¹²they made fifty loops on the one cloth, and they made fifty loops on the edge of the end cloth of the other set, the loops being opposite one another. ¹³And they made fifty gold clasps and coupled the units*a* to one another with the clasps, so that the Tabernacle became one whole.

¹⁴They made cloths of goats' hair for a tent over the Tabernacle; they made the cloths eleven in number. ¹⁵The length of each cloth was thirty cubits, and the width of each cloth was four cubits, the eleven cloths having the same measurements. ¹⁶They joined five of the cloths by themselves, and the other six cloths by themselves. ¹⁷They made fifty loops on the edge of the outermost cloth of the one set, and they made fifty loops on the edge of the end cloth of the other set. ¹⁸They made fifty copper clasps to couple the Tent together so that it might become one whole. ¹⁹And they made a covering of tanned ram skins for the Tent, and a covering of dolphin skins above.

²⁰They made the planks for the Tabernacle of acacia wood, upright. ²¹The length of each plank was ten cubits, the width of

---

a *Lit. "strip of cloth," here used collectively*

173

each plank a cubit and a half. <sup>22</sup>Each plank had two tenons, parallel[b] to each other; they did the same with all the planks of the Tabernacle. <sup>23</sup>Of the planks of the Tabernacle, they made twenty planks for the south side,[c] <sup>24</sup>making forty silver sockets under the twenty planks, two sockets under one plank for its two tenons and two sockets under each following plank for its two tenons; <sup>25</sup>and for the other side wall of the Tabernacle, the north side, twenty planks, <sup>26</sup>with their forty silver sockets, two sockets under one plank and two sockets under each following plank. <sup>27</sup>And for the rear of the Tabernacle, to the west, they made six planks; <sup>28</sup>and they made two planks for the corners of the Tabernacle at the rear. <sup>29d-</sup>They matched at the bottom, but terminated as one at the top into one ring<sup>-d</sup>; they did so with both of them at the two corners. <sup>30</sup>Thus there were eight planks with their sockets of silver: sixteen sockets, two under each plank.

<sup>31</sup>They made bars of acacia wood, five for the planks of the one side wall of the Tabernacle, <sup>32</sup>five bars for the planks of the other side wall of the Tabernacle, and five bars for the planks of the wall of the Tabernacle at the rear, to the west; <sup>33</sup>they made the center bar to run, halfway up the planks, from end to end. <sup>34</sup>They overlaid the planks with gold, and made their rings of gold, as holders for the bars; and they overlaid the bars with gold.

<sup>35</sup>They made the curtain of blue, purple, and crimson yarns, and fine twisted linen, working into it a design of cherubim. <sup>36</sup>They made for it four posts of acacia wood and overlaid them with gold, with their hooks of gold; and they cast for them four silver sockets.

<sup>37</sup>They made the screen for the entrance of the Tent, of blue, purple, and crimson yarns, and fine twisted linen, done in embroidery; <sup>38</sup>and five posts for it with their hooks. They overlaid their tops and their bands with gold; but the five sockets were of copper.

---

b *See note at 26.17*
c *See note at 26.18*
d-d *See note at 26.24*

**37** Bezalel made the ark of acacia wood, two and a half cubits long, a cubit and a half wide, and a cubit and a half high. ²He overlaid it with pure gold, inside and out; and he made a gold molding for it round about. ³He cast four gold rings for it, for its four feet: two rings on one of its side walls and two rings on the other. ⁴He made poles of acacia wood, overlaid them with gold, ⁵and inserted the poles into the rings on the side walls of the ark for carrying the ark.

⁶He made a cover of pure gold, two and a half cubits long and a cubit and a half wide. ⁷He made two cherubim of gold; he made them of hammered work, at the two ends of the cover: ⁸one cherub at one end and the other cherub at the other end; he made the cherubim of one piece with the cover, at its two ends. ⁹The cherubim had their wings spread out above, shielding the cover with their wings. They faced each other; the faces of the cherubim were turned toward the cover.

¹⁰He made the table of acacia wood, two cubits long, one cubit wide, and a cubit and a half high; ¹¹he overlaid it with pure gold and made a gold molding around it. ¹²He made a rim of a hand's breadth around it and made a gold molding for its rim round about. ¹³He cast four gold rings for it and attached the rings to the four corners at its four legs. ¹⁴The rings were next to the rim, as holders for the poles to carry the table. ¹⁵He made the poles of acacia wood for carrying the table, and overlaid them with gold. ¹⁶The utensils that were to be upon the table—its bowls, ladles, jugs, and jars with which to offer libations—he made of pure gold.

¹⁷He made the lampstand of pure gold. He made the lampstand—its base and its shaft—of hammered work; its cups, calyxes, and petals were of one piece with it. ¹⁸Six branches issued from its sides: three branches from one side of the lampstand, and three branches from the other side of the lampstand. ¹⁹There were three cups shaped like almond-blossoms, each

with calyx and petals, on one branch; and there were three cups shaped like almond-blossoms, each with calyx and petals, on the next branch; so for all six branches issuing from the lampstand. ²⁰On the lampstand itself there were four cups shaped like almond-blossoms, each with calyx and petals: ²¹a calyx, of one piece with it, under a pair of branches; and a calyx, of one piece with it, under the second pair of branches; and a calyx, of one piece with it, under the last pair of branches; so for all six branches issuing from it. ²²Their calyxes and their stems were of one piece with it, the whole of it a single hammered piece of pure gold. ²³He made its seven lamps, its tongs, and its fire pans of pure gold. ²⁴He made it and all its furnishings out of a talent of pure gold.

²⁵He made the incense altar of acacia wood, a cubit long and a cubit wide—square—and two cubits high; its horns were of one piece with it. ²⁶He overlaid it with pure gold: its top, its sides round about, and its horns; and he made a gold molding for it round about. ²⁷He made two gold rings for it under its molding, on its two walls—on opposite sides—as holders for the poles with which to carry it. ²⁸He made the poles of acacia wood, and overlaid them with gold. ²⁹He prepared the sacred anointing oil and the pure aromatic incense, expertly blended.

38 He made the altar for burnt offering of acacia wood, five cubits long and five cubits wide—square—and three cubits high. ²He made horns for it on its four corners, the horns being of one piece with it; and he overlaid it with copper. ³He made all the utensils of the altar—the pails, the scrapers, the basins, the flesh hooks, and the fire pans; he made all these utensils of copper. ⁴He made for the altar a grating of meshwork in copper, extending below, under its ledge, to its middle. ⁵He cast four rings, at the four corners of the copper grating, as holders for the poles. ⁶He made the poles of acacia wood and overlaid them

with copper; [7]and he inserted the poles into the rings on the side walls of the altar, to carry it by them. He made it hollow, of boards.

[8]He made the laver of copper and its stand of copper, from the mirrors of the women who performed tasks[a] at the entrance of the Tent of Meeting.

[9]He made the enclosure:

On the south[b] side, a hundred cubits of hangings of fine twisted linen for the enclosure—[10]with their twenty posts and their twenty sockets of copper, the hooks and bands of the posts being silver.

[11]On the north side, a hundred cubits—with their twenty posts and their twenty sockets of copper, the hooks and bands of the posts being silver.

[12]On the west side, fifty cubits of hangings—with their ten posts and their ten sockets, the hooks and bands of the posts being silver.

[13]And on the front side, to the east, fifty cubits: [14]fifteen cubits of hangings on the one flank, with their three posts and their three sockets, [15]and fifteen cubits of hangings on the other flank—on each side of the gate of the enclosure[c]—with their three posts and their three sockets.

[16]All the hangings around the enclosure were of fine twisted linen. [17]The sockets for the posts were of copper, the hooks and bands of the posts were of silver, the overlay of their tops was of silver; all the posts of the enclosure were banded with silver.— [18]The screen of the gate of the enclosure, done in embroidery, was of blue, purple, and crimson yarns, and fine twisted linen. It was twenty cubits long. [d-]Its height—or width—was five cubits, like that of[-d] the hangings of the enclosure. [19]The posts were four; their four sockets were of copper, their hooks of silver; and the overlay of their tops was of silver, as were also their bands.—[20]All the pegs of the Tabernacle and of the enclosure round about were of copper.

---

[a] *Meaning of Heb uncertain*
[b] *Cf. note at 26.18*
[c] *Which accounts for the remaining 20 cubits; cf. v. 18*
[d-d] *Meaning of Heb uncertain*

פקודי

²¹These are the records of the Tabernacle, the Tabernacle of the Pact, which were drawn up at Moses' bidding—the work of the Levites under the direction of Ithamar son of Aaron the priest. ²²Now Bezalel, son of Uri son of Hur, of the tribe of Judah, had made all that the LORD had commanded Moses; ²³at his side was Oholiab son of Ahisamach, of the tribe of Dan, carver and designer, and embroiderer in blue, purple, and crimson yarns and in fine linen.

²⁴All the gold that was used for the work, in all the work of the sanctuary—the elevation offering of gold—came to 29 talents*ᵉ* and 730 shekels by the sanctuary weight. ²⁵The silver of those of the community who were recorded came to 100 talents and 1,775 shekels by the sanctuary weight: ²⁶a half-shekel*ᶠ* a head, half a shekel by the sanctuary weight, for each one who was entered in the records, from the age of twenty years up, 603,550 men. ²⁷The 100 talents of silver were for casting the sockets of the sanctuary and the sockets for the curtain, 100 sockets to the 100 talents, a talent a socket. ²⁸And of the 1,775 shekels he made hooks for the posts, overlay for their tops, and bands around them.

²⁹The copper from the elevation offering came to 70 talents and 2,400 shekels. ³⁰Of it he made the sockets for the entrance of the Tent of Meeting; the copper altar and its copper grating and all the utensils of the altar; ³¹the sockets of the enclosure round about and the sockets of the gate of the enclosure; and all the pegs of the Tabernacle and all the pegs of the enclosure round about.

# 39

Of the blue, purple, and crimson yarns they also*ᵃ* made the service vestments for officiating in the sanctuary; they made Aaron's sacral vestments—as the LORD had commanded Moses.

²The ephod was made*ᵇ* of gold, blue, purple, and crimson

---

ᵉ *A talent here equals 3,000 shekels*   ᶠ *Heb* beqa‘

ᵃ *See 36.8*

ᵇ *Here and elsewhere in this chapter the singular active verb (lit. "he made") is used impersonally* yarns, and fine twisted linen. [3]They hammered out sheets of gold and cut threads to be worked into designs among the blue, the purple, and the crimson yarns, and the fine linen. [4]They made for it attaching shoulder-pieces; they were attached at its two ends. [5]The decorated band that was upon it was made like it, of one piece with it; of gold, blue, purple, and crimson yarns, and fine twisted linen—as the Lord had commanded Moses.

[6]They bordered the lazuli stones with frames of gold, engraved with seal engravings of the names of the sons of Israel. [7]They were set on the shoulder-pieces of the ephod, as stones of remembrance for the Israelites—as the Lord had commanded Moses.

[8]The breastpiece was made in the style of the ephod: of gold, blue, purple, and crimson yarns, and fine twisted linen. [9]It was square; they made the breastpiece doubled—a span in length and a span in width, doubled. [10]They set in it four rows of stones. The first row was a row of ᶜcarnelian, chrysolite, and emerald; [11]the second row: a turquoise, a sapphire, and an amethyst; [12]the third row: a jacinth, an agate, and a crystal; [13]and the fourth row: a beryl, a lapis lazuli, and a jasper. They were encircled in their mountings with frames of gold. [14]The stones corresponded [in number] to the names of the sons of Israel: twelve, corresponding to their names; engraved like seals, each with its name, for the twelve tribes.

[15]On the breastpiece they made braided chains of corded work in pure gold. [16]They made two frames of gold and two rings of gold, and fastened the two rings at the two ends of the breastpiece, [17]attaching the two golden cords to the two rings at the ends of the breastpiece. [18]They then fastened the two ends of the cords to the two frames, attaching them to the shoulder-pieces of the ephod, at the front. [19]They made two rings of gold and attached them to the two ends of the breastpiece, at its inner edge, which faced the ephod. [20]They made two other rings of gold and fastened them on the front of the ephod, low on the two shoulder-pieces, close to its seam above the decorated band.

ᶜ *See note at 28.17*

²¹The breastpiece was held in place by a cord of blue from its rings to the rings of the ephod, so that the breastpiece rested on the decorated band and did not come loose from the ephod—as the LORD had commanded Moses.

²²The robe for the ephod was made of woven work, of pure blue.ᵈ ²³The opening of the robe, in the middle of it, was like the opening of a coat of mail, with a binding around the opening, so that it would not tear. ²⁴On the hem of the robe they made pomegranates of blue, purple, and crimson yarns, twisted. ²⁵They also made bells of pure gold, and attached the bells between the pomegranates, all around the hem of the robe, between the pomegranates: ²⁶a bell and a pomegranate, a bell and a pomegranate, all around the hem of the robe for officiating in—as the LORD had commanded Moses.

²⁷They made the tunics of fine linen, of woven work, for Aaron and his sons; ²⁸and the headdress of fine linen, and the decorated turbans of fine linen, and the linen breeches of fine twisted linen; ²⁹and sashes of fine twisted linen, blue, purple, and crimson yarns, done in embroidery—as the LORD had commanded Moses.

³⁰They made the frontlet for the holy diadem of pure gold, and incised upon it the seal inscription: "Holy to the LORD." ³¹They attached to it a cord of blue to fix it upon the headdress above—as the LORD had commanded Moses.

³²Thus was completed all the work of the Tabernacle of the Tent of Meeting. The Israelites did so; just as the LORD had commanded Moses, so they did.

³³Then they brought the Tabernacle to Moses, with the Tent and all its furnishings: its clasps, its planks, its poles, its posts, and its sockets; ³⁴the covering of tanned ram skins, the covering of dolphin skins, and the curtain for the screen; ³⁵the Ark of the Pact and its poles, and the cover; ³⁶the table and all its utensils, and the bread of display; ³⁷the pure lampstand,ᵉ its lamps—lamps in due order—and all its fittings, and the oil for lighting;

ᵈ *See note at 28.31*
ᵉ *See note at 31.8*

[38]the altar of gold, the oil for anointing, the aromatic incense, and the screen for the entrance of the Tent; [39]the copper altar with its copper grating, its poles and all its utensils, and the laver and its stand; [40]the hangings of the enclosure, its posts and its sockets, the screen for the gate of the enclosure, its cords and its pegs—all the furnishings for the service of the Tabernacle, the Tent of Meeting; [41]the service vestments for officiating in the sanctuary, the sacral vestments of Aaron the priest, and the vestments of his sons for priestly service. [42]Just as the LORD had commanded Moses, so the Israelites had done all the work. [43]And when Moses saw that they had performed all the tasks— as the LORD had commanded, so they had done—Moses blessed them.

# 40 And the LORD spoke to Moses, saying:

[2]On the first day of the first month you shall set up the Tabernacle of the Tent of Meeting. [3]Place there the Ark of the Pact, and screen off the ark with the curtain. [4]Bring in the table and lay out its due setting; bring in the lampstand and light its lamps; [5]and place the gold altar of incense before the Ark of the Pact. Then put up the screen for the entrance of the Tabernacle.

[6]You shall place the altar of burnt offering before the entrance of the Tabernacle of the Tent of Meeting. [7]Place the laver between the Tent of Meeting and the altar, and put water in it. [8]Set up the enclosure round about, and put in place the screen for the gate of the enclosure.

[9]You shall take the anointing oil and anoint the Tabernacle and all that is in it to consecrate it and all its furnishings, so that it shall be holy. [10]Then anoint the altar of burnt offering and all its utensils to consecrate the altar, so that the altar shall be most holy. [11]And anoint the laver and its stand to consecrate it.

[12]You shall bring Aaron and his sons forward to the entrance of the Tent of Meeting and wash them with the water. [13]Put the

sacral vestments on Aaron, and anoint him and consecrate him, that he may serve Me as priest. [14]Then bring his sons forward, put tunics on them, [15]and anoint them as you have anointed their father, that they may serve Me as priests. This their anointing shall serve them for everlasting priesthood throughout the ages.

[16]This Moses did; just as the LORD had commanded him, so he did.

[17]In the first month of the second year, on the first of the month, the Tabernacle was set up. [18]Moses set up the Tabernacle, placing its sockets, setting up its planks, inserting its bars, and erecting its posts. [19]He spread the Tent over the Tabernacle, placing the covering of the Tent on top of it—just as the LORD had commanded Moses.

[20]He took the Pact and placed it in the ark; he fixed the poles to the ark, placed the cover on top of the ark, [21]and brought the ark inside the Tabernacle. Then he put up the curtain for screening, and screened off the Ark of the Pact—just as the LORD had commanded Moses.

[22]He placed the table in the Tent of Meeting, outside the curtain, on the north side of the Tabernacle. [23]Upon it he laid out the setting of bread before the LORD—as the LORD had commanded Moses. [24]He placed the lampstand in the Tent of Meeting opposite the table, on the south side of the Tabernacle. [25]And he lit the lamps before the LORD—as the LORD had commanded Moses. [26]He placed the altar of gold in the Tent of Meeting, before the curtain. [27]On it he burned aromatic incense —as the LORD had commanded Moses.

[28]Then he put up the screen for the entrance of the Tabernacle. [29]At the entrance of the Tabernacle of the Tent of Meeting he placed the altar of burnt offering. On it he offered up the burnt offering and the meal offering—as the LORD had commanded Moses. [30]He placed the laver between the Tent of Meeting and the altar, and put water in it for washing. [31]From it

Moses and Aaron and his sons would wash their hands and feet; [32]they washed when they entered the Tent of Meeting and when they approached the altar—as the LORD had commanded Moses. [33]And he set up the enclosure around the Tabernacle and the altar, and put up the screen for the gate of the enclosure.

When Moses had finished the work, [34]the cloud covered the Tent of Meeting, and the Presence of the LORD filled the Tabernacle. [35]Moses could not enter the Tent of Meeting, because the cloud had settled upon it and the Presence of the LORD filled the Tabernacle. [36]When the cloud lifted from the Tabernacle, the Israelites would set out, on their various journeys; [37]but if the cloud did not lift, they would not set out until such time as it did lift. [38]For over the Tabernacle a cloud of the LORD rested by day, and fire would appear in it[a] by night, in the view of all the house of Israel throughout their journeys.

חזק

---

[a] *I.e. in the cloud*

# ויקרא
# LEVITICUS

# ויקרא

# LEVITICUS

1 The LORD called to Moses and spoke to him from the Tent of Meeting, saying: ²Speak to the Israelite people, and say to them:

When any of you presents an offering of cattle to the LORD, *ᵃ-he shall choose his-ᵃ* offering from the herd or from the flock.

³If his offering is a burnt offering from the herd, he shall make his offering a male without blemish. He shall bring it to the entrance of the Tent of Meeting, for acceptance in his behalf before the LORD. ⁴He shall lay his hand upon the head of the burnt offering, that it may be acceptable in his behalf, in expiation for him. ⁵The bull shall be slaughtered before the LORD; and Aaron's sons, the priests, shall offer the blood, dashing the blood against all sides of the altar which is at the entrance of the Tent of Meeting. ⁶The burnt offering shall be flayed and cut up into sections. ⁷The sons of Aaron the priest shall put fire on the altar and lay out wood upon the fire; ⁸and Aaron's sons, the priests, shall lay out the sections, with the head and the suet, on the wood that is on the fire upon the altar. ⁹Its entrails and legs shall be washed with water, and the priest shall turn the whole into smoke on the altar as a burnt offering, an offering by fire of pleasing odor to the LORD.

¹⁰If his offering for a burnt offering is from the flock, of sheep or of goats, he shall make his offering a male without blemish. ¹¹It shall be slaughtered before the LORD on the north side of the altar, and Aaron's sons, the priests, shall dash its blood against all sides of the altar. ¹²When it has been cut up into sections, the priest shall lay them out, with the head and the suet, on the wood that is on the fire upon the altar. ¹³The

---

ᵃ⁻ᵃ *Lit. "you shall offer your"*

187

entrails and the legs shall be washed with water; the priest shall offer up and turn the whole into smoke on the altar. It is a burnt offering, an offering by fire, of pleasing odor to the LORD.

¹⁴If his offering to the LORD is a burnt offering of birds, he shall choose his offering from turtledoves or pigeons. ¹⁵The priest shall bring it to the altar, pinch off its head, and turn it into smoke on the altar; and its blood shall be drained out against the side of the altar. ¹⁶He shall remove its crop with its contents,[b] and cast it into the place of the ashes, at the east side of the altar. ¹⁷The priest shall tear it open by its wings, without severing it, and turn it into smoke on the altar, upon the wood that is on the fire. It is a burnt offering, an offering by fire, of pleasing odor to the LORD.

**2** When a person presents an offering of meal to the LORD, his offering shall be of choice flour; he shall pour oil upon it, lay frankincense on it, ²and present it to Aaron's sons, the priests. The priest shall scoop out of it a handful of its choice flour and oil, as well as all of its frankincense; and this token portion he shall turn into smoke on the altar, as an offering by fire, of pleasing odor to the LORD. ³And the remainder of the meal offering shall be for Aaron and his sons, a most holy portion from the LORD's offerings by fire.

⁴When you present an offering of meal baked in the oven, [it shall be of] choice flour: unleavened cakes with oil mixed in, or unleavened wafers spread with oil.

⁵If your offering is a meal offering on a griddle, it shall be of choice flour with oil mixed in, unleavened. ⁶Break it into bits and pour oil on it; it is a meal offering.

⁷If your offering is a meal offering in a pan, it shall be made of choice flour in oil.

⁸When you present to the LORD a meal offering that is made in any of these ways, it shall be brought to the priest who shall take it up to the altar. ⁹The priest shall remove the token portion

b *Others "feathers"*

from the meal offering and turn it into smoke on the altar as an offering by fire, of pleasing odor to the Lord. [10]And the remainder of the meal offering shall be for Aaron and his sons, a most holy portion from the Lord's offerings by fire.

[11]No meal offering that you offer to the Lord shall be made with leaven, for no leaven or honey may be turned into smoke as an offering by fire to the Lord. [12]You may bring them to the Lord as an offering of choice products[a]; but they shall not be offered up on the altar for a pleasing odor. [13]You shall season your every offering of meal with salt; you shall not omit from your meal offering the salt of your covenant with God; with all your offerings you must offer salt.

[14]If you bring a meal offering of first fruits to the Lord, you shall bring new ears parched with fire, grits of the fresh grain, as your meal offering of first fruits. [15]You shall add oil to it and lay frankincense on it; it is a meal offering. [16]And the priest shall turn a token portion of it into smoke: some of the grits and oil, with all of the frankincense, as an offering by fire to the Lord.

3 If his offering is a sacrifice of well-being[a]—

If he offers of the herd, whether a male or a female, he shall bring before the Lord one without blemish. [2]He shall lay his hand upon the head of his offering and slaughter it at the entrance of the Tent of Meeting; and Aaron's sons, the priests, shall dash the blood against all sides of the altar. [3]He shall then present from the sacrifice of well-being, as an offering by fire to the Lord, the fat that covers the entrails and all the fat that is about the entrails; [4]the two kidneys and the fat that is on them, that is at the loins; and the protuberance on the liver, which he shall remove with the kidneys. [5]Aaron's sons shall turn these into smoke on the altar, with the burnt offering which is upon the wood that is on the fire, as an offering by fire, of pleasing odor to the Lord.

[6]And if his offering for a sacrifice of well-being to the Lord is

---

a *Exact meaning of Heb uncertain*

a *Others "peace offering." Exact meaning of* shelamim *uncertain* from the flock, whether a male or a female, he shall offer one without blemish. ⁷If he presents a sheep as his offering, he shall bring it before the LORD ⁸and lay his hand upon the head of his offering. It shall be slaughtered before the Tent of Meeting, and Aaron's sons shall dash its blood against all sides of the altar. ⁹He shall then present, as an offering by fire to the LORD, the fat from the sacrifice of well-being: the whole broad tail, which shall be removed close to the backbone; the fat that covers the entrails and all the fat that is about the entrails; ¹⁰the two kidneys and the fat that is on them, that is at the loins; and the protuberance on the liver, which he shall remove with the kidneys. ¹¹The priest shall turn these into smoke on the altar as food, an offering by fire to the LORD.

¹²And if his offering is a goat, he shall bring it before the LORD ¹³and lay his hand upon its head. It shall be slaughtered before the Tent of Meeting, and Aaron's sons shall dash its blood against all sides of the altar. ¹⁴He shall then present as his offering from it, as an offering by fire to the LORD, the fat that covers the entrails and all the fat that is about the entrails; ¹⁵the two kidneys and the fat that is on them, that is at the loins; and the protuberance on the liver, which he shall remove with the kidneys. ¹⁶The priest shall turn these into smoke on the altar as food, an offering by fire, of pleasing odor.

All fat is the LORD's. ¹⁷It is a law for all time throughout the ages, in all your settlements: you must not eat any fat or any blood.

4 The LORD spoke to Moses, saying: ²Speak to the Israelite people thus:

When a person unwittingly incurs guilt in regard to any of the LORD's commandments about things not to be done, and does one of them—

³If it is the anointed priest who has incurred guilt, so that blame falls upon the people, he shall offer for the sin of which he

is guilty a bull of the herd without blemish as a sin offering[a] to the LORD. [4]He shall bring the bull to the entrance of the Tent of Meeting, before the LORD, and lay his hand upon the head of the bull. The bull shall be slaughtered before the LORD, [5]and the anointed priest shall take some of the bull's blood and bring it into the Tent of Meeting. [6]The priest shall dip his finger in the blood, and sprinkle of the blood seven times before the LORD, in front of the curtain of the Shrine. [7]The priest shall put some of the blood on the horns of the altar of aromatic incense, which is in the Tent of Meeting, before the LORD; and all the rest of the bull's blood he shall pour out at the base of the altar of burnt offering, which is at the entrance of the Tent of Meeting. [8]He shall remove all the fat from the bull of sin offering: the fat that covers the entrails and all the fat that is about the entrails; [9]the two kidneys and the fat that is on them, that is at the loins; and the protuberance on the liver, which he shall remove with the kidneys—[10]just as it is removed from the ox of the sacrifice of well-being. The priest shall turn them into smoke on the altar of burnt offering. [11]But the hide of the bull, and all its flesh, as well as its head and legs, its entrails and its dung—[12]all the rest of the bull—he shall carry to a clean place outside the camp, to the ash heap, and burn it up in a wood fire; it shall be burned on the ash heap.

[13]If it is the whole community of Israel that has erred and the matter escapes the notice of the congregation, so that they do any of the things which by the LORD's commandments ought not to be done, and they realize their guilt—[14]when the sin through which they incurred guilt becomes known, the congregation shall offer a bull of the herd as a sin offering, and bring it before the Tent of Meeting. [15]The elders of the community shall lay their hands upon the head of the bull before the LORD, and the bull shall be slaughtered before the LORD. [16]The anointed priest shall bring some of the blood of the bull into the Tent of Meeting, [17]and the priest shall dip his finger in the blood and sprinkle of it seven times before the LORD, in front of the

---

[a] So traditionally; more precisely "offering of purgation"

191

curtain. [18]Some of the blood he shall put on the horns of the altar which is before the LORD in the Tent of Meeting, and all the rest of the blood he shall pour out at the base of the altar of burnt offering, which is at the entrance of the Tent of Meeting. [19]He shall remove all its fat from it and turn it into smoke on the altar. [20]He shall do with this bull just as is done with the [priest's] bull of sin offering; he shall do the same with it. Thus the priest shall make expiation for them, and they shall be forgiven. [21]He shall carry the bull outside the camp and burn it as he burned the first bull; it is the sin offering of the congregation.

[22]In case it is a chieftain who incurs guilt by doing unwittingly any of the things which by the commandment of the LORD his God ought not to be done, and he realizes his guilt—[23]or the sin of which he is guilty is brought to his knowledge—he shall bring as his offering a male goat without blemish. [24]He shall lay his hand upon the goat's head, and it shall be slaughtered at the spot where the burnt offering is slaughtered[b] before the LORD; it is a sin offering. [25]The priest shall take with his finger some of the blood of the sin offering and put it on the horns of the altar of burnt offering; and the rest of its blood he shall pour out at the base of the altar of burnt offering. [26]All its fat he shall turn into smoke on the altar, like the fat of the sacrifice of well-being. Thus the priest shall make expiation on his behalf for his sin, and he shall be forgiven.

[27]If any person from among the populace[c] unwittingly incurs guilt by doing any of the things which by the LORD's commandments ought not to be done, and he realizes his guilt—[28]or the sin of which he is guilty is brought to his knowledge—he shall bring a female goat without blemish as his offering for the sin of which he is guilty. [29]He shall lay his hand upon the head of the sin offering, and the sin offering shall be slaughtered at the place of the burnt offering. [30]The priest shall take with his finger some of its blood and put it on the horns of the altar of burnt offering; and all the rest of its blood he shall pour out at the base of the altar. [31]He shall remove all its fat, just as the fat is

b *Cf. 1.11*
c *Lit. "people of the country"*

removed from the sacrifice of well-being; and the priest shall turn it into smoke on the altar, for a pleasing odor to the Lord. Thus the priest shall make expiation for him, and he shall be forgiven.

³²If the offering he brings as a sin offering is a sheep, he shall bring a female without blemish. ³³He shall lay his hand upon the head of the sin offering, and it shall be slaughtered as a sin offering at the spot where the burnt offering is slaughtered. ³⁴The priest shall take with his finger some of the blood of the sin offering and put it on the horns of the altar of burnt offering, and all the rest of its blood he shall pour out at the base of the altar. ³⁵And all its fat he shall remove just as the fat of the sheep of the sacrifice of well-being is removed; and this the priest shall turn into smoke on the altar, over the Lord's offering by fire. Thus the priest shall make expiation on his behalf for the sin of which he is guilty, and he shall be forgiven.

5 If a person incurs guilt—

When he has heard a public imprecation[a] and—although able to testify as one who has either seen or learned of the matter—he does not give information, so that he is subject to punishment;

²Or when a person touches any unclean thing—be it the carcass of an unclean beast or the carcass of unclean cattle or the carcass of an unclean creeping thing—and the fact has escaped him, and then, being unclean, he realizes his guilt;

³Or when he touches human uncleanness—any such uncleanness whereby one becomes unclean—and, though he has known it, the fact has escaped him, but later he realizes his guilt;

⁴Or when a person utters[b] an oath to bad or good purpose—whatever a man may utter in an oath—and, though he has known it, the fact has escaped him, but later he realizes his guilt in any of these matters—

---

a *Namely, against one who withholds testimony*
b *Lit. "utters with his lips"*

⁵when he realizes his guilt in any of these matters, he shall confess that wherein he has sinned. ⁶And he shall bring as his penalty to the LORD, for the sin of which he is guilty, a female from the flock, sheep or goat, as a sin offering; and the priest shall make expiation on his behalf for his sin.

⁷But if his means do not suffice for a sheep, he shall bring to the LORD, as his penalty for that of which he is guilty, two turtledoves or two pigeons, one for a sin offering and the other for a burnt offering. ⁸He shall bring them to the priest, who shall offer first the one for the sin offering, pinching its head at the nape without severing it. ⁹He shall sprinkle some of the blood of the sin offering on the side of the altar, and what remains of the blood shall be drained out at the base of the altar; it is a sin offering. ¹⁰And the second he shall prepare as a burnt offering, according to regulation. Thus the priest shall make expiation on his behalf for the sin of which he is guilty, and he shall be forgiven.

¹¹And if his means do not suffice for two turtledoves or two pigeons, he shall bring as his offering for that of which he is guilty a tenth of an *ephah* of choice flour for a sin offering; he shall not add oil to it or lay frankincense on it, for it is a sin offering. ¹²He shall bring it to the priest, and the priest shall scoop out of it a handful as a token portion of it and turn it into smoke on the altar, with the LORD's offerings by fire; it is a sin offering. ¹³Thus the priest shall make expiation on his behalf for whichever of these sins he is guilty, and he shall be forgiven. It shall belong to the priest, like the meal offering.

¹⁴And the LORD spoke to Moses, saying:

¹⁵When a person commits a trespass, being unwittingly remiss about any of the LORD's sacred things, he shall bring as his penalty to the LORD a ram without blemish from the flock, convertible into payment in silver by the sanctuary weight, as a guilt offering. ¹⁶He shall make restitution for that wherein he was remiss about the sacred things, and he shall add a fifth part to it and give it to the priest. The priest shall make expiation on

his behalf with the ram of the guilt offering, and he shall be forgiven.

[17]And when a person, without knowing it, sins in regard to any of the LORD's commandments about things not to be done, and then realizes his guilt, he shall be subject to punishment. [18]He shall bring to the priest a ram without blemish from the flock, or the equivalent,[c] as a guilt offering. The priest shall make expiation on his behalf for the error that he committed unwittingly, and he shall be forgiven. [19]It is a guilt offering; he has incurred guilt before the LORD.

[20]The LORD spoke to Moses, saying: [21]When a person sins and commits a trespass against the LORD by dealing deceitfully with his fellow in the matter of a deposit or a pledge,[d] or through robbery, or by defrauding his fellow, [22]or by finding something lost and lying about it; if he swears falsely regarding any one of the various things that one may do and sin thereby—[23]when one has thus sinned and, realizing his guilt, would restore that which he got through robbery or fraud, or the deposit that was entrusted to him, or the lost thing that he found, [24]or anything else about which he swore falsely, he shall repay the principal amount and add a fifth part to it. He shall pay it to its owner when he realizes his guilt. [25]Then he shall bring to the priest, as his penalty to the LORD, a ram without blemish from the flock, or the equivalent,[e] as a guilt offering. [26]The priest shall make expiation on his behalf before the LORD, and he shall be forgiven for whatever he may have done to draw blame thereby.

צו

6 The LORD spoke to Moses, saying: [2]Command Aaron and his sons thus:

This is the ritual of the burnt offering: The burnt offering itself shall remain where it is burned upon the altar all night until morning, while the fire on the altar is kept going on it. [3]The priest shall dress in linen raiment, with linen breeches next to his body; and he shall take up the ashes to which the fire has reduced the burnt offering on the altar and place them beside

c *I.e. in currency; cf. v. 15*
d *Meaning of Heb uncertain*
e *I.e. in currency; cf. v. 15*

the altar. ⁴He shall then take off his vestments and put on other vestments, and carry the ashes outside the camp to a clean place. ⁵The fire on the altar shall be kept burning, not to go out: every morning the priest shall feed wood to it, lay out the burnt offering on it, and turn into smoke the fat parts of the offerings of well-being. ⁶A perpetual fire shall be kept burning on the altar, not to go out.

⁷And this is the ritual of the meal offering: Aaron's sons shall present it before the LORD, in front of the altar. ⁸A handful of the choice flour and oil of the meal offering shall be taken from it, with all the frankincense that is on the meal offering, and this token portion shall be turned into smoke on the altar as a pleasing odor to the LORD. ⁹What is left of it shall be eaten by Aaron and his sons; it shall be eaten as unleavened cakes, in the sacred precinct; they shall eat it in the enclosure of the Tent of Meeting. ¹⁰It shall not be baked with leaven; I have given it as their portion from My offerings by fire; it is most holy, like the sin offering and the guilt offering. ¹¹Only the males among Aaron's descendants may eat of it, as their due for all time throughout the ages from the LORD's offerings by fire. Anything that touches these shall become holy.

¹²The LORD spoke to Moses, saying: ¹³This is the offering that Aaron and his sons shall offer to the LORD on the occasion of his[a] anointment: a tenth of an *ephah* of choice flour as a regular meal offering, half of it in the morning and half of it in the evening, ¹⁴shall be prepared with oil on a griddle. You shall bring it well soaked, and offer it as a meal offering of baked slices,[b] of pleasing odor to the LORD. ¹⁵And so shall the priest, anointed from among his sons to succeed him, prepare it; it is the LORD's—a law for all time—to be turned entirely into smoke. ¹⁶So, too, every meal offering of a priest shall be a whole offering: it shall not be eaten.

¹⁷The LORD spoke to Moses, saying: ¹⁸Speak to Aaron and his sons thus: This is the ritual of the sin offering: the sin offering shall be slaughtered before the LORD, at the spot[c] where the

---

a *Or "their"*
b *Meaning of Heb* tuphine *uncertain*
c *Cf. 1.11*

burnt offering is slaughtered: it is most holy. [19]The priest who offers it as a sin offering shall eat of it; it shall be eaten in the sacred precinct, in the enclosure of the Tent of Meeting. [20]Anything that touches its flesh shall become holy; and if any of its blood is spattered upon a garment, you shall wash the bespattered part in the sacred precinct. [21]An earthen vessel in which it was boiled shall be broken; if it was boiled in a copper vessel, [the vessel] shall be scoured and rinsed with water. [22]Only the males in the priestly line may eat of it: it is most holy. [23]But no sin offering may be eaten from which any blood is brought into the Tent of Meeting for expiation in the sanctuary; any such shall be consumed in fire.

7 This is the ritual of the guilt offering: it is most holy. [2]The guilt offering shall be slaughtered at the spot where the burnt offering is slaughtered, and the blood shall be dashed on all sides of the altar. [3]All its fat shall be offered: the broad tail; the fat that covers the entrails; [4]the two kidneys and the fat that is on them at the loins; and the protuberance on the liver, which shall be removed with the kidneys. [5]The priest shall turn them into smoke on the altar as an offering by fire to the LORD; it is a guilt offering. [6]Only the males in the priestly line may eat of it; it shall be eaten in the sacred precinct: it is most holy.

[7]The guilt offering is like the sin offering. The same rule applies to both: it shall belong to the priest who makes expiation thereby. [8]So, too, the priest who offers a man's burnt offering shall keep the skin of the burnt offering that he offered. [9]Further, any meal offering that is baked in an oven, and any that is prepared in a pan or on a griddle, shall belong to the priest who offers it. [10]But every other meal offering, with oil mixed in or dry, shall go to the sons of Aaron all alike.

[11]This is the ritual of the sacrifice of well-being that one may offer to the LORD:

[12]If he offers it for thanksgiving, he shall offer together with

the sacrifice of thanksgiving unleavened cakes with oil mixed in, unleavened wafers spread with oil, and cakes of choice flour with oil mixed in, well soaked. ¹³This offering, with cakes of leavened bread added, he shall offer along with his thanksgiving sacrifice of well-being. ¹⁴Out of this he shall offer one of each kind*a* as a gift to the LORD; it shall go to the priest who dashes the blood of the offering of well-being. ¹⁵And the flesh of his thanksgiving sacrifice of well-being shall be eaten on the day that it is offered; none of it shall be set aside until morning.

¹⁶If, however, the sacrifice he offers is a votive or a freewill offering, it shall be eaten on the day that he offers his sacrifice, and what is left of it shall be eaten on the morrow. ¹⁷What is then left of the flesh of the sacrifice shall be consumed in fire on the third day. ¹⁸If any of the flesh of his sacrifice of well-being is eaten on the third day, it shall not be acceptable; it shall not count for him who offered it. It is an offensive thing, and the person who eats of it shall bear his guilt.

¹⁹Flesh that touches anything unclean shall not be eaten; it shall be consumed in fire. As for other flesh, only he who is clean may eat such flesh. ²⁰But the person who, in a state of uncleanness, eats flesh from the LORD's sacrifices of well-being, that person shall be cut off from his kin. ²¹When a person touches anything unclean, be it human uncleanness or an unclean animal or any unclean creature,*b* and eats flesh from the LORD's sacrifices of well-being, that person shall be cut off from his kin.

²²And the LORD spoke to Moses, saying: ²³Speak to the Israelite people thus: You shall eat no fat*c* of ox or sheep or goat. ²⁴Fat from animals that died or were torn by beasts may be put to any use, but you must not eat it. ²⁵If anyone eats the fat of animals from which offerings by fire may be made to the LORD, the person who eats it shall be cut off from his kin. ²⁶And you must not consume any blood, either of bird or of animal, in any of your settlements. ²⁷Anyone who eats blood shall be cut off from his kin.

---

a *Lit. "offering"*
b *Heb* sheqeṣ, *lit. "abomination"; several mss. and ancient versions read* shereṣ
  *"swarming things"*    c *I.e. hard, coarse fat (suet); cf. 3.3–5*

<sup>28</sup>And the LORD spoke to Moses, saying: <sup>29</sup>Speak to the Israelite people thus: The offering to the LORD from a sacrifice of well-being must be presented by him who offers his sacrifice of well-being to the LORD: <sup>30</sup>his own hands shall present the LORD's offerings by fire. He shall present the fat with the breast, the breast to be elevated as an elevation offering before the LORD; <sup>31</sup>the priest shall turn the fat into smoke on the altar, and the breast shall go to Aaron and his sons. <sup>32</sup>And the right thigh from your sacrifices of well-being you shall present to the priest as a gift; <sup>33</sup>he from among Aaron's sons who offers the blood and the fat of the offering of well-being shall get the right thigh as his portion. <sup>34</sup>For I have taken the breast of elevation offering and the thigh of gift offering from the Israelites, from their sacrifices of well-being, and given them to Aaron the priest and to his sons as their due from the Israelites for all time.

<sup>35</sup>Those shall be the perquisites<sup>d</sup> of Aaron and the perquisites of his sons from the LORD's offerings by fire, once they have been inducted<sup>e</sup> to serve the LORD as priests; <sup>36</sup>these the LORD commanded to be given them, once they had been anointed, as a due from the Israelites for all time throughout the ages.

<sup>37</sup>Such are the rituals of the burnt offering, the meal offering, the sin offering, the guilt offering, the offering of ordination, and the sacrifice of well-being, <sup>38</sup>with which the LORD charged Moses on Mount Sinai, when He commanded that the Israelites present their offerings to the LORD, in the wilderness of Sinai.

8 The LORD spoke to Moses, saying: <sup>2</sup>Take Aaron along with his sons, and the vestments, the anointing oil, the bull of sin offering, the two rams, and the basket of unleavened bread; <sup>3</sup>and assemble the whole community at the entrance of the Tent of Meeting. <sup>4</sup>Moses did as the LORD commanded him. And when the community was assembled at the entrance of the Tent of Meeting, <sup>5</sup>Moses said to the community, "This is what the LORD has commanded to be done."

---

d *Lit. "anointment," i.e. accruing from anointment*
e *Lit. "brought forward"*

6Then Moses brought Aaron and his sons forward and washed them with water. 7He put the tunic on him, girded him with the sash, clothed him with the robe, and put the ephod on him, girding him with the decorated band with which he tied it to him. 8He put the breastpiece on him, and put into the breastpiece the Urim and Thummim.*a* 9And he set the headdress on his head; and on the headdress, in front, he put the gold frontlet, the holy diadem—as the LORD had commanded Moses.

10Moses took the anointing oil and anointed the Tabernacle and all that was in it, thus consecrating them. 11He sprinkled some of it on the altar seven times, anointing the altar, all its utensils, and the laver with its stand, to consecrate them. 12He poured some of the anointing oil upon Aaron's head and anointed him, to consecrate him. 13Moses then brought Aaron's sons forward, clothed them in tunics, girded them with sashes, and wound turbans upon them, as the LORD had commanded Moses.

14He led forward the bull of sin offering. Aaron and his sons laid their hands upon the head of the bull of sin offering, 15and it was slaughtered. Moses took the blood and with his finger put some on each of the horns of the altar, cleansing the altar; then he poured out the blood at the base of the altar. Thus he consecrated it in order to make expiation upon it.

16Moses then took all the fat that was about the entrails, and the protuberance of the liver, and the two kidneys and their fat, and turned them into smoke on the altar. 17The rest of the bull, its hide, its flesh, and its dung, he put to the fire outside the camp—as the LORD had commanded Moses.

18Then he brought forward the ram of burnt offering. Aaron and his sons laid their hands upon the ram's head, 19and it was slaughtered. Moses dashed the blood against all sides of the altar. 20The ram was cut up into sections and Moses turned the head, the sections, and the suet into smoke on the altar; 21Moses washed the entrails and the legs with water and turned all of the ram into smoke. That was a burnt offering for a pleasing odor, an offering by fire to the LORD—as the LORD had commanded Moses.

a *See note on Exod. 28.30*

²²He brought forward the second ram, the ram of ordination. Aaron and his sons laid their hands upon the ram's head, ²³and it was slaughtered. Moses took some of its blood and put it on the ridge*ᵇ* of Aaron's right ear, and on the thumb of his right hand, and on the big toe of his right foot. ²⁴Moses then brought forward the sons of Aaron, and put some of the blood on the ridges of their right ears, and on the thumbs of their right hands, and on the big toes of their right feet; and the rest of the blood Moses dashed against every side of the altar. ²⁵He took the fat—the broad tail, all the fat about the entrails, the protuberance of the liver, and the two kidneys and their fat—and the right thigh. ²⁶From the basket of unleavened bread that was before the Lord, he took one cake of unleavened bread, one cake of oil bread, and one wafer, and placed them on the fat parts and on the right thigh. ²⁷He placed all these on the palms of Aaron and on the palms of his sons, and elevated them as an elevation offering before the Lord. ²⁸Then Moses took them from their hands and turned them into smoke on the altar with the burnt offering. This was an ordination offering for a pleasing odor; it was an offering by fire to the Lord. ²⁹Moses took the breast and elevated it as an elevation offering before the Lord; it was Moses' portion of the ram of ordination—as the Lord had commanded Moses.

³⁰And Moses took some of the anointing oil and some of the blood that was on the altar and sprinkled it upon Aaron and upon his vestments, and also upon his sons and upon their vestments. Thus he consecrated Aaron and his vestments, and also his sons and their vestments.

³¹Moses said to Aaron and his sons: Boil the flesh at the entrance of the Tent of Meeting and eat it there with the bread that is in the basket of ordination—as I commanded:*ᶜ* Aaron and his sons shall eat it; ³²and what is left over of the flesh and the bread you shall consume in fire. ³³You shall not go outside the entrance of the Tent of Meeting for seven days, until the day that your period of ordination is completed. For your ordination will require seven days. ³⁴Everything done today, the

ᵇ Or "lobe"
ᶜ Or, vocalizing suwwethi, "I have been commanded"; cf. below, vv. 35 and 10.13

LORD has commanded to be done [seven days], to make expiation for you. ³⁵You shall remain at the entrance of the Tent of Meeting day and night for seven days, keeping the LORD's charge—that you may not die—for so I have been commanded.

³⁶And Aaron and his sons did all the things that the LORD had commanded through Moses.

שמיני

9 On the eighth day Moses called Aaron and his sons, and the elders of Israel. ²He said to Aaron: "Take a calf of the herd for a sin offering and a ram for a burnt offering, without blemish, and bring them before the LORD. ³And speak to the Israelites, saying: Take a he-goat for a sin offering; a calf and a lamb, yearlings without blemish, for a burnt offering; ⁴and an ox and a ram for an offering of well-being to sacrifice before the LORD; and a meal offering with oil mixed in. For today the LORD will appear to you."

⁵They brought to the front of the Tent of Meeting the things that Moses had commanded, and the whole community came forward and stood before the LORD. ⁶Moses said: "This is what the LORD has commanded that you do, that the Presence of the LORD may appear to you." ⁷Then Moses said to Aaron: "Come forward to the altar and sacrifice your sin offering and your burnt offering, making expiation for yourself and for the people; and sacrifice the people's offering and make expiation for them, as the LORD has commanded."

⁸Aaron came forward to the altar and slaughtered his calf of sin offering. ⁹Aaron's sons brought the blood to him; he dipped his finger in the blood and put it on the horns of the altar; and he poured out the rest of the blood at the base of the altar. ¹⁰The fat, the kidneys, and the protuberance of the liver from the sin offering he turned into smoke on the altar—as the LORD had commanded Moses; ¹¹and the flesh and the skin were consumed in fire outside the camp. ¹²Then he slaughtered the burnt offering. Aaron's sons passed the blood to him, and he dashed it

against all sides of the altar. [13]They passed the burnt offering to him in sections, as well as the head, and he turned it into smoke on the altar. [14]He washed the entrails and the legs, and turned them into smoke on the altar with the burnt offering.

[15]Next he brought forward the people's offering. He took the goat for the people's sin offering, and slaughtered it, and presented it as a sin offering like the previous one. [16]He brought forward the burnt offering and sacrificed it according to regulation. [17]He then brought forward the meal offering and, taking a handful of it, he turned it into smoke on the altar—in addition to the burnt offering of the morning.[a] [18]He slaughtered the ox and the ram, the people's sacrifice of well-being. Aaron's sons passed the blood to him—which he dashed against every side of the altar—[19]and the fat parts of the ox and the ram: the broad tail, the covering [fat], the kidneys, and the protuberances of the livers. [20]They laid these fat parts over the breasts; and Aaron[b] turned the fat parts into smoke on the altar, [21]and elevated the breasts and the right thighs as an elevation offering before the LORD—as Moses had commanded.

[22]Aaron lifted his hands toward the people and blessed them; and he stepped down after offering the sin offering, the burnt offering, and the offering of well-being. [23]Moses and Aaron then went inside the Tent of Meeting. When they came out, they blessed the people; and the Presence of the Lord appeared to all the people. [24]Fire came forth from before the LORD and consumed the burnt offering and the fat parts on the altar. And all the people saw, and shouted, and fell on their faces.

**10** Now Aaron's sons Nadab and Abihu each took his fire pan, put fire in it, and laid incense on it; and they offered before the LORD alien fire, which He had not enjoined upon them. [2]And fire came forth from the LORD and consumed them; thus they died [a-]at the instance of[-a] the LORD. [3]Then Moses said to Aaron, "This is what the LORD meant when He said:

---

[a] *See Exod. 29.38–46*
[b] *This word moved up from v. 21 for clarity*

[a-a] *Others "before"*

Through those near to Me I show Myself holy,
And gain glory before all the people."
And Aaron was silent.

⁴Moses called Mishael and Elzaphan, sons of Uzziel the uncle of Aaron, and said to them, "Come forward and carry your kinsmen away from the front of the sanctuary to a place outside the camp." ⁵They came forward and carried them out of the camp by their tunics, as Moses had ordered. ⁶And Moses said to Aaron and to his sons Eleazar and Ithamar, "Do not ᵇ⁻bare your heads⁻ᵇ and do not rend your clothes, lest you die and anger strike the whole community. But your kinsmen, all the house of Israel, shall bewail the burning that the LORD has wrought. ⁷And so do not go outside the entrance of the Tent of Meeting, lest you die, for the LORD's anointing oil is upon you." And they did as Moses had bidden.

⁸And the LORD spoke to Aaron, saying: ⁹Drink no wine or other intoxicant, you or your sons, when you enter the Tent of Meeting, that you may not die. This is a law for all time throughout the ages, ¹⁰for you must distinguish between the sacred and the profane, and between the unclean and the clean; ¹¹and you must teach the Israelites all the laws which the LORD has imparted to them through Moses.

¹²Moses spoke to Aaron and to his remaining sons, Eleazar and Ithamar: Take the meal offering that is left over from the LORD's offerings by fire and eat it unleavened beside the altar, for it is most holy. ¹³You shall eat it in the sacred precinct, inasmuch as it is your due, and that of your children, from the LORD's offerings by fire; for so I have been commanded. ¹⁴But the breast of elevation offering and the thigh of gift offering you, and your sons and daughters with you, may eat in any clean place, for they have been assigned as a due to you and your children from the Israelites' sacrifices of well-being. ¹⁵Together with the fat of fire offering, they must present the thigh of gift offering and the breast of elevation offering, which are to be

b-b *Or "dishevel your hair"*

elevated as an elevation offering before the LORD, and which are to be your due and that of your children with you for all time— as the LORD has commanded.

¹⁶Then Moses inquired about the goat of sin offering, and it had already been burned! He was angry with Eleazar and Ithamar, Aaron's remaining sons, and said, ¹⁷"Why did you not eat the sin offering in the sacred area? For it is most holy, and He has given it to you to remove the guilt of the community and to make expiation for them before the LORD. ¹⁸Since its blood was not brought inside the sanctuary,ᶜ you should certainly have eaten it in the sanctuary, as I commanded." ¹⁹And Aaron spoke to Moses, "See, this day they brought their sin offering and their burnt offering before the LORD, and such things have befallen me! Had I eaten sin offering today, would the LORD have approved?" ²⁰And when Moses heard this, he approved.

# 11

The LORD spoke to Moses and Aaron, saying to them: ²Speak to the Israelite people thus:

These are the creatures that you may eat from among all the land animals: ³any animal that has true hoofs, with clefts through the hoofs, and that chewsᵃ the cud—such you may eat. ⁴The following, however, of those that either chew the cud or have true hoofs, you shall not eat: the camel—although it chews the cud, it has no true hoofs: it is unclean for you; ⁵the daman— although it chews the cud, it has no true hoofs: it is unclean for you; ⁶the hare—although it chews the cud, it has no true hoofs: it is unclean for you; ⁷and the swine—although it has true hoofs, with the hoofs cleft through, it does not chew the cud: it is unclean for you. ⁸You shall not eat of their flesh or touch their carcasses; they are unclean for you.

⁹These you may eat of all that live in water: anything in water, whether in the seas or in the streams, that has fins and scales— these you may eat. ¹⁰But anything in the seas or in the streams that has no fins and scales, among all the swarming things of the

ᶜ *As is done in the case of the most solemn offerings; see 4.3–21; 16.11–17*

ᵃ *Lit. "brings up"*

water and among all the other living creatures that are in the water—they are an abomination for you <sup>11</sup>and an abomination for you they shall remain: you shall not eat of their flesh and you shall abominate their carcasses. <sup>12</sup>Everything in water that has no fins and scales shall be an abomination for you.

<sup>13</sup>The following<sup>b</sup> you shall abominate among the birds—they shall not be eaten, they are an abomination: the eagle, the vulture, and the black vulture; <sup>14</sup>the kite, falcons of every variety; <sup>15</sup>all varieties of raven; <sup>16</sup>the ostrich, the nighthawk, the sea gull; hawks of every variety; <sup>17</sup>the little owl, the cormorant, and the great owl; <sup>18</sup>the white owl, the pelican, and the bustard; <sup>19</sup>the stork; herons of every variety; the hoopoe, and the bat.

<sup>20</sup>All winged swarming things that walk on fours shall be an abomination for you. <sup>21</sup>But these you may eat among all the winged swarming things that walk on fours: all that have, above their feet, jointed legs to leap with on the ground—<sup>22</sup>of these you may eat the following<sup>b</sup>: locusts of every variety; all varieties of bald locust; crickets of every variety; and all varieties of grasshopper. <sup>23</sup>But all other winged swarming things that have four legs shall be an abomination for you.

<sup>24</sup>And the following shall make you unclean—whoever touches their carcasses shall be unclean until evening, <sup>25</sup>and whoever carries the carcasses of any of them shall wash his clothes and be unclean until evening—<sup>26</sup>every animal that has true hoofs but without clefts through the hoofs, or that does not chew the cud. They are unclean for you; whoever touches them shall be unclean. <sup>27</sup>Also all animals that walk on paws, among those that walk on fours, are unclean for you; whoever touches their carcasses shall be unclean until evening. <sup>28</sup>And anyone who carries their carcasses shall wash his clothes and remain unclean until evening. They are unclean for you.

<sup>29</sup>The following<sup>b</sup> shall be unclean for you from among the things that swarm on the earth: the mole, the mouse, and great lizards of every variety; <sup>30</sup>the gecko, the land crocodile, the lizard, the sand lizard, and the chameleon. <sup>31</sup>Those are for you

b  *A number of these cannot be identified with certainty*

the unclean among all the swarming things; whoever touches them when they are dead shall be unclean until evening. ³²And anything on which one of them falls when dead shall be unclean: be it any article of wood, or a cloth, or a skin, or a sack—any such article that can be put to use shall be dipped in water, and it shall remain unclean until evening; then it shall be clean. ³³And if any of those falls into an earthen vessel, everything inside it shall be unclean and [the vessel] itself you shall break. ³⁴As to any food that may be eaten, it shall become unclean if it came in contact with water*c*; as to any liquid that may be drunk, it shall become unclean if it was inside any vessel.*d* ³⁵Everything on which the carcass of any of them falls shall be unclean: an oven or stove shall be smashed. They are unclean and unclean they shall remain for you. ³⁶However, a spring or cistern in which water is collected shall be clean, but whoever touches such a carcass in it shall be unclean. ³⁷If such a carcass falls upon seed grain that is to be sown, it is clean; ³⁸but if water is put on the seed and any part of a carcass falls upon it, it shall be unclean for you.

³⁹If an animal that you may eat has died, anyone who touches its carcass shall be unclean until evening; ⁴⁰anyone who eats of its carcass shall wash his clothes and remain unclean until evening; and anyone who carries its carcass shall wash his clothes and remain unclean until evening.

⁴¹All the things that swarm upon the earth are an abomination; they shall not be eaten. ⁴²You shall not eat, among all things that swarm upon the earth, anything that crawls on its belly, or anything that walks on fours, or anything that has many legs; for they are an abomination. ⁴³You shall not draw abomination upon yourselves through anything that swarms; you shall not make yourselves unclean therewith and thus become unclean. ⁴⁴For I the Lord am your God: you shall sanctify yourselves and be holy, for I am holy. You shall not make yourselves unclean through any swarming thing that moves upon the earth. ⁴⁵For I the Lord am He who brought you up

---

*c* I.e. if the food then came in contact with the carcass of any animal named in vv. 29–30

*d* I.e. a vessel that had become contaminated by such contact from the land of Egypt to be your God: you shall be holy, for I am holy.

⁴⁶These are the instructions concerning animals, birds, all living creatures that move in water, and all creatures that swarm on earth, ⁴⁷for distinguishing between the unclean and the clean, between the living things that may be eaten and the living things that may not be eaten.

תזריע

12 The LORD spoke to Moses, saying: ²Speak to the Israelite people thus: When a woman at childbirth*a* bears a male, she shall be unclean seven days; she shall be unclean as at the time of her menstrual infirmity.—³On the eighth day the flesh of his foreskin shall be circumcised.—⁴She shall remain in a state of blood purification for thirty-three days: she shall not touch any consecrated thing, nor enter the sanctuary until her period of purification is completed. ⁵If she bears a female, she shall be unclean two weeks as during her menstruation, and she shall remain in a state of blood purification*b* for sixty-six days.

⁶On the completion of her period of purification, for either son or daughter, she shall bring to the priest, at the entrance of the Tent of Meeting, a lamb in its first year for a burnt offering, and a pigeon or a turtledove for a sin offering.*c* ⁷He shall offer it before the LORD and make expiation on her behalf; she shall then be clean from her flow of blood. Such are the rituals concerning her who bears a child, male or female. ⁸If, however, her means do not suffice for a sheep, she shall take two turtledoves or two pigeons, one for a burnt offering and the other for a sin offering. The priest shall make expiation on her behalf, and she shall be clean.

13 The LORD spoke to Moses and Aaron, saying:

²When a person has on the skin of his body a swelling, a rash, or a discoloration, and it develops into a scaly affection on the

---

a *Heb* tazriaʻ, *lit. "brings forth seed"*
b *Meaning of Heb uncertain*
c *See note at 4.3*

skin of his body, it shall be reported[a] to Aaron the priest or to one of his sons, the priests. ³The priest shall examine the affection on the skin of his body: if hair in the affected patch has turned white and the affection appears to be deeper than the skin of his body, it is a leprous affection[b]; when the priest sees it, he shall pronounce him unclean. ⁴But if it is a white discoloration on the skin of his body which does not appear to be deeper than the skin and the hair in it has not turned white, the priest shall isolate the affected person for seven days. ⁵On the seventh day the priest shall examine him, and if the affection has remained unchanged in color and the disease has not spread on the skin, the priest shall isolate him for another seven days. ⁶On the seventh day the priest shall examine him again: if the affection has faded and has not spread on the skin, the priest shall pronounce him clean. It is a rash; he shall wash his clothes, and he shall be clean. ⁷But if the rash should spread on the skin after he has presented himself to the priest and been pronounced clean, he shall present himself again to the priest. ⁸And if the priest sees that the rash has spread on the skin, the priest shall pronounce him unclean; it is leprosy.

⁹When a person has a scaly affection, it shall be reported[c] to the priest. ¹⁰If the priest finds on the skin a white swelling which has turned some hair white, with [d-a patch of undiscolored flesh-d] in the swelling, ¹¹it is chronic leprosy on the skin of his body, and the priest shall pronounce him unclean; he need not isolate him, for he is unclean. ¹²If the eruption spreads out over the skin so that it covers all the skin of the affected person from head to foot, wherever the priest can see—¹³if the priest sees that the eruption has covered the whole body—he shall pronounce the affected person clean; he is clean, for he has turned all white. ¹⁴But as soon as undiscolored flesh appears in it, he shall be unclean; ¹⁵when the priest sees the undiscolored flesh, he shall pronounce him unclean. The undiscolored flesh is unclean; it is leprosy. ¹⁶But if the undiscolored flesh again turns white, he shall come to the priest, ¹⁷and the priest shall examine him: if

a  Or "he shall be brought"
b  Heb ṣaraʻath is used for a variety of diseases. Where a human being is declared unclean by reason of ṣaraʻath, the traditional translation "leprosy" has been retained without regard to modern medical terminology
c  See note a at 13.2    d-d  Others "quick raw flesh"

the affection has turned white, the priest shall pronounce the affected person clean; he is clean.

18When an inflammation appears on the skin of one's body and it heals, 19and a white swelling or a white discoloration streaked with red develops where the inflammation was, he shall present himself to the priest. 20If the priest finds that it appears lower than the rest of the skin and that the hair in it has turned white, the priest shall pronounce him unclean; it is a leprous affection that has broken out in the inflammation. 21But if the priest finds that there is no white hair in it and it is not lower than the rest of the skin, and it is faded, the priest shall isolate him for seven days. 22If it should spread in the skin, the priest shall pronounce him unclean; it is an affection. 23But if the discoloration remains stationary, not having spread, it is the scar of the inflammation; the priest shall pronounce him clean.

24When the skin of one's body sustains a burn by fire, and the patch from the burn is a discoloration, either white streaked with red, or white, 25the priest shall examine it. If some hair has turned white in the discoloration, which itself appears to go deeper than the skin, it is leprosy that has broken out in the burn. The priest shall pronounce him unclean; it is a leprous affection. 26But if the priest finds that there is no white hair in the discoloration, and that it is not lower than the rest of the skin, and it is faded, the priest shall isolate him for seven days. 27On the seventh day the priest shall examine him: if it has spread in the skin, the priest shall pronounce him unclean; it is a leprous affection. 28But if the discoloration has remained stationary, not having spread on the skin, and it is faded, it is the swelling from the burn. The priest shall pronounce him clean, for it is the scar of the burn.

29If a man or a woman has an affection on the head or in the beard, 30the priest shall examine the affection. If it appears to go deeper than the skin and there is thin yellow hair in it, the priest shall pronounce him unclean; it is a scall, a scaly eruption in the hair or beard. 31But if the priest finds that the scall affection does not appear to go deeper than the skin, yet there is no black hair in it, the priest shall isolate the person with the scall affection for seven days. ³²On the seventh day the priest shall examine the affection. If the scall has not spread and no yellow hair has appeared in it, and the scall does not appear to go deeper than the skin, ³³the person with the scall shall shave himself, but without shaving the scall; the priest shall isolate him for another seven days. ³⁴On the seventh day the priest shall examine the scall. If the scall has not spread on the skin, and does not appear to go deeper than the skin, the priest shall pronounce him clean; he shall wash his clothes, and he shall be clean. ³⁵If, however, the scall should spread on the skin after he has been pronounced clean, ³⁶the priest shall examine him. If the scall has spread on the skin, the priest need not look for yellow hair: he is unclean. ³⁷But if the scall has remained unchanged in color, and black hair has grown in it, the scall is healed; he is clean. The priest shall pronounce him clean.

³⁸If a man or a woman has the skin of the body streaked with white discolorations, ³⁹and the priest sees that the discolorations on the skin of the body are of a dull white, it is a tetter broken out on the skin; he is clean.

⁴⁰If a man loses the hair of his head and becomes bald, he is clean. ⁴¹If he loses the hair on the front part of his head and becomes bald at the forehead, he is clean. ⁴²But if a white affection streaked with red appears on the bald part in the front or at the back of the head, it is a scaly eruption that is spreading over the bald part in the front or at the back of the head. ⁴³The priest shall examine him: if the swollen affection on the bald part in the front or at the back of his head is white streaked with red, like the leprosy of body skin in appearance, ⁴⁴the man is leprous; he is unclean. The priest shall pronounce him unclean; he has the affection on his head.

⁴⁵As for the person with a leprous affection, his clothes shall be rent, his head shall be left bare,ᵉ and he shall cover over his upper lip; and he shall call out, "Unclean! Unclean!" ⁴⁶He shall

---

ᵉ *See note at 10.6*

be unclean as long as the disease is on him. Being unclean, he shall dwell apart; his dwelling shall be outside the camp.

⁴⁷When an eruptive affection occurs in a cloth of wool or linen fabric, ⁴⁸in the warp or in the woof of the linen or the wool, or in a skin or in anything made of skin; ⁴⁹if the affection in the cloth or the skin, in the warp or the woof, or in any article of skin, is streaky green^f or red, it is an eruptive affection. It shall be shown to the priest; ⁵⁰and the priest, after examining the affection, shall isolate the affected article for seven days. ⁵¹On the seventh day he shall examine the affection: if the affection has spread in the cloth—whether in the warp or the woof, or in the skin, for whatever purpose the skin may be used—the affection is a malignant eruption; it is unclean. ⁵²The cloth—whether warp or woof in wool or linen, or any article of skin—in which the affection is found, shall be burned, for it is a malignant eruption; it shall be consumed in fire. ⁵³But if the priest sees that the affection in the cloth—whether in warp or in woof, or in any article of skin—has not spread, ⁵⁴the priest shall order the affected article washed, and he shall isolate it for another seven days. ⁵⁵And if, after the affected article has been washed, the priest sees that the affection has not changed color and that it has not spread, it is unclean. It shall be consumed in fire; it is a fret,^g whether on its inner side or on its outer side. ⁵⁶But if the priest sees that the affected part, after it has been washed, is faded, he shall tear it out from the cloth or skin, whether in the warp or in the woof; ⁵⁷and if it occurs again in the cloth—whether in warp or in woof—or in any article of skin, it is a wild growth; the affected article shall be consumed in fire. ⁵⁸If, however, the affection disappears from the cloth—warp or woof—or from any article of skin that has been washed, it shall be washed again, and it shall be clean.

⁵⁹Such is the procedure for eruptive affections of cloth, woolen or linen, in warp or in woof, or of any article of skin, for pronouncing it clean or unclean.

---

^f *Or "yellow"*
^g *Meaning of Heb* pehetheth *uncertain*

מצרע

14 The LORD spoke to Moses, saying: [2]This shall be the ritual for a leper at the time that he is to be cleansed.

When it has been reported[a] to the priest, [3]the priest shall go outside the camp. If the priest sees that the leper has been healed of his scaly affection, [4]the priest shall order two live clean birds, cedar wood, crimson stuff, and hyssop to be brought for him who is to be cleansed. [5]The priest shall order one of the birds slaughtered over fresh water in an earthen vessel; [6]and he shall take the live bird, along with the cedar wood, the crimson stuff, and the hyssop, and dip them together with the live bird in the blood of the bird that was slaughtered over the fresh water. [7]He shall then sprinkle it seven times on him who is to be cleansed of the eruption and cleanse him; and he shall set the live bird free in the open country. [8]The one to be cleansed shall wash his clothes, shave off all his hair, and bathe in water; then he shall be clean. After that he may enter the camp, but he must remain outside his tent seven days. [9]On the seventh day he shall shave off all his hair—of head, beard, and eyebrows. When he has shaved off all his hair, he shall wash his clothes and bathe his body in water; then he shall be clean. [10]On the eighth day he shall take two male lambs without blemish, one ewe lamb in its first year without blemish, three-tenths of a measure of choice flour with oil mixed in for a meal offering, and one *log* of oil. [11]These shall be presented before the LORD, with the man to be cleansed, at the entrance of the Tent of Meeting, by the priest who performs the cleansing.

[12]The priest shall take one of the male lambs and offer it with the *log* of oil as a guilt offering, and he shall elevate them as an elevation offering before the LORD. [13]The lamb shall be slaughtered at the spot in the sacred area where the sin offering and the burnt offering are slaughtered.[b] For the guilt offering, like the sin offering, goes to the priest; it is most holy. [14]The priest

---

[a] *Cf. note a at 13.2*
[b] *See 1.11; 4.24*

shall take some of the blood of the guilt offering, and the priest shall put it on the ridge of the right ear of him who is being cleansed, and on the thumb of his right hand, and on the big toe of his right foot. ¹⁵The priest shall then take some of the *log* of oil and pour it into the palm of his own left hand. ¹⁶And the priest shall dip his right finger in the oil that is in the palm of his left hand and sprinkle some of the oil with his finger seven times before the LORD. ¹⁷Some of the oil left in his palm shall be put by the priest on the ridge of the right ear of the one being cleansed, on the thumb of his right hand, and on the big toe of his right foot—over the blood of the guilt offering. ¹⁸The rest of the oil in his palm the priest shall put on the head of the one being cleansed. Thus the priest shall make expiation for him before the LORD. ¹⁹The priest shall then offer the sin offering and make expiation for the one being cleansed of his uncleanness. Last, the burnt offering shall be slaughtered, ²⁰and the priest shall offer the burnt offering and the meal offering on the altar, and the priest shall make expiation for him. Then he shall be clean.

²¹If, however, he is poor and his means are insufficient, he shall take one male lamb for a guilt offering, to be elevated in expiation for him, one-tenth of a measure of choice flour with oil mixed in for a meal offering, and a *log* of oil; ²²and two turtledoves or two pigeons, depending on his means, the one to be the sin offering and the other the burnt offering. ²³On the eighth day of his cleansing he shall bring them to the priest at the entrance of the Tent of Meeting, before the LORD. ²⁴The priest shall take the lamb of guilt offering and the *log* of oil, and elevate them as an elevation offering before the LORD. ²⁵When the lamb of guilt offering has been slaughtered, the priest shall take some of the blood of the guilt offering and put it on the ridge of the right ear of the one being cleansed, on the thumb of his right hand, and on the big toe of his right foot. ²⁶The priest shall then pour some of the oil into the palm of his own left hand, ²⁷and with the finger of his right hand the priest shall sprinkle some of the oil that is in the palm of his left hand seven

times before the LORD. <sup>28</sup>Some of the oil in his palm shall be put by the priest on the ridge of the right ear of the one being cleansed, on the thumb of his right hand, and on the big toe of his right foot, over the same places as the blood of the guilt offering; <sup>29</sup>and what is left of the oil in his palm the priest shall put on the head of the one being cleansed, to make expiation for him before the LORD. <sup>30</sup>He shall then offer one of the turtledoves or pigeons, depending on his means—<sup>31</sup>whichever he can afford—the one as a sin offering and the other as a burnt offering, together with the meal offering. Thus the priest shall make expiation before the LORD for the one being cleansed. <sup>32</sup>Such is the ritual for him who has a scaly affection and whose means for his cleansing are limited.

<sup>33</sup>The LORD spoke to Moses and Aaron, saying:

<sup>34</sup>When you enter the land of Canaan that I give you as a possession, and I inflict an eruptive plague upon a house in the land you possess, <sup>35</sup>the owner of the house shall come and tell the priest, saying, "Something like a plague has appeared upon my house." <sup>36</sup>The priest shall order the house cleared before the priest enters to examine the plague, so that nothing in the house may become unclean; after that the priest shall enter to examine the house. <sup>37</sup>If, when he examines the plague, the plague in the walls of the house is found to consist of greenish<sup>c</sup> or reddish streaks<sup>d</sup> that appear to go deep into the wall, <sup>38</sup>the priest shall come out of the house to the entrance of the house, and close up the house for seven days. <sup>39</sup>On the seventh day the priest shall return. If he sees that the plague has spread on the walls of the house, <sup>40</sup>the priest shall order the stones with the plague in them to be pulled out and cast outside the city into an unclean place. <sup>41</sup>The house shall be scraped inside all around, and the coating<sup>e</sup> that is scraped off shall be dumped outside the city in an unclean place. <sup>42</sup>They shall take other stones and replace those stones with them, and take other coating and plaster the house.

<sup>43</sup>If the plague again breaks out in the house, after the stones have been pulled out and after the house has been scraped and

---

<sup>c</sup> Or *"yellowish"*
<sup>d</sup> *Meaning of Heb* sheqaʿaruroth *uncertain*
<sup>e</sup> *Lit.* "dust," "mud"

replastered, ⁴⁴the priest shall come to examine: if the plague has spread in the house, it is a malignant eruption in the house; it is unclean. ⁴⁵The house shall be torn down—its stones and timber and all the coating on the house—and taken to an unclean place outside the city.

⁴⁶Whoever enters the house while it is closed up shall be unclean until evening. ⁴⁷Whoever sleeps in the house must wash his clothes, and whoever eats in the house must wash his clothes.

⁴⁸If, however, the priest comes and sees that the plague has not spread in the house after the house was replastered, the priest shall pronounce the house clean, for the plague has healed. ⁴⁹To purge the house, he shall take two birds, cedar wood, crimson stuff, and hyssop. ⁵⁰He shall slaughter the one bird over fresh water in an earthen vessel. ⁵¹He shall take the cedar wood, the hyssop, the crimson stuff, and the live bird, and dip them in the blood of the slaughtered bird and the fresh water, and sprinkle on the house seven times. ⁵²Having purged the house with the blood of the bird, the fresh water, the live bird, the cedar wood, the hyssop, and the crimson stuff, ⁵³he shall set the live bird free outside the city in the open country. Thus he shall make expiation for the house, and it shall be clean.

⁵⁴Such is the ritual for every eruptive affection—for scalls, ⁵⁵for an eruption on a cloth or a house, ⁵⁶for swellings, for rashes, or for discolorations—⁵⁷to determine when they are unclean and when they are clean.

Such is the ritual concerning eruptions.

15 The Lord spoke to Moses and Aaron, saying: ²Speak to the Israelite people and say to them:

When any man has a discharge issuing from his member,ᵃ he is unclean. ³The uncleanness from his discharge shall mean the following—whether his member runs with the discharge or is stopped up so that there is no discharge, his uncleanness means this: ⁴Any bedding on which the one with the discharge lies shall

---

a  *Lit. "flesh"*

be unclean, and every object on which he sits shall be unclean. [5]Anyone who touches his bedding shall wash his clothes, bathe in water, and remain unclean until evening. [6]Whoever sits on an object on which the one with the discharge has sat shall wash his clothes, bathe in water, and remain unclean until evening. [7]Whoever touches the body of the one with the discharge shall wash his clothes, bathe in water, and remain unclean until evening. [8]If one with a discharge spits on one who is clean, the latter shall wash his clothes, bathe in water, and remain unclean until evening. [9]Any means for riding that one with a discharge has mounted shall be unclean; [10]whoever touches anything that was under him shall be unclean until evening; and whoever carries such things shall wash his clothes, bathe in water, and remain unclean until evening. [11]If one with a discharge, without having rinsed his hands in water, touches another person, that person shall wash his clothes, bathe in water, and remain unclean until evening. [12]An earthen vessel that one with a discharge touches shall be broken; and any wooden implement shall be rinsed with water.

[13]When one with a discharge becomes clean of his discharge, he shall count off seven days for his cleansing, wash his clothes, and bathe his body in fresh water; then he shall be clean. [14]On the eighth day he shall take two turtledoves or two pigeons and come before the LORD at the entrance of the Tent of Meeting and give them to the priest. [15]The priest shall offer them, the one as a sin offering and the other as a burnt offering. Thus the priest shall make expiation on his behalf, for his discharge, before the LORD.

[16]When a man has an emission of semen, he shall bathe his whole body in water and remain unclean until evening. [17]All cloth or leather on which semen falls shall be washed in water and remain unclean until evening. [18]And if a man has carnal relations with a woman, they shall bathe in water and remain unclean until evening.

[19]When a woman has a discharge, her discharge being blood

from her body, she shall remain in her impurity seven days; whoever touches her shall be unclean until evening. [20]Anything that she lies on during her impurity shall be unclean; and anything that she sits on shall be unclean. [21]Anyone who touches her bedding shall wash his clothes, bathe in water, and remain unclean until evening; [22]and anyone who touches any object on which she has sat shall wash his clothes, bathe in water, and remain unclean until evening. [23]Be it the bedding or be it the object on which she has sat, on touching it he shall be unclean until evening. [24]And if a man lies with her, her impurity is communicated to him; he shall be unclean seven days, and any bedding on which he lies shall become unclean.

[25]When a woman has had a discharge of blood for many days, not at the time of her impurity, or when she has a discharge beyond her period of impurity, she shall be unclean, as though at the time of her impurity, as long as her discharge lasts. [26]Any bedding on which she lies while her discharge lasts shall be for her like bedding during her impurity; and any object on which she sits shall become unclean, as it does during her impurity: [27]whoever touches them shall be unclean; he shall wash his clothes, bathe in water, and remain unclean until evening.

[28]When she becomes clean of her discharge, she shall count off seven days, and after that she shall be clean. [29]On the eighth day she shall take two turtledoves or two pigeons, and bring them to the priest at the entrance of the Tent of Meeting. [30]The priest shall offer the one as a sin offering and the other as a burnt offering; and the priest shall make expiation on her behalf, for her unclean discharge, before the LORD.

[31]You shall put the Israelites on guard against their uncleanness, lest they die through their uncleanness by defiling My Tabernacle which is among them.

[32]Such is the ritual concerning him who has a discharge: concerning him who has an emission of semen and becomes unclean thereby, [33]and concerning her who is in menstrual infirmity,

and concerning anyone, male or female, who has a discharge, and concerning a man who lies with an unclean woman.

אחרי מות

**16** The LORD spoke to Moses after the death of the two sons of Aaron who died when they drew too close to the presence of the LORD. [2]The LORD said to Moses:

Tell your brother Aaron that he is not to come at will[a] into the Shrine behind the curtain, in front of the cover that is upon the ark, lest he die; for I appear in the cloud over the cover. [3]Thus only shall Aaron enter the Shrine: with a bull of the herd for a sin offering and a ram for a burnt offering.—[4]He shall be dressed in a sacral linen tunic, with linen breeches next to his flesh, and be girt with a linen sash, and he shall wear a linen turban. They are sacral vestments; he shall bathe his body in water and then put them on.—[5]And from the Israelite community he shall take two he-goats for a sin offering and a ram for a burnt offering.

[6]Aaron is to offer his own bull of sin offering, to make expiation for himself and for his household. [7]Aaron[b] shall take the two he-goats and let them stand before the LORD at the entrance of the Tent of Meeting; [8]and he shall place lots upon the two goats, one marked for the LORD and the other marked for Azazel. [9]Aaron shall bring forward the goat designated by lot for the LORD, which he is to offer as a sin offering; [10]while the goat designated by lot for Azazel shall be left standing alive before the LORD, to make expiation with it and to send it off to the wilderness for Azazel.

[11]Aaron shall then offer his bull of sin offering, to make expiation for himself and his household. He shall slaughter his bull of sin offering, [12]and he shall take a panful of glowing coals scooped from the altar before the LORD, and two handfuls of finely ground aromatic incense, and bring this behind the curtain. [13]He shall put the incense on the fire before the LORD, so

---

[a] Lit. "at any time"
[b] Moved up from v. 8 for clarity

that the cloud from the incense screens the cover that is over [the Ark of] the Pact, lest he die. ¹⁴He shall take some of the blood of the bull and sprinkle it with his finger over the cover on the east side; and in front of the cover he shall sprinkle some of the blood with his finger seven times. ¹⁵He shall then slaughter the people's goat of sin offering, bring its blood behind the curtain, and do with its blood as he has done with the blood of the bull: he shall sprinkle it over the cover and in front of the cover.

¹⁶Thus he shall purge the Shrine of the uncleanness and transgression of the Israelites, whatever their sins; and he shall do the same for the Tent of Meeting, which abides with them in the midst of their uncleanness. ¹⁷When he goes in to make expiation in the Shrine, nobody else shall be in the Tent of Meeting until he comes out.

When he has made expiation for himself and his household, and for the whole congregation of Israel, ¹⁸he shall go out to the altar that is before the LORD and purge it: he shall take some of the blood of the bull and of the goat and apply it to each of the horns of the altar; ¹⁹and the rest of the blood he shall sprinkle on it with his finger seven times. Thus he shall cleanse it of the uncleanness of the Israelites and consecrate it.

²⁰When he has finished purging the Shrine, the Tent of Meeting, and the altar, the live goat shall be brought forward. ²¹Aaron shall lay both his hands upon the head of the live goat and confess over it all the iniquities and transgressions of the Israelites, whatever their sins, putting them on the head of the goat; and it shall be sent off to the wilderness through a designated[c] man. ²²Thus the goat shall carry on it all their iniquities to an inaccessible region; and the goat shall be set free in the wilderness.

²³And Aaron shall go into the Tent of Meeting, take off the linen vestments that he put on when he entered the Shrine, and leave them there. ²⁴He shall bathe his body in water in the holy precinct and put on his vestments; then he shall come out and

[c] Meaning of Heb 'itti uncertain

offer his burnt offering and the burnt offering of the people, making expiation for himself and for the people. ²⁵The fat of the sin offering he shall turn into smoke on the altar.

²⁶He who set the Azazel-goat free shall wash his clothes and bathe his body in water; after that he may reenter the camp.

²⁷The bull of sin offering and the goat of sin offering whose blood was brought in to purge the Shrine shall be taken outside the camp; and their hides, flesh, and dung shall be consumed in fire. ²⁸He who burned them shall wash his clothes and bathe his body in water; after that he may reenter the camp.

²⁹And this shall be to you a law for all time: In the seventh month, on the tenth day of the month, you shall practice self-denial; and you shall do no manner of work, neither the citizen nor the alien who resides among you. ³⁰For on this day atonement shall be made for you to cleanse you of all your sins; you shall be clean before the LORD. ³¹It shall be a sabbath of complete rest for you, and you shall practice self-denial; it is a law for all time. ³²The priest who has been anointed and ordained to serve as priest in place of his father shall make expiation. He shall put on the linen vestments, the sacral vestments. ³³He shall purge the innermost Shrine; he shall purge the Tent of Meeting and the altar; and he shall make expiation for the priests and for all the people of the congregation.

³⁴This shall be to you a law for all time: to make atonement for the Israelites for all their sins once a year.

And Moses did as the LORD had commanded him.

# 17 The LORD spoke to Moses, saying:

²Speak to Aaron and his sons and to all the Israelite people and say to them:

This is what the LORD has commanded: ³if anyone of the house of Israel slaughters an ox or sheep or goat in the camp, or does so outside the camp, ⁴and does not bring it to the entrance of the Tent of Meeting to present it as an offering to the LORD, before the Lord's Tabernacle, bloodguilt shall be imputed to that man: he has shed blood; that man shall be cut off from among his people. ⁵This is in order that the Israelites may bring the sacrifices which they have been making in the open—that they may bring them before the Lord, to the priest, at the entrance of the Tent of Meeting, and offer them as sacrifices of well-being to the Lord; ⁶that the priest may dash the blood against the altar of the Lord at the entrance of the Tent of Meeting, and turn the fat into smoke as a pleasing odor to the Lord; ⁷and that they may offer their sacrifices no more to the goat-demons after whom they stray. This shall be to them a law for all time, throughout the ages.

⁸Say to them further: If anyone of the house of Israel or of the strangers who reside among them offers a burnt offering or a sacrifice, ⁹and does not bring it to the entrance of the Tent of Meeting to offer it to the Lord, that person shall be cut off from his people.

¹⁰And if anyone of the house of Israel or of the strangers who reside among them partakes of any blood, I will set My face against the person who partakes of the blood, and I will cut him off from among his kin. ¹¹For the life of the flesh is in the blood, and I have assigned it to you for making expiation for your lives upon the altar; it is the blood, as life, that effects expiation. ¹²Therefore I say to the Israelite people: No person among you shall partake of blood, nor shall the stranger who resides among you partake of blood.

¹³And if any Israelite or any stranger who resides among them hunts down an animal or a bird that may be eaten, he shall pour out its blood and cover it with earth. ¹⁴For the life of all flesh—its blood is its life. Therefore I say to the Israelite people: You shall not partake of the blood of any flesh, for the life of all flesh is its blood. Anyone who partakes of it shall be cut off.

¹⁵Any person, whether citizen or stranger, who eats what has died or has been torn by beasts shall wash his clothes, bathe in water, and remain unclean until evening; then he shall be clean.

¹⁶But if he does not wash [his clothes] and bathe his body, he shall bear his guilt.

**18** The LORD spoke to Moses, saying: ²Speak to the Israelite people and say to them:

I the LORD am your God. ³You shall not copy the practices of the land of Egypt where you dwelt, or of the land of Canaan to which I am taking you; nor shall you follow their laws. ⁴My rules alone shall you observe, and faithfully follow My laws: I the LORD am your God.

⁵You shall keep My laws and My rules, by the pursuit of which man shall live: I am the LORD.

⁶None of you shall come near anyone of his own flesh to uncover nakedness: I am the LORD.

⁷ᵃ⁻Your father's nakedness, that is, the nakedness of your mother, you shall not uncover; she is your mother—you shall not uncover her nakedness.

⁸Do not uncover the nakedness of your father's wife;⁻ᵃ it is the nakedness of your father.

⁹The nakedness of your sister—your father's daughter or your mother's, whether born into the household or outside—do not uncover their nakedness.

¹⁰The nakedness of your son's daughter, or of your daughter's daughter—do not uncover their nakedness; for their nakedness is yours.ᵇ

¹¹The nakedness of your father's wife's daughter, who was born into your father's household—she is your sister; do not uncover her nakedness.

¹²Do not uncover the nakedness of your father's sister; she is your father's flesh.

¹³Do not uncover the nakedness of your mother's sister; for she is your mother's flesh.

¹⁴Do not uncover the nakedness of your father's brother: do not approach his wife; she is your aunt.

---

ᵃ⁻ᵃ *A man and his wife are one flesh (Gen. 2.24), even if he should die or divorce her*
ᵇ *Meaning uncertain*

¹⁵Do not uncover the nakedness of your daughter-in-law: she is your son's wife; you shall not uncover her nakedness.

¹⁶Do not uncover the nakedness of your brother's wife; it is the nakedness of your brother.

¹⁷Do not uncover the nakedness of a woman and her daughter; nor shall you marry her son's daughter or her daughter's daughter and uncover her nakedness: they are kindred; it is depravity. ¹⁸Do not marry a woman as a rival to her sister and uncover her nakedness in the other's lifetime.

¹⁹Do not come near a woman during her period of uncleanness to uncover her nakedness.

²⁰Do not have carnal relations with your neighbor's wife and defile yourself with her.

²¹Do not allow any of your offspring to be offered up to Molech, and do not profane the name of your God: I am the LORD.

²²Do not lie with a male as one lies with a woman; it is an abhorrence.

²³Do not have carnal relations with any beast and defile yourself thereby; and let no woman lend herself to a beast to mate with it; it is perversion.

²⁴Do not defile yourselves in any of those ways, for it is by such that the nations that I am casting out before you defiled themselves. ²⁵Thus the land became defiled; and I called it to account for its iniquity, and the land spewed out its inhabitants. ²⁶But you must keep My laws and My rules, and you must not do any of those abhorrent things, neither the citizen nor the stranger who resides among you; ²⁷for all those abhorrent things were done by the people who were in the land before you, and the land became defiled. ²⁸So let not the land spew you out for defiling it, as it spewed out the nation that came before you. ²⁹All who do any of those abhorrent things—such persons shall be cut off from their people. ³⁰You shall keep My charge not to engage in any of the abhorrent practices that were carried on before you, and you shall not defile yourselves through them: I the LORD am your God.

קדשים

**19** The LORD spoke to Moses, saying: ²Speak to the whole Israelite community and say to them:

You shall be holy, for I, the LORD your God, am holy.

³You shall each revere his mother and his father, and keep My sabbaths: I the LORD am your God.

⁴Do not turn to idols or make molten gods for yourselves: I the LORD am your God.

⁵When you sacrifice an offering of well-being to the LORD, sacrifice it so that it may be accepted on your behalf. ⁶It shall be eaten on the day you sacrifice it, or on the day following; but what is left by the third day must be consumed in fire. ⁷If it should be eaten on the third day, it is an offensive thing, it will not be acceptable. ⁸And he who eats of it shall bear his guilt, for he has profaned what is sacred to the LORD; that person shall be cut off from his kin.

⁹When you reap the harvest of your land, you shall not reap all the way to the edges of your field, or gather the gleanings of your harvest. ¹⁰You shall not pick your vineyard bare, or gather the fallen fruit of your vineyard; you shall leave them for the poor and the stranger: I the LORD am your God.

¹¹You shall not steal; you shall not deal deceitfully or falsely with one another. ¹²You shall not swear falsely by My name, profaning the name of your God: I am the LORD.

¹³You shall not defraud your fellow. You shall not commit robbery. The wages of a laborer shall not remain with you until morning.

¹⁴You shall not insult the deaf, or place a stumbling block before the blind. You shall fear your God: I am the LORD.

¹⁵You shall not render an unfair decision: do not favor the poor or show deference to the rich; judge your kinsman fairly. ¹⁶Do not ᵃ⁻deal basely with⁻ᵃ your countrymen. Do not ᵇ⁻profit byᵇ the blood of your fellow: I am the LORD.

¹⁷You shall not hate your kinsfolk in your heart. Reprove your kinsman butᶜ incur no guilt because of him. ¹⁸You shall not

ᵃ⁻ᵃ *Others "go about as a talebearer among"; meaning of Heb uncertain*
ᵇ⁻ᵇ *Lit. "stand upon"; precise meaning of Heb phrase uncertain*
ᶜ *Exact force of* we- *uncertain*

take vengeance or bear a grudge against your countrymen. Love your fellow as yourself: I am the LORD.

¹⁹You shall observe My laws.

You shall not let your cattle mate with a different kind; you shall not sow your field with two kinds of seed; you shall not put on cloth from a mixture of two kinds of material.

²⁰If a man has carnal relations with a woman who is a slave and has been designated for another man, but has not been redeemed or given her freedom, there shall be an indemnity; they shall not, however, be put to death, since she has not been freed. ²¹But he must bring to the entrance of the Tent of Meeting, as his guilt offering to the LORD, a ram of guilt offering. ²²With the ram of guilt offering the priest shall make expiation for him before the LORD for the sin that he committed; and the sin that he committed will be forgiven him.

²³When you enter the land and plant any tree for food, you shall regard its fruit as forbidden.ᵈ Three years it shall be forbiddenᵈ for you, not to be eaten. ²⁴In the fourth year all its fruit shall be set aside for jubilation before the LORD; ²⁵and only in the fifth year may you use its fruit—that its yield to you may be increased: I the LORD am your God.

²⁶You shall not eat anything with its blood. You shall not practice divination or soothsaying. ²⁷You shall not round off the side-growth on your head, or destroy the side-growth of your beard. ²⁸You shall not make gashes in your flesh for the dead, or incise any marks on yourselves: I am the LORD.

²⁹Do not degrade your daughter and make her a harlot, lest the land fall into harlotry and the land be filled with depravity. ³⁰You shall keep My sabbaths and venerate My sanctuary: I am the LORD.

³¹Do not turn to ghosts and do not inquire of familiar spirits, to be defiled by them: I the LORD am your God.

³²You shall rise before the aged and show deference to the old; you shall fear your God: I am the LORD.

³³When a stranger resides with you in your land, you shall not wrong him. ³⁴The stranger who resides with you shall be to you

ᵈ *Heb root* ʿrl, *commonly "to be uncircumcised"*

as one of your citizens; you shall love him as yourself, for you were strangers in the land of Egypt: I the LORD am your God. ³⁵You shall not falsify measures of length, weight, or capacity. ³⁶You shall have an honest balance, honest weights, an honest *ephah*, and an honest *hin*.

I the LORD am your God who freed you from the land of Egypt. ³⁷You shall faithfully observe all My laws and all My rules: I am the LORD.

20 And the LORD spoke to Moses: ²Say further to the Israelite people:

Anyone among the Israelites, or among the strangers residing in Israel, who gives any of his offspring to Molech, shall be put to death; the people of the land shall pelt him with stones. ³And I will set My face against that man and will cut him off from among his people, because he gave of his offspring to Molech and so defiled My sanctuary and profaned My holy name. ⁴And if the people of the land should shut their eyes to that man when he gives of his offspring to Molech, and should not put him to death, ⁵I Myself will set My face against that man and his kin, and will cut off from among their people both him and all who follow him in going astray after Molech. ⁶And if any person turns to ghosts and familiar spirits and goes astray after them, I will set My face against that person and cut him off from among his people.

⁷You shall sanctify yourselves and be holy, for I the LORD am your God. ⁸You shall faithfully observe My laws: I the LORD make you holy.

⁹If anyone insults his father or his mother, he shall be put to death; he has insulted his father and his mother—his bloodguilt is upon him.

¹⁰If a man commits adultery with a married woman, committing adultery with another man's wife, the adulterer and the adulteress shall be put to death. ¹¹If a man lies with his father's wife, it is the nakedness of his father that he has uncovered; the

two shall be put to death—their bloodguilt is upon them. [12]If a man lies with his daughter-in-law, both of them shall be put to death; they have committed incest—their bloodguilt is upon them. [13]If a man lies with a male as one lies with a woman, the two of them have done an abhorrent thing; they shall be put to death—their bloodguilt is upon them. [14]If a man marries a woman and her mother, it is depravity; both he and they shall be put to the fire, that there be no depravity among you. [15]If a man has carnal relations with a beast, he shall be put to death; and you shall kill the beast. [16]If a woman approaches any beast to mate with it, you shall kill the woman and the beast; they shall be put to death—their bloodguilt is upon them.

[17]If a man marries his sister, the daughter of either his father or his mother, so that he sees her nakedness and she sees his nakedness, it is a disgrace; they shall be excommunicated[a] in the sight of their kinsfolk. He has uncovered the nakedness of his sister, he shall bear his guilt. [18]If a man lies with a woman in her infirmity and uncovers her nakedness, he has laid bare her flow and she has exposed her blood flow; both of them shall be cut off from among their people. [19]You shall not uncover the nakedness of your mother's sister or of your father's sister, for that is laying bare one's own flesh; they shall bear their guilt. [20]If a man lies with his uncle's wife, it is his uncle's nakedness that he has uncovered. They shall bear their guilt: they shall die childless. [21]If a man marries the wife of his brother, it is indecency. It is the nakedness of his brother that he has uncovered; they shall remain childless.

[22]You shall faithfully observe all My laws and all My regulations, lest the land to which I bring you to settle in spew you out. [23]You shall not follow the practices of the nation that I am driving out before you. For it is because they did all these things that I abhorred them [24]and said to you: You shall possess their land, for I will give it to you to possess, a land flowing with milk and honey. I the LORD am your God who has set you apart from other peoples. [25]So you shall set apart the clean beast from the unclean, the unclean bird from the clean. You shall not draw

a Lit. "cut off"

abomination upon yourselves through beast or bird or anything with which the ground is alive, which I have set apart for you to treat as unclean. ²⁶You shall be holy to Me, for I the LORD am holy, and I have set you apart from other peoples to be Mine.

²⁷A man or a woman who has a ghost or a familiar spirit shall be put to death; they shall be pelted with stones—their blood-guilt shall be upon them.

אמר

21 The LORD said to Moses: Speak to the priests, the sons of Aaron, and say to them:

None shall defile himself for any [dead] person among his kin, ²except for the relatives that are closest to him: his mother, his father, his son, his daughter, and his brother; ³also for a virgin sister, close to him because she has not married, for her he may defile himself. ⁴But he shall not defile himself *ᵃ-as a kinsman by marriage,-ᵃ* and so profane himself.

⁵They shall not shave smooth any part of their heads, or cut the side-growth of their beards, or make gashes in their flesh. ⁶They shall be holy to their God and not profane the name of their God; for they offer the LORD's offerings by fire, the food of their God, and so must be holy.

⁷They shall not marry a woman defiled by harlotry, nor shall they marry one divorced from her husband. For they are holy to their God ⁸and you must treat them as holy, since they offer the food of your God; they shall be holy to you, for I the LORD who sanctify you am holy.

⁹When the daughter of a priest defiles herself through harlotry, it is her father whom she defiles; she shall be put to the fire.

¹⁰The priest who is exalted above his fellows, on whose head the anointing oil has been poured and who has been ordained to wear the vestments, shall not bare his head*ᵇ* or rend his vestments. ¹¹He shall not go in where there is any dead body; he shall not defile himself even for his father or mother. ¹²He shall not go outside the sanctuary and profane the sanctuary of his

---

ᵃ⁻ᵃ *Lit. "as a husband among his kin"; meaning uncertain*
ᵇ *See note at 10.6*

God, for upon him is the distinction of the anointing oil of his God, Mine the LORD's. [13]He may marry only a woman who is a virgin. [14]A widow, or a divorced woman, or one who is degraded by harlotry—such he may not marry. Only a virgin of his own kin may he take to wife—[15]that he may not profane his offspring among his kin, for I the LORD have sanctified him.

[16]The LORD spoke further to Moses: [17]Speak to Aaron and say: No man of your offspring throughout the ages who has a defect shall be qualified to offer the food of his God. [18]No one at all who has a defect shall be qualified: no man who is blind, or lame, or has a limb too short or too long; [19]no man who has a broken leg or a broken arm; [20]or who is a hunchback, or a dwarf, or who has a growth in his eye, or who has a boilscar, or scurvy, or crushed testes. [21]No man among the offspring of Aaron the priest who has a defect shall be qualified to offer the LORD's offering by fire; having a defect, he shall not be qualified to offer the food of his God. [22]He may eat of the food of his God, of the most holy well as of the holy; [23]but he shall not enter behind the curtain or come near the altar, for he has a defect. He shall not profane these places sacred to Me, for I the LORD have sanctified them.

[24]Thus Moses spoke to Aaron and his sons and to all the Israelites.

22 The LORD spoke to Moses, saying: [2]Instruct Aaron and his sons to be scrupulous about the sacred donations that the Israelite people consecrate to Me, lest they profane My holy name, Mine the LORD's. [3]Say to them:

Throughout the ages, if any man among your offspring, while in a state of uncleanness, partakes of any sacred donation that the Israelite people may consecrate to the LORD, that person shall be cut off from before Me: I am the LORD. [4]No man of Aaron's offspring who has an eruption or a discharge[a] shall eat of the sacred donations until he is clean. If one touches anything

---

a *See chapters 13 and 15*

made unclean by a corpse, or if a man has an emission of semen, [5]or if a man touches any swarming thing by which he is made unclean or any human being by whom he is made unclean— whatever his uncleanness—[6]the person who touches such shall be unclean until evening and shall not eat of the sacred donations unless he has washed his body in water. [7]As soon as the sun sets, he shall be clean; and afterward he may eat of the sacred donations, for they are his food. [8]He shall not eat anything that died or was torn by beasts, thereby becoming unclean: I am the LORD. [9]They shall keep My charge, lest they incur guilt thereby and die for it, having committed profanation: I the LORD consecrate them.

[10]No lay person shall eat of the sacred donations. No bound or hired laborer of a priest shall eat of the sacred donations; [11]but a person who is a priest's property by purchase may eat of them; and those that are born into his household may eat of his food. [12]If a priest's daughter marries a layman, she may not eat of the sacred gifts; [13]but if the priest's daughter is widowed or divorced and without offspring, and is back in her father's house as in her youth, she may eat of her father's food. No lay person may eat of it: [14]but if a man eats of a sacred donation unwittingly, he shall pay the priest for the sacred donation, adding one-fifth of its value. [15]But [the priests] must not allow the Israelites to profane the sacred donations that they set aside for the LORD, [16]or to incur guilt requiring a penalty payment, by eating such sacred donations: for it is I the LORD who make them sacred.

[17]The LORD spoke to Moses, saying: [18]Speak to Aaron and his sons, and to all the Israelite people, and say to them:

When any man of the house of Israel or of the strangers in Israel presents a burnt offering as his offering for any of the votive or any of the freewill offerings that they offer to the LORD, [19]it must, to be acceptable in your favor, be a male without blemish, from cattle or sheep or goats. [20]You shall not offer any that has a defect, for it will not be accepted in your favor.

²¹And when a man offers, from the herd or the flock, a sacrifice of well-being to the LORD for an explicit*ᵇ* vow or as a freewill offering, it must, to be acceptable, be without blemish; there must be no defect in it. ²²Anything blind, or injured, or maimed, or with a wen, boil-scar, or scurvy—such you shall not offer to the LORD; you shall not put any of them on the altar as offerings by fire to the LORD. ²³You may, however, present as a freewill offering an ox or a sheep with a limb extended or contracted; but it will not be accepted for a vow. ²⁴You shall not offer to the LORD anything [with its testes] bruised or crushed or torn or cut. You shall have no such practices*ᶜ* in your own land, ²⁵nor shall you accept such [animals] from a foreigner for offering as food for your God, for they are mutilated, they have a defect; they shall not be accepted in your favor.

²⁶The LORD spoke to Moses, saying: ²⁷When an ox or a sheep or a goat is born, it shall stay seven days with its mother, and from the eighth day on it shall be acceptable as an offering by fire to the LORD. ²⁸However, no animal from the herd or from the flock shall be slaughtered on the same day with its young.

²⁹When you sacrifice a thanksgiving offering to the LORD, sacrifice it so that it may be acceptable in your favor. ³⁰It shall be eaten on the same day; you shall not leave any of it until morning: I am the LORD.

³¹You shall faithfully observe My commandments: I am the LORD. ³²You shall not profane My holy name, that I may be sanctified in the midst of the Israelite people—I the LORD who sanctify you, ³³I who brought you out of the land of Egypt to be your God, I the LORD.

23 The LORD spoke to Moses, saying: ²Speak to the Israelite people and say to them:

These are My fixed times, the fixed times of the LORD, which you shall proclaim as sacred occasions.

³On six days work may be done, but on the seventh day there

---

ᵇ Or "unspecified" or "extraordinary"; meaning of Heb lephalle uncertain
ᶜ I.e. mutilations

shall be a sabbath of complete rest, a sacred occasion. You shall do no work; it shall be a sabbath of the LORD throughout your settlements.

⁴These are the set times of the LORD, the sacred occasions, which you shall celebrate each at its appointed time: ⁵In the first month, on the fourteenth day of the month, at twilight, there shall be a passover offering to the LORD, ⁶and on the fifteenth day of that month the LORD's Feast of Unleavened Bread. You shall eat unleavened bread for seven days. ⁷On the first day you shall celebrate a sacred occasion: you shall not work at your occupations. ⁸Seven days you shall make offerings by fire to the LORD. The seventh day shall be a sacred occasion: you shall not work at your occupations.

⁹The LORD spoke to Moses, saying: ¹⁰Speak to the Israelite people and say to them:

When you enter the land that I am giving to you and you reap its harvest, you shall bring the first sheaf of your harvest to the priest. ¹¹He shall elevate the sheaf before the LORD for acceptance in your behalf; the priest shall elevate it on the day after the sabbath. ¹²On the day that you elevate the sheaf, you shall offer as a burnt offering to the LORD a lamb of the first year without blemish. ¹³The meal offering with it shall be two-tenths of a measure of choice flour with oil mixed in, an offering by fire of pleasing odor to the LORD; and the libation with it shall be of wine, a quarter of a *hin*. ¹⁴Until that very day, until you have brought the offering of your God, you shall eat no bread or parched grain or fresh ears*ᵃ*; it is a law for all time throughout the ages in all your settlements.

¹⁵And from the day on which you bring the sheaf of elevation offering—the day after the sabbath—you shall count off seven weeks. They must be complete: ¹⁶you must count until the day after the seventh week—fifty days; then you shall bring an offering of new grain to the LORD. ¹⁷You shall bring from your settlements two loaves of bread as an elevation offering; each

ᵃ *I.e. of the new crop*

shall be made of two-tenths of a measure of choice flour, baked after leavening, as first fruits to the LORD. [18]With the bread you shall present, as burnt offerings to the LORD, seven yearling lambs without blemish, one bull of the herd, and two rams, with their meal offerings and libations, an offering by fire of pleasing odor to the LORD. [19]You shall also offer one he-goat as a sin offering and two yearling lambs as a sacrifice of well-being. [20]The priest shall elevate these—the two lambs[b]—together with the bread of first fruits as an elevation offering before the LORD; they shall be holy to the LORD, for the priest. [21]On that same day you shall hold a celebration; it shall be a sacred occasion for you; you shall not work at your occupations. This is a law for all time in all your settlements, throughout the ages.

[22]And when you reap the harvest of your land, you shall not reap all the way to the edges of your field, or gather the gleanings of your harvest; you shall leave them for the poor and the stranger: I the LORD am your God.

[23]The LORD spoke to Moses, saying: [24]Speak to the Israelite people thus: In the seventh month, on the first day of the month, you shall observe complete rest, a sacred occasion commemorated with loud blasts. [25]You shall not work at your occupations; and you shall bring an offering by fire to the LORD.

[26]The LORD spoke to Moses, saying: [27]Mark, the tenth day of this seventh month is the Day of Atonement. It shall be a sacred occasion for you: you shall practice self-denial, and you shall bring an offering by fire to the LORD; [28]you shall do no work throughout that day. For it is a Day of Atonement, on which expiation is made on your behalf before the LORD your God. [29]Indeed, any person who does not practice self-denial throughout that day shall be cut off from his kin; [30]and whoever does any work throughout that day, I will cause that person to perish from among his people. [31]Do no work whatever; it is a law for all time, throughout the ages in all your settlements. [32]It shall be a sabbath of complete rest for you, and you shall practice self-denial; on the ninth day of the month at evening, from evening to evening, you shall observe this your sabbath.

---

b *Meaning of Heb uncertain*

³³The LORD spoke to Moses, saying: ³⁴Say to the Israelite people:

On the fifteenth day of this seventh month there shall be the Feast of Booths$^c$ to the LORD, [to last] seven days. ³⁵The first day shall be a sacred occasion: you shall not work at your occupations; ³⁶seven days you shall bring offerings by fire to the LORD. On the eighth day you shall observe a sacred occasion and bring an offering by fire to the LORD; it is a solemn gathering$^d$: you shall not work at your occupations.

³⁷Those are the set times of the LORD that you shall celebrate as sacred occasions, bringing offerings by fire to the LORD— burnt offerings, meal offerings, sacrifices, and libations, on each day what is proper to it—³⁸apart from the sabbaths of the LORD, and apart from your gifts and from all your votive offerings and from all your freewill offerings that you give to the LORD.

³⁹Mark, on the fifteenth day of the seventh month, when you have gathered in the yield of your land, you shall observe the festival of the LORD [to last] seven days: a complete rest on the first day, and a complete rest on the eighth day. ⁴⁰On the first day you shall take the product of *hadar*$^e$ trees, branches of palm trees, boughs of leafy$^f$ trees, and willows of the brook, and you shall rejoice before the LORD your God seven days. ⁴¹You shall observe it as a festival of the LORD for seven days in the year; you shall observe it in the seventh month as a law for all time, throughout the ages. ⁴²You shall live in booths seven days; all citizens in Israel shall live in booths, ⁴³in order that future generations may know that I made the Israelite people live in booths when I brought them out of the land of Egypt, I the LORD your God.

⁴⁴So Moses declared to the Israelites the set times of the LORD.

# 24 The LORD spoke to Moses, saying:

²Command the Israelite people to bring you clear oil of beat-

---

$^c$ *Others "Tabernacles"*   $^d$ *Precise meaning of Heb* 'aṣereth *uncertain*
$^e$ *Others "goodly"; exact meaning of Heb* hadar *uncertain. Traditionally the product is understood as "citron"*   $^f$ *Meaning of Heb* 'aboth *uncertain*

en olives for lighting, for kindling lamps regularly. ³Aaron shall set them up in the Tent of Meeting outside the curtain of the Pact [to burn] from evening to morning before the LORD regularly; it is a law for all time throughout the ages. ⁴He shall set up the lamps on the pure*ᵃ* lampstand before the LORD [to burn] regularly.

⁵You shall take choice flour and bake of it twelve loaves, two-tenths of a measure for each loaf. ⁶Place them on the pure*ᵃ* table before the LORD in two rows, six to a row. ⁷With each row you shall place pure frankincense, which is to be a token offering*ᵇ* for the bread, as an offering by fire to the LORD. ⁸He shall arrange them before the LORD regularly every sabbath day—it is a commitment for all time on the part of the Israelites. ⁹They shall belong to Aaron and his sons, who shall eat them in the sacred precinct; for they are his as most holy things from the LORD'S offerings by fire, a due for all time.

¹⁰There came out among the Israelites one whose mother was Israelite and whose father was Egyptian. And a fight broke out in the camp between that half-Israelite*ᶜ* and a certain Israelite. ¹¹The son of the Israelite woman pronounced the Name in blasphemy, and he was brought to Moses—now his mother's name was Shelomith daughter of Dibri of the tribe of Dan— ¹²and he was placed in custody, until the decision of the LORD should be made clear to them.

¹³And the LORD spoke to Moses, saying: ¹⁴Take the blasphemer outside the camp; and let all who were within hearing lay their hands upon his head, and let the whole community stone him.

¹⁵And to the Israelite people speak thus: Anyone who blasphemes his God shall bear his guilt; ¹⁶if he also pronounces the name LORD, he shall be put to death. The whole community shall stone him; stranger or citizen, if he has thus pronounced the Name, he shall be put to death.

¹⁷If anyone kills any human being, he shall be put to death.

---

ᵃ *See note at Exod. 31.8*
ᵇ *See Lev. 2.2*
ᶜ *Lit. "the son of an Israelite woman"*

¹⁸One who kills a beast shall make restitution for it: life for life. ¹⁹If anyone maims his fellow, as he has done so shall it be done to him: ²⁰fracture for fracture, eye for eye, tooth for tooth. The injury he inflicted on another shall be inflicted on him. ²¹One who kills a beast shall make restitution for it; but one who kills a human being shall be put to death. ²²You shall have one standard for stranger and citizen alike: for I the LORD am your God.

²³Moses spoke thus to the Israelites. And they took the blasphemer outside the camp and pelted him with stones. The Israelites did as the LORD had commanded Moses.

בהר

**25** The LORD spoke to Moses on Mount Sinai: ²Speak to the Israelite people and say to them:

When you enter the land that I assign to you, the land shall observe a sabbath of the LORD. ³Six years you may sow your field and six years you may prune your vineyard and gather in the yield. ⁴But in the seventh year the land shall have a sabbath of complete rest, a sabbath of the LORD: you shall not sow your field or prune your vineyard. ⁵You shall not reap the after-growth of your harvest or gather the grapes of your untrimmed vines; it shall be a year of complete rest for the land. ⁶But you may eat whatever the land during its sabbath will produce— you, your male and female slaves, the hired and bound laborers who live with you, ⁷and your cattle and the beasts in your land may eat all its yield.

⁸You shall count off seven weeks of years—seven times seven years—so that the period of seven weeks of years gives you a total of forty-nine years. ⁹Then you shall sound the horn loud; in the seventh month, on the tenth day of the month—the Day of Atonement—you shall have the horn sounded throughout your land ¹⁰and you shall hallow the fiftieth year. You shall proclaim release*ᵃ* throughout the land for all its inhabitants. It shall be a jubilee*ᵇ* for you: each of you shall return to his holding and each of you shall return to his family. ¹¹That fiftieth year shall be a jubilee for you: you shall not sow, neither shall you

ᵃ *Others "liberty"*
ᵇ *Heb yobel, "ram" or "ram's horn"*

reap the aftergrowth or harvest the untrimmed vines, [12]for it is a jubilee. It shall be holy to you: you may only eat the growth direct from the field.

[13]In this year of jubilee, each of you shall return to his holding. [14]When you sell property to your neighbor[c], or buy any from your neighbor, you shall not wrong one another. [15]In buying from your neighbor, you shall deduct only for the number of years since the jubilee; and in selling to you, he shall charge you only for the remaining crop years: [16]the more such years, the higher the price you pay; the fewer such years, the lower the price; for what he is selling you is a number of harvests. [17]Do not wrong one another, but fear your God; for I the LORD am your God.

[18]You shall observe My laws and faithfully keep My rules, that you may live upon the land in security; [19]the land shall yield its fruit and you shall eat your fill, and you shall live upon it in security. [20]And should you ask, "What are we to eat in the seventh year, if we may neither sow nor gather in our crops?" [21]I will ordain My blessing for you in the sixth year, so that it shall yield a crop sufficient for three years. [22]When you sow in the eighth year, you will still be eating old grain of that crop; you will be eating the old until the ninth year, until its crops come in.

[23]But the land must not be sold beyond reclaim, for the land is Mine; you are but strangers resident with Me. [24]Throughout the land that you hold, you must provide for the redemption of the land.

[25]If your kinsman is in straits and has to sell part of his holding, his nearest redeemer[d] shall come and redeem what his kinsman has sold. [26]If a man has no one to redeem for him, but prospers and acquires enough to redeem with, [27]he shall compute the years since its sale, refund the difference to the man to whom he sold it, and return to his holding. [28]If he lacks sufficient means to recover it, what he sold shall remain with the purchaser until the jubilee; in the jubilee year it shall be released, and he shall return to his holding.

[29]If a man sells a dwelling house in a walled city, it may be

c *I.e. fellow Israelite; see v. 46*
d *I.e. the closest relative able to redeem the land*

redeemed until a year has elapsed since its sale; the redemption period shall be a year. [30]If it is not redeemed before a full year has elapsed, the house in the walled city shall pass to the purchaser beyond reclaim throughout the ages; it shall not be released in the jubilee. [31]But houses in villages that have no encircling walls shall be classed as open country: they may be redeemed, and they shall be released through the jubilee. [32]As for the cities of the Levites, the houses in the cities they hold— the Levites shall forever have the right of redemption. [33e]Such property as may be redeemed from the Levites—houses sold in a city they hold—shall be released through the jubilee; for the houses in the cities of the Levites are their holding among the Israelites. [34]But the unenclosed land about their cities cannot be sold, for that is their holding for all time.

[35]If your kinsman, being in straits, comes under your authority, and you hold him as though a resident alien, let him live by your side: [36]do not exact from him advance or accrued interest,[f] but fear your God. Let him live by your side as your kinsman. [37]Do not lend him money at advance interest, or give him your food at accrued interest. [38]I the LORD am your God, who brought you out of the land of Egypt, to give you the land of Canaan, to be your God.

[39]If your kinsman under you continues in straits and must give himself over to you, do not subject him to the treatment of a slave. [40]He shall remain with you as a hired or bound laborer; he shall serve with you only until the jubilee year. [41]Then he and his children with him shall be free of your authority; he shall go back to his family and return to his ancestral holding.—[42]For they are My servants, whom I freed from the land of Egypt; they may not give themselves over into servitude.—[43]You shall not rule over him ruthlessly; you shall fear your God. [44]Such male and female slaves as you may have—it is from the nations round about you that you may acquire male and female slaves. [45]You may also buy them from among the children of aliens resident among you, or from their families that are among you, whom they begot in your land. These shall become your property:

---

[e] Meaning of first half of verse uncertain
[f] I.e. interest deducted in advance, or interest added at the time of repayment

⁴⁶you may keep them as a possession for your children after you, for them to inherit as property for all time. Such you may treat as slaves. But as for your Israelite kinsmen, no one shall rule ruthlessly over the other.

⁴⁷If a resident alien among you has prospered, and your kinsman being in straits, comes under his authority and gives himself over to the resident alien among you, or to an offshoot of an alien's family, ⁴⁸he shall have the right of redemption even after he has given himself over. One of his kinsmen shall redeem him, ⁴⁹or his uncle or his uncle's son shall redeem him, or anyone of his family who is of his own flesh shall redeem him; or, if he prospers, he may redeem himself. ⁵⁰He shall compute with his purchaser the total from the year he gave himself over to him until the jubilee year; the price of his sale shall be applied to the number of years, as though it were for a term as a hired laborer under the other's authority. ⁵¹If many years remain, he shall pay back for his redemption in proportion to his purchase price; ⁵²and if few years remain until the jubilee year, he shall so compute: he shall make payment for his redemption according to the years involved. ⁵³He shall be under his authority as a laborer hired by the year; he shall not rule ruthlessly over him in your sight. ⁵⁴If he has not been redeemed in any of those ways, he and his children with him shall go free in the jubilee year. ⁵⁵For it is to Me that the Israelites are servants: they are My servants, whom I freed from the land of Egypt, I the LORD your God.

26 You shall not make idols for yourselves, or set up for yourselves carved images or pillars, or place figured*a* stones in your land to worship upon, for I the LORD am your God. ²You shall keep My sabbaths and venerate My sanctuary, Mine, the LORD'S.

בחקתי

³If you follow My laws and faithfully observe My command-

___
a *Meaning of Heb* maskith *uncertain*

ments, [4]I will grant your rains in their season, so that the earth shall yield its produce and the trees of the field their fruit. [5]Your threshing shall overtake the vintage, and your vintage shall overtake the sowing; you shall eat your fill of bread and dwell securely in your land.

[6]I will grant peace in the land, and you shall lie down untroubled by anyone; I will give the land respite from vicious beasts, and no sword shall cross your land. [7]You shall give chase to your enemies, and they shall fall before you by the sword. [8]Five of you shall give chase to a hundred, and a hundred of you shall give chase to ten thousand; your enemies shall fall before you by the sword.

[9]I will look with favor upon you, and make you fertile and multiply you; and I will maintain My covenant with you. [10]You shall eat old grain long stored, and you shall have to clear out the old to make room for the new.

[11]I will establish My abode in your midst, and I will not spurn you. [12]I will be ever present in your midst: I will be your God, and you shall be My people. [13]I the LORD am your God who brought you out from the land of the Egyptians to be their slaves no more, who broke the bars of your yoke and made you walk erect.

[14]But if you do not obey Me and do not observe all these commandments, [15]if you reject My laws and spurn My rules, so that you do not observe all My commandments and you break My covenant, [16]I in turn will do this to you: I will wreak misery upon you—[b]consumption and fever, which cause the eyes to pine and the body to languish; you shall sow your seed to no purpose, for your enemies shall eat it. [17]I will set My face against you: you shall be routed by your enemies, and your foes shall dominate you. You shall flee though none pursues.

[18]And if, for all that, you do not obey Me, I will go on to discipline you sevenfold for your sins, [19]and I will break your proud glory. I will make your skies like iron and your earth like copper, [20]so that your strength shall be spent to no purpose.

b *Precise nature of these ills is uncertain*

Your land shall not yield its produce, nor shall the trees of the land yield their fruit.

²¹And if you remain hostile toward Me and refuse to obey Me, I will go on smiting you sevenfold for your sins. ²²I will loose wild beasts against you, and they shall bereave you of your children and wipe out your cattle. They shall decimate you, and your roads shall be deserted.

²³And if these things fail to discipline you for Me, and you remain hostile to Me, ²⁴I too will remain hostile to you: I in turn will smite you sevenfold for your sins. ²⁵I will bring a sword against you to wreak vengeance for the covenant; and if you withdraw into your cities, I will send pestilence among you, and you shall be delivered into enemy hands. ²⁶When I break your staff of bread, ten women shall bake your bread in a single oven; they shall dole out your bread by weight, and though you eat, you shall not be satisfied.

²⁷But if, despite this, you disobey Me and remain hostile to Me, ²⁸I will act against you in wrathful hostility; I, for My part, will discipline you sevenfold for your sins. ²⁹You shall eat the flesh of your sons and the flesh of your daughters. ³⁰I will destroy your cult places and cut down your incense stands, and I will heap your carcasses upon your lifeless fetishes.

I will spurn you. ³¹I will lay your cities in ruin and make your sanctuaries desolate, and I will not savor your pleasing odors. ³²I will make the land desolate, so that your enemies who settle in it shall be appalled by it. ³³And you I will scatter among the nations, and I will unsheath the sword against you. Your land shall become a desolation and your cities a ruin.

³⁴Then shall the land make up for its sabbath years throughout the time that it is desolate and you are in the land of your enemies; then shall the land rest and make up for its sabbath years. ³⁵Throughout the time that it is desolate, it shall observe the rest that it did not observe in your sabbath years while you were dwelling upon it. ³⁶As for those of you who survive, I will cast a faintness into their hearts in the land of their enemies. The sound of a driven leaf shall put them to flight. Fleeing as

though from the sword, they shall fall though none pursues. [37]With no one pursuing, they shall stumble over one another as before the sword. You shall not be able to stand your ground before your enemies, [38]but shall perish among the nations; and the land of your enemies shall consume you.

[39]Those of you who survive shall be heartsick over their iniquity in the land of your enemies; more, they shall be heartsick over the iniquities of their fathers; [40]and they shall confess their iniquity and the iniquity of their fathers, in that they trespassed against Me, yea, were hostile to Me. [41]When I, in turn, have been hostile to them and have removed them into the land of their enemies, then at last shall their obdurate[c] heart humble itself, and they shall atone for their iniquity. [42]Then will I remember My covenant with Jacob; I will remember also My covenant with Isaac, and also My covenant with Abraham; and I will remember the land.

[43]For the land shall be forsaken of them, making up for its sabbath years by being desolate of them, while they atone for their iniquity; for the abundant reason that they rejected My rules and spurned My laws. [44]Yet, even then, when they are in the land of their enemies, I will not reject them or spurn them so as to destroy them, annulling My covenant with them: for I the LORD am their God. [45]I will remember in their favor the covenant with the ancients, whom I freed from the land of Egypt in the sight of the nations to be their God: I, the LORD.

[46]These are the laws, rules, and instructions that the LORD established, through Moses on Mount Sinai, between Himself and the Israelite people.

# 27

The LORD spoke to Moses, saying:
[2]Speak to the Israelite people and say to them: When anyone explicitly[a] vows to the LORD the equivalent for a human being, [3]the following scale shall apply: If it is a male from twenty to sixty years of age, the equivalent is fifty shekels of silver by the

---

[c] Others "uncircumcised," lit. "blocked"

[a] Cf. note at Lev. 22.21

sanctuary weight; [4]if it is a female, the equivalent is thirty shekels. [5]If the age is from five years to twenty years, the equivalent is twenty shekels for a male and ten shekels for a female. [6]If the age is from one month to five years, the equivalent for a male is five shekels of silver, and the equivalent for a female is three shekels of silver. [7]If the age is sixty years or over, the equivalent is fifteen shekels in the case of a male and ten shekels for a female. [8]But if one cannot afford the equivalent, he shall be presented before the priest, and the priest shall assess him; the priest shall assess him according to what the vower can afford.

[9]If [the vow concerns] any animal that may be brought as an offering to the LORD, any such that may be given to the LORD shall be holy. [10]One may not exchange or substitute another for it, either good for bad, or bad for good; if one does substitute one animal for another, the thing vowed and its substitute shall both be holy. [11]If [the vow concerns] any unclean animal that may not be brought as an offering to the LORD, the animal shall be presented before the priest, [12]and the priest shall assess it. Whether [b-]high or low,[-b] whatever assessment is set by the priest shall stand; [13]and if he wishes to redeem it, he must add one-fifth to its assessment.

[14]If anyone consecrates his house to the LORD, the priest shall assess it. Whether high or low, as the priest assesses it, so it shall stand; [15]and if he who has consecrated his house wishes to redeem it, he must add one-fifth to the sum at which it was assessed, and it shall be his.

[16]If anyone consecrates to the LORD any land that he holds, its assessment shall be in accordance with its seed requirement: fifty shekels of silver to a *homer* of barley seed. [17]If he consecrates his land as of the jubilee year, its assessment stands. [18]But if he consecrates his land after the jubilee, the priest shall compute the price according to the years that are left until the jubilee year, and its assessment shall be so reduced; [19]and if he who consecrated the land wishes to redeem it, he must add one-fifth to the sum at which it was assessed, and it shall pass to him. [20]But if he does not redeem the land, and the land is sold to another, it

b-b *Lit. "good or bad"*

shall no longer be redeemable: [21]when it is released in the jubilee, the land shall be holy to the LORD, as land proscribed; it becomes the priest's holding.

[22]If he consecrates to the LORD land that he purchased, which is not land of his holding, [23]the priest shall compute for him the proportionate assessment up to the jubilee year, and he shall pay the assessment as of that day, a sacred donation to the LORD. [24]In the jubilee year the land shall revert to him from whom it was bought, whose holding the land is. [25]All assessments shall be by the sanctuary weight, the shekel being twenty *gerahs*.

[26]A firstling of animals, however, which—as a firstling—is the LORD'S, cannot be consecrated by anybody; whether ox or sheep, it is the LORD's. [27]But if it is of unclean animals, it may be ransomed as its assessment, with one-fifth added; if it is not redeemed, it shall be sold at its assessment.

[28]But of all that anyone owns, be it man or beast or land of his holding, nothing that he has proscribed for the LORD may be sold or redeemed; every proscribed thing is totally consecrated to the LORD. [29]No human being who has been proscribed can be ransomed: he shall be put to death.

[30]All tithes from the land, whether seed from the ground or fruit from the tree, are the LORD's; they are holy to the LORD. [31]If anyone wishes to redeem any of his tithes, he must add one-fifth to them. [32]All tithes of the herd or flock—of all that passes under the shepherd's staff, every tenth one—shall be holy to the LORD. [33]He must not look out for good as against bad, or make substitution for it. If he does make substitution for it, then it and its substitute shall both be holy: it cannot be redeemed.

[34]These are the commandments that the LORD gave Moses for the Israelite people on Mount Sinai.

חזק

במדבר

# NUMBERS

# במדבר

# NUMBERS

1 On the first day of the second month, in the second year following the exodus from the land of Egypt, the LORD spoke to Moses in the wilderness of Sinai, in the Tent of Meeting, saying: ²Take a census of the whole Israelite community by the clans of *ª⁻its ancestral houses,⁻ª* listing the names, every male, head by head. ³You and Aaron shall record them by their groups, from the age of twenty years up, all those in Israel who are able to bear arms. ⁴Associated with you shall be a man from each tribe, each one the head of his ancestral house.

⁵These are the names of the men who shall assist you:

From Reuben, Elizur son of Shedeur.

⁶From Simeon, Shelumiel son of Zurishaddai.

⁷From Judah, Nahshon son of Amminadab.

⁸From Issachar, Nethanel son of Zuar.

⁹From Zebulun, Eliab son of Helon.

¹⁰From the sons of Joseph:

from Ephraim, Elishama son of Ammihud:

from Manasseh, Gamaliel son of Pedahzur.

¹¹From Benjamin, Abidan son of Gideoni.

¹²From Dan, Ahiezer son of Ammishaddai.

¹³From Asher, Pagiel son of Ochran.

¹⁴From Gad, Eliasaph son of Deuel.

¹⁵From Naphtali, Ahira son of Enan.

¹⁶Those are the elected of the assembly, the chieftains of their ancestral tribes: they are the heads of the contingents of Israel.

¹⁷So Moses and Aaron took those men, who were designated by name, ¹⁸and on the first day of the second month they convoked the whole community, who were registered by the

---

ª⁻ª *I.e. of its tribes*

clans of their ancestral houses—the names of those aged twenty years and over being listed head by head. <sup>19</sup>As the LORD had commanded Moses, so he recorded them in the wilderness of Sinai.

<sup>20</sup>They totaled as follows:

The descendants of Reuben, Israel's first-born, the registration of the clans of their ancestral house, as listed by name, head by head, all males aged twenty years and over, all who were able to bear arms—<sup>21</sup>those enrolled from the tribe of Reuben: 46,500.

<sup>22</sup>Of the descendants of Simeon, the registration of the clans of their ancestral house, their enrollment as listed by name, head by head, all males aged twenty years and over, all who were able to bear arms—<sup>23</sup>those enrolled from the tribe of Simeon: 59,300.

<sup>24</sup>Of the descendants of Gad, the registration of the clans of their ancestral house, as listed by name, aged twenty years and over, all who were able to bear arms—<sup>25</sup>those enrolled from the tribe of Gad: 45,650.

<sup>26</sup>Of the descendants of Judah, the registration of the clans of their ancestral house, as listed by name, aged twenty years and over, all who were able to bear arms—<sup>27</sup>those enrolled from the tribe of Judah: 74,600.

<sup>28</sup>Of the descendants of Issachar, the registration of the clans of their ancestral house, as listed by name, aged twenty years and over, all who were able to bear arms—<sup>29</sup>those enrolled from the tribe of Issachar: 54,400.

<sup>30</sup>Of the descendants of Zebulun, the registration of the clans of their ancestral house, as listed by name, aged twenty years and over, all who were able to bear arms—<sup>31</sup>those enrolled from the tribe of Zebulun: 57,400.

<sup>32</sup>Of the descendants of Joseph:

Of the descendants of Ephraim, the registration of the clans of their ancestral house, as listed by name, aged twenty years and over, all who were able to bear arms—<sup>33</sup>those enrolled from the tribe of Ephraim: 40,500.

³⁴Of the descendants of Manasseh, the registration of the clans of their ancestral house, as listed by name, aged twenty years and over, all who were able to bear arms—³⁵those enolled from the tribe of Manasseh: 32,200.

³⁶Of the descendants of Benjamin, the registration of the clans of their ancestral house, as listed by name, aged twenty years and over, all who were able to bear arms—²⁷those enrolled from the tribe of Benjamin: 35,400.

³⁸Of the descendants of Dan, the registration of the clans of their ancestral house, as listed by name, aged twenty years and over, all who were able to bear arms—³⁹those enrolled from the tribe of Dan: 62,700.

⁴⁰Of the descendants of Asher, the registration of the clans of their ancestral house, as listed by name, aged twenty years and over, all who were able to bear arms—⁴¹those enrolled from the tribe of Asher: 41,500.

⁴²[Of] the descendants of Naphtali, the registration of the clans of their ancestral house as listed by name, aged twenty years and over, all who were able to bear arms—⁴³those enrolled from the tribe of Naphtali: 53,400.

⁴⁴Those are the enrollments recorded by Moses and Aaron and by the chieftains of Israel, who were twelve in number, one man to each ancestral house. ⁴⁵All the Israelites, aged twenty years and over, enrolled by ancestral houses, all those in Israel who were able to bear arms—⁴⁶all who were enrolled came to 603,550.

⁴⁷The Levites, however, were not recorded among them by their ancestral tribe. ⁴⁸For the LORD had spoken to Moses, saying: ⁴⁹Do not on any account enroll the tribe of Levi or take a census of them with the Israelites. ⁵⁰You shall put the Levites in charge of the Tabernacle of the Pact, all its furnishings, and everything that pertains to it: they shall carry the Tabernacle and all its furnishings, and they shall tend it; and they shall camp around the Tabernacle. ⁵¹When the Tabernacle is to set out, the Levites shall take it down, and when the Tabernacle is to be pitched, the Levites shall set it up; any outsider who encroaches

shall be put to death. [52]The Israelites shall encamp troop by troop, each man with his division and each under his standard. [53]The Levites, however, shall camp around the Tabernacle of the Pact, that wrath may not strike the Israelite community; the Levites shall stand guard around the Tabernacle of the Pact.

[54]The Israelites did accordingly; just as the LORD had commanded Moses, so they did.

2 The LORD spoke to Moses and Aaron, saying: [2]The Israelites shall camp each with his standard, under the banners of their ancestral house; they shall camp around the Tent of Meeting at a distance.

[3]Camped on the front, or east side: the standard of the division of Judah, troop by troop.
   Chieftain of the Judites: Nahshon son of Amminadab. [4]His troop, as enrolled: 74,600.
   [5]Camping next to it:
      the tribe of Issachar.
      Chieftain of the Issacharites: Nethanel son of Zuar. [6]His troop, as enrolled: 54,400.
      [7]The tribe of Zebulun.
      Chieftain of the Zebulunites: Eliab son of Helon. [8]His troop, as enrolled: 57,400.
[9]The total enrolled in the division of Judah: 186,400, for all troops. These shall march first.

[10]On the south: the standard of the division of Reuben, troop by troop. Chieftain of the Reubenites: Elizur son of Shedeur. [11]His troop, as enrolled: 46,500.
   [12]Camping next to it:
      The tribe of Simeon.
      Chieftain of the Simeonites: Shelumiel son of Zurishaddai. [13]His troop, as enrolled: 59,300.

<sup>14</sup>And the tribe of Gad.

Chieftain of the Gadites: Eliasaph son of Reuel. <sup>15</sup>His troop, as enrolled: 45,650.

<sup>16</sup>The total enrolled in the division of Reuben: 151,450, for all troops. These shall march second.

<sup>17</sup>Then, midway between the divisions, the Tent of Meeting, the division of the Levites, shall move. As they camp, so they shall march, each in position, by their standards.

<sup>18</sup>On the west: the standard of the division of Ephraim, troop by troop. Chieftain of the Ephraimites: Elishama son of Ammihud. <sup>19</sup>His troop, as enrolled: 40,500.
<sup>20</sup>Next to it:

The tribe of Manasseh.

Chieftain of the Manassites: Gamaliel son of Pedahzur. <sup>21</sup>His troop, as enrolled: 32,200.

<sup>22</sup>And the tribe of Benjamin.

Chieftain of the Benjaminites: Abidan son of Gideoni. <sup>23</sup>His troop, as enrolled: 35,400.

<sup>24</sup>The total enrolled in the division of Ephraim: 108,100 for all troops. These shall march third.

<sup>25</sup>On the north: the standard of the division of Dan, troop by troop. Chieftain of the Danites: Ahiezer son of Ammishaddai. <sup>26</sup>His troop, as enrolled: 62,700.
<sup>27</sup>Camping next to it:

The tribe of Asher.

Chieftain of the Asherites: Pagiel son of Ochran. <sup>28</sup>His troop, as enrolled: 41,500.

<sup>29</sup>And the tribe of Naphtali.

Chieftain of the Naphtalites: Ahira son of Enan. <sup>30</sup>His troop, as enrolled: 53,400.

<sup>31</sup>The total enrolled in the division of Dan: 157,600. These shall march last, by their standards.

³²Those are the enrollments of the Israelites by ancestral houses. The total enrolled in the divisions, for all troops: 603,550. ³³The Levites, however, were not recorded among the Israelites, as the LORD had commanded Moses.

³⁴The Israelites did accordingly; just as the LORD had commanded Moses, so they camped by their standards, and so they marched, each with his clan according to his ancestral house.

3 This is the line of Aaron and Moses at the time that the LORD spoke with Moses on Mount Sinai. ²These were the names of Aaron's sons: Nadab, the first-born, and Abihu, Eleazar and Ithamar; ³those were the names of Aaron's sons, the anointed priests who were ordained for priesthood. ⁴But Nadab and Abihu died *-by the will-* of the LORD, when they offered alien fire before the LORD in the wilderness of Sinai; and they left no sons. So it was Eleazar and Ithamar who served as priests in the lifetime of their father Aaron.

⁵The LORD spoke to Moses, saying: ⁶Advance the tribe of Levi and place them in attendance upon Aaron the priest to serve him. ⁷They shall perform duties for him and for the whole community before the Tent of Meeting, doing the work of the Tabernacle. ⁸They shall take charge of all the furnishings of the Tent of Meeting—a duty on behalf of the Israelites—doing the work of the Tabernacle. ⁹You shall assign the Levites to Aaron and to his sons: they are formally assigned to him from among the Israelites. ¹⁰You shall make Aaron and his sons responsible for observing their priestly duties; and any outsider who encroaches shall be put to death.

¹¹The LORD spoke to Moses, saying: ¹²I hereby take the Levites from among the Israelites in place of all the first-born, the first issue of the womb among the Israelites: the Levites shall be Mine. ¹³For every first-born is Mine: at the time that I smote every first-born in the land of Egypt, I consecrated every first-born in Israel, man and beast, to Myself, to be Mine, the LORD's.

¹⁴The LORD spoke to Moses in the wilderness of Sinai, saying:

a-a Others "before"

254

¹⁵Record the Levites by ancestral house and by clan; record every male among them from the age of one month up. ¹⁶So Moses recorded them at the command of the LORD, as he was bidden. ¹⁷These were the sons of Levi by name: Gershon, Kohath, and Merari. ¹⁸These were the names of the sons of Gershon by clan: Libni and Shimei. ¹⁹The sons of Kohath by clan: Amram and Izhar, Hebron and Uzziel. ²⁰The sons of Merari by clan: Mahli and Mushi.

These were the clans of the Levites within their ancestral houses:

²¹To Gershon belonged the clan of the Libnites and the clan of the Shimeites; those were the clans of the Gershonites. ²²The recorded entries of all their males from the age of one month up, as recorded, came to 7,500. ²³The clans of the Gershonites were to camp behind the Tabernacle, to the west. ²⁴The chieftain of the ancestral house of the Gershonites was Eliasaph son of Lael. ²⁵The duties of the Gershonites in the Tent of Meeting comprised: the tabernacle,ᵇ the tent, its covering, and the screen for the entrance of the Tent of Meeting; ²⁶the hangings of the enclosure, the screen for the entrance of the enclosure which surrounds the Tabernacle, the cords thereof, and the altar—all the service connected with these.

²⁷To Kohath belonged the clan of the Amramites, the clan of the Izharites, the clan of the Hebronites, and the clan of the Uzzielites; those were the clans of the Kohathites. ²⁸All the listed males from the age of one month up came to 8,600, attending to the duties of the sanctuary. ²⁹The clans of the Kohathites were to camp along the south side of the Tabernacle. ³⁰The chieftain of the ancestral house of the Kohathite clans was Elizaphan son of Uzziel. ³¹Their duties comprised: the ark, the table, the lampstand, the altars, and the sacred utensils that were used with them, and the screenᶜ—all the service connected with these. ³²The head chieftain of the Levites was Eleazar son of Aaron the priest, in charge of those attending to the duties of the sanctuary.

³³To Merari belonged the clan of the Mahlites and the clan of

ᵇ *See note on Exod. 26.1*
ᶜ *I.e. the screening curtain; cf. 4–5*

the Mushites; those were the clans of Merari. ³⁴The recorded entries of all their males from the age of one month up came to 6,200. ³⁵The chieftain of the ancestral house of the clans of Merari was Zuriel son of Abihail. They were to camp along the north side of the Tabernacle. ³⁶The assigned duties of the Merarites comprised: the planks of the Tabernacle, its bars, posts, and sockets, and all its furnishings—all the service connected with these; ³⁷also the posts around the enclosure and their sockets, pegs, and cords.

³⁸Those who were to camp before the Tabernacle, in front—before the Tent of Meeting, on the east—were Moses and Aaron and his sons, attending to the duties of the sanctuary, as a duty on behalf of the Israelites; and any outsider who encroached was to be put to death. ³⁹All the Levites who were recorded, whom at the LORD's command Moses and Aaron recorded by their clans, all the males from the age of one month up, came to 22,000.

⁴⁰The LORD said to Moses: Record every first-born male of the Israelite people from the age of one month up, and make a list of their names; ⁴¹and take the Levites for Me, the LORD, in place of every first-born among the Israelite people, and the cattle of the Levites in place of every first-born among the cattle of the Israelites. ⁴²So Moses recorded all the first-born among the Israelites, as the LORD had commanded him. ⁴³All the first-born males as listed by name, recorded from the age of one month up, came to 22,273.

⁴⁴The LORD spoke to Moses, saying: ⁴⁵Take the Levites in place of all the first-born among the Israelite people, and the cattle of the Levites in place of their cattle; and the Levites shall be Mine, the LORD's. ⁴⁶And as the redemption price of the 273 Israelite first-born over and above the number of the Levites, ⁴⁷take five shekels per head—take this by the sanctuary weight, twenty *gerahs* to the shekel—⁴⁸and give the money to Aaron and his sons as the redemption price for those who are in excess. ⁴⁹So Moses took the redemption money from those over and above

the ones redeemed by the Levites; [50]he took the money from the first-born of the Israelites, 1,365 sanctuary shekels. [51]And Moses gave the redemption money to Aaron and his sons at the Lord's bidding, as the Lord had commanded Moses.

**4** The Lord spoke to Moses and Aaron, saying:
[2]Take a [separate] census of the Kohathites among the Levites, by the clans of their ancestral house, [3]from the age of thirty years up to the age of fifty, all who are subject to service, to perform tasks for the Tent of Meeting. [4]This is the responsibility of the Kohathites in the Tent of Meeting: the most sacred objects.

[5]At the breaking of camp, Aaron and his sons shall go in and take down the screening curtain and cover the Ark of the Pact with it. [6]They shall lay a covering of dolphin skin over it and spread a cloth of pure blue on top; and they shall put its poles in place.
[7]Over the table of display they shall spread a blue cloth; they shall place upon it the bowls, the ladles, the jars, and the libation jugs; and the regular bread shall rest upon it. [8]They shall spread over these a crimson cloth which they shall cover with a covering of dolphin skin; and they shall put the poles in place.
[9]Then they shall take a blue cloth and cover the lampstand for lighting, with its lamps, its tongs, and its fire pans, as well as all the oil vessels that are used in its service. [10]They shall put it and all its furnishings into a covering of dolphin skin,[a] which they shall then place on a carrying frame.
[11]Next they shall spread a blue cloth over the altar of gold and cover it with a covering of dolphin skin; and they shall put its poles in place. [12]They shall take all the service vessels with which the service in the sanctuary is performed, put them into a blue cloth and cover them with a covering of dolphin skin, which they shall then place on a carrying frame. [13]They shall remove

[a] *See note b at Exod. 25.5*

the ashes from the [copper] altar and spread a purple cloth over it. [14]Upon it they shall place all the vessels that are used in its service: the fire pans, the flesh hooks, the scrapers, and the basins—all the vessels of the altar—and over it they shall spread a covering of dolphin skin; and they shall put its poles in place.

[15b]When Aaron and his sons have finished covering the sacred objects and all the furnishings of the sacred objects at the breaking of camp, only then shall the Kohathites come and lift them, so that they do not come in contact with the sacred objects and die. These things in the Tent of Meeting shall be the porterage of the Kohathites.

[16]Responsibility shall rest with Eleazar son of Aaron the priest for the lighting oil, the aromatic incense, the regular meal offering, and the anointing oil—responsibility for the whole Tabernacle and for everything consecrated that is in it or in its vessels.

[17]The LORD spoke to Moses and Aaron, saying: [18]Do not let the group of Kohathite clans be cut off from the Levites. [19]Do this with them, that they may live and not die when they approach the most sacred objects: let Aaron and his sons go in and assign each of them to his duties and to his porterage. [20]But let not [the Kohathites] go inside and [c]witness the dismantling of the sanctuary,[c] lest they die.

נשא

[21]The LORD spoke to Moses: [22]Take a census of the Gershonites also, by their ancestral house and by their clans. [23]Record them from the age of thirty years up to the age of fifty, all who are subject to service in the performance of tasks for the Tent of Meeting. [24]These are the duties of the Gershonite clans as to labor and porterage: [25]they shall carry the cloths of the Tabernacle, the Tent of Meeting with its covering, the covering of dolphin skin that is on top of it, and the screen for the entrance of the Tent of Meeting; [26]the hangings of the enclosure, the screen at the entrance of the gate of the enclosure that sur-

b *Continuing v. 4*
c-c *Others "look at the sacred objects even for a moment"*

rounds the Tabernacle, the cords thereof, and the altar, and all their service equipment and all their accessories; and they shall perform the service. [27]All the duties of the Gershonites, all their porterage and all their service, shall be performed on orders from Aaron and his sons; you shall make them responsible for attending to all their porterage. [28]Those are the duties of the Gershonite clans for the Tent of Meeting; they shall attend to them under the direction of Ithamar son of Aaron the priest.

[29]As for the Merarites, you shall record them by the clans of their ancestral house; [30]you shall record them from the age of thirty years up to the age of fifty, all who are subject to service in the performance of the duties for the Tent of Meeting. [31]These are their porterage tasks in connection with their various duties for the Tent of Meeting: the planks, the bars, the posts, and the sockets of the Tabernacle; [32]the posts around the enclosure and their sockets, pegs, and cords—all these furnishings and their service: you shall list by name the objects that are their porterage tasks. [33]Those are the duties of the Merarite clans, pertaining to their various duties in the Tent of Meeting under the direction of Ithamar son of Aaron the priest.

[34]So Moses, Aaron, and the chieftains of the community recorded the Kohathites by the clans of their ancestral house, [35]from the age of thirty years up to the age of fifty, all who were subject to service for work relating to the Tent of Meeting. [36]Those recorded by their clans came to 2,750. [37]That was the enrollment of the Kohathite clans, all those who performed duties relating to the Tent of Meeting, whom Moses and Aaron recorded at the command of the LORD through Moses.

[38]The Gershonites who were recorded by the clans of their ancestral house, [39]from the age of thirty years up to the age of fifty, all who were subject to service for work relating to the Tent of Meeting—[40]those recorded by the clans of their ancestral house came to 2,630. [41]That was the enrollment of the Gershonite clans, all those performing duties relating to the Tent of Meeting whom Moses and Aaron recorded at the command of the LORD.

⁴²The enrollment of the Merarite clans by the clans of their ancestral house, ⁴³from the age of thirty years up to the age of fifty, all who were subject to service for work relating to the Tent of Meeting—⁴⁴those recorded by their clans came to 3,200. ⁴⁵That was the enrollment of the Merarite clans which Moses and Aaron recorded at the command of the LORD through Moses.

⁴⁶All the Levites whom Moses, Aaron, and the chieftains of Israel recorded by the clans of their ancestral houses, ⁴⁷from the age of thirty years up to the age of fifty, all who were subject to duties of service and porterage relating to the Tent of Meeting —⁴⁸those recorded came to 8,580. ⁴⁹Each one was given responsibility for his service and porterage at the command of the LORD through Moses, and each was recorded as the LORD had commanded Moses.

5 The LORD spoke to Moses, saying: ²Instruct the Israelites to remove from camp anyone with an ᵃ‑eruption or a discharge‑ᵃ and anyone defiled by a corpse. ³Remove male and female alike; put them outside the camp so that they do not defile the camp of those in whose midst I dwell.

⁴The Israelites did so, putting them outside the camp; as the LORD had spoken to Moses, so the Israelites did.

⁵The LORD spoke to Moses, saying: ⁶Speak to the Israelites: When a man or woman commits any wrong toward a fellow man, thus breaking faith with the LORD, and that person realizes his guilt, ⁷he shall confess the wrong that he has done. He shall make restitution in the principal amount and add one-fifth to it, giving it to him whom he has wronged. ⁸If the man has no kinsmanᵇ to whom restitution can be made, the amount repaid shall go to the LORD for the priest—in addition to the ram of expiation with which expiation is made on his behalf.ᶜ ⁹So, too, any gift among the sacred donations that the Israelites offer

a-a *See Lev. 13, 15*
b *Lit. "redeemer"*
c *Cf. Lev. 5.15 f.*

shall be the priest's. ¹⁰And each shall retain his sacred donations: each priest shall keep what is given to him.

¹¹The LORD spoke to Moses, saying: ¹²Speak to the Israelite people and say to them:

If any man's wife has gone astray and broken faith with him ¹³in that a man has had carnal relations with her unbeknown to her husband, and she keeps secret the fact that she has defiled herself without being forced, and there is no witness against her—¹⁴but a fit of jealousy comes over him and he is wrought up about the wife who has defiled herself; or if a fit of jealousy comes over one and he is wrought up about his wife although she has not defiled herself—¹⁵the man shall bring his wife to the priest. And he shall bring as an offering for her one-tenth of an *ephah* of barley flour. No oil shall be poured upon it and no frankincense shall be laid on it, for it is a meal offering of jealousy, a meal offering of remembrance which recalls wrong-doing.

¹⁶The priest shall bring her forward and have her stand before the LORD. ¹⁷The priest shall take sacral water in an earthen vessel and, taking some of the earth that is on the floor of the Tabernacle, the priest shall put it into the water. ¹⁸After he has made the woman stand before the LORD, the priest shall bare the woman's head*ᵈ* and place upon her hands the meal offering of remembrance, which is a meal offering of jealousy. And in the priest's hands shall be the water of bitterness ᵉ·that induces the spell.·ᵉ ¹⁹The priest shall adjure the woman, saying to her, "If no man has lain with you, if you have not gone astray in defilement while married to your husband, be immune to harm from this water of bitterness that induces the spell. ²⁰But if you have gone astray while married to your husband and have defiled yourself, if a man other than your husband has had carnal relations with you"—²¹here the priest shall administer the curse of adjuration to the woman, as the priest goes on to say to the woman—"may

ᵈ *See note at Lev. 10.6*
ᵉ⁻ᵉ *Meaning of Heb uncertain*

261

the Lord make you a curse and an imprecation among your people, as the Lord causes your thigh to sag and your belly to distend; ²²may this water that induces the spell enter your body, causing the belly to distend and the thigh to sag." And the woman shall say, "Amen, amen!"

²³The priest shall put these curses down in writing and rub it off into the water of bitterness. ²⁴He is to make the woman drink the water of bitterness that induces the spell, so that the spell-inducing water may enter into her to bring on bitterness. ²⁵Then the priest shall take from the woman's hand the meal offering of jealousy, elevate the meal offering before the Lord, and present it on the altar. ²⁶The priest shall scoop out of the meal offering a token part of it and turn it into smoke on the altar. Last, he shall make the woman drink the water. ²⁷Once he has made her drink the water—if she has defiled herself by breaking faith with her husband, the spell-inducing water shall enter into her to bring on bitterness, so that her belly shall distend and her thigh shall sag; and the woman shall become a curse among her people. ²⁸But if the woman has not defiled herself and is pure, she shall be unharmed and able to retain seed.

²⁹This is the ritual in cases of jealousy, when a woman goes astray while married to her husband and defiles herself, ³⁰or when a fit of jealousy comes over a man and he is wrought up over his wife: the woman shall be made to stand before the Lord and the priest shall carry out all this ritual with her. ³¹The man shall be clear of guilt; but that woman shall suffer for her guilt.

6 The Lord spoke to Moses, saying: ²Speak to the Israelites and say to them: If anyone, man or woman, explicitly*a* utters a nazirite's vow, to set himself apart for the Lord, ³he shall abstain from wine and any other intoxicant; he shall not drink vinegar of wine or of any other intoxicant, neither shall he drink anything in which grapes have been steeped, nor eat grapes fresh or

---

a *See note at Lev. 22.21*

dried. ⁴Throughout his term as nazirite, he may not eat anything that is obtained from the grapevine, even seeds or skin.ᵇ

⁵Throughout the term of his vow as nazirite, no razor shall touch his head; it shall remain consecrated until the completion of his term as nazirite of the LORD, the hair of his head being left to grow untrimmed. ⁶Throughout the term that he has set apart for the LORD, he shall not go in where there is a dead person. ⁷Even if his father or mother, or his brother or sister should die, he must not defile himself for them, ᶜ‑since hair set apart for his God‑ᶜ is upon his head: ⁸throughout his term as nazirite he is consecrated to the LORD.

⁹If a person dies suddenly near him,ᵈ defiling his consecrated hair, he shall shave his head on the day he becomes clean; he shall shave it on the seventh day. ¹⁰On the eighth day he shall bring two turtledoves or two pigeons to the priest, at the entrance of the Tent of Meeting. ¹¹The priest shall offer one as a sin offering and the other as a burnt offering, and make expiation on his behalf for the guilt that he incurred through the corpse. That same day he shall reconsecrate his head ¹²and rededicate to the LORD his term as nazirite; and he shall bring a lamb in its first year as a penalty offering. The previous period shall be void, since his consecrated hair was defiled.

¹³This is the ritual for the nazirite: On the day that his term as nazirite is completed, heᵉ shall be brought to the entrance of the Tent of Meeting. ¹⁴As his offering to the LORD he shall present: one male lamb in its first year without blemish, for a burnt offering; one ewe lamb in its first year, without blemish, for a sin offering; one ram without blemish for an offering of well-being; ¹⁵a basket of unleavened cakes of choice flour with oil mixed in, and unleavened wafers spread with oil; and the proper meal offerings and libations.

¹⁶The priest shall present them before the LORD and offer the sin offering and the burnt offering. ¹⁷He shall offer the ram as a sacrifice of well-being to the LORD, together with the basket of unleavened cakes; the priest shall also offer the meal offerings

ᵇ *Meaning of Heb* ḥarṣannim *and* zag *uncertain*
ᶜ‑ᶜ *Others "his consecration unto God"*
ᵈ *Cf. Num. 19.14–16*
ᵉ *Or "it," i.e. the consecrated hair; cf. v. 19*

and the libations. [18]The nazirite shall then shave his consecrated hair, at the entrance of the Tent of Meeting, and take the locks of his consecrated hair and put them on the fire that is under the sacrifice of well-being.

[19]The priest shall take the shoulder of the ram when it has been boiled, one unleavened cake from the basket, and one unleavened wafer, and place them on the hands of the nazirite after he has shaved his consecrated hair. [20]The priest shall elevate them as an elevation offering before the LORD; and this shall be a sacred donation for the priest, in addition to the breast of the elevation offering and the thigh of gift offering. After that the nazirite may drink wine.

[21]Such is the obligation of a nazirite; except that he who vows an offering to the LORD of what he can afford, beyond his nazirite requirements, must do exactly according to the vow that he has made beyond his obligation as a nazirite.

[22]The LORD spoke to Moses: [23]Speak to Aaron and his sons: Thus shall you bless the people of Israel. Say to them:

[24]The LORD bless you and protect you!

[25]The LORD [f]deal kindly and graciously with you![f]

[26]The LORD [g]bestow His favor[g] upon you and grant you peace![h]

[27]Thus they shall link My name with the people of Israel, and I will bless them.

7 On the day that Moses finished setting up the Tabernacle, he anointed and consecrated it and all its furnishings, as well as the altar and its utensils. When he had anointed and consecrated them, [2]the chieftains of Israel, the heads of ancestral houses, namely, the chieftains of the tribes, those who were in charge of enrollment, drew near[a] [3]and brought their offering before the LORD: six draught carts and twelve oxen, a cart for every two chieftains and an ox for each one.

When they had brought them before the Tabernacle, [4]the

---

[f-f] Others *"make His face to shine upon thee and be gracious to thee"*
[g-g] Others *"lift up His countenance"*    [h] Or *"friendship"*

[a] Cf. Exod. 14.10

LORD said to Moses: ⁵Accept these from them for use in the service of the Tent of Meeting, and give them to the Levites according to their respective services.

⁶Moses took the carts and the oxen and gave them to the Levites. ⁷Two carts and four oxen he gave to the Gershonites, as required for their service, ⁸and four carts and eight oxen he gave to the Merarites, as required for their service—under the direction of Ithamar son of Aaron the priest. ⁹But to the Kohathites he did not give any; since theirs was the service of the [most] sacred objects, their porterage was by shoulder.

¹⁰The chieftains also brought the dedication offering for the altar upon its being anointed. As the chieftains were presenting their offerings before the altar, ¹¹the LORD said to Moses: Let them present their offerings for the dedication of the altar, one chieftain each day.

¹²The one who presented his offering on the first day was Nahshon son of Amminadab of the tribe of Judah. ¹³His offering: one silver bowl weighing 130 shekels and one silver basin of 70 shekels by the sanctuary weight, both filled with choice flour with oil mixed in, for a meal offering; ¹⁴one gold ladle of 10 shekels, filled with incense; ¹⁵one bull of the herd, one ram, and one lamb in its first year, for a burnt offering; ¹⁶one goat for a sin offering; ¹⁷and for his sacrifice of well-being: two oxen, five rams, five he-goats, and five yearling lambs. That was the offering of Nahshon son of Amminadab.

¹⁸On the second day, Nethanel son of Zuar, chieftain of Issachar, made his offering. ¹⁹He presented as his offering: one silver bowl weighing 130 shekels and one silver basin of 70 shekels by the sanctuary weight, both filled with choice flour with oil mixed in, for a meal offering; ²⁰one gold ladle of 10 shekels, filled with incense; ²¹one bull of the herd, one ram, and one lamb in its first year, for a burnt offering; ²²one goat for a sin offering; ²³and for his sacrifice of well-being: two oxen, five rams, five he-goats, and five yearling lambs. That was the offering of Nethanel son of Zuar.

²⁴On the third day, it was the chieftain of the Zebulunites,

Eliab son of Helon. [25]His offering: one silver bowl weighing 130 shekels and one silver basin of 70 shekels by the sanctuary weight, both filled with choice flour with oil mixed in, for a meal offering; [26]one gold ladle of 10 shekels, filled with incense; [27]one bull of the herd, one ram, and one lamb in its first year, for a burnt offering; [28]one goat for a sin offering; [29]and for his sacrifice of well-being: two oxen, five rams, five he-goats, and five yearling lambs. That was the offering of Eliab son of Helon.

[30]On the fourth day, it was the chieftain of the Reubenites, Elizur son of Shedeur. [31]His offering: one silver bowl weighing 130 shekels and one silver basin of 70 shekels by the sanctuary weight, both filled with choice flour with oil mixed in, for a meal offering; [32]one gold ladle of 10 shekels, filled with incense; [33]one bull of the herd, one ram, and one lamb in its first year, for a burnt offering; [34]one goat for a sin offering; [35]and for his sacrifice of well-being: two oxen, five rams, five he-goats, and five yearling lambs. That was the offering of Elizur son of Shedeur.

[36]On the fifth day, it was the chieftain of the Simeonites, Shelumiel son of Zurishaddai. [37]His offering: one silver bowl weighing 130 shekels and one silver basin of 70 shekels by the sanctuary weight, both filled with choice flour with oil mixed in, for a meal offering; [38]one gold ladle of 10 shekels, filled with incense; [39]one bull of the herd, one ram, and one lamb in its first year, for a burnt offering; [40]one goat for a sin offering; [41]and for his sacrifice of well-being: two oxen, five rams, five he-goats, and five yearling lambs. That was the offering of Shelumiel son of Zurishaddai.

[42]On the sixth day, it was the chieftain of the Gadites, Eliasaph son of Deuel. [43]His offering: one silver bowl weighing 130 shekels and one silver basin of 70 shekels by the sanctuary weight, both filled with choice flour with oil mixed in, for a meal offering; [44]one gold ladle of 10 shekels, filled with incense; [45]one bull of the herd, one ram, and one lamb in its first year, for a burnt offering; [46]one goat for a sin offering; [47]and for his sacrifice of well-being: two oxen, five rams, five he-goats, and five yearling lambs. That was the offering of Eliasaph son of Deuel.

⁴⁸On the seventh day, it was the chieftain of the Ephraimites, Elishama son of Ammihud. ⁴⁹His offering: one silver bowl weighing 130 shekels and one silver basin of 70 shekels by the sanctuary weight, both filled with choice flour with oil mixed in, for a meal offering; ⁵⁰one gold ladle of 10 shekels, filled with incense; ⁵¹one bull of the herd, one ram, and one lamb in its first year, for a burnt offering; ⁵²one goat for a sin offering; ⁵³and for his sacrifice of well-being: two oxen, five rams, five he-goats, and five yearling lambs. That was the offering of Elishama son of Ammihud.

⁵⁴On the eighth day, it was the chieftain of the Manasites, Gamaliel son of Pedahzur. ⁵⁵His offering: one silver bowl weighing 130 shekels and one silver basin of 70 shekels by the sanctuary weight, both filled with choice flour with oil mixed in, for a meal offering; ⁵⁶one gold ladle of 10 shekels, filled with incense; ⁵⁷one bull of the herd, one ram, and one lamb in its first year, for a burnt offering; ⁵⁸one goat for a sin offering; ⁵⁹and for his sacrifice of well-being: two oxen, five rams, five he-goats, and five yearling lambs. That was the offering of Gamaliel son of Pedahzur.

⁶⁰On the ninth day, it was the chieftain of the Benjaminites, Abidan son of Gideoni. ⁶¹His offering: one silver bowl weighing 130 shekels and one silver basin of 70 shekels by the sanctuary weight, both filled with choice flour with oil mixed in, for a meal offering; ⁶²one gold ladle of 10 shekels, filled with incense; ⁶³one bull of the herd, one ram, and one lamb in its first year, for a burnt offering; ⁶⁴one goat for a sin offering; ⁶⁵and for his sacrifice of well-being: two oxen, five rams, five he-goats, and five yearling lambs. That was the offering of Abidan son of Gideoni.

⁶⁶On the tenth day, it was the chieftain of the Danites, Ahiezer son of Ammishaddai. ⁶⁷His offering: one silver bowl weighing 130 shekels and one silver basin of 70 shekels by the sanctuary weight, both filled with choice flour with oil mixed in, for a meal offering; ⁶⁸one gold ladle of 10 shekels, filled with incense; ⁶⁹one bull of the herd, one ram, and one lamb in its first year, for a burnt offering; ⁷⁰one goat for a sin offering; ⁷¹and for his sac-

rifice of well-being: two oxen, five rams, five he-goats, and five yearling lambs. That was the offering of Ahiezer son of Ammishaddai.

[72]On the eleventh day, it was the chieftain of the Asherites, Pagiel son of Ochran. [73]His offering: one silver bowl weighing 130 shekels and one silver basin of 70 shekels by the sanctuary weight, both filled with choice flour with oil mixed in, for a meal offering; [74]one gold ladle of 10 shekels, filled with incense; [75]one bull of the herd, one ram, and one lamb in its first year, for a burnt offering; [76]one goat for a sin offering; [77]and for his sacrifice of well-being: two oxen, five rams, five he-goats, and five yearling lambs. That was the offering of Pagiel son of Ochran.

[78]On the twelfth day, it was the chieftain of the Naphtalites, Ahira son of Enan. [79]His offering: one silver bowl weighing 130 shekels and one silver basin of 70 shekels by the sanctuary weight, both filled with choice flour with oil mixed in, for a meal offering; [80]one gold ladle of 10 shekels, filled with incense; [81]one bull of the herd, one ram, and one lamb in its first year, for a burnt offering; [82]one goat for a sin offering; [83]and for his sacrifice of well-being: two oxen, five rams, five he-goats, and five yearling lambs. That was the offering of Ahira son of Enan.

[84]This was the dedication offering for the altar from the chieftains of Israel upon its being anointed: silver bowls, 12; silver basins, 12; gold ladles, 12. [85]Silver per bowl, 130; per basin, 70. Total silver of vessels, 2,400 sanctuary shekels. [86]The 12 gold ladles filled with incense—10 sanctuary shekels per ladle—total gold of the ladles, 120.

[87]Total of herd animals for burnt offerings, 12 bulls; of rams, 12; of yearling lambs, 12—with their proper meal offerings; of goats for sin offerings, 12. [88]Total of herd animals for sacrifices of well-being, 24 bulls; of rams, 60; of he-goats, 60; of yearling lambs, 60. That was the dedication offering for the altar after its anointing.

[89]When Moses went into the Tent of Meeting to speak with Him, he would hear the Voice addressing him from above the

cover that was on top of the Ark of the Pact between the two
cherubim; thus He spoke to him.

בהעלתך

**8** The LORD spoke to Moses, saying: ²Speak to Aaron and say
to him, "When you mount*a* the lamps, let the seven lamps give
light at the front of the lampstand." ³Aaron did so; he mounted
the lamps at the front of the lampstand, as the LORD had commanded Moses.—⁴Now this is how the lampstand was made: it
was hammered work of gold, hammered from base to petal.
According to the pattern that the LORD had shown Moses, so
was the lampstand made.

⁵The LORD spoke to Moses, saying: ⁶Take the Levites from
among the Israelites and cleanse them. ⁷This is what you shall do
to them to cleanse them: sprinkle on them water of purification,
and let them go over their whole body with a razor, and wash
their clothes; thus they shall be cleansed. ⁸Let them take a bull of
the herd, and with it a meal offering of choice flour with oil
mixed in, and you take a second bull of the herd for a sin
offering. ⁹You shall bring the Levites forward before the Tent
of Meeting. Assemble the whole Israelite community, ¹⁰and
bring the Levites forward before the LORD. Let the Israelites lay
their hands upon the Levites, ¹¹and let Aaron designate*b* the
Levites before the LORD as an elevation offering from the Israelites, that they may perform the service of the LORD. ¹²The
Levites shall now lay their hands upon the heads of the bulls;
one shall be offered to the LORD as a sin offering and the other as
a burnt offering, to make expiation for the Levites.

¹³You shall place the Levites in attendance upon Aaron and
his sons, and designate them as an elevation offering to the
LORD. ¹⁴Thus you shall set the Levites apart from the Israelites,
and the Levites shall be Mine. ¹⁵Thereafter the Levites shall be
qualified for the service of the Tent of Meeting, once you have
cleansed them and designated them as an elevation offering.
¹⁶For they are formally assigned to Me from among the Israel-

---

a *Cf. Exod. 25.37*
b *Lit. "elevate"*

ites: I have taken them for Myself in place of all the first issue of the womb, of all the first-born of the Israelites. [17]For every first-born among the Israelites, man as well as beast, is Mine; I consecrated them to Myself at the time that I smote every first-born in the land of Egypt. [18]Now I take the Levites instead of every first-born of the Israelites; [19]and from among the Israelites I formally assign the Levites to Aaron and his sons, to perform the service for the Israelites in the Tent of Meeting and to make expiation for the Israelites, so that no plague may afflict the Israelites ʿfor comingʿ too near the sanctuary.

[20]Moses, Aaron, and the whole Israelite community did with the Levites accordingly; just as the LORD had commanded Moses in regard to the Levites, so the Israelites did with them. [21]The Levites purified themselves and washed their clothes; and Aaron designated them as an elevation offering before the LORD, and Aaron made expiation for them to cleanse them. [22]Thereafter the Levites were qualified to perform their service in the Tent of Meeting, under Aaron and his sons. As the LORD had commanded Moses in regard to the Levites, so they did to them.

[23]The LORD spoke to Moses, saying: [24]This is the rule for the Levites. From twenty-five years of age up they shall participate in the work force in the service of the Tent of Meeting; [25]but at the age of fifty they shall retire from the work force and shall serve no more. [26]They may assist their brother Levites at the Tent of Meeting by standing guard, but they shall perform no labor. Thus you shall deal with the Levites in regard to their duties.

9 The LORD spoke to Moses in the wilderness of Sinai, on the first new moon of the second year following the exodus from the land of Egypt, saying: [2]Let the Israelite people offer the passover sacrifice at its set time: [3]you shall offer it on the fourteenth

c-c *Lit. "when the Israelites come"*

day of this month, at twilight, at its set time; you shall offer it in accordance with all its rules and rites.

⁴Moses instructed the Israelites to offer the passover sacrifice; ⁵and they offered the passover sacrifice in the first month, on the fourteenth day of the month, at twilight, in the wilderness of Sinai. Just as the LORD had commanded Moses, so the Israelites did.

⁶But there were some men who were unclean by reason of a corpse and could not offer the passover sacrifice on that day. Appearing that same day before Moses and Aaron, ⁷those men said to them,ᵃ "Unclean though we are by reason of a corpse, why must we be debarred from presenting the LORD's offering at its set time with the rest of the Israelites?" ⁸Moses said to them, "Stand by, and let me hear what instructions the LORD gives about you."

⁹And the LORD spoke to Moses, saying: ¹⁰Speak to the Israelite people, saying: When any of you or of your posterity who are defiled by a corpse or are on a long journey would offer a passover sacrifice to the LORD, ¹¹they shall offer it in the second month, on the fourteenth day of the month, at twilight. They shall eat it with unleavened bread and bitter herbs, ¹²and they shall not leave any of it over until morning. They shall not break a bone of it. They shall offer it in strict accord with the law of the passover sacrifice. ¹³But if a man who is clean and not on a journey refrains from offering the passover sacrifice, that person shall be cut off from his kin, for he did not present the LORD's offering at its set time; that man shall bear his guilt.

¹⁴And when a stranger who resides with you would offer a passover sacrifice to the LORD, he must offer it in accordance with the rules and rites of the passover sacrifice. There shall be one law for you, whether stranger or citizen of the country.

¹⁵On the day that the Tabernacle was set up, the cloud covered the Tabernacle, the Tent of the Pact; and in the evening it rested over the Tabernacle in the likeness of fire until morning.

ᵃ Lit. "him"

271

¹⁶It was always so: the cloud covered it, appearing as fire by night. ¹⁷And whenever the cloud lifted from the Tent, the Israelites would set out accordingly; and at the spot where the cloud settled, there the Israelites would make camp. ¹⁸At a command of the LORD the Israelites broke camp, and at a command of the LORD they made camp: they remained encamped as long as the cloud stayed over the Tabernacle. ¹⁹When the cloud lingered over the Tabernacle many days, the Israelites observed the LORD's mandate and did not journey on. ²⁰At such times as the cloud rested over the Tabernacle for but a few days, they remained encamped at a command of the LORD, and broke camp at a command of the LORD. ²¹And at such times as the cloud stayed from evening until morning, they broke camp as soon as the cloud lifted in the morning. Day or night, whenever the cloud lifted, they would break camp. ²²Whether it was two days or a month or a year—however long the cloud lingered over the Tabernacle—the Israelites remained encamped and did not set out; only when it lifted did they break camp. ²³On a sign from the LORD they made camp and on a sign from the LORD they broke camp; they observed the LORD's mandate at the LORD's bidding through Moses.

10 The LORD spoke to Moses, saying: ²Have two silver trumpets made; make them of hammered work. They shall serve you to summon the community and to set the divisions in motion. ³When both are blown in long blasts,ᵃ the whole community shall assemble before you at the entrance of the Tent of Meeting; ⁴and if only one is blown, the chieftains, heads of Israel's contingents, shall assemble before you. ⁵But when you sound short blasts, the divisions encamped on the east shall move forward; ⁶and when you sound short blasts a second time, those encamped on the south shall move forward. Thus short blasts shall be blown for setting them in motion, ⁷while to convoke the

---

ᵃ *Meaning of Heb uncertain*

congregation you shall blow long blasts, not short ones. [8]The trumpets shall be blown by Aaron's sons, the priests; they shall be for you an institution for all time throughout the ages.

[9]When you are at war in your land against an aggressor who attacks you, you shall sound short blasts on the trumpets, that you may be remembered before the LORD your God and be delivered from your enemies. [10]And on your joyous occasions— your fixed festivals and new moon days—you shall sound the trumpets over your burnt offerings and your sacrifices of well-being. They shall be a reminder of you before your God: I, the LORD, am your God.

[11]In the second year, on the twentieth day of the second month, the cloud lifted from the Tabernacle of the Pact [12]and the Israelites set out on their journeys from the wilderness of Sinai. The cloud came to rest in the wilderness of Paran.

[13]When the march was to begin, at the LORD's command through Moses, [14]the first standard to set out, troop by troop, was the division of Judah. In command of its troops was Nahshon son of Amminadab; [15]in command of the tribal troop of Issachar, Nethanel son of Zuar; [16]and in command of the tribal troop of Zebulun, Eliab son of Helon.

[17]Then the Tabernacle would be taken apart; and the Gershonites and the Merarites, who carried the Tabernacle, would set out.

[18]The next standard to set out, troop by troop, was the division of Reuben. In command of its troop was Elizur son of Shedeur; [19]in command of the tribal troop of Simeon, Shelumiel son of Zurishaddai; [20]and in command of the tribal troop of Gad, Eliasaph son of Deuel.

[21]Then the Kohathites, who carried the sacred objects, would set out; and by the time they arrived, the Tabernacle would be set up again.

[22]The next standard to set out, troop by troop, was the di-

vision of Ephraim. In command of its troop was Elishama son of Ammihud; <sup>23</sup>in command of the tribal troop of Manasseh, Gamaliel son of Pedahzur; <sup>24</sup>and in command of the tribal troop of Benjamin, Abidan son of Gideoni.

<sup>25</sup>Then, as the rear guard of all the divisions, the standard of the division of Dan would set out, troop by troop. In command of its troop was Ahiezer son of Ammishaddai; <sup>26</sup>in command of the tribal troop of Asher, Pagiel son of Ochran; <sup>27</sup>and in command of the tribal troop of Naphtali, Ahira son of Enan.

<sup>28</sup>Such was the order of march of the Israelites, as they marched troop by troop.

<sup>29</sup>Moses said to Hobab son of Reuel the Midianite, Moses' father-in-law, "We are setting out for the place of which the LORD has said, 'I will give it to you.' Come with us and we will be generous with you; for the LORD has promised to be generous to Israel."

<sup>30</sup>"I will not go," he replied to him, "but will return to my native land." <sup>31</sup>He said, "Please do not leave us, inasmuch as you know where we should camp in the wilderness and can be our guide.<sup>b</sup> So if you come with us, we will extend to you the same bounty that the LORD grants us."

<sup>33</sup>They marched from the mountain of the LORD a distance of three days. The Ark of the Covenant of the LORD traveled in front of them on that three days' journey to seek out a resting place for them; <sup>34</sup>and the LORD's cloud kept above them by day, as they moved on from camp.

<sup>35</sup>When the Ark was to set out, Moses would say:

> Advance, O LORD!
> May Your enemies be scattered,
> And may Your foes flee before You!

<sup>36</sup>And when it halted, he would say:

> <sup>c-</sup>Return, O LORD,
> You who are Israel's myriads of thousands!<sup>-c</sup>

---

<sup>b</sup> Lit. "eyes"
<sup>c-c</sup> Others "Return, O LORD, unto the ten thousands of the families of Israel!"

11 The people took to complaining bitterly before the LORD. The LORD heard and was incensed: a fire of the LORD broke out against them, ravaging the outskirts of the camp. ²The people cried out to Moses. Moses prayed to the LORD, and the fire died down. ³That place was named Taberah,ᵃ because a fire of the LORD had broken out against them.

⁴The riffraff in their midst felt a gluttonous craving; and then the Israelites wept and said, "If only we had meat to eat! ⁵We remember the fish that we used to eat free in Egypt, the cucumbers, the melons, the leeks, the onions, and the garlic. ⁶Now our gullets are shriveled. There is nothing at all! Nothing but this manna to look to!"

⁷Now the manna was like coriander seed, and in color it was like bdellium. ⁸The people would go about and gather it, grind it between millstones or pound it in a mortar, boil it in a pot, and make it into cakes. It tasted like rich cream.ᵇ ⁹When the dew fell on the camp at night, the manna would fall upon it.

¹⁰Moses heard the people weeping, every clan apart, each person at the entrance of his tent. The LORD was very angry, and Moses was distressed. ¹¹And Moses said to the LORD, "Why have You dealt ill with Your servant, and why have I not enjoyed Your favor, that You have laid the burden of all this people upon me? ¹²Did I conceive all this people, did I bear them, that You should say to me, 'Carry them in your bosom as a nurse carries an infant,' to the land that You have promised on oath to their fathers? ¹³Where am I to get meat to give to all this people, when they whine before me and say, 'Give us meat to eat!' ¹⁴I cannot carry all this people by myself, for it is too much for me. ¹⁵If You would deal thus with me, kill me rather, I beg You, and let me see no more of my wretchedness!"

¹⁶Then the LORD said to Moses, "Gather for Me seventy of Israel's elders of whom you have experience as elders and officers of the people, and bring them to the Tent of Meeting and

ᵃ *From root* bʿr, *"to burn"*
ᵇ *Lit. "cream of oil (or, fat)"*

275

let them take their place there with you. ¹⁷I will come down and speak with you there, and I will draw upon the spirit that is on you and put it upon them; they shall share the burden of the people with you, and you shall not bear it alone. ¹⁸And say to the people: ᶜ-Purify yourselves-ᶜ for tomorrow and you shall eat meat, for you have kept whining before the LORD and saying, 'If only we had meat to eat! Indeed, we were better off in Egypt!' The LORD will give you meat and you shall eat. ¹⁹You shall eat not one day, not two, not even five days or ten or twenty, ²⁰but a whole month, until it comes out of your nostrils and becomes loathsome to you. For you have rejected the LORD who is among you, by whining before Him and saying, 'Oh, why did we ever leave Egypt!' "

²¹But Moses said, "The people ᵈ-who are with me-ᵈ number six hundred thousand men; yet You say, 'I will give them enough meat to eat for a whole month.' ²²Could enough flocks and herds be slaughtered to suffice them? Or could all the fish of the sea be gathered for them to suffice them?" ²³And the LORD answered Moses, ᵉ-"Is there a limit to the LORD'S power?-ᵉ You shall soon see whether what I have said happens to you or not!"

²⁴Moses went out and reported the words of the LORD to the people. He gathered seventy of the people's elders and stationed them around the Tent. ²⁵Then the LORD came down in a cloud and spoke to him; He drew upon the spirit that was on him and put it upon the seventy elders. And when the spirit rested upon them, they ᶠ-spoke in ecstasy,-ᶠ but did not continue.

²⁶Two men, one named Eldad and the other Medad, had remained in camp; yet the spirit rested upon them—they were among those recorded, but they had not gone out to the Tent— and they ᶠ-spoke in ecstasy-ᶠ in the camp. ²⁷A youth ran out and told Moses, saying, "Eldad and Medad are acting the prophet in the camp!" ²⁸And Joshua son of Nun, Moses' attendant from his youth, spoke up and said, "My lord Moses, restrain them!" ²⁹But Moses said to him, "Are you wrought up on my account? Would that all the LORD'S people were prophets, that the LORD put His

---

ᶜ-ᶜ *I.e. as for a sacrificial meal*
ᵈ-ᵈ *Lit. "in whose midst I am"*
ᵉ-ᵉ *Lit. "Is the* LORD'S *hand too short?"*
ᶠ-ᶠ *Others "prophesied"*

spirit upon them!" ³⁰Moses then reentered the camp together with the elders of Israel.

³¹A wind from the LORD started up, swept quail from the sea and strewed them over the camp, about a day's journey on this side and about a day's journey on that side, all around the camp, and some two cubits deep on the ground. ³²The people set to gathering quail all that day and night and all the next day—even he who gathered least had ten *homers*—and they spread them out all around the camp. ³³The meat was still between their teeth, nor yet chewed,ᵍ when the anger of the LORD blazed forth against the people and the LORD struck the people with a very severe plague. ³⁴That place was named Kibroth-hattaavah,ʰ because the people who had the craving were buried there.

³⁵Then the people set out from Kibroth-hattaavah for Hazeroth.

# 12

When they were in Hazeroth, ¹Miriam and Aaron spoke against Moses because of the Cushite woman he had married: "He married a Cushite woman!"

²They said, "Has the LORD spoken only through Moses? Has He not spoken through us as well?" The LORD heard it. ³Now Moses was a very humble man, more so than any other man on earth. ⁴Suddenly the LORD called to Moses, Aaron, and Miriam, "Come out, you three, to the Tent of Meeting." So the three of them went out. ⁵The LORD came down in a pillar of cloud, stopped at the entrance of the Tent, and called out, "Aaron and Miriam!" The two of them came forward; ⁶and He said, "Hear these My words: *ᵃ*When a prophet of the LORD arises among you, I*ᵃ* make Myself known to him in a vision, I speak with him in a dream. ⁷Not so with My servant Moses; he is trusted throughout My household. ⁸With him I speak mouth to mouth, plainly and not in riddles, and he beholds the likeness of the

---

ᵍ *Exact nuance of Heb* yikkareth *uncertain*

ʰ *I.e. "the graves of craving"*

ᵃ⁻ᵃ *Meaning of Heb uncertain. Others "If there be a prophet among you, I the* LORD*"*

LORD. How then did you not shrink from speaking against My servant Moses!" ⁹Still incensed with them, the LORD departed.

¹⁰As the cloud withdrew from the Tent, there was Miriam stricken with snow-white scales!*ᵇ* When Aaron turned toward Miriam, he saw that she was stricken with scales. ¹¹And Aaron said to Moses, "O my lord, account not to us the sin which we committed in our folly. ¹²Let her not be as one dead, who emerges from his mother's womb with half his flesh eaten away." ¹³So Moses cried out to the LORD, saying, "O God, pray heal her!"

¹⁴But the LORD said to Moses, "If her father spat in her face, would she not bear her shame for seven days? Let her be shut out of camp for seven days, and then let her be readmitted." ¹⁵So Miriam was shut out of camp seven days; and the people did not march on until Miriam was readmitted. ¹⁶After that the people set out from Hazeroth and encamped in the wilderness of Paran.

שלח לך

**13** The LORD spoke to Moses, saying, ²"Send men to scout the land of Canaan, which I am giving to the Israelite people; send one man from each of their ancestral tribes, each one a chieftain among them." ³So Moses, by the LORD's command, sent them out from the wilderness of Paran, all the men being leaders of the Israelites. ⁴And these were their names:

From the tribe of Reuben, Shammua son of Zaccur.

⁵From the tribe of Simeon, Shaphat son of Hori.

⁶From the tribe of Judah, Caleb son of Jephunneh.

⁷From the tribe of Issachar, Igal son of Joseph.

⁸From the tribe of Ephraim, Hosea*ᵃ* son of Nun.

⁹From the tribe of Benjamin, Palti son of Rafu.

¹⁰From the tribe of Zebulun, Gaddiel son of Sodi.

¹¹From the tribe of Joseph, namely, the tribe of Manasseh, Gaddi son of Susi.

¹²From the tribe of Dan, Ammiel son of Gemalli.

ᵇ *Cf. Lev. 13.2–3*

ᵃ *Or "Hoshea"*

¹³From the tribe of Asher, Sethur son of Michael.

¹⁴From the tribe of Naphtali, Nahbi son of Vophsi.

¹⁵From the tribe of Gad, Geuel son of Machi.

¹⁶Those were the names of the men whom Moses sent to scout the land; but Moses changed the name of Hosea[a] son of Nun to Joshua.

¹⁷When Moses sent them to scout the land of Canaan, he said to them, "Go up there into the Negeb and on into the hill country, ¹⁸and see what kind of country it is. Are the people who dwell in it strong or weak, few or many? ¹⁹Is the country in which they dwell good or bad? Are the towns they live in open or fortified? ²⁰Is the soil rich or poor? Is it wooded or not? And take pains to bring back some of the fruit of the land."—Now it happened to be the season of the first ripe grapes.

²¹They went up and scouted the land, from the wilderness of Zin to Rehob, at Lebo-hamath.[b] ²²They went up into the Negeb and came to Hebron, where lived Ahiman, Sheshai, and Talmai, the Anakites.—Now Hebron was founded seven years before Zoan of Egypt.—²³They reached the wadi Eshcol, and there they cut down a branch with a single cluster of grapes—it had to be borne on a carrying frame by two of them—and some pomegranates and figs. ²⁴That place was named the wadi Eshcol[c] because of the cluster that the Israelites cut down there.

²⁵At the end of forty days they returned from scouting the land. ²⁶They went straight to Moses and Aaron and the whole Israelite community at Kadesh in the wilderness of Paran, and they made their report to them and to the whole community, as they showed them the fruit of the land. ²⁷This is what they told him: "We came to the land you sent us to; it does indeed flow with milk and honey, and this is its fruit. ²⁸However, the people who inhabit the country are powerful, and the cities are fortified and very large; moreover, we saw the Anakites there. ²⁹Amalekites dwell in the Negeb region; Hittites, Jebusites, and Amorites inhabit the hill country; and Canaanites dwell by the Sea and along the Jordan."

b *Others "the entrance to Hamath"*

c *I.e. "cluster"*

³⁰Caleb hushed the people before Moses and said, "Let us by all means go up, and we shall gain possession of it, for we shall surely overcome it."

³¹But the men who had gone up with him said, "We cannot attack that people, for it is stronger than we." ³²Thus they spread calumnies among the Israelites about the land they had scouted, saying, "The country that we traversed and scouted is one that devours its settlers. All the people that we saw in it are men of great size; ³³we saw the Nephilim*ᵈ* there—the Anakites are part of the Nephilim—and we looked like grasshoppers to ourselves, and so we must have looked to them."

14 The whole community broke into loud cries, and the people wept that night. ²All the Israelites railed against Moses and Aaron. "If only we had died in the land of Egypt," the whole community shouted at them, "or if only we might die in this wilderness! ³Why is the LORD taking us to that land to fall by the sword? Our wives and children will be carried off! It would be better for us to go back to Egypt!" ⁴And they said to one another, "Let us *ᵃ*head back for*ᵃ* Egypt."

⁵Then Moses and Aaron fell on their faces before all the assembled congregation of the Israelites. ⁶And Joshua son of Nun and Caleb son of Jephunneh, of those who had scouted the land, rent their clothes ⁷and exhorted the whole Israelite community: "The land that we traversed and scouted is an exceedingly good land. ⁸If the LORD is pleased with us, He will bring us into that land, a land that flows with milk and honey, and give it to us; ⁹only you must not rebel against the LORD. Have no fear then of the people of the country, for they are our prey*ᵇ*: their protection has departed from them, but the LORD is with us. Have no fear of them!" ¹⁰As the whole community threatened to pelt them with stones, the Presence of the LORD appeared in the Tent of Meeting to all the Israelites.

¹¹And the LORD said to Moses, "How long will this people

---

ᵈ *See Gen. 6.4*

ᵃ⁻ᵃ *Lit. "set the head and return to"; cf. Neh. 9.17. Others, "Let us make a captain and return to"*

ᵇ *Lit. "food (or, bread)"*

spurn Me, and how long will they have no faith in Me despite all the signs that I have performed in their midst? [12]I will strike them with pestilence and disown them, and I will make of you a nation far more numerous than they!" [13]But Moses said to the LORD, "When the Egyptians, from whose midst You brought up this people in Your might, hear the news, [14]they will tell it to the inhabitants of that land. Now they have heard that You, O LORD, are in the midst of this people; that You, O LORD, appear in plain sight when Your cloud rests over them and when You go before them in a pillar of cloud by day and in a pillar of fire by night. [15]If then You slay this people to a man, the nations who have heard Your fame will say, [16]'It must be because the LORD was powerless to bring that people into the land He had promised them on oath that He slaughtered them in the wilderness.' [17]Therefore, I pray, let my LORD's forbearance be great, as You have declared, saying,[c] [18]'The LORD! slow to anger and abounding in kindness; forgiving iniquity and transgression; yet not remitting all punishment, but visiting the iniquity of fathers upon children, upon the third and fourth generations.' [19]Pardon, I pray, the iniquity of this people according to Your great kindness, as You have forgiven this people ever since Egypt."

[20]And the LORD said, "I pardon, as you have asked. [21]Nevertheless, as I live and as the LORD's Presence fills the whole world, [22]none of the men who have seen My Presence and the signs that I have performed in Egypt and in the wilderness, and who have tried Me these many[d] times and have disobeyed Me, [23]shall see the land that I promised on oath to their fathers; none of those who spurn Me shall see it. [24]But My servant Caleb, because he was imbued with a different spirit and remained loyal to Me— him will I bring into the land that he entered, and his offspring shall hold it as a possession. [25]Now the Amalekites and the Canaanites occupy the valleys. Start out, then, tomorrow and march into the wilderness by way of the Sea of Reeds."[e]

[26]The LORD spoke further to Moses and Aaron, [27]"How much longer shall that wicked community keep muttering against Me?

---

c *Cf. Exod. 34.6–7*
d *Lit. "ten"; cf. note at Gen. 31.41*
e *See note at Exod. 10.19*

Very well, I have heeded the incessant muttering of the Israelites against Me. [28]Say to them: 'As I live,' says the LORD, 'I will
do to you just as you have urged Me. [29]In this very wilderness
shall your carcasses drop. Of all of you who were recorded in
your various lists from the age of twenty years up, you who have
muttered against Me, [30]not one shall enter the land in which I
swore[f] to settle you—save Caleb son of Jephunneh and Joshua
son of Nun. [31]Your children who, you said, would be carried
off—these will I allow to enter; they shall know the land that you
have rejected. [32]But your carcasses shall drop in this wilderness,
[33]while your children roam the wilderness for forty years, suffering for your faithlessness, until the last of your carcasses is
down in the wilderness. [34]You shall bear your punishment for
forty years, corresponding to the number of days—forty days—
that you scouted the land: a year for each day. Thus you shall
know what it means to thwart Me. [35]I the LORD have spoken:
Thus will I do to all that wicked band that has banded together
against Me: in this very wilderness they shall die to the last
man.'"

[36]As for the men whom Moses sent to scout the land, those
who came back and caused the whole community to mutter
against him by spreading calumnies about the land—[37]those
who spread such calumnies about the land died of plague, by the
will of the LORD. [38]Of those men who had gone to scout the
land, only Joshua son of Nun and Caleb son of Jephunneh
survived.

[39]When Moses repeated these words to all the Israelites, the
people were overcome by grief. [40]Early next morning they set
out toward the crest of the hill country, saying, "We are prepared to go up to the place that the LORD has spoken of, for we
were wrong." [41]But Moses said, "Why do you transgress the
LORD's command? This will not succeed. [42]Do not go up, lest you
be routed by your enemies, for the LORD is not in your midst.
[43]For the Amalekites and the Canaanites will be there to face
you, and you will fall by the sword, inasmuch as you have turned
from following the LORD and the LORD will not be with you."

[f] *Lit. "raised my hand"*

⁴⁴Yet defiantly*g* they marched toward the crest of the hill country, though neither the LORD's Ark of the Covenant nor Moses stirred from the camp. ⁴⁵And the Amalekites and the Canaanites who dwelt in that hill country came down and dealt them a shattering blow at Hormah.

# 15 The LORD spoke to Moses, saying: ²Speak to the Israelite people and say to them:

When you enter the land that I am giving you to settle in, ³and would present an offering by fire to the LORD from the herd or from the flock, be it burnt offering or sacrifice, in fulfillment of a vow explicitly uttered,*a* or as a freewill offering, or at your fixed occasions, producing an odor pleasing to the LORD:

⁴The person who presents the offering to the LORD shall bring as a meal offering: a tenth of a measure of choice flour with a quarter of a *hin* of oil mixed in. ⁵You shall also offer, with the burnt offering or the sacrifice, a quarter of a *hin* of wine as a libation for each sheep.

⁶In the case of a ram, you shall present as a meal offering: two-tenths of a measure of choice flour with a third of a *hin* of oil mixed in; ⁷and a third of a *hin* of wine as a libation—as an offering of pleasing odor to the LORD.

⁸And if it is an animal from the herd that you offer to the LORD as a burnt offering or as a sacrifice, in fulfillment of a vow explicitly uttered or as an offering of well-being, ⁹there shall be offered a meal offering along with the animal: three-tenths of a measure of choice flour with half a *hin* of oil mixed in; ¹⁰and as libation you shall offer half a *hin* of wine—these being offerings by fire of pleasing odor to the LORD.

¹¹Thus shall be done with each ox, with each ram, and with any sheep or goat, ¹²as many as you offer; you shall do thus with each one, as many as there are. ¹³Every citizen, when presenting an offering by fire of pleasing odor to the LORD, shall do so with them.

g *Meaning of Heb uncertain*

a *See note at Lev. 22.21*

¹⁴And when, throughout the ages, a stranger who has taken up residence with you, or one who lives among you, would present an offering by fire of pleasing odor to the LORD—as you do, so *ᵇ⁻*shall it be done by ¹⁵the rest of the congregation.*⁻ᵇ* There shall be one law for you and for the resident stranger; it shall be a law for all time throughout the ages. You and the stranger shall be alike before the LORD; ¹⁶the same ritual and the same rule shall apply to you and to the stranger who resides among you.

¹⁷The LORD spoke to Moses, saying: ¹⁸Speak to the Israelite people and say to them:

When you enter the land to which I am taking you ¹⁹and you eat of the bread of the land, you shall set some aside as a gift to the LORD: ²⁰as the first yield of your baking,*ᶜ* you shall set aside a loaf as a gift; you shall set it aside as a gift like the gift from the threshing floor. ²¹You shall make a gift to the LORD from the first yield of your baking, throughout the ages.

²²If you unwittingly fail to observe any one of the commandments that the LORD has declared to Moses ²³—anything that the LORD has enjoined upon you through Moses—from the day that the LORD gave the commandment and on through the ages:

²⁴If this was done unwittingly, through the inadvertence of the community, the whole community shall present one bull of the herd as a burnt offering of pleasing odor to the LORD, with its proper meal offering and libation, and one he-goat as a sin offering. ²⁵The priest shall make expiation for the whole Israelite community and they shall be forgiven; for it was an error, and for their error they have brought their offering, an offering by fire to the LORD and their sin offering before the LORD. ²⁶The whole Israelite community and the stranger residing among them shall be forgiven, for it happened to the entire people through error.

²⁷In case it is an individual who has sinned unwittingly, he shall offer a she-goat in its first year as a sin offering. ²⁸The priest

ᵇ⁻ᵇ *Meaning of Heb uncertain*
ᶜ *Meaning of Heb* ʿarisah *uncertain*

shall make expiation before the LORD on behalf of the person who erred, for he sinned unwittingly, making such expiation for him that he may be forgiven. <sup>29</sup>For the citizen among the Israelites and for the stranger who resides among them—you shall have one ritual for anyone who acts in error.

<sup>30</sup>But the person, be he citizen or stranger, who acts defiantly<sup>d</sup> reviles the LORD; that person shall be cut off from among his people. <sup>31</sup>Because he has spurned the word of the LORD and violated His commandment, that person shall be cut off—he bears his guilt.

<sup>32</sup>Once, when the Israelites were in the wilderness, they came upon a man gathering wood on the sabbath day. <sup>33</sup>Those who found him as he was gathering wood brought him before Moses, Aaron, and the whole community. <sup>34</sup>He was placed in custody, for it had not been specified what should be done to him. <sup>35</sup>Then the LORD said to Moses, "The man shall be put to death: the whole community shall pelt him with stones outside the camp." <sup>36</sup>So the whole community took him outside the camp and stoned him to death—as the LORD had commanded Moses.

<sup>37</sup>The LORD said to Moses as follows: <sup>38</sup>Speak to the Israelite people and instruct them to make for themselves fringes on the corners of their garments throughout the ages; let them attach a cord of blue to the fringe at each corner. <sup>39</sup>That shall be your fringe; look at it and recall all the commandments of the LORD and observe them, so that you do not follow your heart and eyes in your lustful urge. <sup>40</sup>Thus you shall be reminded to observe all My commandments and to be holy to your God. <sup>41</sup>I the LORD am your God, who brought you out of the land of Egypt to be your God: I, the LORD your God.

קרח

**16** Now Korah, son of Izhar son of Kohath son of Levi, <sup>a</sup>betook himself,<sup>-a</sup> along with Dathan and Abiram sons of Eliab, <sup>b</sup>and On son of Peleth—descendants of Reuben<sup>-b</sup>—<sup>2</sup>to rise up

---

<sup>d</sup> *Lit. "with upraised hand"*

<sup>a-a</sup> *Lit. "took"; meaning of Heb uncertain*

<sup>b-b</sup> *According to Num. 26.5, 8–9, Eliab was son of Pallu, son of Reuben*

against Moses, together with two hundred and fifty Israelites, chieftains of the community, chosen in the assembly, men of repute. ³They combined against Moses and Aaron and said to them, "You have gone too far! For all the community are holy, all of them, and the LORD is in their midst. Why then do you raise yourselves above the LORD's congregation?"

⁴When Moses heard this, he fell on his face.ᶜ ⁵Then he spoke to Korah and all his company, saying, "Come morning, the LORD will make known who is His and who is holy, and will grant him access to Himself; He will grant access to the one He has chosen. ⁶Do this: You, Korah and all yourᵈ band, take fire pans, ⁷and tomorrow put fire in them and lay incense on them before the LORD. Then the man whom the LORD chooses, he shall be the holy one. You have gone too far, sons of Levi!"

⁸Moses said further to Korah, "Hear me, sons of Levi. ⁹Is it not enough for you that the God of Israel has set you apart from the community of Israel and given you access to Him, to perform the duties of the LORD's Tabernacle and to minister to the community and serve them? ¹⁰Now that He has advanced you and all your fellow Levites with you, do you seek the priesthood too? ¹¹Truly, it is against the LORD that you and all your company have banded together. For who is Aaron that you should rail against him?"

¹²Moses sent for Dathan and Abiram, sons of Eliab; but they said, "We will not come! ¹³Is it not enough that you brought us from a land flowing with milk and honey to have us die in the wilderness, that you would also lord it over us? ¹⁴ᵉ⁻Even if you hadᵉ brought us to a land flowing with milk and honey, and given us possession of fields and vineyards, should you gouge out those men's eyesᶠ? We will not come!" ¹⁵Moses was much aggrieved and he said to the LORD, "Pay no regard to their oblation. I have not taken the ass of any one of them, nor have I wronged any one of them."

¹⁶And Moses said to Korah, "Tomorrow, you and all your company appear before the LORD, you and they and Aaron.

---

ᶜ Perhaps in the sense of "his face fell"   ᵈ Lit. "his"

ᵉ⁻ᵉ Lit. "You have not even"

ᶠ "Those men's" is a euphemism for "our"; cf. I Sam. 29.4. Gouging out the eyes was punishment for runaway slaves and rebellious vassals; cf. II Kings 25.4-7; Jer. 39.4-7; 52.7-11

¹⁷Each of you take his fire pan and lay incense on it, and each of you bring his fire pan before the Lord, two hundred and fifty fire pans; you and Aaron also [bring] your fire pans." ¹⁸Each of them took his fire pan, put fire in it, laid incense on it, and took his place at the entrance of the Tent of Meeting, as did Moses and Aaron. ¹⁹Korah gathered the whole community against them at the entrance of the Tent of Meeting.

Then the Presence of the Lord appeared to the whole community, ²⁰and the Lord spoke to Moses and Aaron, saying, ²¹"Stand back from this community that I may annihilate them in an instant!" ²²But they fell on their faces and said, "O God, Source$^g$ of the breath of all flesh! When one man sins, will You be wrathful with the whole community?"

²³The Lord spoke to Moses, saying, ²⁴"Speak to the community and say: Withdraw from about the abodes of Korah, Dathan, and Abiram."

²⁵Moses rose and went to Dathan and Abiram, the elders of Israel following him. ²⁶He addressed the community, saying, "Move away from the tents of these wicked men and touch nothing that belongs to them, lest you be wiped out for all their sins." ²⁷So they withdrew from about the abodes of Korah, Dathan, and Abiram.

Now Dathan and Abiram had come out and they stood at the entrance of their tents, with their wives, their children, and their little ones. ²⁸And Moses said, "By this you shall know that it was the Lord who sent me to do all these things; that they are not of my own devising: ²⁹if these men die as all men do, if their lot be the common fate of all mankind, it was not the Lord who sent me. ³⁰But if the Lord brings about something unheard-of, so that the ground opens its mouth and swallows them up with all that belongs to them, and they go down alive into Sheol, you shall know that these men have spurned the Lord." ³¹Scarcely had he finished speaking all these words when the ground under them burst asunder, ³²and the earth opened its mouth and swallowed them up with their households, all Korah's people

g *Lit. "God"*

and all their possessions. ³³They went down alive into Sheol, with all that belonged to them; the earth closed over them and they vanished from the midst of the congregation. ³⁴All Israel around them fled at their shrieks, for they said, "The earth might swallow us!"

³⁵And a fire went forth from the LORD and consumed the two hundred and fifty men offering the incense.

**17** The LORD spoke to Moses, saying: ²Order Eleazar son of Aaron the priest to remove the fire pans—for they have become sacred—from among the charred remains; and scatter the coals abroad. ³ ᵃ[Remove] the fire pans of those who have sinned at the cost of their lives, and let them be made into hammered sheets as plating for the altar—for once they have been used for offering to the LORD, they have become sacred—and let them serve as a warning to the people of Israel. ⁴Eleazar the priest took the copper fire pans which had been used for offering by those who died in the fire; and they were hammered into plating for the altar, ⁵as the LORD had ordered him through Moses. It was to be a reminder to the Israelites, so that no outsider—one not of Aaron's offspring—should presume to offer incense before the LORD and suffer the fate of Korah and his band.

⁶Next day the whole Israelite community railed against Moses and Aaron, saying, "You two have brought death upon the LORD's people!" ⁷But as the community gathered against them, Moses and Aaron turned toward the Tent of Meeting; the cloud had covered it and the Presence of the LORD appeared.

⁸When Moses and Aaron reached the Tent of Meeting, ⁹the LORD spoke to Moses, saying, ¹⁰"Remove yourselves from this community, that I may annihilate them in an instant." They fell on their faces. ¹¹Then Moses said to Aaron, "Take the fire pan, and put on it fire from the altar. Add incense and take it quickly to the community and make expiation for them. For wrath has gone forth from the LORD: the plague has begun!" ¹²Aaron took it, as Moses had ordered, and ran to the midst of the congre-

ᵃ *Meaning of parts of verse uncertain*

gation, where the plague had begun among the people. He put on the incense and made expiation for the people; ¹³he stood between the dead and the living until the plague was checked. ¹⁴Those who died of the plague came to fourteen thousand and seven hundred, aside from those who died on account of Korah. ¹⁵Aaron then returned to Moses at the entrance of the Tent of Meeting, since the plague was checked.

¹⁶The LORD spoke to Moses, saying: ¹⁷Speak to the Israelite people and take from them—from the chieftains of their ancestral houses*b*—one staff for each chieftain of an ancestral house: twelve staffs in all. Inscribe each man's name on his staff, ¹⁸there being one staff for each head of an ancestral house; also inscribe Aaron's name on the staff of Levi. ¹⁹Deposit them in the Tent of Meeting before the Pact, where I meet with you. ²⁰The staff of the man whom I choose shall sprout, and I will rid*c* Myself of the incessant mutterings of the Israelites against you.

²¹Moses spoke thus to the Israelites. Their chieftains gave him a staff for each chieftain of an ancestral house, twelve staffs in all; among these staffs was that of Aaron. ²²Moses deposited the staffs before the LORD, in the Tent of the Pact. ²³The next day Moses entered the Tent of the Pact, and there the staff of Aaron of the house of Levi had sprouted: it had brought forth sprouts, produced blossoms, and borne almonds. ²⁴Moses then brought out all the staffs from before the LORD to all the Israelites; each identified and recovered his staff.

²⁵The LORD said to Moses, "Put Aaron's staff back before the Pact, to be kept as a lesson to rebels, so that their mutterings against Me may cease, lest they die." ²⁶This Moses did; just as the LORD had commanded him, so he did.

²⁷But the Israelites said to Moses, "Lo, we perish! We are lost, all of us lost! ²⁸Everyone who so much as ventures near the LORD's Tabernacle must die. Alas, we are doomed to perish!"

18 The LORD said to Aaron: You and your sons and the ancestral house under your charge shall bear any guilt con-

b *I.e. of their tribes*
c *Meaning of Heb* wahashikkothi *uncertain*

nected with the sanctuary; you and your sons alone shall bear any guilt connected with your priesthood. ²You shall also associate with yourself your kinsmen the tribe of Levi, your ancestral tribe, to be attached to you and to minister to you, while you and your sons under your charge are before the Tent of the Pact.ᵃ ³They shall discharge their duties to you and to the Tent as a whole, but they must not have any contact with the furnishings of the Shrine or with the altar, lest both they and you die. ⁴They shall be attached to you and discharge the duties of the Tent of Meeting, all the service of the Tent; but no outsider shall intrude upon you ⁵as you discharge the duties connected with the Shrine and the altar, that wrath may not again strike the Israelites.

⁶I hereby take your fellow Levites from among the Israelites; they are assigned to you in dedication to the LORD, to do the work of the Tent of Meeting; ⁷while you and your sons shall be careful to perform your priestly duties in everything pertaining to the altar and to what is behind the curtain. I make your priesthood a service of dedication; any outsider who encroaches shall be put to death.

⁸The LORD spoke further to Aaron: I hereby give you charge of My gifts, all the sacred donations of the Israelites; I grant them to you and to your sons as a perquisite,ᵇ a due for all time. ⁹This shall be yours from the most holy sacrifices, ᶜthe offerings by fireᶜ: every such offering that they render to Me as most holy sacrifices, namely, every meal offering, sin offering, and guilt offering of theirs, shall belong to you and your sons. ¹⁰You shall partake of them as most sacred donations: only males may eat them; you shall treat them as consecrated.ᵈ

¹¹This, too, shall be yours: the gift offeringsᵉ of their contributions, all the elevation offerings of the Israelites, I give to you, to your sons, and to the daughters that are with you, as a due for all time; everyone of your household who is clean may eat it.

¹²All the best of the new oil, wine, and grain—the choice parts

---

ᵃ *Meaning of latter part of verse uncertain*
ᵇ *See note at Lev. 7.35*
ᶜ⁻ᶜ *Meaning of Heb uncertain; lit. "from the fire"*
ᵈ *Or "they are consecrated for your use"*   ᵉ *Cf. Lev. 7.29 ff.*

that they present to the LORD—I give to you. ¹³The first fruits of everything in their land, that they bring to the LORD, shall be yours; everyone of your household who is clean may eat them. ¹⁴Everything that has been proscribed in Israel*f* shall be yours. ¹⁵The first issue of the womb of every being, man or beast, that is offered to the LORD, shall be yours; but you shall have the first-born of man redeemed, and you shall also have the firstling of unclean animals redeemed. ¹⁶Take as their redemption price,*g* from the age of one month up, the money equivalent of five shekels by the sanctuary weight, which is twenty *gerahs.* ¹⁷But the firstlings of cattle, sheep, or goats may not be redeemed; they are consecrated. You shall dash their blood against the altar, and turn their fat into smoke as an offering by fire for a pleasing odor to the LORD. ¹⁸But their meat shall be yours: it shall be yours like the breast of elevation offering and like the right thigh.

¹⁹All the sacred gifts that the Israelites set aside for the LORD I give to you, to your sons, and to the daughters that are with you, as a due for all time. It shall be an everlasting covenant of salt*h* before the LORD for you and for your offspring as well. ²⁰And the LORD said to Aaron: You shall, however, have no territorial share among them or own any portion in their midst; I am your portion and your share among the Israelites.

²¹And to the Levites I hereby give all the tithes in Israel as their share in return for the services that they perform, the services of the Tent of Meeting. ²²Henceforth, Israelites shall not trespass on the Tent of Meeting, and thus incur guilt and die: ²³only Levites shall perform the services of the Tent of Meeting; others*i* would incur guilt. It is the law for all time throughout the ages. But they shall have no territorial share among the Israelites; ²⁴for it is the tithes set aside by the Israelites as a gift to the LORD that I give to the Levites as their share. Therefore I have said concerning them: They shall have no territorial share among the Israelites.

²⁵The LORD spoke to Moses, saying: ²⁶Speak to the Levites

f *See Lev. 27.28*
g *I.e. for human first-born; cf. Num. 3.44 ff. For animals see Exod. 34.19 f.*
h *See Lev. 2.13*
i *Lit. "they"*

and say to them: When you receive from the Israelites their tithes, which I have assigned to you as your share, you shall set aside from them one-tenth of the tithe as a gift to the LORD. <sup>27</sup>This shall be accounted to you as your gift. As with the new grain from the threshing floor or the flow from the vat, <sup>28</sup>so shall you on your part set aside a gift for the LORD from all the tithes that you receive from the Israelites; and from them you shall bring the gift for the LORD to Aaron the priest. <sup>29</sup>You shall set aside all gifts due to the LORD from everything that is donated to you, from each thing its best portion, the part thereof that is to be consecrated.

<sup>30</sup>Say to them further: When you have removed the best part from it, you Levites may consider it the same as the yield of threshing floor or vat. <sup>31</sup>You and your households may eat it anywhere, for it is your recompense for your services in the Tent of Meeting. <sup>32</sup>You will incur no guilt through it, once you have removed the best part from it; but you must not profane the sacred donations of the Israelites, lest you die.

חקת

**19** The LORD spoke to Moses and Aaron, saying: <sup>2</sup>This is the ritual law that the LORD has commanded:

Instruct the Israelite people to bring you a red cow without blemish, in which there is no defect and on which no yoke has been laid. <sup>3</sup>You shall give it to Eleazar the priest. It shall be taken outside the camp and slaughtered in his presence. <sup>4</sup>Eleazar the priest shall take some of its blood with his finger and sprinkle it seven times toward the front of the Tent of Meeting. <sup>5</sup>The cow shall be burned in his sight—its hide, flesh, and blood shall be burned, its dung included—<sup>6</sup>and the priest shall take cedar wood, hyssop, and crimson stuff, and throw them into the fire consuming the cow. <sup>7</sup>The priest shall wash his garments and bathe his body in water; after that the priest may reenter the camp, but he shall be unclean until evening. <sup>8</sup>He who performed the burning shall also wash his garments in water, bathe his body in water, and be unclean until evening. <sup>9</sup>A man who is clean shall gather up the ashes of the cow and deposit them outside the camp in a clean place, to be kept for water of lustration[a] for the Israelite community. It is for cleansing. [10]He who gathers up the ashes of the cow shall also wash his clothes and be unclean until evening.

This shall be a permanent law for the Israelites and for the strangers who reside among you.

[11]He who touches the corpse of any human being shall be unclean for seven days. [12]He shall cleanse himself with it[b] on the third day and on the seventh day, and then be clean; if he fails to cleanse himself on the third and seventh days, he shall not be clean. [13]Whoever touches a corpse, the body of a person who has died, and does not cleanse himself, defiles the LORD's Tabernacle; that person shall be cut off from Israel. Since the water of lustration was not dashed on him, he remains unclean; his uncleanness is still upon him.

[14]This is the ritual: When a person dies in a tent, whoever enters the tent and whoever is in the tent shall be unclean seven days; [15]and every open vessel, with no lid fastened down, shall be unclean. [16]And in the open, anyone who touches a person who was killed[c] or who died naturally, or human bone, or a grave, shall be unclean seven days. [17]Some of the ashes[d] from the fire of cleansing shall be taken for the unclean person, and fresh water shall be added to them in a vessel. [18]A person who is clean shall take hyssop, dip it in the water, and sprinkle on the tent and on all the vessels and people who were there, or on him who touched the bones or the person who was killed or died naturally or the grave. [19]The clean person shall sprinkle it upon the unclean person on the third day and on the seventh day, thus cleansing him by the seventh day. He[e] shall then wash his clothes and bathe in water, and at nightfall he shall be clean. [20]If anyone who has become unclean fails to cleanse himself, that person shall be cut off from the congregation, for he has defiled the LORD's sanctuary. The water of lustration was not dashed on him: he is unclean.

[21]That shall be for them a law for all time. Further, he who

---

[a] Lit. "water for impurity"
[b] I.e. the ashes, as in v. 9
[c] Lit. "slain by the sword"
[d] Lit. "earth" or "dust"    [e] I.e. the person being cleansed

sprinkled the water of lustration shall wash his clothes; and whoever touches the water of lustration shall be unclean until evening. ²²Whatever that unclean person touches shall be unclean; and the person who touches him shall be unclean until evening.

20 The Israelites arrived in a body at the wilderness of Zin on the first new moon,ᵃ and the people stayed at Kadesh. Miriam died there and was buried there.

²The community was without water, and they joined against Moses and Aaron. ³The people quarreled with Moses, saying, "If only we had perished when our brothers perished at the instance of the LORD! ⁴Why have you brought the LORD's congregation into this wilderness for us and our beasts to die there? ⁵Why did you make us leave Egypt to bring us to this wretched place, a place with no grain or figs or vines or pomegranates? There is not even water to drink!"

⁶Moses and Aaron came away from the congregation to the entrance of the Tent of Meeting, and fell on their faces. The Presence of the LORD appeared to them, ⁷and the LORD spoke to Moses, saying, ⁸"You and your brother Aaron take the rod and assemble the community, and before their very eyes order the rock to yield its water. Thus you shall produce water for them from the rock and provide drink for the congregation and their beasts."

⁹Moses took the rod from before the LORD, as He had commanded him. ¹⁰Moses and Aaron assembled the congregation in front of the rock; and he said to them, "Listen, you rebels, shall we get water for you out of this rock?" ¹¹And Moses raised his hand and struck the rock twice with his rod. Out came copious water, and the community and their beasts drank.

¹²But the LORD said to Moses and Aaron, "Because you did not trust Me enough to affirm My sanctity in the sight of the Israelite people, therefore you shall not lead this congregation into the land that I have given them." ¹³Those are the Waters of

ᵃ *Of the fortieth year; cf. Num. 33.36–38*

Meribah*b*—meaning that the Israelites quarrelled with the LORD—through which He affirmed His sanctity.

<sup>14</sup>From Kadesh, Moses sent messengers to the king of Edom: "Thus says your brother Israel: You know all the hardships that have befallen us; <sup>15</sup>that our ancestors went down to Egypt, that we dwelt in Egypt a long time, and that the Egyptians dealt harshly with us and our ancestors. <sup>16</sup>We cried to the LORD and He heard our plea, and He sent a messenger*c* who freed us from Egypt. Now we are in Kadesh, the town on the border of your territory. <sup>17</sup>Allow us, then, to cross your country. We will not pass through fields or vineyards, and we will not drink water from wells. We will follow the king's highway, turning off neither to the right nor to the left until we have crossed your territory."

<sup>18</sup>But Edom answered him, "You shall not pass through us, else we will go out against you with the sword." <sup>19</sup>"We will keep to the beaten track," the Israelites said to them, "and if we or our cattle drink your water, we will pay for it. We ask only for passage on foot—it is but a small matter." <sup>20</sup>But they replied, "You shall not pass through!" And Edom went out against them in heavy force, strongly armed. <sup>21</sup>So Edom would not let Israel cross their territory, and Israel turned away from them.

<sup>22</sup>Setting out from Kadesh, the Israelites arrived in a body at Mount Hor. <sup>23</sup>At Mount Hor, on the boundary of the land of Edom, the LORD said to Moses and Aaron, <sup>24</sup>"Let Aaron be gathered to his kin: he is not to enter the land that I have assigned to the Israelite people, because you disobeyed my command about the waters of Meribah. <sup>25</sup>Take Aaron and his son Eleazar and bring them up on Mount Hor. <sup>26</sup>Strip Aaron of his vestments and put them on his son Eleazar. There Aaron shall be gathered *d*-unto the dead."-*d*

<sup>27</sup>Moses did as the LORD had commanded. They ascended Mount Hor in the sight of the whole community. <sup>28</sup>Moses stripped Aaron of his vestments and put them on his son Eleazar, and Aaron died there on the summit of the mountain.

---

b *I.e. "Quarrel"; cf. Exod. 17.7 and note b there*
c *Or "angel"*
d-d *Lit. "and die"*

When Moses and Eleazar came down from the mountain, ²⁹the whole community knew that Aaron had breathed his last. All the house of Israel bewailed Aaron thirty days.

# 21

When the Canaanite, king of Arad, who dwelt in the Negeb, learned that Israel was coming by the way of Atharim,ᵃ he engaged Israel in battle and took some of them captive. ²Then Israel made a vow to the LORD and said, "If You deliver this people into our hand, we will proscribeᵇ their towns." ³The LORD heeded Israel's plea and delivered up the Canaanites; and they and their cities were proscribed. So that place was named Hormah.ᶜ

⁴They set out from Mount Hor by way of the Sea of Reedsᵈ to skirt the land of Edom. But the people grew restive on the journey, ⁵and the people spoke against God and against Moses, "Why did you make us leave Egypt to die in the wilderness? There is no bread and no water, and we have come to loathe this miserable food." ⁶The LORD sent *seraph*ᵉ serpents against the people. They bit the people and many of the Israelites died. ⁷The people came to Moses and said, "We sinned by speaking against the LORD and against you. Intercede with the LORD to take away the serpents from us!" And Moses interceded for the people. ⁸Then the LORD said to Moses, "Make a *seraph* figure and mount it on a standard. And if anyone who is bitten looks at it, he shall recover." ⁹Moses made a copper serpent and mounted it on a standard; and when anyone was bitten by a serpent, he would look at the copper serpent and recover.

¹⁰The Israelites marched on and encamped at Oboth. ¹¹They set out from Oboth and encamped at Iye-abarim, in the wilderness bordering on Moab to the east. ¹²From there they set out and encamped at the wadi Zered. ¹³From there they set out and encamped beyond the Arnon, that is, in the wilderness that

---

ᵃ *Meaning of Heb* ha'atharim *uncertain. Targum and other ancient versions render* "the way [taken by] the scouts"

ᵇ *I.e. utterly destroy, reserving no booty except what is deposited in the Sanctuary; see Josh. 6.24*   ᶜ *Connected with* heḥerim *"to proscribe"*   ᵈ *See Exod. 10.19 note*

ᵉ *Cf. Isa. 14.29; 30.6. Others "fiery"; exact meaning of Heb* saraph *uncertain* extends from the territory of the Amorites. For the Arnon is the boundary of Moab, between Moab and the Amorites. [14]Therefore the Book of the Wars of the LORD speaks of [f]". . . Waheb in Suphah, and the wadis: the Arnon [15]with its tributary wadis, stretched along the settled country of Ar, hugging the territory of Moab . . ."

[16]And from there to Beer,[g] which is the well where the LORD said to Moses, "Assemble the people that I may give them water." [17]Then Israel sang this song:

Spring up, O well—sing to it—
[18]The well which the chieftains dug,
Which the nobles of the people started
With maces, with their own staffs.

And from Midbar[h] to Mattanah, [19]and from Mattanah to Nahaliel, and from Nahaliel to Bamoth, [20]and from Bamoth to the valley that is in the country of Moab, at the peak of Pisgah, overlooking the wasteland.[i]

[21]Israel now sent messengers to Sihon king of the Amorites, saying, [22]"Let me pass through your country. We will not turn off into fields or vineyards, and we will not drink water from wells. We will follow the king's highway until we have crossed your territory." [23]But Sihon would not let Israel pass through his territory. Sihon gathered all his people and went out against Israel in the wilderness. He came to Jahaz and engaged Israel in battle. [24]But Israel put them to the sword, and took possession of their land, from the Arnon to the Jabbok, as far as [Az] of the Ammonites, for Az[j] marked the boundary of the Ammonites. [25]Israel took all those towns. And Israel settled in all the towns of the Amorites, in Heshbon and all its dependencies.

[26]Now Heshbon was the city of Sihon king of the Amorites, who had fought against a former king of Moab and taken all his land from him as far as the Arnon. [27]Therefore the bards would recite:

"[k]Come to Heshbon; firmly built

---

[f] *The quotation that follows is a fragment; text and meaning are uncertain*
[g] *Lit. "well"*   [h] *Septuagint "the well" (=Beer); cf. v. 16*
[i] *Or "Jeshimon"*
[j] *Septuagint "Jazer," cf. v. 32. Others "for the boundary of the Ammonites was strong"*
[k] *The meaning of several parts of this ancient poem is no longer certain*

And well founded is Sihon's city.
<sup>28</sup>For fire went forth from Heshbon,
Flame from Sihon's city,
Consuming Ar of Moab,
The lords of Bamoth<sup>l</sup> by the Arnon.
<sup>29</sup>Woe to you, O Moab!
You are undone, O people of Chemosh!
His sons are rendered fugitive
And his daughters captive
By an Amorite king, Sihon."
<sup>30m</sup>Yet we have cast them down utterly,
Heshbon along with Dibon;
We have wrought desolation at Nophah,
Which is hard by Medeba.

<sup>31</sup>So Israel occupied the land of the Amorites. <sup>32</sup>Then Moses sent to spy out Jazer, and they captured its dependencies and dispossessed the Amorites who were there.

<sup>33</sup>They marched on and went up the road to Bashan, and King Og of Bashan, with all his people, came out to Edrei to engage them in battle. <sup>34</sup>But the LORD said to Moses, "Do not fear him, for I give him and all his people and his land into your hand. You shall do to him as you did to Sihon king of the Amorites who dwelt in Heshbon." <sup>35</sup>They defeated him and his sons and **22** all his people, until no remnant was left him; and they took possession of his country. <sup>1</sup>The Israelites then marched on and encamped in the steppes of Moab, across the Jordan from Jericho.

בלק

<sup>2</sup>Balak son of Zippor saw all that Israel had done to the Amorites.

<sup>3</sup>Moab was alarmed because that people was so numerous. Moab dreaded the Israelites, <sup>4</sup>and Moab said to the elders of

---

<sup>l</sup> *Cf. vv. 19 and 20 and Num. 22.21*
<sup>m</sup> *Meaning of verse uncertain. Alternatively:*

*"Their dominion is at an end      And from Nashim to Nophah,*
*From Heshbon to Dibon            Which is hard by Medeba."*

Midian, "Now this horde will lick clean all that is about us as an ox licks up the grass of the field."

Balak son of Zippor, who was king of Moab at that time, [5]sent messengers to Balaam son of Beor in Pethor, which is by the Euphrates,[a] in the land of his kinsfolk, to invite him, saying, "There is a people that came out of Egypt; it hides the earth from view, and it is settled next to me. [6]Come then, put a curse upon this people for me, since they are too numerous for me; perhaps I can thus defeat them and drive them out of the land. For I know that he whom you bless is blessed indeed, and he whom you curse is cursed."

[7]The elders of Moab and the elders of Midian, [b]versed in divination,[-b] set out. They came to Balaam and gave him Balak's message. [8]He said to them, "Spend the night here, and I shall reply to you as the LORD may instruct me." So the Moabite dignitaries stayed with Balaam.

[9]God came to Balaam and said, "What do these people want of you?" [10]Balaam said to God, "Balak son of Zippor, king of Moab, sent me this message: [11]Here is a people that came out from Egypt and hides the earth from view. Come now and curse them for me; perhaps I can engage them in battle and drive them off." [12]But God said to Balaam, "Do not go with them. You must not curse that people, for they are blessed."

[13]Balaam arose in the morning and said to Balak's dignitaries, "Go back to your own country, for the LORD will not let me go with you." [14]The Moabite dignitaries left, and they came to Balak and said, "Balaam refused to come with us."

[15]Then Balak sent other dignitaries, more numerous and distinguished than the first. [16]They came to Balaam and said to him, "Thus says Balak son of Zippor: Please do not refuse to come to me. [17]I will reward you richly and I will do anything you ask of me. Only come and damn this people for me." [18]Balaam replied to Balak's officials, "Though Balak were to give me his house full of silver and gold, I could not do anything, big or

---

a *Lit. "the River"*
b-b *Lit. "with divination in their power (hand)"*

little, contrary to the command of the LORD my God. ¹⁹So you, too, stay here overnight, and let me find out what else the LORD may say to me." ²⁰That night God came to Balaam and said to him, "If these men have come to invite you, you may go with them. But whatever I command you, that you shall do."

²¹When he arose in the morning, Balaam saddled his ass and departed with the Moabite dignitaries. ²²But God was incensed at his going; so an angel of the LORD placed himself in his way as an adversary.

He was riding on his she-ass, with his two servants alongside, ²³when the ass caught sight of the angel of the LORD standing in the way, with his drawn sword in his hand. The ass swerved from the road and went into the fields; and Balaam beat the ass to turn her back onto the road. ²⁴The angel of the LORD then stationed himself in a lane between the vineyards, with a fence on either side. ²⁵The ass, seeing the angel of the LORD, pressed herself against the wall and squeezed Balaam's foot against the wall; so he beat her again. ²⁶Once more the angel of the LORD moved forward and stationed himself on a spot so narrow that there was no room to swerve right or left. ²⁷When the ass now saw the angel of the LORD, she lay down under Balaam; and Balaam was furious and beat the ass with his stick.

²⁸Then the LORD opened the ass's mouth, and she said to Balaam, "What have I done to you that you have beaten me these three times?" ²⁹Balaam said to the ass, "You have made a mockery of me! If I had a sword with me, I'd kill you." ³⁰The ass said to Balaam, "Look, I am the ass that you have been riding all along until this day! Have I been in the habit of doing thus to you?" And he answered, "No."

³¹Then the LORD uncovered Balaam's eyes, and he saw the angel of the LORD standing in the way, his drawn sword in his hand; thereupon he bowed ꜛright down to the ground.ꜛ ³²The angel of the LORD said to him, "Why have you beaten your ass these three times? It is I who came out as an adversary, for the

---

c-c *Lit. "and prostrated himself to his nostrils"*

errand is obnoxious[d] to me. 33And when the ass saw me, she shied away because of me those three times. If she had not shied away from me, you are the one I should have killed, while sparing her." 34Balaam said to the angel of the LORD, "I erred because I did not know that you were standing in my way. If you still disapprove, I will turn back." 35But the angel of the LORD said to Balaam, "Go with the men. But you must say nothing except what I tell you." So Balaam went on with Balak's dignitaries.

36When Balak heard that Balaam was coming, he went out to meet him at Ir-moab, which is on the Arnon border, at its farthest point. 37Balak said to Balaam, "When I first sent to invite you, why didn't you come to me? Am I really unable to reward you?" 38But Balaam said to Balak, "And now that I have come to you, have I the power to speak freely? I can utter only the word that God puts into my mouth."

39Balaam went with Balak and they came to Kiriath-huzoth. 40Balak sacrificed oxen and sheep, and had them served to Balaam and the dignitaries with him. 41In the morning Balak took Balaam up to Bamoth-baal. From there he could see a portion of the people.

**23** Balaam said to Balak, "Build me seven altars here and have seven bulls and seven rams ready here for me." 2Balak did as Balaam directed; and Balak and Balaam offered up a bull and a ram on each altar. 3Then Balaam said to Balak, "Stay here beside your offerings while I am gone. Perhaps the LORD will grant me a manifestation, and whatever He reveals to me I will tell you." And he went off alone.[a]

4God manifested Himself to Balaam, who said to Him, "I have set up the seven altars and offered up a bull and a ram on each altar." 5And the LORD put a word in Balaam's mouth and said, "Return to Balak and speak thus."

d *Precise meaning of Heb uncertain*
a *Others "to a bare height"; exact meaning of Heb* shephi *uncertain*

⁶So he returned to him and found him standing beside his offerings, and all the Moabite dignitaries with him. ⁷He took up his theme, and said:

> From Aram has Balak brought me,
> Moab's king from the hills of the East:
> Come, curse me Jacob,
> Come, tell Israel's doom!
> ⁸How can I damn whom God*ᵇ* has not damned,
> How doom when the LORD has not doomed?
> ⁹As I see them from the mountain tops,
> Gaze on them from the heights,
> There is a people that dwells apart,
> Not reckoned among the nations,
> ¹⁰Who can count the dust*ᶜ* of Jacob,
> Number*ᵈ* the dust-cloud of Israel?
> May I die the death of the upright,*ᵉ*
> May my fate be like theirs!

¹¹Then Balak said to Balaam, "What have you done to me? Here I brought you to damn my enemies, and instead you have blessed them!" ¹²He replied, "I can only repeat faithfully what the LORD puts in my mouth." ¹³Then Balak said to him, "Come with me to another place from which you can see them—you will see only a portion of them; you will not see all of them—and damn them for me from there." ¹⁴With that, he took him to Sedehzophim,*ᶠ* on the summit of Pisgah. He built seven altars and offered a bull and a ram on each altar. ¹⁵And [Balaam] said to Balak, "Stay here beside your offerings, while I seek a manifestation yonder."

¹⁶The LORD manifested Himself to Balaam and put a word in his mouth, saying, "Return to Balak and speak thus." ¹⁷He went to him and found him standing beside his offerings, and the Moabite dignitaries with him. Balak asked him, "What did the LORD say?" ¹⁸And he took up his theme, and said:

---

ᵇ *Heb El, as often in these poems*
ᶜ *Cf. Gen. 13.16*
ᵈ *Lit. "and the number of"*
ᵉ *Heb yesharim, a play on yeshurun (Jeshurun in Deut. 32.15), a name for Israel*
ᶠ *Or "Lookout Point"*

Up, Balak, attend,
Give ear unto me, son of Zippor!
<sup>19</sup>God is not man to be capricious,
Or mortal to change His mind.
Would He speak and not act,
Promise and not fulfill?
<sup>20</sup>My message was to bless:
When He blesses, I cannot reverse it.
<sup>21</sup>No harm is in sight for Jacob,
No woe in view for Israel.
The LORD their God is with them,
And their King's acclaim in their midst.
<sup>22</sup>God who freed them from Egypt
Is for them like the horns<sup>g</sup> of the wild ox.
<sup>23</sup>Lo, there is no augury in Jacob,
No divining in Israel:<sup>h</sup>
Jacob is told at once,
Yea Israel, what God has planned.<sup>i</sup>
<sup>24</sup>Lo, a people that rises like a lion,
Leaps up like the <sup>j</sup>king of beasts,<sup>j</sup>
Rests not till it has feasted on prey
And drunk the blood of the slain.

<sup>25</sup>Thereupon Balak said to Balaam, "Don't curse them and don't bless them!" <sup>26</sup>In reply, Balaam said to Balak, "But I told you: Whatever the LORD says, that I must do." <sup>27</sup>Then Balak said to Balaam, "Come now, I will take you to another place. Perhaps God will deem it right that you damn them for me there." <sup>28</sup>Balak took Balaam to the peak of Peor, which overlooks the wasteland.<sup>k</sup> <sup>29</sup>Balaam said to Balak, "Build me here seven altars, and have seven bulls and seven rams ready for me here." <sup>30</sup>Balak did as Balaam said: he offered up a bull and a ram on each altar.

# 24 Now Balaam, seeing that it pleased the LORD to bless

---

<sup>g</sup> *Lit. "eminences," used figuratively*
<sup>h</sup> *Cf. Deut. 18.10–15*
<sup>i</sup> *Or, "Else would it be told to Jacob, / Yea to Israel, what God has planned"*
<sup>j-j</sup> *Heb 'ari, another term for "lion"*
<sup>k</sup> *Cf. note on 21.20*

Israel, did not, as on previous occasions, go in search of omens, but turned his face toward the wilderness. ²As Balaam looked up and saw Israel encamped tribe by tribe, the spirit of God came upon him. ³Taking up his theme, he said:

> ᵃWord of Balaam son of Beor,
> Word of the man whose eye is true,ᵇ
> ⁴Word of him who hears God's speech,
> Who beholds visions from the Almighty,
> Prostrate, but with eyes unveiled:
> ⁵How fair are your tents, O Jacob,
> Your dwellings, O Israel!
> ⁶Like palm-groves that stretch out,
> Like gardens beside a river,
> Like aloes planted by the LORD,
> Like cedars beside the water;
> ⁷Their boughs drip with moisture,
> Their rootsᶜ have abundant water.
> Their king shall rise above Agag,
> Their kingdom shall be exalted.
> ⁸God who freed them from Egypt
> Is for them like the hornsᵈ of the wild ox.
> They shall devour enemy nations,
> Crush their bones,
> And smash their arrows.
> ⁹They crouch, they lie down like a lion,
> Like the king of beastsᵉ; who dare rouse them?
> Blessed are they who bless you,
> Accursed they who curse you!

¹⁰Enraged at Balaam, Balak struck his hands together. "I called you," Balak said to Balaam, "to damn my enemies, and instead you have blessed them these three times! ¹¹Back with

---

ᵃ *Some of the poetic portions of this chapter are unclear*
ᵇ *Others "whose eye is (or, eyes are) open"; meaning of Heb uncertain*
ᶜ *Lit. "and its seed"*
ᵈ *See note at 23.22*
ᵉ *Heb* labi, *another word for "lion"; cf. note at 23.24*

you at once to your own place! I was going to reward you richly, but the LORD has denied you the reward." 12Balaam replied to Balak, "But I even told the messengers you sent to me, 13'Though Balak were to give me his house full of silver and gold, I could not of my own accord do anything good or bad contrary to the LORD's command. What the LORD says, that I must say.' 14And now, as I go back to my people, let me inform you of what this people will do to your people in days to come." 15He took up his theme, and said:

> Word of Balaam son of Beor,
> Word of the man whose eye is true,*b*
> 16Word of him who hears God's speech,
> Who obtains knowledge from the Most High,
> And beholds visions from the Almighty,
> Prostrate, but with eyes unveiled:
> 17What I see for them is not yet,
> What I behold will not be soon:
> A star rises from Jacob,
> A scepter comes forth from Israel;
> It smashes the brow of Moab,
> The foundation of*f* all children of Seth.
> 18Edom becomes a possession,
> Yea, Seir a possession of its enemies;
> But Israel is triumphant.
> 19A victor issues from Jacob
> To wipe out what is left of Ir.

20He saw Amalek and, taking up his theme, he said:
> A leading nation is Amalek;
> But its fate is to perish forever.

21He saw the Kenites and, taking up his theme, he said:
> Though your abode be secure,

---

b Others "whose eye is (or, eyes are) open"; meaning of Heb uncertain
f Samaritan "the pate of," cf. Jer. 48.45; others "breaks down"

And your nest be set among cliffs,
²²Yet shall Kainᵍ be consumed,
When Asshur takes you captive.

²³He took up his theme and said:
Alas, who can survive except God has willed it!
²⁴Ships come from the quarter of Kittim;
They subject Asshur, subject Eber.
They, too, shall perish forever.

²⁵Then Balaam set out on his journey back home; and Balak also went his way.

**25** While Israel was staying at Shittim, the people ᵃ‑profaned themselves by whoring‑ᵃ with the Moabite women, ²who invited the people to the sacrifices for their god. The people partook of them and worshiped that god. ³Thus Israel attached itself to Baal-peor, and the LORD was incensed with Israel. ⁴The LORD said to Moses, "Take all the ringleadersᵇ and have them publiclyᶜ impaled before the LORD, so that the LORD's wrath may turn away from Israel." ⁵So Moses said to Israel's officials, "Each of you slay those of his men who attached themselves to Baal-peor."

⁶Just then one of the Israelites came and brought a Midianite woman over to his companions, in the sight of Moses and of the whole Israelite community who were weeping at the entrance of the Tent of Meeting. ⁷When Phinehas, son of Eleazar son of Aaron the priest, saw this, he left the assembly and, taking a spear in his hand, ⁸he followed the Israelite into the chamber and stabbed both of them, the Israelite and the woman, through the belly. Then the plague against the Israelites was checked. ⁹Those who died of the plague numbered twenty-four thousand.

---

ᵍ I.e. the Kenites

ᵃ⁻ᵃ Others "began to commit harlotry"
ᵇ Lit. "heads of the people"
ᶜ Others "in face of the sun"

¹⁰The LORD spoke to Moses, saying, ¹¹"Phinehas, son of Eleazar son of Aaron the priest, has turned back My wrath from the Israelites by displaying among them his passion for Me, so that I did not wipe out the Israelite people in My passion. ¹²Say, therefore, 'I grant him My pact of friendship. ¹³It shall be for him and his descendants after him a pact of priesthood for all time, because he took impassioned action for his God, thus making expiation for the Israelites.'"

¹⁴The name of the Israelite who was killed, the one who was killed with the Midianite woman, was Zimri son of Salu, chieftain of a Simeonite ancestral house. ¹⁵The name of the Midianite woman who was killed was Cozbi daughter of Zur; he was the tribal head of an ancestral house in Midian.

¹⁶The LORD spoke to Moses, saying, ¹⁷"Assail the Midianites and defeat them—¹⁸for they assailed you by the trickery they practiced against you—because of the affair of Peor and because of the affair of their kinswoman Cozbi, daughter of the Midianite chieftain, who was killed at the time of the plague on account of Peor."

# 26

¹⁹When the plague was over, ¹the LORD said to Moses and to Eleazar son of Aaron the priest, ²"Take a census of the whole Israelite community from the age of twenty years up, by their ancestral houses, all Israelites able to bear arms." ³ ᵃSo Moses and Eleazar the priest, on the steppes of Moab, at the Jordan near Jericho, gave instructions about them, namely, ⁴those from twenty years up, as the LORD had commanded Moses.

The descendants of the Israelites who came out of the land of Egypt were:

⁵Reuben, Israel's first-born. Descendants of Reuben: [Of] Enoch,ᵇ the clan of the Enochites; of Pallu, the clan of the

---

ᵃ *Meaning of parts of vv. 3 and 4 uncertain*
ᵇ *Or "Hanoch"*

Palluites; [6]of Hezron, the clan of the Hezronites; of Carmi, the clan of the Carmites. [7]Those are the clans of the Reubenites. The persons enrolled came to 43,730.

[8] [c]Born to[c] Pallu: Eliab. [9]The sons of Eliab were Nemuel, and Dathan and Abiram. These are the same Dathan and Abiram, chosen in the assembly, who agitated against Moses and Aaron as part of Korah's band when they agitated against the LORD. [10]Whereupon the earth opened its mouth and swallowed them up with Korah—when that band died, when the fire consumed the two hundred and fifty men—and they became an example. [11]The sons of Korah, however, did not die.

[12]Descendants of Simeon by their clans: Of Nemuel, the clan of the Nemuelites; of Jamin, the clan of the Jaminites; of Jachin, the clan of the Jachinites; [13]of Zerah, the clan of the Zerahites; of Saul,[d] the clan of the Saulites. [14]Those are the clans of the Simeonites; [persons enrolled:] 22,200.

[15]Descendants of Gad by their clans: Of Zephon, the clan of the Zephonites; of Haggi, the clan of the Haggites; of Shuni, the clan of the Shunites; [16]of Ozni, the clan of the Oznites; of Eri, the clan of the Erites; [17]of Arod, the clan of the Arodites; of Areli, the clan of the Arelites. [18]Those are the clans of Gad's descendants; persons enrolled: 40,500.

[19] [c]Born to[c] Judah: Er and Onan. Er and Onan died in the land of Canaan.

[20]Descendants of Judah by their clans: Of Shelah, the clan of the Shelanites; of Perez, the clan of the Perezites; of Zerah, the clan of the Zerahites. [21]Descendants of Perez: of Hezron, the clan of the Hezronites; of Hamul, the clan of the Hamulites. [22]Those are the clans of Judah; persons enrolled: 76,500.

[23]Descendants of Issachar by their clans: [Of] Tola, the clan of the Tolaites; of Puvah, the clan of the Punites; [24]of Jashub, the clan of the Jashubites; of Shimron, the clan of the Shimronites. [25]Those are the clans of Issachar; persons enrolled: 64,300.

[26]Descendants of Zebulun by their clans: Of Sered, the clan of the Seredites; of Elon, the clan of the Elonites; of Jahleel, the

c-c Or "descendants of"
d Or "Shaul"

clan of the Jahleelites. <sup>27</sup>Those are the clans of the Zebulunites; persons enrolled: 60,500.

<sup>28</sup>The sons of Joseph were Manasseh and Ephraim—by their clans.

<sup>29</sup>Descendants of Manasseh: Of Machir, the clan of the Machirites.—Machir begot Gilead.—Of Gilead, the clan of the Gileadites. <sup>30</sup>These were the descendants of Gilead: [Of] Iezer, the clan of the Iezerites; of Helek, the clan of the Helekites; <sup>31</sup>[of] Asriel, the clan of the Asrielites; [of] Shechem, the clan of the Shechemites; <sup>32</sup>[of] Shemida, the clan of the Shemidaites; [of] Hepher, the clan of the Hepherites. <sup>33</sup>—Now Zelophehad son of Hepher had no sons, only daughters. The names of Zelophehad's daughters were Mahlah, Noah, Hoglah, Milcah, and Tirzah.—<sup>34</sup>Those are the clans of Manasseh; persons enrolled: 52,700.

<sup>35</sup>These are the descendants of Ephraim by their clans: Of Shuthelah, the clan of the Shuthelahites; of Becher, the clan of the Becherites; of Tahan, the clan of the Tahanites. <sup>36</sup>These are the descendants of Shuthelah: Of Eran, the clan of the Eranites. <sup>37</sup>Those are the clans of Ephraim's descendants; persons enrolled: 32,500.

Those are the descendants of Joseph by their clans.

<sup>38</sup>The descendants of Benjamin by their clans: Of Bela, the clan of the Belaites; of Ashbel, the clan of the Ashbelites; of Ahiram, the clan of the Ahiramites; <sup>39</sup>of Shephupham, the clan of the Shuphamites; of Hupham, the clan of the Huphamites. <sup>40</sup>The sons of Bela were Ard and Naaman: [Of Ard,] the clan of the Ardites; of Naaman, the clan of the Naamanites. <sup>41</sup>Those are the descendants of Benjamin by their clans; persons enrolled: 45,600.

<sup>42</sup>These are the descendants of Dan by their clans: Of Shuham, the clan of the Shuhamites. Those are the clans of Dan,<sup>e</sup> by their clans. <sup>43</sup>All the clans of the Shuhamites; persons enrolled: 64,400.

<sup>44</sup>Descendants of Asher by their clans: Of Imnah, the clan of

e *Meaning of parts of vv. 42 and 43 uncertain*

the Imnites; of Ishvi, the clan of the Ishvites; of Beriah, the clan of the Beriites. <sup>45</sup>Of the descendants of Beriah: Of Heber, the clan of the Heberites; of Malchiel, the clan of the Malchielites. <sup>46</sup>—The name of Asher's daughter was Serah.—<sup>47</sup>These are the clans of Asher's descendants; persons enrolled: 53,400.

<sup>48</sup>Descendants of Naphtali by their clans: Of Jahzeel, the clan of the Jahzeelites; of Guni, the clan of the Gunites; <sup>49</sup>of Jezer, the clan of the Jezerites; of Shillem, the clan of the Shillemites. <sup>50</sup>Those are the clans of the Naphtalites, clan by clan; persons enrolled: 45,400.

<sup>51</sup>This is the enrollment of the Israelites: 601,730.

<sup>52</sup>The LORD spoke to Moses, saying, <sup>53</sup>"Among these shall the land be apportioned as shares, according to the listed names: <sup>54</sup>with larger groups increase the share, with smaller groups reduce the share. Each is to be assigned its share according to its enrollment. <sup>55</sup>The land, moreover, is to be apportioned by lot; and the allotment shall be made according to the listings of their ancestral tribes. <sup>56</sup>Each portion shall be assigned by lot, whether for larger or smaller groups."

<sup>57</sup>This is the enrollment of the Levites by their clans: Of Gershon, the clan of the Gershonites; of Kohath, the clan of the Kohathites; of Merari, the clan of the Merarites. <sup>58</sup>These are the clans of Levi: The clan of the Libnites, the clan of the Hebronites, the clan of the Mahlites, the clan of the Mushites, the clan of the Korahites.—Kohath begot Amram. <sup>59</sup>The name of Amram's wife was Jochebed daughter of Levi, who was born to Levi in Egypt; she bore to Amram Aaron and Moses and their sister Miriam. <sup>60</sup>To Aaron were born Nadab and Abihu, Eleazar and Ithamar. <sup>61</sup>Nadab and Abihu died when they offered alien fire before the LORD.—<sup>62</sup>Their enrollment of 23,000 comprised all males from a month up. They were not part of the regular enrollment of the Israelites, since no share was assigned to them among the Israelites.

<sup>63</sup>These are the persons enrolled by Moses and Eleazar the priest who registered the Israelites on the steppes of Moab, at

the Jordan near Jericho. ⁶⁴Among these there was not one of those enrolled by Moses and Aaron the priest when they recorded the Israelites in the wilderness of Sinai. ⁶⁵For the LORD had said of them, "They shall die in the wilderness." Not one of them survived, except Caleb son of Jephunneh and Joshua son of Nun.

27 The daughters of Zelophehad, of Manassite family—son of Hepher son of Gilead son of Machir son of Manasseh son of Joseph—came forward. The names of the daughters were Mahlah, Noah, Hoglah, Milcah, and Tirzah. ²They stood before Moses, Eleazar the priest, the chieftains, and the whole assembly, at the entrance of the Tent of Meeting, and they said, ³"Our father died in the wilderness. He was not one of the faction, Korah's faction, which banded together against the LORD, but died for his own sin; and he has left no sons. ⁴Let not our father's name be lost to his clan just because he had no son! Give us a holding among our father's kinsmen!"

⁵Moses brought their case before the LORD.

⁶And the LORD said to Moses, ⁷"The plea of Zelophehad's daughters is just: you should give them a hereditary holding among their father's kinsmen; transfer their father's share to them.

⁸"Further, speak to the Israelite people as follows: 'If a man dies without leaving a son, you shall transfer his property to his daughter. ⁹If he has no daughter, you shall assign his property to his brothers. ¹⁰If he has no brothers, you shall assign his property to his father's brothers. ¹¹If his father had no brothers, you shall assign his property to his nearest relative in his own clan, and he shall inherit it.' This shall be the law of procedure for the Israelites, in accordance with the LORD's command to Moses."

¹²The LORD said to Moses, "Ascend these heights of Abarim and view the land that I have given to the Israelite people. ¹³When you have seen it, you too shall be gathered to your kin,

311

just as your brother Aaron was. ¹⁴For, in the wilderness of Zin, when the community was contentious, you disobeyed My command to uphold My sanctity in their sight by means of the water." Those are the Waters of Meribath-kadesh,ᵃ in the wilderness of Zin.

¹⁵Moses spoke to the LORD, saying, ¹⁶"Let the LORD, Source of the breath of all flesh, appoint someone over the community ¹⁷ ᵇ⁻who shall go out before them and come in before them, and who shall take them out and bring them in,⁻ᵇ so that the LORD's community may not be like sheep that have no shepherd." ¹⁸And the LORD answered Moses, "Single out Joshua son of Nun, an inspired man, and lay your hand upon him. ¹⁹Have him stand before Eleazar the priest and before the whole community, and commission him in their sight. ²⁰Invest him with some of your authority, so that the whole Israelite community may obey. ²¹But he shall present himself to Eleazar the priest, who shall on his behalf seek the decision of the Urim before the LORD. By such instruction they shall go out and by such instruction they shall come in, he and all the Israelites, the whole community."

²²Moses did as the LORD commanded him. He took Joshua and had him stand before Eleazar the priest and before the whole community. ²³He laid his hands upon him and commissioned him—as the LORD had spoken through Moses.

# 28

The LORD spoke to Moses, saying: ²Command the Israelite people and say to them: Be punctilious in presenting to Me at stated times ᵃ⁻the offerings of food due Me,⁻ᵃ as offerings by fire of pleasing odor to Me.

³Say to them: These are the offerings by fire that you are to present to the LORD:

As a regular burnt offering every day, two yearling lambs without blemish. ⁴You shall offer one lamb in the morning, and the other lamb you shall offer at twilight. ⁵And as a meal offering, there shall be a tenth of an *ephah* of choice flour with a

ᵃ *See note at 20.13*
ᵇ⁻ᵇ *I.e. who shall lead them in all matters and whom they shall follow in all matters*
ᵃ⁻ᵃ *Lit. "My offering, My food"*

quarter of a *hin* of beaten oil mixed in [6]—the regular burnt offering instituted at Mount Sinai[b]—an offering by fire of pleasing odor to the LORD.

[7]The libation with it shall be a quarter of a *hin* for each lamb, to be poured in the sacred precinct as an offering of fermented drink[c] to the LORD. [8]The other lamb you shall offer at twilight, preparing the same meal offering and libation as in the morning —an offering by fire of pleasing odor to the LORD.

[9]On the sabbath day: two yearling lambs without blemish, together with two-tenths of a measure[d] of choice flour with oil mixed in as a meal offering, and with the proper libation—[10]a burnt offering for every sabbath, in addition to the regular burnt offering and its libation.

[11]On your new moons you shall present a burnt offering to the LORD: two bulls of the herd, one ram, and seven yearling lambs, without blemish. [12]As meal offering for each bull: three-tenths of a measure of choice flour with oil mixed in. As meal offering for each ram: two-tenths of a measure of choice flour with oil mixed in. [13]As meal offering for each lamb: a tenth of a measure of fine flour with oil mixed in. Such shall be the burnt offering of pleasing odor, an offering by fire to the LORD. [14]Their libations shall be: half a *hin* of wine for a bull, a third of a *hin* for a ram, and a quarter of a *hin* for a lamb. That shall be the monthly burnt offering for each new moon of the year. [15]And there shall be one goat as a sin offering to the LORD, to be offered in addition to the regular burnt offering and its libation.

[16]In the first month, on the fourteenth day of the month, there shall be a passover sacrifice to the LORD, [17]and on the fifteenth day of that month a festival. Unleavened bread shall be eaten for seven days. [18]The first day shall be a sacred occasion: you shall not work at your occupations. [19]You shall present an offering by fire, a burnt offering, to the LORD: two bulls of the herd, one ram, and seven yearling lambs—[e-]see that they are[-e] without blemish. [20]The meal offering with them shall be of choice flour with oil mixed in: prepare three-tenths of a measure for a bull, two-tenths for a ram; [21]and for each of the seven

---

b *Exod. 29.38–41*    c *I.e. wine*
d *I.e. of an* ephah
e-e *Lit. "they shall be to you"*

lambs prepare one-tenth of a measure. <sup>22</sup>And there shall be one goat for a sin offering, to make expiation in your behalf. <sup>23</sup>You shall present these in addition to the morning portion of the regular burnt offering. <sup>24</sup>You shall offer the like daily for seven days as food, an offering by fire of pleasing odor to the LORD; they shall be offered, with their libations, in addition to the regular burnt offering. <sup>25</sup>And the seventh day shall be a sacred occasion for you: you shall not work at your occupations.

<sup>26</sup>On the day of the first fruits, your Feast of Weeks, when you bring an offering of new grain to the LORD, you shall observe a sacred occasion: you shall not work at your occupations. <sup>27</sup>You shall present a burnt offering of pleasing odor to the LORD: two bulls of the herd, one ram, seven yearling lambs. <sup>28</sup>The meal offering with them shall be of choice flour with oil mixed in, three-tenths of a measure for a bull, two-tenths for a ram, <sup>29</sup>and one-tenth for each of the seven lambs. <sup>30</sup>And there shall be one goat for expiation in your behalf. <sup>31</sup>You shall present them—see that they are without blemish—with their libations, in addition to the regular burnt offering and its meal offering.

# 29

In the seventh month, on the first day of the month, you shall observe a sacred occasion: you shall not work at your occupations. You shall observe it as <sup>a-</sup>a day when the horn is sounded.<sup>-a</sup> <sup>2</sup>You shall present a burnt offering of pleasing odor to the LORD: one bull of the herd, one ram, and seven yearling lambs, without blemish. <sup>3</sup>The meal offering with them—choice flour with oil mixed in—shall be: three-tenths of a measure for a bull, two-tenths for a ram, <sup>4</sup>and one-tenth for each of the seven lambs. <sup>5</sup>And there shall be one goat for a sin offering, to make expiation in your behalf—<sup>6</sup>in addition to the burnt offering of the new moon with its meal offering and the regular burnt offering with its meal offering, each with its libation as prescribed, offerings by fire of pleasing odor to the LORD.

<sup>7</sup>On the tenth day of the same seventh month you shall ob-

---

<sup>a-a</sup> Or "a day of festivity"

serve a sacred occasion when you shall practice self-denial. You shall do no work. ⁸You shall present to the Lord a burnt offering of pleasing odor: one bull of the herd, one ram, seven yearling lambs; see that they are*b* without blemish. ⁹The meal offering with them—of choice flour with oil mixed in—shall be: three-tenths of a measure for a bull, two-tenths for the one ram, ¹⁰one-tenth for each of the seven lambs. ¹¹And there shall be one goat for a sin offering, in addition to the sin offering of expiation and the regular burnt offering with its meal offering, each with its libation.

¹²On the fifteenth day of the seventh month, you shall observe a sacred occasion: you shall not work at your occupations.— Seven days you shall observe a festival of the Lord.—¹³You shall present a burnt offering, an offering by fire of pleasing odor to the Lord: Thirteen bulls of the herd, two rams, fourteen yearling lambs; they shall be without blemish. ¹⁴The meal offerings with them—of choice flour with oil mixed in—shall be: three-tenths of a measure for each of the thirteen bulls, two-tenths for each of the two rams, ¹⁵and one-tenth for each of the fourteen lambs. ¹⁶And there shall be one goat for a sin offering —in addition to the regular burnt offering, its meal offering and libation.

¹⁷Second day: Twelve bulls of the herd, two rams, fourteen yearling lambs, without blemish; ¹⁸the meal offerings and libations for the bulls, rams, and lambs, in the quantities prescribed; ¹⁹and one goat for a sin offering—in addition to the regular burnt offering, its meal offering and libations.

²⁰Third day: Eleven bulls, two rams, fourteen yearling lambs, without blemish; ²¹the meal offerings and libations for the bulls, rams, and lambs, in the quantities prescribed; ²²and one goat for a sin offering—in addition to the regular burnt offering, its meal offering and libation.

²³Fourth day: Ten bulls, two rams, fourteen yearling lambs, without blemish; ²⁴the meal offerings and libations for the bulls, rams, and lambs, in the quantities prescribed; ²⁵and one goat for

---

b *See note at 28.19*

a sin offering—in addition to the regular burnt offering, its meal offering and libation.

²⁶Fifth day: Nine bulls, two rams, fourteen yearling lambs, without blemish; ²⁷the meal offerings and libations for the bulls, rams, and lambs, in the quantities prescribed; ²⁸and one goat for a sin offering—in addition to the regular burnt offering, its meal offering and libation.

²⁹Sixth day: Eight bulls, two rams, fourteen yearling lambs, without blemish; ³⁰the meal offerings and libations for the bulls, rams, and lambs, in the quantities prescribed; ³¹and one goat for a sin offering—in addition to the regular burnt offering, its meal offering and libations.

³²Seventh day: Seven bulls, two rams, fourteen yearling lambs, without blemish; ³³the meal offerings and libations for the bulls, rams, and lambs, in the quantities prescribed; ³⁴and one goat for a sin offering—in addition to the regular burnt offering, its meal offering and libation.

³⁵On the eighth day you shall hold a solemn gathering$^c$; you shall not work at your occupations. ³⁶You shall present a burnt offering, an offering by fire of pleasing odor to the LORD; one bull, one ram, seven yearling lambs, without blemish; ³⁷the meal offerings and libations for the bull, the ram, and the lambs, in the quantities prescribed; ³⁸and one goat for a sin offering—in addition to the regular burnt offering, its meal offering and libation.

³⁹All these you shall offer to the LORD at the stated times, in addition to your votive and freewill offerings, be they burnt

30 offerings, meal offerings, libations, or offerings of well-being. ¹So Moses spoke to the Israelites just as the LORD had commanded Moses.

מטות

²Moses spoke to the heads of the Israelite tribes, saying: This is what the LORD has commanded:

---

$^c$ *See note at Lev. 23.36*

³If a man makes a vow to the LORD or takes an oath imposing an obligation*ᵃ* on himself, he shall not break his pledge; he must carry out all that has *ᵇ*crossed his lips.*⁻ᵇ*

⁴If a woman makes a vow to the LORD or assumes an obligation while still in her father's household by reason of her youth, ⁵and her father learns of her vow or her self-imposed obligation and offers no objection, all her vows shall stand and every self-imposed obligation shall stand. ⁶But if her father restrains her on the day he finds out, none of her vows or self-imposed obligations shall stand; and the LORD will forgive her, since her father restrained her.

⁷If she should marry while her vow or the commitment to which she bound herself is still in force, ⁸and her husband learns of it and offers no objection on the day he finds out, her vows shall stand and her self-imposed obligations shall stand. ⁹But if her husband restrains her on the day that he learns of it, he thereby annuls her vow which was in force or the commitment*ᶜ* to which she bound herself; and the LORD will forgive her. ¹⁰— The vow of a widow or of a divorced woman, however, whatever she has imposed on herself, shall be binding upon her.— ¹¹So, too, if, while in her husband's household, she makes a vow or imposes an obligation on herself by oath, ¹²and her husband learns of it, yet offers no objection—thus failing to restrain her—all her vows shall stand and all her self-imposed obligations shall stand. ¹³But if her husband does annul them on the day he finds out, then nothing that has crossed her lips shall stand, whether vows or self-imposed obligations. Her husband has annulled them, and the LORD will forgive her. ¹⁴Every vow and every sworn obligation of self-denial may be upheld by her husband or annulled by her husband. ¹⁵If her husband offers no objection from that day to the next, he has upheld all the vows or obligations she has assumed: he has upheld them by offering no objection on the day he found out. ¹⁶But if he annuls them after [the day] he finds out, he shall bear her guilt.

---

ᵃ *Or "a prohibition"*
ᵇ⁻ᵇ *Lit. "come out of his mouth"*
ᶜ *Lit. "utterance of her lips"*

¹⁷Those are the laws that the LORD enjoined upon Moses between a man and his wife, and as between a father and his daughter while in her father's household by reason of her youth.

**31** The LORD spoke to Moses, saying, ²"Avenge the Israelite people on the Midianites; then you shall be gathered to your kin."

³Moses spoke to the people, saying, "Let men be picked out from among you for a campaign, and let them fall upon Midian to wreak the LORD's vengeance on Midian. ⁴You shall dispatch on the campaign a thousand from every one of the tribes of Israel."

⁵So a thousand from each tribe were furnished from the divisions of Israel, twelve thousand picked for the campaign. ⁶Moses dispatched them on the campaign, a thousand from each tribe, with Phinehas son of Eleazar serving as a priest on the campaign, equipped with the sacred utensils*a* and the trumpets for sounding the blasts. ⁷They took the field against Midian, as the LORD had commanded Moses, and slew every male. ⁸Along with their other victims, they slew the kings of Midian: Evi, Rekem, Zur, Hur, and Reba, the five kings of Midian. They also put Balaam son of Beor to the sword.

⁹The Israelites took the women and children of the Midianites captive, and seized as booty all their beasts, all their herds, and all their wealth. ¹⁰And they destroyed by fire all the towns in which they were settled, and their encampments. ¹¹They gathered all the spoil and all the booty, man and beast, ¹²and they brought the captives, the booty, and the spoil to Moses, Eleazar the priest, and the whole Israelite community, at the camp in the steppes of Moab, at the Jordan near Jericho.

¹³Moses, Eleazar the priest, and all the chieftains of the community came out to meet them outside the camp. ¹⁴Moses be-

---

a *Perhaps the Urim; cf. 27.21*

came angry with the commanders of the army, the officers of thousands and the officers of hundreds, who had come back from the military campaign. ¹⁵Moses said to them, "You have spared every female! ¹⁶Yet they are the very ones who, at the bidding of Balaam, induced*ᵇ* the Israelites to trespass against the LORD in the matter of Peor, so that the LORD's community was struck by the plague. ¹⁷Now, therefore, slay every male among the children, and slay also every woman who has known a man carnally; ¹⁸but spare every young woman who has not had carnal relations with a man.

¹⁹"You shall then stay outside the camp seven days; every one among you or among your captives who has slain a person or touched a corpse shall cleanse himself on the third and seventh days. ²⁰You shall also cleanse every cloth, every article of skin, everything made of goats' hair, and every object of wood."

²¹Eleazar the priest said to the troops who had taken part in the fighting, "This is the ritual law that the LORD has enjoined upon Moses: ²²Gold and silver, copper, iron, tin, and lead²³— any article that can withstand fire—these you shall pass through fire and they shall be clean, except that they must be cleansed with water of lustration; and anything that cannot withstand fire you must pass through water. ²⁴On the seventh day you shall wash your clothes and be clean, and after that you may enter the camp."

²⁵The LORD said to Moses: ²⁶"You and Eleazar the priest and the family heads of the community take an inventory of the booty that was captured, man and beast, ²⁷and divide the booty equally between the combatants who engaged in the campaign and the rest of the community. ²⁸You shall exact a levy for the LORD: in the case of the warriors who engaged in the campaign, one item in five hundred, of persons, oxen, asses, and sheep, ²⁹shall be taken from their half-share and given to Eleazar the priest as a contribution to the LORD; ³⁰and from the half-share of the other Israelites you shall withhold one in every fifty human

---

ᵇ *Meaning of Heb* hayu . . . limsor *uncertain*

beings as well as cattle, asses, and sheep—all the animals—and give them to the Levites, who attend to the duties of the LORD's Tabernacle."

[31]Moses and Eleazar the priest did as the LORD commanded Moses. [32]The amount of booty, other than the spoil that the troops had plundered, came to 675,000 sheep, [33]72,000 head of cattle, [34]61,000 asses, [35]and a total of 32,000 human beings, namely, the women who had not had carnal relations.

[36]Thus, the half-share of those who had engaged in the campaign [was as follows]: The number of sheep was 337,500, [37]and the LORD's levy from the sheep was 675; [38]the cattle came to 36,000, from which the LORD's levy was 72; [39]the asses came to 30,500, from which the LORD's levy was 61. [40]And the number of human beings was 16,000, from which the LORD's levy was 32. [41]Moses gave the contributions levied for the LORD to Eleazar the priest, as the LORD had commanded Moses.

[42]As for the half-share of the other Israelites, which Moses withdrew from the men who had taken the field, [43]that half-share of the community consisted of 337,500 sheep, [44]36,000 head of cattle, [45]30,500 asses, [46]and 16,000 human beings. [47]From this half-share of the Israelites, Moses withheld one in every fifty humans and animals; and he gave them to the Levites, who attended to the duties of the LORD's Tabernacle, as the LORD had commanded Moses.

[48]The commanders of the troop divisions, the officers of thousands and the officers of hundreds, approached Moses. [49]They said to Moses, "Your servants have made a check of the warriors in our charge, and not one of us is missing. [50]So we have brought as an offering to the LORD such articles of gold as each of us came upon: armlets, bracelets, signet rings, earrings, and pendants,[c] that expiation may be made for our persons before the LORD." [51]Moses and Eleazar the priest accepted the gold from them, all kinds of wrought articles. [52]All the gold that was offered by the officers of thousands and the officers of hundreds as a contribution to the LORD came to 16,750 shekels. [53]—But

[c] *See note at Exod. 35.22*

in the ranks, everyone kept his booty for himself.—⁵⁴So Moses and Eleazar the priest accepted the gold from the officers of thousands and the officers of hundreds and brought it to the Tent of Meeting, as a reminder in behalf of the Israelites before the LORD.

32 The Reubenites and the Gadites owned cattle in very great numbers. Noting that the lands of Jazer and Gilead were a region suitable for cattle, ²the Gadites and the Reubenites came to Moses, Eleazar the priest, and the chieftains of the community, and said, ³"Ataroth, Dibon, Jazer, Nimrah, Heshbon, Elealeh, Sebam, Nebo, and Beon—⁴the land that the LORD has conquered for the community of Israel is cattle country, and your servants have cattle. ⁵It would be a favor to us," they continued, "if this land were given to your servants as a holding; do not move us across the Jordan."

⁶Moses replied to the Gadites and the Reubenites, "Are your brothers to go to war while you stay here? ⁷Why will you turn the minds of the Israelites from crossing into the land that the LORD has given them? ⁸That is what your fathers did when I sent them from Kadesh-barnea to survey the land. ⁹After going up to the wadi Eshcol and surveying the land, they turned the minds of the Israelites from invading the land that the LORD had given them. ¹⁰Thereupon the LORD was incensed and He swore, ¹¹'None of the men from twenty years up who came out of Egypt shall see the land that I promised on oath to Abraham, Isaac, and Jacob, for they did not remain loyal to Me—¹²none except Caleb son of Jephunneh the Kenizzite and Joshua son of Nun, for they remained loyal to the LORD.' ¹³The LORD was incensed at Israel, and for forty years He made them wander in the wilderness, until the whole generation that had provoked the LORD's displeasure was gone. ¹⁴And now you, a breed of sinful men, have replaced your fathers, to add still further to the LORD's wrath against Israel. ¹⁵If you turn away from Him and

He abandons them once more in the wilderness, you will bring calamity upon all this people."

[16]Then they stepped up to him and said, "We will build here sheepfolds for our flocks and towns for our children. [17]And we will hasten[a] as shock-troops in the van of the Israelites until we have established them in their home, while our children stay in the fortified towns because of the inhabitants of the land. [18]We will not return to our homes until every one of the Israelites is in possession of his portion. [19]But we will not have a share with them in the territory beyond the Jordan, for we have received our share on the east side of the Jordan."

[20]Moses said to them, "If you do this, if you go to battle as shock-troops, at the instance of the LORD, [21]and every shock-fighter among you crosses the Jordan, at the instance of the LORD, until He has dispossessed His enemies before Him, [22]and the land has been subdued, at the instance of the LORD, and then you return—you shall be clear before the LORD and before Israel; and this land shall be your holding under the LORD. [23]But if you do not do so, you will have sinned against the LORD; and know that your sin will overtake you. [24]Build towns for your children and sheepfolds for your flocks, but do what you have promised."

[25]The Gadites and the Reubenites answered Moses, "Your servants will do as my lord commands. [26]Our children, our wives, our flocks, and all our other livestock will stay behind[b] in the towns of Gilead; [27]while your servants, all those recruited for war, cross over, at the instance of the LORD, to engage in battle—as my lord orders."

[28]Then Moses gave instructions concerning them to Eleazar the priest, Joshua son of Nun, and the family heads of the Israelite tribes. [29]Moses said to them, "If every shock-fighter among the Gadites and the Reubenites crosses the Jordan with you to do battle, at the instance of the LORD, and the land is subdued before you, you shall give them the land of Gilead as a holding. [30]But if they do not cross over with you as shock-troops, they shall receive holdings among you in the land of Canaan."

[a] *Meaning of Heb* hushim *uncertain*
[b] *Lit. "there"*

³¹The Gadites and the Reubenites said in reply, "Whatever the LORD has spoken concerning your servants, that we will do. ³²We ourselves will cross over as shock-troops, at the instance of the LORD, into the land of Canaan; and we shall keep our hereditary holding across the Jordan."ᶜ

³³So Moses assigned to them—to the Gadites, the Reubenites, and the half-tribe of Manasseh son of Joseph—the kingdom of Sihon king of the Amorites and the kingdom of King Og of Bashan, the land with its various cities and the territories of their surrounding towns. ³⁴The Gadites rebuilt Dibon, Ataroth, Aroer, ³⁵Atroth-shophan, Jazer, Jogbehah, ³⁶Beth-nimrah, and Beth-haran as fortified towns or as enclosures for flocks. ³⁷The Reubenites rebuilt Heshbon, Elealeh, Kiriathaim, ³⁸Nebo, Baal-meon—some names being changed—and Sibmah; they gave [their own] names to towns that they rebuilt.ᵈ ³⁹The descendants of Machir son of Manasseh went to Gilead and captured it, dispossessing the Amorites who were there; ⁴⁰so Moses gave Gilead to Machir son of Manasseh, and he settled there. ⁴¹Jair son of Manasseh went and captured ᵉ‑their villages,‑ᵉ which he re-named Havvoth-jair.ᶠ ⁴²And Nobah went and captured Kenath and its dependencies, renaming it Nobah after himself.

מסעי

**33** These were the marches of the Israelites who started out from the land of Egypt, troop by troop, in the charge of Moses and Aaron. ²Moses recorded the starting points of their various marches as directed by the LORD. Their marches, by starting points, were as follows:

³They set out from Rameses in the first month, on the fif-teenth day of the first month. It was on the morrow of the passover offering that the Israelites started out defiantly,ᵃ in plain view of all the Egyptians. ⁴The Egyptians meanwhile were burying those among them whom the LORD had struck down, every first-born—whereby the LORD executed judgment on their gods.

⁵The Israelites set out from Rameses and encamped at Suc-

---

ᶜ *I.e. in Transjordan*    ᵈ *Cf. vv. 41, 42*
ᵉ‑ᵉ *Or "the villages of Ham"; cf. Gen. 14.5*    ᶠ *I.e. "the villages of Jair"*
ᵃ *See note at Exod. 14.8*

coth. <sup>6</sup>They set out from Succoth and encamped at Etham, which is on the edge of the wilderness. <sup>7</sup>They set out from Etham and turned about toward Pi-hahiroth, which faces Baal-zephon, and they encamped before Migdol. <sup>8</sup>They set out from Pene<sup>b</sup>-hahiroth and passed through the sea into the wilderness; and they made a three-days' journey in the wilderness of Etham and encamped at Marah. <sup>9</sup>They set out from Marah and came to Elim. There were twelve springs in Elim and seventy palm trees, so they encamped there. <sup>10</sup>They set out from Elim and encamped by the Sea of Reeds.<sup>c</sup> <sup>11</sup>They set out from the Sea of Reeds and encamped in the wilderness of Sin. <sup>12</sup>They set out from the wilderness of Sin and encamped at Dophkah. <sup>13</sup>They set out from Dophkah and encamped at Alush. <sup>14</sup>They set out from Alush and encamped at Rephidim; it was there that the people had no water to drink. <sup>15</sup>They set out from Rephidim and encamped in the wilderness of Sinai. <sup>16</sup>They set out from the wilderness of Sinai and encamped at Kibroth-hattaavah. <sup>17</sup>They set out from Kibroth-hattaavah and encamped at Hazeroth. <sup>18</sup>They set out from Hazeroth and encamped at Rithmah. <sup>19</sup>They set out from Rithmah and encamped at Rimmon-perez. <sup>20</sup>They set out from Rimmon-perez and encamped at Libnah. <sup>21</sup>They set out from Libnah and encamped at Rissah. <sup>22</sup>They set out from Rissah and encamped at Kehelath. <sup>23</sup>They set out from Kehelath and encamped at Mount Shepher. <sup>24</sup>They set out from Mount Shepher and encamped at Haradah. <sup>25</sup>They set out from Haradah and encamped at Makheloth. <sup>26</sup>They set out from Makheloth and encamped at Tahath. <sup>27</sup>They set out from Tahath and encamped at Terah. <sup>28</sup>They set out from Terah and encamped at Mithkah. <sup>29</sup>They set out from Mithkah and encamped at Hashmonah. <sup>30</sup>They set out from Hashmonah and encamped at Moseroth. <sup>31</sup>They set out from Moseroth and encamped at Bene-jaakan. <sup>32</sup>They set out from Bene-jaakan and encamped at Hor-haggidgad. <sup>33</sup>They set out from Hor-haggidgad and encamped at Jotbath. <sup>34</sup>They set out from Jotbath and encamped at Abronah. <sup>35</sup>They set out from Abronah and

---

<sup>b</sup> *Many Hebrew manuscripts and ancient versions read "Pi"*
<sup>c</sup> *See note at Exod. 10.19*

encamped at Ezion-geber. ³⁶They set out from Ezion-geber and encamped in the wilderness of Zin, that is, Kadesh. ³⁷They set out from Kadesh and encamped at Mount Hor, on the edge of the land of Edom.

³⁸Aaron the priest ascended Mount Hor at the command of the LORD and died there, in the fortieth year after the Israelites had left the land of Egypt, on the first day of the fifth month. ³⁹Aaron was a hundred and twenty-three years old when he died on Mount Hor. ⁴⁰And the Canaanite, king of Arad, who dwelt in the Negeb, in the land of Canaan, learned of the coming of the Israelites.ᵈ

⁴¹They set out from Mount Hor and encamped at Zalmonah. ⁴²They set out from Zalmonah and encamped at Punon. ⁴³They set out from Punon and encamped at Oboth. ⁴⁴They set out from Oboth and encamped at Iye-abarim, in the territory of Moab. ⁴⁵They set out from Iyim and encamped at Dibon-gad. ⁴⁶They set out from Dibon-gad and encamped at Almon-diblathaim. ⁴⁷They set out from Almon-diblathaim and encamped in the hills of Abarim, before Nebo. ⁴⁸They set out from the hills of Abarim and encamped in the steppes of Moab, at the Jordan near Jericho; ⁴⁹they encamped by the Jordan from Beth-jeshimoth as far as Abel-shittim, in the steppes of Moab.

⁵⁰In the steppes of Moab, at the Jordan near Jericho, the LORD spoke to Moses, saying: ⁵¹Speak to the Israelite people and say to them: When you cross the Jordan into the land of Canaan, ⁵²you shall dispossess all the inhabitants of the land; you shall destroy all their figuredᵉ objects; you shall destroy all their molten images, and you shall demolish all their cult places. ⁵³And you shall take possession of the land and settle in it, for I have assigned the land to you to possess. ⁵⁴You shall apportion the land among yourselves by lot, clan by clan: with larger groups increase the share, with smaller groups reduce the share. Wherever the lot falls for anyone, that shall be his. You shall have your portions according to your ancestral tribes. ⁵⁵But if you do

ᵈ *See 21.1–3*
ᵉ *See note at Lev. 26.1*

not dispossess the inhabitants of the land, those whom you allow to remain shall be stings in your eyes and thorns in your sides, and they shall harass you in the land in which you live; [56]so that I will do to you what I planned to do to them.

34 The LORD spoke to Moses, saying: [2]Instruct the Israelite people and say to them: When you enter the land of Canaan, this is the land that shall fall to you as your portion, the land of Canaan with its various boundaries:

[3]Your southern sector shall extend from the wilderness of Zin alongside Edom. Your southern boundary shall start on the east from the tip of the Dead Sea. [4]Your boundary shall then turn to pass south of the ascent of Akrabbim and continue to Zin, and its limits shall be south of Kadesh-barnea, reaching Hazar-addar and continuing to Azmon. [5]From Azmon the boundary shall turn toward the Wadi of Egypt and terminate at the Sea.[a]

[6]For the western boundary you shall have the coast of the Great Sea[a]; that shall serve as your western boundary.

[7]This shall be your northern boundary: Draw a line from the Great Sea to Mount Hor; [8]from Mount Hor draw a line to Lebo-hamath,[b] and let the boundary reach Zedad. [9]The boundary shall then run to Ziphron and terminate at Hazar-enan. That shall be your northern boundary.

[10]For your eastern boundary you shall draw a line from Hazar-enan to Shepham. [11]From Shepham the boundary shall descend to Riblah on the east side of Ain; from there the boundary shall continue downward and abut on the eastern slopes of the Sea of Chinnereth.[c] [12]The boundary shall then descend along the Jordan and terminate at the Dead Sea.

That shall be your land as defined by its boundaries on all sides.

[13]Moses instructed the Israelites, saying: This is the land you are to receive by lot as your hereditary portion, which the LORD has commanded to be given to the nine and a half tribes. [14]For

---

[a] *I.e. the Mediterranean Sea*
[b] *See note at 13.21*
[c] *I.e. the Sea (or Lake) of Galilee*

the Reubenite tribe by its ancestral houses, the Gadite tribe by its ancestral houses, and the half-tribe of Manasseh have already received their portions: ¹⁵those two and a half tribes have received their portions across the Jordan, opposite Jericho, on the east, the orient side.

¹⁶The LORD spoke to Moses, saying: ¹⁷These are the names of the men through whom the land shall be apportioned for you: Eleazar the priest and Joshua son of Nun. ¹⁸And you shall also take a chieftain from each tribe through whom the land shall be apportioned. ¹⁹These are the names of the men: from the tribe of Judah: Caleb son of Jephunneh. ²⁰From the Simeonite tribe: Samuel*d* son of Ammihud. ²¹From the tribe of Benjamin: Elidad son of Chislon. ²²From the Danite tribe: a chieftain, Bukki son of Jogli. ²³For the descendants of Joseph: from the Manassite tribe: a chieftain, Hanniel son of Ephod; ²⁴and from the Ephraimite tribe: a chieftain, Kemuel son of Shiphtan. ²⁵From the Zebulunite tribe: a chieftain, Elizaphan son of Parnach. ²⁶From the Issacharite tribe: a chieftain, Paltiel son of Azzan. ²⁷From the Asherite tribe: a chieftain, Ahihud son of Shelomi. ²⁸From the Naphtalite tribe: a chieftain, Pedahel son of Ammihud.

²⁹It was these whom the LORD designated to allot portions to the Israelites in the land of Canaan.

**35** The LORD spoke to Moses in the steppes of Moab at the Jordan near Jericho, saying: ²Instruct the Israelite people to assign, out of the holdings apportioned to them, towns for the Levites to dwell in; you shall also assign to the Levites pasture land around their towns. ³The towns shall be theirs to dwell in, and the pasture shall be for the cattle they own and all their other beasts. ⁴The town pasture that you are to assign to the Levites shall extend a thousand cubits outside the town wall all around. ⁵You shall measure off two thousand cubits outside the town on the east side, two thousand on the south side, two thousand on the west side, and two thousand on the north side, with the town in the center. That shall be the pasture for their towns.

d  *Or "Shemuel"*

⁶The towns that you assign to the Levites shall comprise the six cities of refuge that you are to designate for a manslayer to flee to, to which you shall add forty-two towns. ⁷Thus the total of the towns that you assign to the Levites shall be forty-eight towns, with their pasture. ⁸In assigning towns from the holdings of the Israelites, take more from the larger groups and less from the smaller, so that each assigns towns to the Levites in proportion to the share it receives.

⁹The LORD spoke further to Moses: ¹⁰Speak to the Israelite people and say to them: When you cross the Jordan into the land of Canaan, ¹¹you shall provide yourselves with places to serve you as cities of refuge to which a manslayer who has killed a person unintentionally may flee. ¹²The cities shall serve you as a refuge from the avenger,ᵃ so that the manslayer may not die unless he has stood trial before the assembly.

¹³The towns that you thus assign shall be six cities of refuge in all. ¹⁴Three cities shall be designated beyond the Jordan, and the other three shall be designated in the land of Canaan: they shall serve as cities of refuge. ¹⁵These six cities shall serve the Israelites and the resident aliens among them for refuge, so that anyone who kills a person unintentionally may flee there.

¹⁶Anyone, however, who strikes another with an iron object so that death results is a murderer; the murderer must be put to death. ¹⁷If he struck him with a stone toolᵇ that could cause death, and death resulted, he is a murderer; the murderer must be put to death. ¹⁸Similarly, if the object with which he struck him was a wooden toolᵇ that could cause death, and death resulted, he is a murderer; the murderer must be put to death. ¹⁹The blood-avenger himself shall put the murderer to death; it is he who shall put him to death upon encounter. ²⁰So, too, if he pushed him in hate or hurled something at him on purpose and death resulted, ²¹or if he struck him with his hand in enmity and death resulted, the assailant shall be put to death; he is a murderer. The blood-avenger shall put the murderer to death upon encounter. ²²But if he pushed him without malice aforethought

ᵃ *Lit. "redeemer," i.e. next of kin; cf. note at Lev. 25.25*
ᵇ *Lit. "of the hand"*

or hurled any object at him unintentionally, ²³or inadvertently[c] dropped upon him any deadly object of stone, and death resulted—though he was not an enemy of his and did not seek his harm—²⁴in such cases the assembly shall decide between the slayer and the blood-avenger. ²⁵The assembly shall protect the manslayer from the blood-avenger, and the assembly shall restore him to the city of refuge to which he fled, and there he shall remain until the death of the high priest who was anointed with the sacred oil. ²⁶But if the manslayer ever goes outside the limits of the city of refuge to which he has fled,²⁷and the blood-avenger comes upon him outside the limits of his city of refuge, and the blood-avenger kills the manslayer, there is no bloodguilt on his account. ²⁸For he must remain inside his city of refuge until the death of the high priest; after the death of the high priest, the manslayer may return to his land holding.

²⁹Such shall be your law of procedure throughout the ages in all your settlements.

³⁰If anyone kills a person, the manslayer may be executed only on the evidence of witnesses; the testimony of a single witness against a person shall not suffice for a sentence of death. ³¹You may not accept a ransom for the life of a murderer who is guilty of a capital crime; he must be put to death. ³²Nor may you accept ransom in lieu of flight to a city of refuge, enabling one to return to live on his land before the death of the priest. ³³You shall not pollute the land in which you live; for blood pollutes the land, and the land can have no expiation for blood that is shed on it, except by the blood of him who shed it. ³⁴You shall not defile the land in which you live, in which I Myself abide, for I the LORD abide among the Israelite people.

**36** The family heads in the clan of the descendants of Gilead son of Machir son of Manasseh, one of the Josephite clans, came forward and appealed to Moses and the chieftains, family heads[a] of the Israelites. ²They said, "The LORD commanded my lord to assign the land to the Israelites as shares by lot, and my lord was

---

[c] *Lit. "without seeing"*

[a] *I.e. tribal heads*

further commanded by the LORD to assign the share of our kinsman Zelophehad to his daughters. ³Now, if they marry persons from another Israelite tribe, their share will be cut off from our ancestral portion and be added to the portion of the tribe into which they marry; thus our allotted portion will be diminished. ⁴And even when the Israelites observe the jubilee, their share will be added to that of the tribe into which they marry, and their share will be cut off from the ancestral portion of our tribe."

⁵So Moses, at the LORD's bidding, instructed the Israelites, saying: "The plea of the Josephite tribe is just. ⁶This is what the LORD has commanded concerning the daughters of Zelophehad: They may marry anyone they wish, provided they marry into a clan of their father's tribe. ⁷No inheritance of the Israelites may pass over from one tribe to another, but the Israelites must remain bound each to the ancestral portion of his tribe. ⁸Every daughter among the Israelite tribes who inherits a share must marry someone from a clan of her father's tribe, in order that every Israelite may keep his ancestral share. ⁹Thus no inheritance shall pass over from one tribe to another, but the Israelite tribes shall remain bound each to its portion."

¹⁰The daughters of Zelophehad did as the LORD had commanded Moses: ¹¹Mahlah, Tirzah, Hoglah, Milcah, and Noah, Zelophehad's daughters, were married to sons of their uncles, ¹²marrying into clans of descendants of Manasseh son of Joseph; and so their share remained in the tribe of their father's clan.

¹³These are the commandments and regulations that the LORD enjoined upon the Israelites, through Moses, on the steppes of Moab, at the Jordan near Jericho.

חזק

# דברים

# DEUTERONOMY

# דברים
# DEUTERONOMY

1 These are the words that Moses addressed to all Israel on the other side of the Jordan.—*Through the wilderness, in the Arabah near Suph, between Paran and Tophel, Laban, Hazeroth, and Di-zahab, ²it is eleven days from Horeb to Kadesh-barnea by the Mount Seir route.—³It was in the fortieth year, on the first day of the eleventh month, that Moses addressed the Israelites in accordance with the instructions that the LORD had given him for them, ⁴after he had defeated Sihon king of the Amorites, who dwelt in Heshbon, and King Og of Bashan, who dwelt at Ashtaroth [and*ᵇ*] Edrei. ⁵On the other side of the Jordan, in the land of Moab, Moses undertook to expound this Teaching. He said:

⁶The LORD our God spoke to us at Horeb, saying: You have stayed long enough at this mountain. ⁷Start out and make your way to the hill country of the Amorites and to all their neighbors in the Arabah, the hill country, the Shephelah,*ᶜ* the Negeb, the seacoast, the land of the Canaanites,*ᵈ* and the Lebanon, as far as the Great River, the river Euphrates. ⁸See, I place the land at your disposal. Go, take possession of the land that the LORD swore to your fathers, Abraham, Isaac, and Jacob, to assign to them and to their heirs after them.

⁹Thereupon I said to you, "I cannot bear the burden of you by myself. ¹⁰The LORD your God has multiplied you until you are today as numerous as the stars in the sky.—¹¹May the LORD, the God of your fathers, increase your numbers a thousandfold, and bless you as He promised you.—¹²How can I bear unaided the trouble of you, and the burden, and the bickering! ¹³Pick from

---

ᵃ *The rest of this verse and v. 2 are unclear; cf. v. 19 and Num. 33.16–36*
ᵇ *Cf. Josh. 12.4; 13.21, 31*
ᶜ *Others "Lowland"*
ᵈ *I.e. Phoenicia*

each of your tribes men who are wise, discerning, and experienced, and I will appoint them as your heads." ¹⁴You answered me and said, "What you propose to do is good." ¹⁵So I took your tribal leaders, wise and experienced men, and appointed them heads over you: chiefs of thousands, chiefs of hundreds, chiefs of fifties, and chiefs of tens, and officials for your tribes. ¹⁶I charged your magistrates at that time as follows, "Hear out your fellow men, and decide justly between any man and a fellow Israelite or a stranger. ¹⁷You shall not be partial in judgment: hear out low and high alike. Fear no man, for judgment is God's. And any matter that is too difficult for you, you shall bring to me and I will hear it." ¹⁸Thus I instructed you, at that time, about the various things that you should do.

¹⁹We set out from Horeb and traveled the great and terrible wilderness that you saw, along the road to the hill country of the Amorites, as the LORD our God had commanded us. When we reached Kadesh-barnea, ²⁰I said to you, "You have come to the hill country of the Amorites which the LORD our God is giving to us. ²¹See, the LORD your God has placed the land at your disposal. Go up, take possession, as the LORD, the God of your fathers, promised you. Fear not and be not dismayed."

²²Then all of you came to me and said, "Let us send men ahead to reconnoiter the land for us and bring back word on the route we shall follow and the cities we shall come to." ²³I approved of the plan, and so I selected twelve of your men, one from each tribe. ²⁴They made for the hill country, came to the wadi Eshcol, and spied it out. ²⁵They took some of the fruit of the land with them and brought it down to us. And they gave us this report: "It is a good land that the LORD our God is giving to us."

²⁶Yet you refused to go up, and flouted the command of the LORD your God. ²⁷You sulked*ᵉ* in your tents and said, "It is because the LORD hates us that He brought us out of the land of Egypt, to hand us over to the Amorites to wipe us out. ²⁸ ᶠ*What kind of place*ᶠ are we going to? Our kinsmen have taken the

---

ᵉ *Precise meaning of Heb uncertain*
ᶠ⁻ᶠ *Lit. "Where"*

heart out of us, saying, 'We saw there a people stronger and taller than we, large cities with walls sky-high, and even Anakites.'"

<sup>29</sup>I said to you, "Have no dread or fear of them. <sup>30</sup>None other than the LORD your God, who goes before you, will fight for you, just as He did for you in Egypt before your very eyes, <sup>31</sup>and in the wilderness, where you saw how the LORD your God carried you, as a man carries his son, all the way that you traveled until you came to this place. <sup>32</sup>Yet for all that, you have no faith in the LORD your God, <sup>33</sup>who goes before you on your journeys—to scout the place where you are to encamp—in fire by night and in cloud by day, in order to guide you on the route you are to follow."

<sup>34</sup>When the LORD heard your loud complaint, He was angry. He vowed: <sup>35</sup>Not one of these men, this evil generation, shall see the good land that I swore to give to your fathers—<sup>36</sup>none except Caleb son of Jephunneh; he shall see it, and to him and his descendants will I give the land on which he set foot, because he remained loyal to the LORD.—<sup>37</sup>Because of you the LORD was incensed with me too, and He said: You shall not enter it either. <sup>38</sup>Joshua son of Nun, who attends you, he shall enter it. Imbue him with strength, for he shall allot it to Israel.— <sup>39</sup>Moreover, your little ones who you said would be carried off, your children who do not yet know good from bad, they shall enter it; to them will I give it and they shall possess it. <sup>40</sup>As for you, turn about and march into the wilderness by the way of the Sea of Reeds.

<sup>41</sup>You replied to me, saying, "We stand guilty before the LORD. We will go up now and fight, just as the LORD our God commanded us." And you all girded yourselves with war gear and recklessly<sup>g</sup> started for the hill country. <sup>42</sup>But the LORD said to me, "Warn them: Do not go up and do not fight, since I am not in your midst; else you will be routed by your enemies." <sup>43</sup>I spoke to you, but you would not listen; you flouted the LORD's command and willfully marched into the hill country. <sup>44</sup>Then

---

<sup>g</sup> *Meaning of Heb uncertain*

the Amorites who lived in those hills came out against you like so many bees and chased you, and they crushed you at Hormah in Seir. ⁴⁵Again you wept before the LORD; but the LORD would not heed your cry or give ear to you.

**2** ⁴⁶Thus, after you had remained at Kadesh *ʰ-*all that long time,*-ʰ* ¹we marched back into the wilderness by the way of the Sea of Reeds, as the LORD had spoken to me, and skirted the hill country of Seir a long time.

²Then the LORD said to me: ³You have been skirting this hill country long enough; now turn north. ⁴And charge the people as follows: You will be passing through the territory of your kinsmen, the descendants of Esau, who live in Seir. Though they will be afraid of you, be very careful ⁵not to provoke them. For I will not give you of their land so much as a foot can tread on; I have given the hill country of Seir as a possession to Esau. ⁶ *ᵃ-*What food you eat you shall obtain from them for money; even the water you drink you shall procure from them for money.*-ᵃ* ⁷Indeed, the LORD your God has blessed you in all your undertakings. He has watched over your wanderings through this great wilderness; the LORD your God has been with you these past forty years: you have lacked nothing.

⁸We then moved on, away from our kinsmen, the descendants of Esau, who live in Seir, away from the road of the Arabah, away from Elath and Ezion-geber; and we marched on in the direction of the wilderness of Moab. ⁹And the LORD said to me: Do not harass the Moabites or provoke them to war. For I will not give you any of their land as a possession; I have assigned Ar as a possession to the descendants of Lot.—

¹⁰It was formerly inhabited by the Emim, a people great and numerous, and as tall as the Anakites. ¹¹Like the Anakites, they are counted as Rephaim; but the Moabites call them Emim. ¹²Similarly, Seir was formerly inhabited by the Horites; but the descendants of Esau dispossessed them, wiping

h-h *Lit. "many days, like the days that you remained"*

a-a *Or "You may obtain food from them to eat for money; and you may also procure water from them to drink for money"* them out and settling in their place, just as Israel did in the land they were to possess, which the LORD had given to them.—

¹³Up now! Cross the wadi Zered!

So we crossed the wadi Zered. ¹⁴The time that we spent in travel from Kadesh-barnea until we crossed the wadi Zered was thirty-eight years, until that whole generation of warriors had perished from the camp, as the LORD had sworn concerning them. ¹⁵Indeed, the hand of the LORD struck them, to root them out from the camp to the last man.

¹⁶When all the warriors among the people had died off, ¹⁷the LORD spoke to me, saying: ¹⁸You are now passing through the territory of Moab, through Ar. ¹⁹You will then be close to the Ammonites; do not harass them or start a fight with them. For I will not give any part of the land of the Ammonites to you as a possession; I have assigned it as a possession to the descendants of Lot.—

²⁰It, too, is counted as Rephaim country. It was formerly inhabited by Rephaim, whom the Ammonites call Zamzum-mim, ²¹a people great and numerous and as tall as the Anakites. The LORD wiped them out, so that [the Ammonites] dispossessed them and settled in their place, ²²as He did for the descendants of Esau who live in Seir, when He wiped out the Horites before them, so that they dispossessed them and settled in their place, as is still the case.ᵇ ²³So, too, with the Avvim who dwelt in villages in the vicinity of Gaza: the Caphtorim, who came from Crete,ᶜ wiped them out and settled in their place.—

²⁴Up! Set out across the wadi Arnon! See, I give into your power Sihon the Amorite, king of Heshbon, and his land. Begin the occupation: engage him in battle. ²⁵This day I begin to put the dread and fear of you upon the peoples everywhere under heaven, so that they shall tremble and quake because of you whenever they hear you mentioned.

²⁶Then I sent messengers from the wilderness of Kedemoth to

---

ᵇ *Lit. "until this day"*
ᶜ *Heb "Caphtor"*

King Sihon of Heshbon with an offer of peace, as follows, [27]"Let me pass through your country. I will keep strictly to the highway, turning off neither to the right nor to the left. [28]What food I eat you will supply for money, and what water I drink you will furnish for money; just let me pass through[d]—[29]as the descendants of Esau who dwell in Seir did for me, and the Moabites who dwell in Ar—that I may cross the Jordan into the land that the LORD our God is giving us."

[30]But King Sihon of Heshbon refused to let us pass through, because the LORD had stiffened his will and hardened his heart in order to deliver him into your power—as is now the case. [31]And the LORD said to me: See, I begin by placing Sihon and his land at your disposal. Begin the occupation; take possession of his land.

[32]Sihon with all his men took the field against us at Jahaz, [33]and the LORD our God delivered him to us and we defeated him and his sons and all his men. [34]At that time we captured all his towns, and we doomed[e] every town—men, women, and children—leaving no survivor. [35]We retained as booty only the cattle and the spoil of the cities that we captured. [36]From Aroer on the edge of the Arnon valley, including the town[f] in the valley itself, to Gilead, not a city was too mighty for us; the LORD our God delivered everything to us. [37]But you did not encroach upon the land of the Ammonites, all along the wadi Jabbok and the towns of the hill country, just as the LORD our God had commanded.

3 We made our way up the road toward Bashan, and King Og of Bashan with all his men took the field against us at Edrei. [2]But the LORD said to me: Do not fear him, for I am delivering him and all his men and his country into your power, and you will do to him as you did to Sihon king of the Amorites, who lived in Heshbon.

[3]So the LORD our God also delivered into our power King Og

---

d *Lit. "with my feet"*

e *I.e. placed under* ḥerem, *which meant the annihilation of the population. Cf. note b at Num. 21.2; Josh. 6.24*

f *Meaning of Heb uncertain*

of Bashan, with all his men, and we dealt them such a blow that no survivor was left. ⁴At that time we captured all his towns; there was not a town that we did not take from them: sixty towns, the whole district of Argob, the kingdom of Og in Bashan ⁵—all those towns were fortified with high walls, gates,ᵃ and bars—apart from a great number of unwalled towns. ⁶We doomed them as we had done in the case of King Sihon of Heshbon; we doomed every town—men, women, and children —⁷and retained as booty all the cattle and the spoil of the towns.

⁸Thus we seized, at that time, from the two Amorite kings, the country beyond the Jordan, from the wadi Arnon to Mount Hermon—⁹Sidonians called Hermon Sirion, and the Amorites call it Senir—¹⁰all the towns of the Tableland and the whole of Gilead and Bashan as far as Salcahᵇ and Edrei, the towns of Og's kingdom in Bashan. ¹¹Only King Og of Bashan was left of the remaining Rephaim. His bedstead, an iron bedstead, is now in Rabbah of the Ammonites; it is nine cubits long and four cubits wide, by ᶜthe standard cubit!ᶜ

¹² ᵈAnd this is the land which we apportioned at that time: The part from Aroer along the wadi Arnon, with part of the hill country of Gilead and its towns, I assigned to the Reubenites and the Gadites. ¹³The rest of Gilead, and all of Bashan under Og's rule—the whole Argob district, all that part of Bashan which is called Rephaim country—I assigned to the half-tribe of Manasseh. ¹⁴Jair son of Manasseh received the whole Argob district (that is, Bashan) as far as the boundary of the Geshurites and the Maacathites, and named it after himself: Havvoth-jairᵉ—as is still the case. ¹⁵To Machir I assigned Gilead. ¹⁶And to the Reubenites and the Gadites I assigned the part from Gilead down to the wadi Arnon, the middle of the wadi being the boundary, and up to the wadi Jabbok, the boundary of the Ammonites.

¹⁷ ᶠ[We also seized] the Arabah, from the foot of the slopes of Pisgah on the east, to the edge of the Jordan, and from Chinnereth down to the sea of the Arabah, the Dead Sea.

---

ᵃ *I.e. two-leaf doors*   ᵇ *Others "Salecah" or "Salchah"*
ᶜ⁻ᶜ *Lit. "by a man's forearm"*
ᵈ *Vv. 12–13 proceed from south to north; vv. 14–16 from north to south*
ᵉ *I.e. "villages of Jair"*   ᶠ *Continuing vv. 8–10; cf. 4.47–49*

¹⁸At that time I charged you,ᵍ saying, "The LORD your God has given you this country to possess. You must go as shock-troops, warriors all, at the head of your Israelite kinsmen. ¹⁹Only your wives, children, and livestock—I know that you have much livestock—shall be left in the towns I have assigned to you, ²⁰until the LORD has granted your kinsmen a haven such as you have, and they too have taken possession of the land that the LORD your God is assigning them, beyond the Jordan. Then you may return each to the homestead that I have assigned to him."

²¹I also charged Joshua at that time, saying, "You have seen with your own eyes all that the LORD your God has done to these two kings; so shall the LORD do to all the kingdoms into which you shall cross over. ²²Do not fear them, for it is the LORD your God who will battle for you."

ואתחנן

²³I pleaded with the LORD at that time, saying, ²⁴"O Lord GOD, You who let Your servant see the first works of Your greatness and Your mighty hand, You whose powerful deeds no god in heaven or on earth can equal! ²⁵Let me, I pray, cross over and see the good land on the other side of the Jordan, that good hill country, and the Lebanon." ²⁶But the LORD was wrathful with me on your account and would not listen to me. The LORD said to me, "Enough! Never speak to Me of this matter again! ²⁷Go up to the summit of Pisgah and gaze about, to the west, the north, the south, and the east. Look at it well, for you shall not go across yonder Jordan. ²⁸Give Joshua his instructions, and imbue him with strength and courage, for he shall go across at the head of this people, and he shall allot to them the land that you may only see."

²⁹Meanwhile we stayed on in the valley near Beth-peor.

4 And now, O Israel, give heed to the laws and rules that I am instructing you to observe, so that you may live to enter and

ᵍ *I.e. the two and a half tribes*

occupy the land that the LORD, the God of your fathers, is giving you. ²You shall not add anything to what I command you or take anything away from it, but keep the commandments of the LORD your God that I enjoin upon you. ³You saw with your own eyes what the LORD did in the matter of Baal-peor, that the LORD your God wiped out from among you every person who followed Baal-peor; ⁴while you, who held fast to the LORD your God, are all alive today.

⁵See, I have imparted to you laws and rules, as the LORD my God has commanded me, for you to abide by in the land that you are about to enter and occupy. ⁶Observe them faithfully, for that will be proof of your wisdom and discernment to other peoples, who on hearing of all these laws will say, "Surely, that great nation is a wise and discerning people." ⁷For what great nation is there that has a god so close at hand as is the LORD our God whenever we call upon Him? ⁸Or what great nation has laws and rules as perfect as all this Teaching that I set before you this day?

⁹But take utmost care and watch yourselves scrupulously, so that you do not forget the things that you saw with your own eyes and so that they do not fade from your mind as long as you live. And make them known to your children and to your children's children: ¹⁰The day you stood before the LORD your God at Horeb, when the LORD said to me, "Gather the people to Me that I may let them hear My words, in order that they may learn to revere Me as long as they live on earth, and may so teach their children." ¹¹You came forward and stood at the foot of the mountain. The mountain was ablaze with flames to the very skies, dark with densest clouds. ¹²The LORD spoke to you out of the fire; you heard the sound of words but perceived no shape— nothing but a voice. ¹³He declared to you the covenant that He commanded you to observe, the Ten Commandments; and He inscribed them on two tablets of stone. ¹⁴At the same time the LORD commanded me to impart to you laws and rules for you to observe in the land that you are about to cross into and occupy.

¹⁵For your own sake, therefore, be most careful—since you saw no shape when the LORD your God spoke to you at Horeb out of the fire—¹⁶not to act wickedly and make for yourselves a sculptured image in any likeness whatever: the form of a man or a woman, ¹⁷the form of any beast on earth, the form of any winged bird that flies in the sky, ¹⁸the form of anything that creeps on the ground, the form of any fish that is in the waters below the earth.—¹⁹And when you look up to the sky and behold the sun and the moon and the stars, the whole heavenly host, you must not be lured into bowing down to them or serving them. These the LORD your God allotted to other peoples everywhere under heaven; ²⁰but you the LORD took and brought out of Egypt, that iron blast furnace, to be His very own people, as is now the case.

²¹Now the LORD was angry with me on your account and swore that I should not cross the Jordan and enter the good land that the LORD your God is assigning you as a heritage. ²²For I must die in this land; I shall not cross the Jordan. But you will cross and take possession of that good land.

²³Take care, then, not to forget the covenant that the LORD your God concluded with you, and not to make for yourselves a sculptured image in any likeness, against which the LORD your God has enjoined you. ²⁴For the LORD your God is a consuming fire, an impassioned God.

²⁵When you have begotten children and children's children and are long established in the land, should you act wickedly and make for yourselves a sculptured image in any likeness, causing the LORD your God displeasure and vexation, ²⁶I call heaven and earth this day to witness against you that you shall soon perish from the land that you are crossing the Jordan to possess; you shall not long endure in it, but shall be utterly wiped out. ²⁷The LORD will scatter you among the peoples, and only a scant few of you shall be left among the nations to which the LORD will drive you. ²⁸There you will serve man-made gods of wood and stone, that cannot see or hear or eat or smell.

²⁹But if you search there for the LORD your God, you will find Him, if only you seek Him with all your heart and soul—³⁰when you are in distress because all these things have befallen you and, in the end, return to the LORD your God and obey Him. ³¹For the LORD your God is a compassionate God: He will not fail you nor will He let you perish; He will not forget the covenant which He made on oath with your fathers.

³²You have but to inquire about bygone ages that came before you, ever since God created man on earth, from one end of heaven to the other: has anything as grand as this ever happened, or has its like ever been known? ³³Has any people heard the voice of a god speaking out of a fire, as you have, and survived? ³⁴Or has any god ventured to go and take for himself one nation from the midst of another by prodigious acts, by signs and portents, by war, by a mighty hand and an outstretched arm and awesome power, as the LORD your God did for you in Egypt before your very eyes? ³⁵ᵃ⁻It has been clearly demonstrated to you⁻ᵃ that the LORD alone is God; there is none beside Him. ³⁶From the heavens He let you hear His voice to discipline you; on earth He let you see His great fire; and from amidst that fire you heard His words. ³⁷And because He loved your fathers, He chose their heirs after them; He Himself,ᵇ in His great might, led you out of Egypt, ³⁸to drive from your path nations greater and more populous than you, to take you into their land and assign it to you as a heritage, as is still the case. ³⁹Know therefore this day and keep in mind that the LORD alone is God in heaven above and on earth below; there is no other. ⁴⁰Observe His laws and commandments, which I enjoin upon you this day, that it may go well with you and your children after you, and that you may long remain in the land that the LORD your God is assigning to you for all time.

⁴¹Then Moses set aside three cities on the east side of the Jordan ⁴²to which a manslayer could escape, one who unwittingly slew a fellow man without having been hostile to him in

a-a *Lit. "You have been shown to know"*
b *Lit. "With His face (or, Presence)"; cf. note at Exod. 33.14*

the past; he could flee to one of these cities and live: ⁴³Bezer, in the wilderness in the Tableland, belonging to the Reubenites; Ramoth, in Gilead, belonging to the Gadites; and Golan, in Bashan, belonging to the Manassites.

⁴⁴This is the Teaching that Moses set before the Israelites: ⁴⁵these are the decrees, laws, and rules that Moses addressed to the people of Israel, after they had left Egypt, ⁴⁶beyond the Jordan, in the valley at Beth-peor, in the land of King Sihon of the Amorites, who dwelt in Heshbon, whom Moses and the Israelites defeated after they had left Egypt. ⁴⁷They had taken possession of his country and that of King Og of Bashan—the two kings of the Amorites—which were on the east side of the Jordan ⁴⁸from Aroer on the banks of the wadi Arnon, as far as Mount Sion,ᶜ that is, Hermon; ⁴⁹also the whole Arabah on the east side of the Jordan, as far as the Sea of the Arabah, at the foot of the slopes of Pisgah.

5 Moses summoned all the Israelites and said to them: Hear, O Israel, the laws and rules that I proclaim to you this day! Study them and observe them faithfully!

²The LORD our God made a covenant with us at Horeb. ³It was not with our fathers that the LORD made this covenant, but with us, the living, every one of us who is here today. ⁴Face to face the LORD spoke to you on the mountain out of the fire—⁵I stood between the LORD and you at that time to convey the LORD'S words to you, for you were afraid of the fire and did not go up the mountain—saying:

⁶ ᵃI the LORD am your God who brought you out of the land of Egypt, the house of bondage: ⁷You shall have no other gods beside Me.

⁸You shall not make for yourself a sculptured image, any likeness of what is in the heavens above, or on the earth below,

---

ᶜ *Cf. "Sirion," 3.9*

ᵃ *Tradition varies as to the divisions of the Commandments in vv. 6–18 and the numbering of the verses. Cf. Exod. 20, note a* or in the waters below the earth. [9]You shall not bow down to them or serve them. For I the LORD your God am an impassioned God, visiting the guilt of the parents upon the children, upon the third and upon the fourth generations of those who reject Me, [10]but showing kindness to the thousandth generation of those who love Me and keep My commandments.

[11]You shall not swear falsely by the name of the LORD your God; for the LORD will not clear one who swears falsely by His name.

[12]Observe the sabbath day and keep it holy, as the LORD your God has commanded you. [13]Six days you shall labor and do all your work, [14]but the seventh day is a sabbath of the LORD your God; you shall not do any work—you, your son or your daughter, your male or female slave, your ox or your ass, or any of your cattle, or the stranger in your settlements, so that your male and female slave may rest as you do. [15]Remember that you were a slave in the land of Egypt and the LORD your God freed you from there with a mighty hand and an outstretched arm; therefore the LORD your God has commanded you to observe the sabbath day.

[16]Honor your father and your mother, as the LORD your God has commanded you, that you may long endure, and that you may fare well, in the land that the LORD your God is assigning to you.

[17]You shall not murder.

You shall not commit adultery.

You shall not steal.

You shall not bear false witness against your neighbor.

[18]You shall not covet your neighbor's wife. You shall not crave your neighbor's house, or his field, or his male or female slave, or his ox, or his ass, or anything that is your neighbor's.

[19]The LORD spoke those words—those and no more—to your whole congregation at the mountain, with a mighty voice out of the fire and the dense clouds. He inscribed them on two tablets

of stone, which He gave to me. ²⁰When you heard the voice out of the darkness, while the mountain was ablaze with fire, you came up to me, all your tribal heads and elders, ²¹and said, "The LORD our God has just shown us His majestic Presence, and we have heard His voice out of the fire; we have seen this day that man may live though God has spoken to him. ²²Let us not die, then, for this fearsome fire will consume us; if we hear the voice of the LORD our God any longer, we shall die. ²³For what mortal ever heard the voice of the living God speak out of the fire, as we did, and lived? ²⁴You go closer and hear all that the LORD our God says, and then you tell us everything that the LORD our God tells you, and we will willingly do it."

²⁵The LORD heard the plea that you made to me, and the LORD said to me, "I have heard the plea that this people made to you; they did well to speak thus. ²⁶May they always be of such mind, to revere Me and follow all My commandments, that it may go well with them and with their children forever! ²⁷Go, say to them, 'Return to your tents.' ²⁸But you remain here with Me, and I will give you the whole Instruction—the laws and the rules—that you shall impart to them, for them to observe in the land that I am giving them to possess."

²⁹Be careful, then, to do as the LORD your God has commanded you. Do not turn aside to the right or to the left: ³⁰follow only the path that the LORD your God has enjoined upon you, so that you may thrive and that it may go well with you, and that you may long endure in the land you are to possess.

**6** And this is the Instruction—the laws and the rules—that the LORD your God has commanded [me] to impart to you, to be observed in the land that you are about to cross into and occupy, ²so that you, your children, and your children's children may revere the LORD your God and follow, as long as you live, all His laws and commandments that I enjoin upon you, to the end that you may long endure. ³Obey, O Israel, willingly and faithfully, that it may go well with you and that you may increase greatly [in] *ᵃ-a land flowing with milk and honey,-ᵃ* as the LORD, the God of your fathers, spoke to you.

⁴Hear, O Israel! The LORD is our God, the LORD alone.ᵇ ⁵You shall love the LORD your God with all your heart and with all your soul and with all your might. ⁶Take to heart these instructions with which I charge you this day. ⁷Impress them upon your children. Recite them when you stay at home and when you are away, when you lie down and when you get up. ⁸Bind them as a sign on your hand and let them serve as a symbolᶜ on your foreheadᵈ; ⁹inscribe them on the doorposts of your house and on your gates.

¹⁰When the LORD your God brings you into the land that He swore to your fathers, Abraham, Isaac, and Jacob, to assign to you—great and flourishing cities that you did not build, ¹¹houses full of all good things that you did not fill, hewn cisterns that you did not hew, vineyards and olive groves that you did not plant—and you eat your fill, ¹²take heed that you do not forget the LORD who freed you from the land of Egypt, the house of bondage. ¹³Revere only the LORD your God and worship Him alone, and swear only by His name. ¹⁴Do not follow other gods, any gods of the peoples about you ¹⁵—for the LORD your God in your midst is an impassioned God—lest the anger of the LORD your God blaze forth against you and He wipe you off the face of the earth.

¹⁶Do not try the LORD your God, as you did at Massah.ᵉ ¹⁷Be sure to keep the commandments, decrees, and laws that the LORD your God has enjoined upon you. ¹⁸Do what is right and good in the sight of the LORD, that it may go well with you and that you may be able to possess the good land that the LORD your God promised on oath to your fathers, ¹⁹and that all your enemies may be driven out before you, as the LORD has spoken.

---

ᵃ⁻ᵃ *According to Ibn Ezra, this phrase connects with the end of v. 1*
ᵇ *Cf. Rashbam and Ibn Ezra; see Zech. 14.9. Others "The LORD our God, the LORD is one"*
ᶜ *Others "frontlet"; cf. Exod. 13.16*
ᵈ *Lit. "between your eyes"; cf. Exod. 13.9*     ᵉ *Cf. Exod. 17.1–7*

²⁰When, in time to come, your children ask you, "What mean the decrees, laws, and rules that the LORD our God has enjoined upon you?ᶠ" ²¹you shall say to your children, "We were slaves to Pharaoh in Egypt and the LORD freed us from Egypt with a mighty hand. ²²The LORD wrought before our eyes marvelous and destructive signs and portents in Egypt, against Pharaoh and all his household; ²³and us He freed from there, that He might take us and give us the land that He had promised on oath to our fathers. ²⁴Then the LORD commanded us to observe all these laws, to revere the LORD our God, for our lasting good and for our survival, as is now the case. ²⁵It will be therefore to our merit before the LORD our God to observe faithfully this whole Instruction, as He has commanded us."

7 When the LORD your God brings you to the land that you are about to enter and possess, and He dislodges many nations before you—the Hittites, Girgashites, Amorites, Canaanites, Perizzites, Hivites, and Jebusites, seven nations much larger than you—²and the LORD your God delivers them to you and you defeat them, you must doom them to destruction: grant them no terms and give them no quarter. ³You shall not intermarry with them: do not give your daughters to their sons or take their daughters for your sons. ⁴For they will turn your children away from Me to worship other gods, and the LORD's anger will blaze forth against you and He will promptly wipe you out. ⁵Instead, this is what you shall do to them: you shall tear down their altars, smash their pillars, cut down their sacred posts, and consign their images to the fire.

⁶For you are a people consecrated to the LORD your God: of all the peoples on earth the LORD your God chose you to be His treasured people. ⁷It is not because you are the most numerous of peoples that the LORD set His heart on you and chose you— indeed, you are the smallest of peoples; ⁸but it was because the

ᶠ *Septuagint and rabbinic quotations read "us"*

LORD favored you and kept the oath He made to your fathers that the LORD freed you with a mighty hand and rescued you from the house of bondage, from the power of Pharaoh king of Egypt.

⁹Know, therefore, that only the LORD your God is God, the steadfast God who keeps His covenant faithfully to the thousandth generation of those who love Him and keep His commandments, ¹⁰but who instantly requites with destruction those who reject Him—never slow with those who reject Him, but requiting them instantly. ¹¹Therefore, observe faithfully the Instruction—the laws and the rules—with which I charge you today.

עקב

¹²And if you do obey these rules and observe them carefully, the LORD your God will maintain faithfully for you the covenant that He made on oath with your fathers: ¹³He will favor you and bless you and multiply you; He will bless the issue of your womb and the produce of your soil, your new grain and wine and oil, the calving of your herd and the lambing of your flock, in the land that He swore to your fathers to assign to you. ¹⁴You shall be blessed above all other peoples: there shall be no sterile male or female among you or among your livestock. ¹⁵The LORD will ward off from you all sickness; He will not bring upon you any of the dreadful diseases of Egypt, about which you know, but will inflict them upon all your enemies.

¹⁶You shall destroy all the peoples that the LORD your God delivers to you, showing them no pity. And you shall not worship their gods, for that would be a snare to you. ¹⁷Should you say to yourselves, "These nations are more numerous than we; how can we dispossess them?" ¹⁸You need have no fear of them. You have but to bear in mind what the LORD your God did to Pharaoh and all the Egyptians: ¹⁹the wondrous acts that you saw with your own eyes, the signs and the portents, the mighty hand,

and the outstretched arm by which the LORD your God liberated you. Thus will the LORD your God do to all the peoples you now fear. ²⁰The LORD your God will also send a plague*ᵃ* against them, until those who are left in hiding perish before you. ²¹Do not stand in dread of them, for the LORD your God is in your midst, a great and awesome God.

²²The LORD your God will dislodge those peoples before you little by little; you will not be able to put an end to them at once, else the wild beasts would multiply to your hurt. ²³The LORD your God will deliver them up to you, throwing them into utter panic until they are wiped out. ²⁴He will deliver their kings into your hand, and you shall obliterate their name from under the heavens; no man shall stand up to you, until you have wiped them out.

²⁵You shall consign the images of their gods to the fire; you shall not covet the silver and gold on them and keep it for yourselves, lest you be ensnared thereby; for that is abhorrent to the LORD your God. ²⁶You must not bring an abhorrent thing into your house, or you will be proscribed like it; you must reject it as abominable and abhorrent, for it is proscribed.

8 You shall faithfully observe all the Instruction that I enjoin upon you today, that you may thrive and increase and be able to possess the land that the LORD promised on oath to your fathers.

²Remember the long way that the LORD your God has made you travel in the wilderness these past forty years, that He might test you by hardships to learn what was in your hearts: whether you would keep His commandments or not. ³He subjected you to the hardship of hunger and then gave you manna to eat, which neither you nor your fathers had ever known, in order to teach you that man does not live on bread alone, but that man may live on anything that the LORD decrees. ⁴The clothes upon you did not wear out, nor did your feet swell these forty years.

---

ᵃ *Others "hornet"; meaning of Heb uncertain. Cf. note at Exod. 23.28*

⁵Bear in mind that the LORD your God disciplines you just as a man disciplines his son. ⁶Therefore keep the commandments of the LORD your God: walk in His ways and revere Him.

⁷For the LORD your God is bringing you into a good land, a land with streams and springs and fountains issuing from plain and hill; ⁸a land of wheat and barley, of vines, figs, and pomegranates, a land of olive trees and honey; ⁹a land where you may eat food without stint, where you will lack nothing; a land whose rocks are iron and from whose hills you can mine copper. ¹⁰When you have eaten your fill, give thanks to the LORD your God for the good land which He has given you.

¹¹Take care lest you forget the LORD your God and fail to keep His commandments, His rules, and His laws, which I enjoin upon you today. ¹²When you have eaten your fill, and have built fine houses to live in, ¹³and your herds and flocks have multiplied, and your silver and gold have increased, and everything you own has prospered, ¹⁴beware lest<sup>a</sup> your heart grow haughty and you forget the LORD your God—who freed you from the land of Egypt, the house of bondage; ¹⁵who led you through the great and terrible wilderness with its *seraph*<sup>b</sup> serpents and scorpions, a parched land with no water in it, who brought forth water for you from the flinty rock; ¹⁶who fed you in the wilderness with manna, which your fathers had never known, in order to test you by hardships only to benefit you in the end—¹⁷and you say to yourselves, "My own power and the might of my own hand have won this wealth for me." ¹⁸Remember that it is the LORD your God who gives you the power to get wealth, in fulfillment of the covenant that He made on oath with your fathers, as is still the case.

¹⁹If you do forget the LORD your God and follow other gods to serve them or bow down to them, I warn you this day that you shall certainly perish; ²⁰like the nations that the LORD will cause to perish before you, so shall you perish—because you did not heed the LORD your God.

---

<sup>a</sup> *Heb* pen *moved down from v. 12 for clarity*
<sup>b</sup> *See note at Num. 21.6*

9 Hear, O Israel! You are about to cross the Jordan to go in and dispossess nations greater and more populous than you: great cities with walls sky-high; ²a people great and tall, the Anakites, of whom you have knowledge; for you have heard it said, "Who can stand up to the children of Anak?" ³Know then this day that none other than the LORD your God is crossing at your head, a devouring fire; it is He who will wipe them out. He will subdue them before you, that you may quickly dispossess and destroy them, as the LORD promised you. ⁴And when the LORD your God has thrust them from your path, say not to yourselves, "The LORD has enabled us to possess this land because of our virtues"; it is rather because of the wickedness of those nations that the LORD is dispossessing them before you. ⁵It is not because of your virtues and your rectitude that you will be able to possess their country; but it is because of their wickedness that the LORD your God is dispossessing those nations before you, and in order to fulfill the oath that the LORD made to your fathers, Abraham, Isaac, and Jacob.

⁶Know, then, that it is not for any virtue of yours that the LORD your God is giving you this good land to possess; for you are a stiffnecked people. ⁷Remember, never forget, how you provoked the LORD your God to anger in the wilderness: from the day that you left the land of Egypt until you reached this place, you have continued defiant toward the LORD.

⁸At Horeb you so provoked the LORD that the LORD was angry enough with you to have destroyed you. ⁹I had ascended the mountain to receive the tablets of stone, the Tablets of the Covenant that the LORD had made with you, and I stayed on the mountain forty days and forty nights, eating no bread and drinking no water. ¹⁰And the LORD gave me the two tablets of stone inscribed by the finger of God, with the exact words that the LORD had addressed to you on the mountain out of the fire on the day of the Assembly.

<sup>11</sup>At the end of those forty days and forty nights, the Lord gave me the two tablets of stone, the Tablets of the Covenant. <sup>12</sup>And the Lord said to me, "Hurry, go down from here at once, for the people whom you brought out of Egypt have acted wickedly; they have been quick to stray from the path that I enjoined upon them; they have made themselves a molten image." <sup>13</sup>The Lord further said to me, "I see that this is a stiff-necked people. <sup>14</sup>Let Me alone and I will destroy them and blot out their name from under heaven, and I will make you a nation far more numerous than they."

<sup>15</sup>I started down the mountain, a mountain ablaze with fire, the two Tablets of the Covenant in my two hands. <sup>16</sup>I saw how you had sinned against the Lord your God: you had made yourselves a molten calf; you had been quick to stray from the path that the Lord had enjoined upon you. <sup>17</sup>Thereupon I gripped the two tablets and flung them away with both my hands, smashing them before your eyes. <sup>18</sup>I threw myself down before the Lord—eating no bread and drinking no water forty days and forty nights, as before—because of the great wrong you had committed, doing what displeased the Lord and vexing Him. <sup>19</sup>For I was in dread of the Lord's fierce anger against you, which moved Him to wipe you out. And that time, too, the Lord gave heed to me.—<sup>20</sup>Moreover, the Lord was angry enough with Aaron to have destroyed him; so I also interceded for Aaron at that time.—<sup>21</sup>As for that sinful thing you had made, the calf, I took it and put it to the fire; I broke it to bits and ground it thoroughly until it was fine as dust, and I threw its dust into the brook that comes down from the mountain.

<sup>22</sup>Again you provoked the Lord at Taberah, and at Massah, and at Kibroth-hattaavah.

<sup>23</sup>And when the Lord sent you on from Kadesh-barnea, saying, "Go up and take possession of the land that I am giving you," you flouted the command of the Lord your God; you did not put your trust in Him and did not obey Him.

<sup>24</sup>As long as I have known you, you have been defiant toward the LORD.

<sup>25</sup>When I lay prostrate before the LORD <sup>a-</sup>those forty days and forty nights,<sup>-a</sup> because the LORD was determined to destroy you, <sup>26</sup>I prayed to the LORD and said, "O Lord God, do not annihilate Your very own people, whom You redeemed in Your majesty and whom You freed from Egypt with a mighty hand. <sup>27</sup>Give thought to Your servants, Abraham, Isaac, and Jacob, and pay no heed to the stubbornness of this people, its wickedness, and its sinfulness. <sup>28</sup>Else the country from which You freed us will say, 'It was because the LORD was powerless to bring them into the land that He had promised them, and because He rejected them, that He brought them out to have them die in the wilderness.' <sup>29</sup>Yet they are Your very own people, whom You freed with Your great might and Your outstretched arm."

# 10 Thereupon the LORD said to me, "Carve out two tablets of stone like the first, and come up to Me on the mountain; and make an ark of wood. <sup>2</sup>I will inscribe on the tablets the commandments that were on the first tablets that you smashed, and you shall deposit them in the ark."

<sup>3</sup>I made an ark of acacia wood and carved out two tablets of stone like the first; I took the two tablets with me and went up the mountain. <sup>4</sup>The LORD inscribed on the tablets the same text as on the first, the Ten Commandments that He addressed to you on the mountain out of the fire on the day of the Assembly; and the LORD gave them to me. <sup>5</sup>Then I left and went down from the mountain, and I deposited the tablets in the ark that I had made, where they still are, as the LORD had commanded me.

<sup>6</sup>From Beeroth-bene-jaakan<sup>a</sup> the Israelites marched to Moserah. Aaron died there and was buried there; and his son Eleazar became priest in his stead. <sup>7</sup>From there they marched to

---

<sup>a-a</sup> Lit. "the forty days and forty nights that I lay prostrate"

<sup>a</sup> Lit. "wells of Bene-jaakan"; cf. Num. 33.31–32

<sup>b</sup> "Hor-haggidgad" in Num. 33.32–33

Gudgod,*b* and from Gudgod to Jotbath, a region of running brooks.

⁸At that time the LORD set apart the tribe of Levi to carry the Ark of the LORD's Covenant, to stand in attendance upon the LORD, and to bless in His name, as is still the case. ⁹That is why the Levites have received no hereditary portion along with their kinsmen: the LORD is their portion, as the LORD your God spoke concerning them.

¹⁰I had stayed on the mountain, as I did the first time, forty days and forty nights; and the LORD heeded me once again: the LORD agreed not to destroy you. ¹¹And the LORD said to me, "Up, resume the march at the head of the people, that they may go in and possess the land that I swore to their fathers to give them."

¹²And now, O Israel, what does the LORD your God demand of you? Only this: to revere the LORD your God, to walk only in His paths, to love Him, and to serve the LORD your God with all your heart and soul, ¹³keeping the LORD's commandments and laws, which I enjoin upon you today, for your good. ¹⁴Mark, the heavens *ᶜto their uttermost reachesᶜ* belong to the LORD your God, the earth and all that is on it! ¹⁵Yet it was to your fathers that the LORD was drawn in His love for them, so that He chose you, their lineal descendants, from among all peoples—as is now the case. ¹⁶Cut away, therefore, the thickening about your hearts and stiffen your necks no more. ¹⁷For the LORD your God is *ᵈGod supreme and Lord supreme,ᵈ* the great, the mighty, and the awesome God, who shows no favor and takes no bribe, ¹⁸but upholds the cause of the fatherless and the widow, and befriends the stranger, providing him with food and clothing.—¹⁹You too must befriend the stranger, for you were strangers in the land of Egypt.

²⁰You must revere the LORD your God: only Him shall you

---

ᶜ⁻ᶜ *Lit. "and the heaven of heavens"*
ᵈ⁻ᵈ *Lit. "the God of gods and the Lord of lords"*

worship, to Him shall you hold fast, and by His name shall you swear. [21]He is your glory and He is your God, who wrought for you those marvelous, awesome deeds that you saw with your own eyes. [22]Your ancestors went down to Egypt seventy persons in all; and now the LORD your God has made you as numerous as the stars of heaven.

# 11 Love, therefore, the LORD your God, and always keep His charge, His laws, His rules, and His commandments.

[2] [a]Take thought this day that it was not your children, who neither experienced nor witnessed the lesson of the LORD your God—

His majesty, His mighty hand, His outstretched arm; [3]the signs and the deeds that He performed in Egypt against Pharaoh king of Egypt and all his land; [4]what He did to Egypt's army, its horses and chariots; how the LORD rolled back upon them the waters of the Sea of Reeds when they were pursuing you, thus destroying them [b]once and for all[b]; [5]what He did for you in the wilderness before you arrived in this place; [6]and what He did to Dathan and Abiram, sons of Eliab son of Reuben, when the earth opened her mouth and swallowed them, along with their households, their tents, and every living thing in their train, from amidst all Israel—

[7]but that it was you who saw with your own eyes all the marvelous deeds that the LORD performed.

[8]Keep, therefore, all the Instruction that I enjoin upon you today, so that you may have the strength to enter and take possession of the land that you are about to cross into and possess, [9]and that you may long endure upon the soil that the LORD swore to your fathers to assign to them and to their heirs, a land flowing with milk and honey.

[10]For the land that you are about to enter and possess is not

---

[a] *Syntax of Heb uncertain*
[b-b] *Lit. "to this day"*

like the land of Egypt from which you have come. There the grain you sowed had to be watered by your own labors,*c* like a vegetable garden; ¹¹but the land you are about to cross into and possess, a land of hills and valleys, soaks up its water from the rains of heaven. ¹²It is a land which the LORD your God looks after, on which the LORD your God always keeps His eye, from year's beginning to year's end.

¹³If, then, you obey the commandments that I enjoin upon you this day, loving the LORD your God and serving Him with all your heart and soul, ¹⁴*d*I will grant the rain for your land in season, the early rain and the late. You shall gather in your new grain and wine and oil—¹⁵I*d* will also provide grass in the fields for your cattle—and thus you shall eat your fill. ¹⁶Take care not to be lured away to serve other gods and bow to them. ¹⁷For the LORD's anger will flare up against you, and He will shut up the skies so that there will be no rain and the ground will not yield its produce; and you will soon perish from the good land that the LORD is assigning to you.

¹⁸Therefore impress these My words upon your *e*~very heart*e*: bind them as a sign on your hand and let them serve as a *f*symbol on your forehead,*⁻f* ¹⁹and teach them to your children—reciting them when you stay at home and when you are away, when you lie down and when you get up; ²⁰and inscribe them on the doorposts of your house and on your gates—²¹to the end that you and your children may endure, in the land that the LORD swore to your fathers to assign to them, as long as there is a heaven over the earth.

²²If, then, you faithfully keep all this Instruction that I command you, loving the LORD your God, walking in all His ways, and holding fast to Him, ²³the LORD will dislodge before you all these nations: you will dispossess nations greater and more numerous than you. ²⁴Every spot on which your foot treads shall be yours; your territory shall extend from the wilderness to the Lebanon and from the River—the Euphrates—to the Western*g*

---

c  Lit. *"by your foot"*
d  I.e. the LORD; Samaritan reads *"He"*
e-e  Lit. *"heart and self"*
f-f  See notes on 6.8
g  I.e. Mediterranean

Sea. <sup>25</sup>No man shall stand up to you: the LORD your God will put the dread and the fear of you over the whole land in which you set foot, as He promised you.

ראה

<sup>26</sup>See, this day I set before you blessing and curse: <sup>27</sup>blessing, if you obey the commandments of the LORD your God that I enjoin upon you this day; <sup>28</sup>and curse, if you do not obey the commandments of the LORD your God, but turn away from the path that I enjoin upon you this day and follow other gods, <sup>h-</sup>whom you have not experienced.<sup>-h</sup> <sup>29</sup>When the LORD your God brings you into the land that you are about to enter and possess, you shall pronounce the blessing at Mount Gerizim and the curse at Mount Ebal.—<sup>30</sup>Both are on the other side of the Jordan, beyond the west road that is in the land of the Canaanites who dwell in the Arabah—near Gilgal, by the terebinths of Moreh.

<sup>31</sup>For you are about to cross the Jordan to enter and possess the land that the LORD your God is assigning to you. When you have occupied it and are settled in it, <sup>32</sup>take care to observe all the laws and rules that I have set before you this day.

**12** These are the laws and rules that you must carefully observe in the land that the LORD, God of your fathers, is giving you to possess, as long as you live on earth.

<sup>2</sup>You must destroy all the sites at which the nations you are to dispossess worshiped their gods, whether on lofty mountains and on hills or under any luxuriant tree. <sup>3</sup>Tear down their altars, smash their pillars, put their sacred posts to the fire, and cut down the images of their gods, obliterating their name from that site.

<sup>4</sup>Do not worship the LORD your God in like manner, <sup>5</sup>but look only to the site that the LORD your God will choose amidst all your tribes as His habitation, to establish His name there. There

---

h-h *I.e. who have not proved themselves to you; cf. Hos. 13.4* you are to go, [6]and there you are to bring your burnt offerings and other sacrifices, your tithes and contributions,[a] your votive and freewill offerings, and the firstlings of your herds and flocks. [7]Together with your households, you shall feast there before the LORD your God, happy in all the undertakings in which the LORD your God has blessed you.

[8]You shall not act at all as we now act here, every man as he pleases, [9]because you have not yet come to the allotted haven that the LORD your God is giving you. [10]When you cross the Jordan and settle in the land that the LORD your God is allotting to you, and He grants you safety from all your enemies around you and you live in security, [11]then you must bring everything that I command you to the site where the LORD your God will choose to establish His name: your burnt offerings and other sacrifices, your tithes and contributions,[a] and all the choice votive offerings that you vow to the LORD. [12]And you shall rejoice before the LORD your God with your sons and daughters and with your male and female slaves, along with the Levite in your settlements, for he has no territorial allotment among you.

[13]Take care not to sacrifice your burnt offerings in any place you like, [14]but only in the place that the LORD will choose in one of your tribal territories. There you shall sacrifice your burnt offerings and there you shall observe all that I enjoin upon you. [15]But whenever you desire, you may slaughter and eat meat in any of your settlements, according to the blessing that the LORD your God has granted you. The unclean and the clean alike may partake of it, as of the gazelle and the deer.[b] [16]But you must not partake of the blood; you shall pour it out on the ground like water.

[17]You may not partake in your settlements of the tithes of your new grain or wine or oil, or of the firstlings of your herds and flocks, or of any of the votive offerings that you vow, or of your freewill offerings, or of your contributions.[a] [18]These you must consume before the LORD your God in the place that the LORD your God will choose—you and your sons and your

---

[a] Lit. "the contribution(s) of your hands"
[b] I.e. animals that may be eaten (cf. 14.5; Lev. 11.1 ff.), but not sacrificed (Lev 1.1 ff.)

daughters, your male and female slaves, and the Levite in your settlements—happy before the LORD your God in all your undertakings. [19]Be sure not to neglect the Levite as long as you live in your land.

[20]When the LORD enlarges your territory, as He has promised you, and you say, "I shall eat some meat," for you have the urge to eat meat, you may eat meat whenever you wish. [21]If the place where the LORD has chosen to establish His name is too far from you, you may slaughter any of the cattle or sheep that the LORD gives you, as I have instructed you; and you may eat to your heart's content in your settlements. [22]Eat it, however, as the gazelle and the deer are eaten: the unclean may eat it together with the clean. [23]But make sure that you do not partake of the blood; for the blood is the life, and you must not consume the life with the flesh. [24]You must not partake of it; you must pour it out on the ground like water: [25]you must not partake of it, in order that it may go well with you and with your descendants to come, for you will be doing what is right in the sight of the LORD.

[26]But such sacred and votive donations as you may have ⸢shall be taken by you⸣ to the site that the LORD will choose. [27]You shall offer your burnt offerings, both the flesh and the blood, on the altar of the LORD your God; and of your other sacrifices, the blood shall be poured out on the altar of the LORD your God, and you shall eat the flesh.

[28]Be careful to heed all these commandments that I enjoin upon you; thus it will go well with you and with your descendants after you forever, for you will be doing what is good and right in the sight of the LORD your God.

[29]When the LORD your God has cut down before you the nations that you are about to enter and dispossess, and you have dispossessed them and settled in their land, [30]beware of being lured into their ways after they have been wiped out before you! Do not inquire about their gods, saying, "How did those nations worship their gods? I too will follow those practices." [31]You shall

⸢⸣ *Lit. "you shall pick up and come"*

not act thus toward the LORD your God, for they perform for their gods every abhorrent act that the LORD detests; they even

**13** offer up their sons and daughters in fire to their gods. [1]Be careful to observe only that which I enjoin upon you: neither add to it nor take away from it.

[2]If there appears among you a prophet or a dream-diviner and he gives you a sign or a portent, [3]saying, "Let us follow and worship another god"—whom you have not experienced[a]— even if the sign or portent that he named to you comes true, [4]do not heed the words of that prophet or that dream-diviner. For the LORD your God is testing you to see whether you really love the LORD your God with all your heart and soul. [5]Follow none but the LORD your God, and revere none but Him; observe His commandments alone, and heed only His orders; worship none but Him, and hold fast to Him. [6]As for that prophet or dream-diviner, he shall be put to death; for he urged disloyalty to the LORD your God—who freed you from the land of Egypt and who redeemed you from the house of bondage—to make you stray from the path that the LORD your God commanded you to follow. Thus you will sweep out evil from your midst.

[7]If your brother, [b]your own mother's son,[b] or your son or daughter, or the wife of your bosom, or your [c]closest friend[c] entices you in secret, saying, "Come let us worship other gods"—whom neither you nor your fathers have experienced[a]—[8]from among the gods of the peoples around you, either near to you or distant, anywhere from one end of the earth to the other: [9]do not assent or give heed to him. Show him no pity or compassion, and do not shield him; [10]but take his life. Let your hand be the first against him to put him to death, and the hand of the rest of the people thereafter. [11]Stone him to death, for he sought to make you stray from the LORD your God, who brought you out of the land of Egypt, out of the house of bondage. [12]Thus all Israel will hear and be afraid, and such evil things will not be done again in your midst.

[13]If you hear it said, of one of the towns that the LORD your God is giving you to dwell in, [14]that some scoundrels from

a *See note on 11.28*
b-b *Samaritan reads, "the son of your father or the son of your mother"*
c-c *Lit. "your friend who is as yourself"*

361

among you have gone and subverted the inhabitants of their town, saying, "Come let us worship other gods"—whom you have not experienced—¹⁵you shall investigate and inquire and interrogate thoroughly. If it is true, the fact is established—that abhorrent thing was perpetrated in your midst—¹⁶put the inhabitants of that town to the sword and put its cattle to the sword. Doom it and all that is in it to destruction: ¹⁷gather all its spoil into the open square, and burn the town and all its spoil as a holocaust to the LORD your God. And it shall remain an everlasting ruin, never to be rebuilt. ¹⁸Let nothing that has been doomed stick to your hand, in order that the LORD may turn from His blazing anger and show you compassion, and in His compassion increase you as He promised your fathers on oath—¹⁹for you will be heeding the LORD your God, obeying all His commandments that I enjoin upon you this day, doing what is right in the sight of the LORD your God.

**14** You are children of the LORD your God. You shall not gash yourselves or shave the front of your heads because of the dead. ²For you are a people consecrated to the LORD your God: the LORD your God chose you from among all other peoples on earth to be His treasured people.

³You shall not eat anything abhorrent. ⁴These are the animals that you may eat: the ox, the sheep, and the goat; ⁵ ᵃthe deer, the gazelle, the roebuck, the wild goat, the ibex, the antelope, the mountain sheep, ⁶and any other animal that has true hoofs which are cleft in two and brings up the cud—such you may eat. ⁷But the following, which do bring up the cud or have true hoofs which are cleft through, you may not eat: the camel, the hare, and the daman—for although they bring up the cud, they have no true hoofs—they are unclean for you; ⁸also the swine—for although it has true hoofs, it does not bring up the cud—is unclean for you. You shall not eat of their flesh or touch their carcasses.

---

ᵃ *A number of these creatures cannot be identified with certainty*

⁹These you may eat of all that live in water: you may eat anything that has fins and scales. ¹⁰But you may not eat anything that has no fins and scales: it is unclean for you.

¹¹You may eat any clean bird. ¹²The following you may not eat: ᵃthe eagle, the vulture, and the black vulture; ¹³the kite, the falcon, and the buzzard of any variety; ¹⁴every variety of raven; ¹⁵the ostrich, the nighthawk, the sea gull, and the hawk of any variety; ¹⁶the little owl, the great owl, and the white owl; ¹⁷the pelican, the bustard, and the cormorant; ¹⁸the stork, any variety of heron, the hoopoe, and the bat.

¹⁹All winged swarming things are unclean for you: they may not be eaten. ²⁰You may eat only clean winged creatures.

²¹You shall not eat anything that has died a natural death; give it to the stranger in your community to eat, or you may sell it to a foreigner. For you are a people consecrated to the LORD your God.

You shall not boil a kid in its mother's milk.

²²You shall set aside every year a tenth part of all the yield of your sowing that is brought from the field. ²³You shall consume the tithes of your new grain and wine and oil, and the firstlings of your herds and flocks, in the presence of the LORD your God, in the place where He will choose to establish His name, so that you may learn to revere the LORD your God forever. ²⁴Should the distance be too great for you, should you be unable to transport them, because the place where the LORD your God has chosen to establish His name is far from you and because the LORD your God has blessed you,ᵇ ²⁵you may convert them into money. Wrap up the money and take it with you to the place that the LORD your God has chosen, ²⁶and spend the money on anything you want—cattle, sheep, wine, or other intoxicant, or anything you may desire. And you shall feast there, in the presence of the LORD your God, and rejoice with your household.

²⁷But do not neglect the Levite in your community, for he has

ᵇ *I.e. with abundant crops*

no hereditary portion as you have. <sup>28c-</sup>Every third year<sup>-c</sup> you shall bring out the full tithe of your yield of that year, but leave it within your settlements. <sup>29</sup>Then the Levite, who has no hereditary portion as you have, and the stranger, the fatherless, and the widow in your settlements shall come and eat their fill, so that the LORD your God may bless you in all the enterprises you undertake.

**15** <sup>a-</sup>Every seventh year<sup>-a</sup> you shall practice remission of debts. <sup>2</sup>This shall be the nature of the remission: every creditor shall remit the due that he claims from his fellow; he shall not dun his fellow or kinsman, for the remission proclaimed is of the LORD. <sup>3</sup>You may dun the foreigner; but you must remit whatever is due you from your kinsmen.

<sup>4</sup>There shall be no needy among you—since the LORD your God will bless you in the land that the LORD your God is giving you as a hereditary portion—<sup>5</sup>if only you heed the LORD your God and take care to keep all this Instruction that I enjoin upon you this day. <sup>6</sup>For the LORD your God will bless you as He has promised you: you will extend loans to many nations, but require none yourself; you will dominate many nations, but they will not dominate you.

<sup>7</sup>If, however, there is a needy person among you, one of your kinsmen in any of your settlements in the land that the LORD your God is giving you, do not harden your heart and shut your hand against your needy kinsman. <sup>8</sup>Rather, you must open your hand and lend him sufficient for whatever he needs. <sup>9</sup>Beware lest you harbor the base thought, "The seventh year, the year of remission, is approaching," so that you are mean to your needy kinsman and give him nothing. He will cry out to the LORD against you, and you will incur guilt. <sup>10</sup>Give to him readily and have no regrets when you do so, for in return the LORD your God will bless you in all your efforts and in all your undertakings. <sup>11</sup>For there will never cease to be needy ones in your

c-c *Lit. "After a period of three years"; cf. Deut. 26.12*

a-a *Cf. 14.28*

land, which is why I command you: open your hand to the poor and needy kinsman in your land.

¹²If a fellow Hebrew, man or woman, is sold to you, he shall serve you six years, and in the seventh year you shall set him free. ¹³When you set him free, do not let him go empty-handed: ¹⁴Furnish him out of the flock, threshing floor, and vat, with which the Lord your God has blessed you. ¹⁵Bear in mind that you were slaves in the land of Egypt and the Lord your God redeemed you; therefore I enjoin this commandment upon you today.

¹⁶But should he say to you, "I do not want to leave you"—for he loves you and your household and is happy with you—¹⁷you shall take an awl and put it through his ear into the door, and he shall become your slave in perpetuity. Do the same with your female slave. ¹⁸When you do set him free, do not feel aggrieved; for in the six years he has given you double the service of a hired man. Moreover, the Lord your God will bless you in all you do.

¹⁹You shall consecrate to the Lord your God all male firstlings that are born in your herd and in your flock: you must not work your firstling ox or shear your firstling sheep. ²⁰You and your household shall eat it annually before the Lord your God in the place that the Lord will choose. ²¹But if it has a defect, lameness or blindness, any serious defect, you shall not sacrifice it to the Lord your God. ²²Eat it in your settlements, the unclean among you no less than the clean, just like the gazelle and the deer. ²³Only you must not partake of its blood; you shall pour it out on the ground like water.

16 Observe the month*a* of Abib and offer a passover sacrifice to the Lord your God, for it was in the month of Abib, at night, that the Lord your God freed you from Egypt. ²You shall slaughter the passover sacrifice for the Lord your God, from the flock and the herd, in the place where the Lord will choose to establish His name. ³You shall not eat anything leavened with

---

a *Cf. Exod. 13.4; 23.15; 34.18*

it; for seven days thereafter[b] you shall eat unleavened bread, bread of distress—for you departed from the land of Egypt hurriedly—so that you may remember the day of your departure from the land of Egypt as long as you live. [4]For seven days no leaven shall be found with you in all your territory, and none of the flesh of what you slaughter on the evening of the first day shall be left until morning.

[5]You are not permitted to slaughter the passover sacrifice in any of the settlements that the LORD your God is giving you; [6]but at the place where the LORD your God will choose to establish His name, there alone shall you slaughter the passover sacrifice, in the evening, at sundown, the time of day when you departed from Egypt. [7]You shall cook and eat it at the place that the LORD your God will choose; and in the morning you may start back on your journey home. [8]After eating unleavened bread six days, you shall hold a solemn gathering[c] for the LORD your God on the seventh day: you shall do no work.

[9]You shall count off seven weeks; start to count the seven weeks when the sickle is first put to the standing grain. [10]Then you shall observe the Feast of Weeks for the LORD your God, offering your freewill contribution according as the LORD your God has blessed you. [11]You shall rejoice before the LORD your God with your son and daughter, your male and female slave, the Levite in your communities, and the stranger, the fatherless, and the widow in your midst, at the place where the LORD your God will choose to establish His name. [12]Bear in mind that you were slaves in Egypt, and take care to obey these laws.

[13]After the ingathering from your threshing floor and your vat, you shall hold the Feast of Booths for seven days. [14]You shall rejoice in your festival, with your son and daughter, your male and female slave, the Levite, the stranger, the fatherless, and the widow in your communities. [15]You shall hold a festival for the LORD your God seven days, in the place that the LORD will choose; for the LORD your God will bless all[d] your crops and all your undertakings, and you shall have nothing but joy.

[16]Three times a year—on the Feast of Unleavened Bread, on

b *Lit. "upon it"*
c *See note at Lev. 23.36*
d *Lit. "you in all"*

the Feast of Weeks, and on the Feast of Booths—all your males shall appear before the LORD your God in the place that He will choose. They shall not appear before the LORD empty-handed, [17]but each with his own gift, according to the blessing that the LORD your God has bestowed upon you.

שפטים

[18]You shall appoint magistrates and officials for your tribes, in all the settlements that the LORD your God is giving you, and they shall govern the people with due justice. [19]You shall not judge unfairly: you shall show no partiality; you shall not take bribes, for bribes blind the eyes of the discerning and upset the plea of the just. [20]Justice, justice shall you pursue, that you may thrive and occupy the land that the LORD your God is giving you.

[21]You shall not set up a sacred post—any kind of pole beside the altar of the LORD your God that you may make—[22]or erect a stone pillar; for such the LORD your God detests.

17 You shall not sacrifice to the LORD your God an ox or a sheep that has any defect of a serious kind, for that is abhorrent to the LORD your God.

[2]If there is found among you, in one of the settlements that the LORD your God is giving you, a man or woman who has affronted the LORD your God and transgressed His covenant— [3]turning to the worship of other gods and bowing down to them, to the sun or the moon or any of the heavenly host, something I never commanded—[4]and you have been informed or have learned of it, then you shall make a thorough inquiry. If it is true, the fact is established, that abhorrent thing was perpetrated in Israel, [5]you shall take the man or the woman who did that wicked thing out to the public place, and you shall stone them, man or woman, to death.—[6]A person shall be put to death only on the testimony of two or more[a] witnesses; he must

---

[a] Lit. "three"

not be put to death on the testimony of a single witness.—[7]Let the hands of the witnesses be the first against him to put him to death, and the hands of the rest of the people thereafter. Thus you will sweep out evil from your midst.

[8]If a case is too baffling for you to decide, be it a controversy over homicide, civil law, or assault—matters of dispute in your courts—you shall promptly repair to the place that the LORD your God will have chosen, [9]and appear before the levitical priests, or the magistrate in charge at the time, and present your problem. When they have announced to you the verdict in the case, [10]you shall carry out the verdict that is announced to you from that place that the LORD chose, observing scrupulously all their instructions to you. [11]You shall act in accordance with the instructions given you and the ruling handed down to you; you must not deviate from the verdict that they announce to you either to the right or to the left. [12]Should a man act presumptuously and disregard the priest charged with serving there the LORD your God, or the magistrate, that man shall die. Thus you will sweep out evil from Israel: [13]all the people will hear and be afraid and will not act presumptuously again.

[14]If, after you have entered the land that the LORD your God has assigned to you, and taken possession of it and settled in it, you decide, "I will set a king over me, as do all the nations about me," [15]you shall be free to set a king over yourself, one chosen by the LORD your God. Be sure to set as king over yourself one of your own people; you must not set a foreigner over you, one who is not your kinsman. [16]Moreover, he shall not keep many horses or send people back to Egypt to add to his horses, since the LORD has warned you, "You must not go back that way again." [17]And he shall not have many wives, lest his heart go astray; nor shall he amass silver and gold to excess.

[18]When he is seated on his royal throne, he shall have a copy of this Teaching written for him on a scroll by[b] the levitical priests. [19]Let it remain with him and let him read in it all his life, so that he may learn to revere the LORD his God, to observe faithfully every word of this Teaching as well as these laws.

b *Nuance of Heb* milliphne *uncertain*

²⁰Thus he will not act haughtily toward his fellows or deviate from the Instruction to the right or to the left, to the end that he and his descendants may reign long in the midst of Israel.

18 The levitical priests, the whole tribe of Levi, shall have no territorial portion with Israel. They shall live only off the LORD's offerings by fire as their*ᵃ* portion, ²and shall have no portion among their brother tribes: the LORD is their portion, as He promised them.

³This then shall be the priests' due from the people: Everyone who offers a sacrifice, whether an ox or a sheep, must give the shoulder, the cheeks, and the stomach to the priest. ⁴You shall also give him the first fruits of your new grain and wine and oil, and the first shearing of your sheep. ⁵For the LORD your God has chosen him and his descendants, out of all your tribes, to be in attendance for service in the name of the LORD for all time.

⁶If a Levite would go, from any of the settlements throughout Israel where he has been residing, to the place that the LORD has chosen, he may do so whenever he pleases. ⁷He may serve in the name of the LORD his God like all his fellow Levites who are there in attendance before the LORD. ⁸They shall receive equal shares of the dues, *ᵇ*without regard to personal gifts or patrimonies.*⁻ᵇ*

⁹When you enter the land that the LORD your God is giving you, you shall not learn to imitate the abhorrent practices of those nations. ¹⁰Let no one be found among you who consigns his son or daughter to the fire, or who is an augur, a soothsayer, a diviner, a sorcerer, ¹¹one who casts spells, or one who consults ghosts or familiar spirits, or one who inquires of the dead. ¹²For anyone who does such things is abhorrent to the LORD, and it is because of these abhorrent things that the LORD your God is dispossessing them before you. ¹³You must be wholehearted with the LORD your God. ¹⁴Those nations that you are about to

---

ᵃ *Lit. "its," i.e. the tribe's*
ᵇ⁻ᵇ *Meaning of Heb uncertain*

dispossess do indeed resort to soothsayers and augurs; to you, however, the LORD your God has not assigned the like.

¹⁵The LORD your God will raise up for you a prophet from among your own people, like myself; him you shall heed. ¹⁶This is just what you asked of the LORD your God at Horeb, on the day of the Assembly, saying, "Let me not hear the voice of the LORD my God any longer or see this wondrous fire any more, lest I die." ¹⁷Whereupon the LORD said to me, "They have done well in speaking thus. ¹⁸I will raise up a prophet for them from among their own people, like yourself: I will put My words in his mouth and he will speak to them all that I command him; ¹⁹and if anybody fails to heed the words he speaks in My name, I Myself will call him to account. ²⁰But any prophet who presumes to speak in My name an oracle that I did not command him to utter, or who speaks in the name of other gods—that prophet shall die." ²¹And should you ask yourselves, "How can we know that the oracle was not spoken by the LORD?"—²²if the prophet speaks in the name of the LORD and the oracle does not come true, that oracle was not spoken by the LORD; the prophet has uttered it presumptuously: do not stand in dread of him.

19 When the LORD your God has cut down the nations whose land the LORD your God is assigning to you, and you have dispossessed them and settled in their towns and homes, ²you shall set aside three cities in the land that the LORD your God is giving you to possess. ³You shall survey the distances, and divide into three parts the territory of the country that the LORD your God has allotted to you, so that any manslayer may have a place to flee to. ⁴—Now this is the case of the manslayer who may flee there and live: one who has killed another unwittingly, without having been his enemy in the past. ⁵For instance, a man goes with his neighbor into a grove to cut wood; as his hand swings the ax to cut down a tree, the ax-head flies off the handle and strikes the other so that he dies. That man shall flee to one of these cities and live.—⁶Otherwise, when the distance is great,

the blood-avenger, pursuing the manslayer in hot anger, may overtake him and kill him; yet he did not incur the death penalty, since he had never been the other's enemy. [7]That is why I command you: set aside three cities.

[8]And when the LORD your God enlarges your territory, as He swore to your fathers, and gives you all the land that He promised to give your fathers—[9]if you faithfully observe all this Instruction that I enjoin upon you this day, to love the LORD your God and to walk in His ways at all times—then you shall add three more towns to those three. [10]Thus blood of the innocent will not be shed, bringing bloodguilt upon you in the land that the LORD your God is allotting to you.

[11]If, however, a person who is the enemy of another lies in wait for him and sets upon him and strikes him a fatal blow and then flees to one of these towns, [12]the elders of his town shall have him brought back from there and shall hand him over to the blood-avenger to be put to death; [13]you must show him no pity. Thus you will purge Israel of the blood of the innocent,[a] and it will go well with you.

[14]You shall not move your countryman's landmarks, set up by previous generations, in the property that will be allotted to you in the land that the LORD your God is giving you to possess.

[15]A single witness may not validate against a person any guilt or blame for any offense that may be committed; a case can be valid only on the testimony of two witnesses or more.[b] [16]If a man appears against another to testify maliciously and gives false testimony against him, [17]the two parties to the dispute shall appear before the LORD, before the priests or magistrates in authority at the time, [18]and the magistrates shall make a thorough investigation. If the man who testified is a false witness, if he has testified falsely against his fellow, [19]you shall do to him as he schemed to do to his fellow. Thus you will sweep out evil from your midst; [20]others will hear and be afraid, and such evil things will not again be done in your midst. [21]Nor must you show pity: life for life, eye for eye, tooth for tooth, hand for hand, foot for foot.

---

[a] *Cf. Num. 35.33–34*
[b] *See note at 17.6*

20 When you take the field against your enemies, and see horses and chariots—forces larger than yours—have no fear of them, for the LORD your God, who brought you from the land of Egypt, is with you. ²Before you join battle, the priest shall come forward and address the troops. ³He shall say to them, "Hear, O Israel! You are about to join battle with your enemy. Let not your courage falter. Do not be in fear, or in panic, or in dread of them. ⁴For it is the LORD your God who marches with you to do battle for you against your enemy, to bring you victory."

⁵Then the officials shall address the troops, as follows: "Is there anyone who has built a new house but has not dedicated it? Let him go back to his home, lest he die in battle and another dedicate it. ⁶Is there anyone who has planted a vineyard but has never harvested it? Let him go back to his home, lest he die in battle and another harvest it. ⁷Is there anyone who has paid the bride-price for a wife*ᵃ*, but who has not yet married her? Let him go back to his home, lest he die in battle and another marry her." ⁸The officials shall go on addressing the troops and say, "Is there anyone afraid and disheartened? Let him go back to his home, lest the courage of his comrades flag like his." ⁹When the officials have finished addressing the troops, army commanders shall assume command of the troops.

¹⁰When you approach a town to attack it, you shall ᵇ-offer it terms of peace.-ᵇ ¹¹If it responds peaceably and lets you in, all the people present there shall serve you at forced labor. ¹²If it does not surrender to you, but would join battle with you, you shall lay siege to it; ¹³and when the LORD your God delivers it into your hand, you shall put all its males to the sword. ¹⁴You may, however, take as your booty the women, the children, the livestock, and everything in the town—all its spoil—and enjoy the use of the spoil of your enemy, which the LORD your God gives you.

¹⁵Thus you shall deal with all towns that lie very far from you,

---

ᵃ *Thereby making her his wife legally, even though the marriage has not yet taken place*
ᵇ⁻ᵇ *Or, "call on it to surrender"*

towns that do not belong to nations hereabout. [16]In the towns of the latter peoples, however, which the LORD your God is giving you as a heritage, you shall not let a soul remain alive. [17]No, you must proscribe[c] them—the Hittites and the Amorites, the Canaanites and the Perizzites, the Hivites and the Jebusites—as the LORD your God has commanded you, [18]lest they lead you into doing all the abhorrent things that they have done for their gods and you stand guilty before the LORD your God.

[19]When in your war against a city you have to besiege it a long time in order to capture it, you must not destroy its trees, wielding the ax against them. You may eat of them, but you must not cut them down. Are trees of the field human to withdraw before you into the besieged city? [20]Only trees that you know do not yield food may be destroyed; you may cut them down for constructing siegeworks against the city that is waging war on you, until it has been reduced.

# 21

If, in the land that the LORD your God is assigning you to possess, someone slain is found lying in the open, the identity of the slayer not being known, [2]your elders and magistrates shall go out and measure the distances from the corpse to the nearby towns. [3]The elders of the town nearest to the corpse shall then take a heifer which has never been worked, which has never pulled in a yoke; [4]and the elders of that town shall bring the heifer down to an everflowing wadi, which is not tilled or sown. There, in the wadi, they shall break the heifer's neck. [5]The priests, sons of Levi, shall come forward; for the LORD your God has chosen them to minister to Him and to pronounce blessing in the name of the LORD, and every lawsuit and case of assault[a] is subject to their ruling. [6]Then all the elders of the town nearest to the corpse shall wash their hands over the heifer whose neck was broken in the wadi. [7]And they shall make this declaration: "Our hands did not shed this blood, nor did our eyes see it done. [8]Absolve, O LORD, Your people Israel whom You redeemed,

---

c *See Lev. 27.29*

a *Cf. 17.8. Or "skin affection"; cf. 24.8*

and do not let guilt for the blood of the innocent remain among Your people Israel." And they will be absolved of bloodguilt. ⁹Thus you will remove from your midst guilt for the blood of the innocent, for you will be doing what is right in the sight of the LORD.

כי תצא

¹⁰When you take the field against your enemies, and the LORD your God delivers them into your power and you take some of them captive, ¹¹and you see among the captives a beautiful woman and you desire her and would take her to wife, ¹²you shall bring her into your house, and she shall trim her hair, pare her nails, ¹³and discard her captive's garb. She shall spend a month's time in your house lamenting her father and mother; after that you may come to her and possess her, and she shall be your wife. ¹⁴Then, should you no longer want her, you must release her outright. You must not sell her for money: since you had your will of her, you must not enslave her.

¹⁵If a man has two wives, one loved and the other unloved, and both the loved and the unloved have borne him sons, but the first-born is the son of the unloved one—¹⁶when he wills his property to his sons, he may not treat as first-born the son of the loved one in disregard of the son of the unloved one who is older. ¹⁷Instead, he must accept the first-born, the son of the unloved one, and allot to him a double portion*b* of all he possesses; since he is the first fruit of his vigor, the birthright is his due.

¹⁸If a man has a wayward and defiant son, who does not heed his father or mother and does not obey them even after they discipline him, ¹⁹his father and mother shall take hold of him and bring him out to the elders of his town at the public place of his community. ²⁰They shall say to the elders of his town, "This

b  *Lit. two-thirds*

son of ours is disloyal and defiant; he does not heed us. He is a glutton and a drunkard." <sup>21</sup>Thereupon the men of his town shall stone him to death. Thus you will sweep out evil from your midst: all Israel will hear and be afraid.

<sup>22</sup>If a man is guilty of a capital offense and is put to death, and you impale him on a stake, <sup>23</sup>you must not let his corpse remain on the stake overnight, but must bury him the same day. For an impaled body is an affront to God: you shall not defile the land that the LORD your God is giving you to possess.

**22** If you see your fellow's ox or sheep gone astray, do not ignore it; you must take it back to your fellow. <sup>2</sup>If your fellow does not live near you or you do not know who he is, you shall bring it home and it shall remain with you until your fellow claims it; then you shall give it back to him. <sup>3</sup>You shall do the same with his ass; you shall do the same with his garment; and so too shall you do with anything that your fellow loses and you find: you must not remain indifferent.

<sup>4</sup>If you see your fellow's ass or ox fallen on the road, do not ignore it; you must help him raise it.

<sup>5</sup>A woman must not put on man's apparel, nor shall a man wear woman's clothing; for whoever does these things is abhorrent to the LORD your God.

<sup>6</sup>If, along the road, you chance upon a bird's nest, in any tree or on the ground, with fledglings or eggs and the mother sitting over the fledglings or on the eggs, do not take the mother together with her young. <sup>7</sup>Let the mother go, and take only the young, in order that you may fare well and have a long life.

<sup>8</sup>When you build a new house, you shall make a parapet for your roof, so that you do not bring bloodguilt on your house if anyone should fall from it.

<sup>9</sup>You shall not sow your vineyard with a second kind of seed, else the crop—from the seed you have sown—and the yield of

the vineyard may not be used. ¹⁰You shall not plow with an ox and an ass together. ¹¹You shall not wear cloth combining wool and linen.

¹²You shall make tassels on the four corners of the garment with which you cover yourself.

¹³A man marries a woman and cohabits with her. Then he takes an aversion to her ¹⁴and makes up charges against her and defames her, saying, "I married this woman; but when I approached her, I found that she was not a virgin." ¹⁵In such a case, the girl's father and mother shall produce the evidence of the girl's virginity before the elders of the town at the gate. ¹⁶And the girl's father shall say to the elders, "I gave this man my daughter to wife, but he has taken an aversion to her; ¹⁷so he has made up charges, saying, 'I did not find your daughter a virgin.' But here is the evidence of my daughter's virginity!" And they shall spread out the cloth before the elders of the town. ¹⁸The elders of that town shall then take the man and flog him, ¹⁹and they shall fine him a hundred [shekels of] silver and give it to the girl's father; for the man has defamed a virgin in Israel. Moreover, she shall remain his wife; he shall never have the right to divorce her.

²⁰But if the charge proves true, the girl was found not to have been a virgin, ²¹then the girl shall be brought out to the entrance of her father's house, and the men of her town shall stone her to death; for she did a shameful thing in Israel, committing fornication while under her father's authority. Thus you will sweep away evil from your midst.

²²If a man is found lying with another man's wife, both of them—the man and the woman with whom he lay—shall die. Thus you will sweep away evil from Israel.

²³In the case of a virgin who is ᵃ‑engaged to a manᵃ—if a man comes upon her in town and lies with her, ²⁴you shall take the two of them out to the gate of that town and stone them to

---

a-a *I.e. for whom a bride-price had been paid; see 20.7*

death: the girl because she did not cry for help in the town, and the man because he violated another man's wife. Thus you will sweep away evil from your midst. ²⁵But if the man comes upon the engaged girl in the open country, and the man lies with her by force, only the man who lay with her shall die, ²⁶but you shall do nothing to the girl. The girl did not incur the death penalty, for this case is like that of a man attacking another and murdering him. ²⁷He came upon her in the open; though the engaged girl cried for help, there was no one to save her.

²⁸If a man comes upon a virgin who is not engaged and he seizes her and lies with her, and they are discovered, ²⁹the man who lay with her shall pay the girl's father fifty [shekels of] silver and she shall be his wife. Because he has violated her, he ca never have the right to divorce her.

**23** No man shall marry his father's former wife, so as ᵃ remove his father's garment.⁻ᵃ

²No one whose testes are crushed or whose member is cut shall be admitted into the congregation of the LORD.

³No one misbegottenᵇ shall be admitted into the congregat of the LORD; none of his descendants, even in the tenth ¡ eration, shall be admitted into the congregation of the LOR

⁴No Ammonite or Moabite shall be admitted into the gregation of the LORD; none of their descendants, even in tenth generation, shall ever be admitted into the congreg of the LORD, ⁵because they did not meet you with food water on your journey after you left Egypt, and because hired Balaam son of Beor, from Pethor of Aram-nahara curse you.—⁶But the LORD your God refused to heed B¡ instead, the LORD your God turned the curse into a bless¡ you, for the LORD your God loves you.—⁷You shall nev cern yourself with their welfare or benefit as long as you

⁸You shall not abhor an Edomite, for he is your kinsm¡

---

ᵃ⁻ᵃ *I.e. lay claim to what his father had possessed. See Lev. 18.8, 20.11;*
*Ruth 3.9*
ᵇ *Meaning of Heb* mamzer *uncertain; in Jewish law, the offspring of adul*
*between Jews*

shall not abhor an Egyptian, for you were a stranger in his land.
⁹Children born to them may be admitted into the congregation
of the Lord in the third generation.ᶜ

¹⁰When you go out as a troop against your enemies, be on
your guard against anything untoward. ¹¹If anyone among you
has been rendered unclean by a nocturnal emission, he must
leave the camp, and he must not reenter the camp. ¹²Toward
evening he shall bathe in water, and at sundown he may reenter
the camp. ¹³Further, there shall be an area for you outside the
camp, where you may relieve yourself. ¹⁴With your gear you
shall have a spike, and when you have squatted you shall dig a
hole with it and cover up your excrement. ¹⁵Since the Lord
your God moves about in your camp to protect you and to
deliver your enemies to you, let your camp be holy; let Him not
find anything unseemly among you and turn away from you.

¹⁶You shall not turn over to his master a slave who seeks
refuge with you from his master. ¹⁷He shall live with you in any
place he may choose among the settlements in your midst,
wherever he pleases; you must not ill-treat him.

¹⁸No Israelite woman shall be a cult prostitute, nor shall any
Israelite man be a cult prostitute. ¹⁹You shall not bring the fee of
a whore or the pay of a dogᵈ into the house of the Lord your
God in fulfillment of any vow, for both are abhorrent to the
Lord your God.

²⁰You shall not deduct interest from loans to your countrymen, whether in money or food or anything else that can be
deducted as interest; ²¹but you may deduct interest from loans
to foreigners. Do not deduct interest from loans to your countrymen, so that the Lord your God may bless you in all your
undertakings in the land that you are about to enter and possess.

²²When you make a vow to the Lord your God, do not put off
fulfilling it, for the Lord your God will require it of you, and
you will have incurred guilt; ²³whereas you incur no guilt if you
refrain from vowing. ²⁴You must fulfill what has crossed your

ᶜ *I.e. of residence in Israel's territory*
ᵈ *I.e. a male prostitute*

lips and perform what you have voluntarily vowed to the LORD your God, having made the promise with your own mouth.

25When you enter another man's vineyard, you may eat as many grapes as you want, until you are full, but you must not put any in your vessel. 26When you enter another man's field of standing grain, you may pluck ears with your hand; but you must not put a sickle to your neighbor's grain.

**24** A man takes a wife and possesses her. She fails to please him because he finds something obnoxious about her, and he writes her a bill of divorcement, hands it to her, and sends her away from his house; 2she leaves his household and becomes the wife of another man; 3then this latter man rejects her, writes her a bill of divorcement, hands it to her, and sends her away from his house; or the man who married her last dies. 4Then the first husband who divorced her shall not take her to wife again, since she has been defiled*a*—for that would be abhorrent to the LORD. You must not bring sin upon the land that the LORD your God is giving you as a heritage.

5When a man has taken a bride, he shall not go out with the army or be assigned to it for any purpose; he shall be exempt one year for the sake of his household, to give happiness to the woman he has married.

6A handmill or an upper millstone shall not be taken in pawn, for that would be taking someone's life in pawn.

7If a man is found to have kidnapped a fellow Israelite, enslaving him or selling him, that kidnapper shall die; thus you will sweep out evil from your midst.

8In cases of a skin affection*b* be most careful to do exactly as the levitical priests instruct you. Take care to do as I have commanded them. 9Remember what the LORD your God did to Miriam on the journey after you left Egypt.*c*

10When you make a loan of any sort to your countryman, you must not enter his house to seize his pledge. 11You must remain

---

a *I.e. disqualified for him*
b *Cf. Lev. 13.1 ff.*
c *See Num. 12.10 ff.*

outside, while the man to whom you made the loan brings the pledge out to you. [12]If he is a needy man, you shall not go to sleep in his pledge; [13]you must return the pledge to him at sundown, that he may sleep in his cloth and bless you; and it will be to your merit before the LORD your God.

[14]You shall not abuse a needy and destitute laborer, whether a fellow countryman or a stranger in one of the communities of your land. [15]You must pay him his wages on the same day, before the sun sets, for he is needy and urgently depends on it; else he will cry to the LORD against you and you will incur guilt.

[16]Parents shall not be put to death for children, nor children be put to death for parents: a person shall be put to death only for his own crime.

[17]You shall not subvert the rights of the stranger or the fatherless; you shall not take a widow's garment in pawn. [18]Remember that you were a slave in Egypt and that the LORD your God redeemed you from there; therefore do I enjoin you to observe this commandment.

[19]When you reap the harvest in your field and overlook a sheaf in the field, do not turn back to get it; it shall go to the stranger, the fatherless, and the widow—in order that the LORD your God may bless you in all your undertakings.

[20]When you beat down the fruit of your olive trees, do not go over them again; that shall go to the stranger, the fatherless, and the widow. [21]When you gather the grapes of your vineyard, do not pick it over again; that shall go to the stranger, the fatherless, and the widow. [22]Always remember that you were a slave in the land of Egypt; therefore do I enjoin you to observe this commandment.

25 When there is a dispute between men and they go to law, and a decision is rendered declaring the one in the right and the other in the wrong—[2]if the guilty one is to be flogged, the magistrate shall have him lie down and be given lashes in his presence, by count, as his guilt warrants. [3]He may be given up to

forty lashes, but not more, lest being flogged further, to excess, your brother be degraded before your eyes.

⁴You shall not muzzle an ox while it is threshing.

⁵When brothers dwell together and one of them dies and leaves no son, the wife of the deceased shall not be married to a stranger, outside the family. Her husband's brother shall unite with her: he shall take her as his wife and perform the levir's duty. ⁶The first son that she bears shall be accounted to the dead brother, that his name may not be blotted out in Israel. ⁷But if the man does not want to marry his brother's widow, his brother's widow shall appear before the elders in the gate and declare, "My husband's brother refuses to establish a name in Israel for his brother; he will not perform the duty of a levir." ⁸The elders of his town shall then summon him and talk to him. If he insists, saying, "I do not want to marry her," ⁹his brother's widow shall go up to him in the presence of the elders, pull the sandal off his foot, spit in his face, and make this declaration: Thus shall be done to the man who will not build up his brother's house! ¹⁰And he shall go in Israel by the name of "the family of the unsandaled one."

¹¹If two men get into a fight with each other, and the wife of one comes up to save her husband from his antagonist and puts out her hand and seizes him by his genitals, ¹²you shall cut off her hand; show no pity.

¹³You shall not have in your pouch alternate weights, larger and smaller. ¹⁴You shall not have in your house alternate measures, a larger and a smaller. ¹⁵You must have completely honest weights and completely honest measures, if you are to endure long on the soil that the LORD your God is giving you. ¹⁶For everyone who does those things, everyone who deals dishonestly, is abhorrent to the LORD your God.

¹⁷Remember what Amalek did to you on your journey, after you left Egypt—¹⁸how, undeterred by fear of God, he surprised you on the march, when you were famished and weary, and cut

down all the stragglers in your rear. [19]Therefore, when the LORD your God grants you safety from all your enemies around you, in the land that the LORD your God is giving you as a hereditary portion, you shall blot out the memory of Amalek from under heaven. Do not forget!

כי תבוא

26 When you enter the land that the LORD your God is giving you as a heritage, and you possess it and settle in it, [2]you shall take some of every first fruit of the soil, which you harvest from the land that the LORD your God is giving you, put it in a basket and go to the place where the LORD your God will choose to establish His name. [3]You shall go to the priest in charge at that time and say to him, "I acknowledge this day before the LORD your God that I have entered the land that the LORD swore to our fathers to assign us."

[4]The priest shall take the basket from your hand and set it down in front of the altar of the LORD your God.

[5]You shall then recite as follows before the LORD your God: "My father was a fugitive Aramean. He went down to Egypt with meager numbers and sojourned there; but there he became a great and very populous nation. [6]The Egyptians dealt harshly with us and oppressed us; they imposed heavy labor upon us. [7]We cried to the LORD, the God of our fathers, and the LORD heard our plea and saw our plight, our misery, and our oppression. [8]The LORD freed us from Egypt by a mighty hand, by an outstretched arm and awesome power, and by signs and portents. [9]He brought us to this place and gave us this land, a land flowing with milk and honey. [10]Wherefore I now bring the first fruits of the soil which You, O LORD, have given me."

You shall leave it[a] before the LORD your God and bow low before the LORD your God. [11]And you shall enjoy, together with the Levite and the stranger in your midst, all the bounty that the LORD your God has bestowed upon you and your household.

[12]When you have set aside in full the tenth part of your

---

a *I.e. the basket of v. 4*

yield—in the third year, the year of the tithe[b]—and have given it to the Levite, the stranger, the fatherless, and the widow, that they may eat their fill in your settlements, [13]you shall declare before the Lord your God: "I have cleared out the consecrated portion from the house; and I have given it to the Levite, the stranger, the fatherless, and the widow, just as You commanded me; I have neither transgressed nor neglected any of Your commandments:[c] [14] 'I have not eaten of it while in mourning, I have not cleared out any of it while I was unclean, and I have not deposited any of it with the dead.[d] I have obeyed the Lord my God; I have done just as You commanded me. [15]Look down from Your holy abode, from heaven, and bless Your people Israel and the soil You have given us, a land flowing with milk and honey, as You swore to our fathers."

[16]The Lord your God commands you this day to observe these laws and rules; observe them faithfully with all your heart and soul. [17]You have affirmed[e] this day that the Lord is your God, that you will walk in His ways, that you will observe His laws and commandments and rules, and that you will obey Him. [18]And the Lord has affirmed[e] this day that you are, as He promised you, His treasured people who shall observe all His commandments, [19]and that He will set you, in fame and renown and glory, high above all the nations that He has made; and that you shall be, as He promised, a holy people to the Lord your God.

# 27

Moses and the elders of Israel charged the people, saying: Observe all the Instruction that I enjoin upon you this day. [2] [a]As soon as you have crossed the Jordan into the land that the Lord your God is giving you, you shall set up large stones. Coat them with plaster [3]and inscribe upon them all the words of this Teaching. When you cross over to enter the land that the Lord your God is giving you, a land flowing with milk and honey, as the Lord, the God of your fathers, promised you—[4]upon crossing

---

[b] *See Deut. 14.28–29*   [c] *Meaning of first part of verse uncertain*

[d] *No part of the tithe may be left as food for the dead*

[e] *Exact nuance of Heb uncertain*

[a] *Construction of vv. 2–4 uncertain*

the Jordan, you shall set up these stones, about which I charge you this day, on Mount Ebal, and coat them with plaster. ⁵There, too, you shall build an altar to the LORD your God, an altar of stones. Do not wield an iron tool over them; ⁶you must build the altar of the LORD your God of unhewn*ᵇ* stones. You shall offer on it burnt offerings to the LORD your God, ⁷and you shall sacrifice there offerings of well-being and eat them, rejoicing before the LORD your God. ⁸And on those stones you shall inscribe every word of this Teaching most distinctly.

⁹Moses and the levitical priests spoke to all Israel, saying: Silence! Hear, O Israel! Today you have become the people of the LORD your God: ¹⁰Heed the LORD your God and observe His commandments and His laws, which I enjoin upon you this day.

¹¹Thereupon Moses charged the people, saying: ¹² *ᶜ*After you have crossed the Jordan, the following shall stand on Mount Gerizim when the blessing for the people is spoken: Simeon, Levi, Judah, Issachar, Joseph, and Benjamin. ¹³And for the curse, the following shall stand on Mount Ebal: Reuben, Gad, Asher, Zebulun, Dan, and Naphthali. ¹⁴The Levites shall then proclaim in a loud voice to all the people of Israel:

¹⁵Cursed be anyone who makes a sculptured or molten image, abhorred by the LORD, a craftsman's handiwork, and sets it up in secret.—And all the people shall respond, Amen.

¹⁶Cursed be he who insults his father or mother.—And all the people shall say, Amen.

¹⁷Cursed be he who moves his fellow countryman's landmark.—And all the people shall say, Amen.

¹⁸Cursed be he who misdirects a blind person on his way.—And all the people shall say, Amen.

¹⁹Cursed be he who subverts the rights of the stranger, the fatherless, and the widow.—And all the people shall say, Amen.

²⁰Cursed be he who lies with his father's wife, for he has removed his father's garment.*ᵈ*—And all the people shall say, Amen.

---

ᵇ *Lit. "whole"*
ᶜ *Construction of vv. 12–13 uncertain*
ᵈ *See note at 23.1*

²¹Cursed be he who lies with any beast.—And all the people shall say, Amen.

²²Cursed be he who lies with his sister, whether daughter of his father or of his mother.—And all the people shall say, Amen.

²³Cursed be he who lies with his mother-in-law.—And all the people shall say, Amen.

²⁴Cursed be he who strikes down his fellow countryman in secret.—And all the people shall say, Amen.

²⁵Cursed be he who accepts a bribe *ᵉin the case of the murder ofᵉ* an innocent person.—And all the people shall say, Amen.

²⁶Cursed be he who will not uphold the terms of this Teaching and observe them.—And all the people shall say, Amen.

**28** Now, if you obey the LORD your God, to observe faithfully all His commandments which I enjoin upon you this day, the LORD your God will set you high above all the nations of the earth. ²All these blessings shall come upon you and take effect, if you will but heed the word of the LORD your God:

³Blessed shall you be in the city and blessed shall you be in the country.

⁴Blessed shall be the issue of your womb, the produce of your soil, and the offspring of your cattle, the calving of your herd and the lambing of your flock.

⁵Blessed shall be your basket and your kneading bowl.

⁶Blessed shall you be in your comings and blessed shall you be in your goings.

⁷The LORD will put to rout before you the enemies who attack you; they will march out against you by a single road, but flee from you by many*ᵃ* roads. ⁸The LORD will ordain blessings for you upon your barns and upon all your undertakings: He will bless you in the land that the LORD your God is giving you. ⁹The LORD will establish you as His holy people, as He swore to you, if you keep the commandments of the LORD your God and walk in

---

ᵉ⁻ᵉ *I.e. to acquit the murderer; others "to slay"*

ᵃ *Lit. "seven"*

His ways. [10]And all the peoples of the earth shall see that the LORD's name is proclaimed over you,[b] and they shall stand in fear of you. [11]The LORD will give you abounding prosperity in the issue of your womb, the offspring of your cattle, and the produce of your soil in the land that the LORD swore to your fathers to assign to you. [12]The LORD will open for you His bounteous store, the heavens, to provide rain for your land in season and to bless all your undertakings. You will be creditor to many nations, but debtor to none.

[13]The LORD will make you the head, not the tail; you will always be at the top and never at the bottom—if only you obey and faithfully observe the commandments of the LORD your God that I enjoin upon you this day, [14]and do not deviate to the right or to the left from any of the commandments that I enjoin upon you this day and turn to the worship of other gods.

[15]But if you do not obey the LORD your God to observe faithfully all His commandments and laws which I enjoin upon you this day, all these curses shall come upon you and take effect:

[16]Cursed shall you be in the city and cursed shall you be in the country.

[17]Cursed shall be your basket and your kneading bowl.

[18]Cursed shall be the issue of your womb and the produce of your soil, the calving of your herd and the lambing of your flock.

[19]Cursed shall you be in your comings and cursed shall you be in your goings.

[20]The LORD will let loose against you calamity, panic, and frustration in all the enterprises you undertake, so that you shall soon be utterly wiped out because of your evildoing in forsaking Me. [21]The LORD will make pestilence cling to you, until He has put an end to you in the land that you are entering to possess. [22]The LORD will strike you with [c]consumption, fever, and inflammation, with scorching heat and drought, with blight and

---

[b] *I.e. the LORD recognizes you as His own; cf. Isa. 4.1*
[c] *Exact nature of these afflictions uncertain*

mildew; they shall hound you until you perish. [23]The skies above your head shall be copper and the earth under you iron. [24]The LORD will make the rain of your land dust, and sand shall drop on you from the sky, until you are wiped out.

[25]The LORD will put you to rout before your enemies; you shall march out against them by a single road, but flee from them by many roads; and you shall become a horror to all the kingdoms of the earth. [26]Your carcasses shall become food for all the birds of the sky and all the beasts of the earth, with none to frighten them off.

[27]The LORD will strike you with the Egyptian inflammation,[d] with hemorrhoids, boil-scars, and itch, from which you shall never recover.

[28]The LORD will strike you with madness, blindness, and dismay.[e] [29]You shall grope at noon as a blind man gropes in the dark; you shall not prosper in your ventures, but shall be constantly abused and robbed, with none to give help.

[30]If you pay the bride-price for a wife, another man shall enjoy her. If you build a house, you shall not live in it. If you plant a vineyard, you shall not harvest it.[f] [31]Your ox shall be slaughtered before your eyes, but you shall not eat of it; your ass shall be seized in front of you, and it shall not be returned to you; your flock shall be delivered to your enemies, with none to help you. [32]Your sons and daughters shall be delivered to another people, while you look on; and your eyes shall strain for them constantly, but you shall be helpless. [33]A people you do not know shall eat up the produce of your soil and all your gains; you shall be abused and downtrodden continually, [34]until you are driven mad by what your eyes behold. [35]The LORD will afflict you at the knees and thighs with a severe inflammation, from which you shall never recover—from the sole of your foot to the crown of your head.

[36]The LORD will drive you, and the king you have set over you, to a nation unknown to you or your fathers, where you shall serve other gods, of wood and stone. [37]You shall be a

---

d *See Exod. 9.9–10*
e *Lit. "numbness of heart"*
f *Cf. 20.6*

consternation, a proverb, and a byword among all the peoples to which the LORD will drive you.

38Though you take much seed out to the field, you shall gather in little, for the locust shall consume it. 39Though you plant vineyards and till them, you shall have no wine to drink or store, for the worm shall devour them. 40Though you have olive trees throughout your territory, you shall have no oil for anointment, for your olives shall drop off. 41Though you beget sons and daughters, they shall not remain with you, for they shall go into captivity. 42The cricket shall take over all the trees and produce of your land.

43The stranger in your midst shall rise above you higher and higher, while you sink lower and lower: 44he shall be your creditor, but you shall not be his; he shall be the head and you the tail.

45All these curses shall befall you; they shall pursue you and overtake you, until you are wiped out, because you did not heed the LORD your God and keep the commandments and laws that He enjoined upon you. 46They shall serve as signs and proofs against you and your offspring for all time. 47Because you would not serve the LORD your God in joy and gladness over the abundance of everything, 48you shall have to serve—in hunger and thirst, naked and lacking everything—the enemies whom the LORD will let loose against you. He will put an iron yoke upon your neck until He has wiped you out.

49The LORD will bring a nation against you from afar, from the end of the earth, which will swoop down like the eagle—a nation whose language you do not understand, 50a ruthless nation, that will show the old no regard and the young no mercy. 51It shall devour the offspring of your cattle and the produce of your soil, until you have been wiped out, leaving you nothing of new grain, wine, or oil, of the calving of your herds and the lambing of your flocks, until it has brought you to ruin. 52It shall shut you up in all your towns throughout your land until every mighty, towering wall in which you trust has come down. And when you are shut up in all your towns throughout your land that the LORD your God has assigned to you, <sup>53</sup>you shall eat your own issue, the flesh of your sons and daughters that the LORD your God has assigned to you, because of the desperate straits to which your enemy shall reduce you. <sup>54</sup>He who is most tender and fastidious among you shall be too mean to his brother and the wife of his bosom and the children he has spared <sup>55</sup>to share with any of them the flesh of the children that he eats, because he has nothing else left as a result of the desperate straits to which your enemy shall reduce you in all your towns. <sup>56</sup>And she who is most tender and dainty among you, so tender and dainty that she would never venture to set a foot on the ground, shall begrudge the husband of her bosom, and her son and her daughter, <sup>57</sup>the afterbirth that issues from between her legs and the babies she bears; she shall eat them secretly, because of utter want, in the desperate straits to which your enemy shall reduce you in your towns.

<sup>58</sup>If you fail to observe faithfully all the terms of this Teaching that are written in this book, to reverence this honored and awesome Name, the LORD your God, <sup>59</sup>the LORD will inflict extraordinary plagues upon you and your offspring, strange and lasting plagues, malignant and chronic diseases. <sup>60</sup>He will bring back upon you all the sicknesses of Egypt that you dreaded so, and they shall cling to you. <sup>61</sup>Moreover, the LORD will bring upon you all the other diseases and plagues that are not mentioned in this book of Teaching, until you are wiped out. <sup>62</sup>You shall be left a scant few, after having been as numerous as the stars in the skies, because you did not heed the command of the LORD your God. <sup>63</sup>And as the LORD once delighted in making you prosperous and many, so will the LORD now delight in causing you to perish and in wiping you out; you shall be torn from the land that you are about to enter and possess.

<sup>64</sup>The LORD will scatter you among all the peoples from one end of the earth to the other, and there you shall serve other gods, wood and stone, whom neither you nor your ancestors

have experienced.[g] 65Yet even among those nations you shall find no peace, nor shall your foot find a place to rest. The LORD will give you there an anguished heart and eyes that pine and a despondent spirit. 66The life you face shall be precarious; you shall be in terror, night and day, with no assurance of survival. 67In the morning you shall say, "If only it were evening!" and in the evening you shall say, "If only it were morning!"—because of what your heart shall dread and your eyes shall see. 68The LORD will send you back to Egypt in galleys, by a route which I told you you should not see again. There you shall offer yourselves for sale to your enemies as male and female slaves, but none will buy.

69These are the terms of the covenant which the LORD commanded Moses to conclude with the Israelites in the land of Moab, in addition to the covenant which He had made with them at Horeb.

# 29 Moses summoned all Israel and said to them:

You have seen all that the LORD did before your very eyes in the land of Egypt, to Pharaoh and to all his courtiers and to his whole country: 2the wondrous feats that you saw with your own eyes, those prodigious signs and marvels. 3Yet to this day the LORD has not given you a mind to understand or eyes to see or ears to hear.

4I led you through the wilderness forty years; the clothes on your back did not wear out, nor did the sandals on your feet; 5you had no bread to eat and no wine or other intoxicant to drink—that you might know that I the LORD am your God.

6When you reached this place, King Sihon of Heshbon and King Og of Bashan came out to engage us in battle, but we defeated them. 7We took their land and gave it to the Reubenites, the Gadites, and the half-tribe of Manasseh as their heritage. 8Therefore observe faithfully all the terms of this covenant, that you may succeed in all that you undertake.

g *See note at 11.28*

נצבים

⁹You stand this day, all of you, before the LORD your God—your tribal heads, your elders and your officials, all the men of Israel, ¹⁰your children, your wives, even the stranger within your camp, from woodchopper to waterdrawer—¹¹to enter into the covenant of the LORD your God, which the LORD your God is concluding with you this day, with its sanctions*; ¹²to the end that He may establish you this day as His people and be your God, as He promised you and as He swore to your fathers, Abraham, Isaac, and Jacob. ¹³I make this covenant, with its sanctions, not with you alone, ¹⁴but both with those who are standing here with us this day before the LORD our God and with those who are not with us here this day.

¹⁵Well you know that we dwelt in the land of Egypt and that we passed through the midst of various other nations; ¹⁶and you have seen the detestable things and the fetishes of wood and stone, silver and gold, that they keep. ¹⁷Perchance there is among you some man or woman, or some clan or tribe, whose heart is even now turning away from the LORD our God to go and worship the gods of those nations—perchance there is among you a stock sprouting poison weed and wormwood. ¹⁸When such a one hears the words of these sanctions, he may fancy himself immune, thinking, "I shall be safe, though I follow my own willful heart"—to the utter ruin of moist and dry alike.*

¹⁹The LORD will never forgive him; rather will the LORD's anger and passion rage against that man, till every sanction recorded in this book comes down upon him, and the LORD blots out his name from under heaven.

²⁰The LORD will single them* out from all the tribes of Israel for misfortune, in accordance with all the sanctions of the covenant recorded in this book of Teaching. ²¹And later generations will ask—the children who succeed you, and foreigners who come from distant lands and see the plagues and diseases that the LORD has inflicted upon that land, ²²all its soil devastated by sulfur and salt, beyond sowing and producing, no

---

ª *I.e. the curses that violations of the covenant will entail*
ᵇ *I.e. everything*
ᶜ *I.e. clan or tribe, v. 17*

grass growing in it, just like the upheaval of Sodom and Gomorrah, Admah and Zeboiim, which the Lord overthrew in His fierce anger—²³all nations will ask, "Why did the Lord do thus to this land? Wherefore that awful wrath?" ²⁴They will be told, "Because they forsook the covenant that the Lord, God of their fathers, made with them when He freed them from the land of Egypt; ²⁵they turned to the service of other gods and worshiped them, gods whom they had not experienced*ᵈ* and whom He had not allotted*ᵉ* to them. ²⁶So the Lord was incensed at that land and brought upon it all the curses recorded in this book. ²⁷The Lord uprooted them from their soil in anger, fury, and great wrath, and cast them into another land, as is still the case."

²⁸Concealed acts concern the Lord our God; but with overt acts, it is for us and our children ever to apply all the provisions of this Teaching.

# 30

When all these things befall you—the blessing and the curse that I have set before you—and you take them to heart amidst the various nations to which the Lord your God has banished you, ²and you return to the Lord your God, and you and your children heed His command with all your heart and soul, just as I enjoin upon you this day, ³then the Lord your God will restore your fortunes*ᵃ* and take you back in love. He will bring you together again from all the peoples where the Lord your God has scattered you. ⁴Even if your outcasts are at the ends of the world,*ᵇ* from there the Lord your God will gather you, from there He will fetch you. ⁵And the Lord your God will bring you to the land that your fathers possessed, and you shall possess it; and He will make you more prosperous and more numerous than your fathers.

⁶Then the Lord your God will open up*ᶜ* your heart and the hearts of your offspring to love the Lord your God with all your heart and soul, in order that you may live. ⁷The Lord your God

---

ᵈ *See note at 11.28*
ᵉ *See 4.19–20*

ᵃ *Others "captivity"*
ᵇ *Lit. "sky"*   ᶜ *Others "circumcise"*

will inflict all those curses upon the enemies and foes who persecuted you. ⁸You, however, will again heed the LORD and obey all His commandments that I enjoin upon you this day. ⁹And the LORD your God will grant you abounding prosperity in all your undertakings, in the issue of your womb, the offspring of your cattle, and the produce of your soil. For the LORD will again delight in your well-being, as He did in that of your fathers, ¹⁰since you will be heeding the LORD your God and keeping His commandments and laws that are recorded in this book of the Teaching—once you return to the LORD your God with all your heart and soul.

¹¹Surely, this Instruction which I enjoin upon you this day is not too baffling for you, nor is it beyond reach. ¹²It is not in the heavens, that you should say, "Who among us can go up to the heavens and get it for us and impart it to us, that we may observe it?" ¹³Neither is it beyond the sea, that you should say, "Who among us can cross to the other side of the sea and get it for us and impart it to us, that we may observe it?" ¹⁴No, the thing is very close to you, in your mouth and in your heart, to observe it.

¹⁵See, I set before you this day life and prosperity, death and adversity. ¹⁶For*ᵈ* I command you this day, to love the LORD your God, to walk in His ways, and to keep His commandments, His laws, and His rules, that you may thrive and increase, and that the LORD your God may bless you in the land that you are about to enter and possess. ¹⁷But if your heart turns away and you give no heed, and are lured into the worship and service of other gods, ¹⁸I declare to you this day that you shall certainly perish; you shall not long endure on the soil that you are crossing the Jordan to enter and possess. ¹⁹I call heaven and earth to witness against you this day: I have put before you life and death, blessing and curse. Choose life—if you and your offspring would live—²⁰by loving the LORD your God, heeding His commands, and holding fast to Him. For thereby you shall have life and shall long endure upon the soil that the LORD swore to your ancestors, Abraham, Isaac, and Jacob, to give to them.

---

ᵈ *Septuagint reads "If you obey the commandments of the LORD your God, which"*

וילך

**31** *a-*Moses went and spoke*-a* these things to all Israel. ²He said to them:

I am now one hundred and twenty years old, I can no longer *b-*be active.*-b* Moreover, the LORD has said to me, "You shall not go across yonder Jordan." ³The LORD your God Himself will cross over before you; and He Himself will wipe out those nations from your path and you shall dispossess them.—Joshua is the one who shall cross before you, as the LORD has spoken.— ⁴The LORD will do to them as He did to Sihon and Og, kings of the Amorites, and to their countries, when He wiped them out. ⁵The LORD will deliver them up to you, and you shall deal with them in full accordance with the Instruction that I have enjoined upon you. ⁶Be strong and resolute, be not in fear or in dread of them; for the LORD your God Himself marches with you: He will not fail you or forsake you.

⁷Then Moses called Joshua and said to him in the sight of all Israel: "Be strong and resolute, for it is you who shall go with this people into the land that the LORD swore to their fathers to give them, and it is you who shall apportion it to them. ⁸And the LORD Himself will go before you. He will be with you; He will not fail you or forsake you. Fear not and be not dismayed!"

⁹Moses wrote down this Teaching and gave it to the priests, sons of Levi, who carried the Ark of the LORD's Covenant, and to all the elders of Israel.

¹⁰And Moses instructed them as follows: Every seventh year,*c* the year set for remission, at the Feast of Booths, ¹¹when all Israel comes to appear before the LORD your God in the place that He will choose, you shall read this Teaching aloud in the presence of all Israel. ¹²Gather the people—men, women, children, and the strangers in your communities—that they may hear and so learn to revere the LORD your God and to observe faithfully every word of this Teaching. ¹³Their children, too,

---

a-a *An ancient Heb ms. and the Septuagint read: "When Moses had finished speaking . . ."; cf. 29.1*
b-b *Lit. "come and go"*
c *See note at 15.1*

who have not had the experience, shall hear and learn to revere the LORD your God as long as they live in the land that you are about to cross the Jordan to possess.

[14]The LORD said to Moses: The time is drawing near for you to die. Call Joshua and present yourselves in the Tent of Meeting, that I may instruct him. Moses and Joshua went and presented themselves in the Tent of Meeting. [15]The LORD appeared in the Tent, in a pillar of cloud, the pillar of cloud having come to rest at the entrance of the tent.

[16]The LORD said to Moses: You are soon to lie with your fathers. This people will thereupon go astray after the alien gods in their midst, in the land that they are about to enter; they will forsake Me and break My covenant that I made with them. [17]Then My anger will flare up against them, and I will abandon them and hide My countenance from them. They shall be ready prey; and many evils and troubles shall befall them. And they shall say on that day, "Surely it is because our God is not in our midst that these evils have befallen us." [18]Yet I will keep My countenance hidden on that day, because of all the evil they have done in turning to other gods. [19]Therefore, write down this poem and teach it to the people of Israel; put it in their mouths, in order that this poem may be My witness against the people of Israel. [20]When I bring them into the land flowing with milk and honey that I promised on oath to their fathers, and they eat their fill and grow fat and turn to other gods and serve them, spurning Me and breaking My covenant, [21]and the many evils and troubles befall them—then this poem shall confront them as a witness, since it will never be lost from the mouth of their offspring. For I know what plans they are devising even now, before I bring them into the land that I promised on oath.

[22]That day, Moses wrote down this poem and taught it to the Israelites.

[23]And He charged Joshua son of Nun: "Be strong and res-

olute: for you shall bring the Israelites into the land that I promised them on oath, and I will be with you."

²⁴When Moses had put down in writing the words of this Teaching to the very end, ²⁵Moses charged the Levites who carried the Ark of the Covenant of the LORD, saying: ²⁶Take this book of Teaching and place it beside the Ark of the Covenant of the LORD your God, and let it remain there as a witness against you. ²⁷Well I know how defiant and stiffnecked you are: even now, while I am still alive in your midst, you have been defiant toward the LORD; how much more, then, when I am dead! ²⁸Gather to me all the elders of your tribes and your officials, that I may speak all these words to them and that I may call heaven and earth to witness against them. ²⁹For I know that, when I am dead, you will act wickedly and turn away from the path that I enjoined upon you, and that in time to come misfortune will befall you for having done evil in the sight of the LORD and vexed Him by your deeds.

³⁰Then Moses recited the words of this poem to the very end, in the hearing of the whole congregation of Israel:

האזינו

**32** Give ear, O heavens, let me speak;
Let the earth hear the words I utter!
²May my discourse come down as the rain,
My speech distill as the dew,
Like showers on young growth,
Like droplets on the grass.ᵃ
³For the name of the LORD I proclaim;
Give glory to our God!

⁴The Rock!—His deeds are perfect,
Yea, all His ways are just;
A faithful God, never false,
True and upright is He.
⁵ ᵇChildren unworthy of Him—
That crooked, perverse generation—

---

ᵃ *I.e. may my words be received eagerly; cf. Job 29.22–23*
ᵇ *Meaning of Heb uncertain*

Their baseness has played Him false.
⁶Do you thus requite the LORD,
O dull and witless people?
Is not He the Father who created you,
Fashioned you and made you endure!

⁷Remember the days of old,
Consider the years of ages past;
Ask your father, he will inform you,
Your elders, they will tell you:
⁸When the Most High gave nations their homes
And set the divisions of man,
He fixed the boundaries of peoples
In relation to Israel's numbers.
⁹For the LORD's portion is His people,
Jacob His own allotment.

¹⁰He found him in a desert region,
In an empty howling waste.
He engirded him, watched over him,
Guarded him as the pupil of His eye.
¹¹Like an eagle who rouses his nestlings,
Gliding down to his young,
So did He spread His wings and take him,
Bear him along on His pinions;
¹²The LORD alone did guide him,
No alien god at His side.

¹³He set him atop the highlands,
To feast on the yield of the earth;
He fed him honey from the crag,
And oil from the flinty rock,
¹⁴Curd of kine and milk of flocks;
With the best^c of lambs,
And rams of Bashan, and he-goats;
With the ^d-very finest^d wheat—
And foaming grape-blood was your drink.

---

^c *Lit. "fat"*
d-d *"kidney fat of"*

397

<sup>15</sup>So Jeshurun grew fat and kicked—
You grew fat and gross and coarse<sup>e</sup>—
He forsook the God who made him
And spurned the Rock of his support.
<sup>16</sup>They incensed Him with alien things,
Vexed Him with abominations.
<sup>17</sup>They sacrificed to demons, no-gods,
Gods they had never known,
New ones, who came but lately,
<sup>f</sup>Who stirred not your fathers' fears.<sup>f</sup>
<sup>18</sup>You neglected the Rock that begot you,
Forgot the God who brought you forth.

<sup>19</sup>The LORD saw and was vexed
And spurned His sons and His daughters.
<sup>20</sup>He said:
I will hide My countenance from them,
And see how they fare in the end.
For they are a treacherous breed,
Children with no loyalty in them.
<sup>21</sup>They incensed Me with no-gods,
Vexed Me with their futilities; <sup>g</sup>
I'll incense them with a no-folk,
Vex them with a nation of fools.
<sup>22</sup>For a fire has flared in My wrath
And burned to the bottom of Sheol,
Has consumed the earth and its increase,
Eaten down to the base of the hills.
<sup>23</sup>I will sweep<sup>e</sup> misfortunes on them,
Use up My arrows on them:
<sup>24</sup>Wasting famine, ravaging plague,
Deadly pestilence, and fanged beasts
Will I let loose against them,
With venomous creepers in dust.
<sup>25</sup>The sword shall deal death without,

---

<sup>e</sup> *Meaning of Heb uncertain*
<sup>f-f</sup> *Meaning of Heb uncertain. Arabic* sha'ara *suggests the rendering, "Whom your fathers did not know"*
<sup>g</sup> *I.e. idols*

As shall the terror within,
To youth and maiden alike,
The suckling as well as the aged.

²⁶ʰ⁻I might have reduced them to naught,⁻ʰ
Made their memory cease among men,
²⁷But for fear of the taunts of the foe,
Their enemies who might misjudge
And say, "Our own hand has prevailed;
None of this was wrought by the LORD!"
²⁸ ⁱFor they are a folk void of sense,
Lacking in all discernment.
²⁹Were they wise, they would think upon this,
Gain insight into their future:
³⁰"How could one have routed a thousand,
Or two put ten thousand to flight,
Unless their Rock had sold them,
The LORD had given them up?"
³¹For their rock is not like our Rock,
ʲ⁻In our enemies' ownᵏ estimation.⁻ʲ

³²Ah! The vine for them is from Sodom,
From the vineyards of Gomorrah;
The grapes for them are poison,
A bitter growth their clusters.
³³Their wine is the venom of asps,
The pitiless poison of vipers.
³⁴Lo, I have it all put away,
Sealed up in My storehouses,
³⁵To be My vengeance and recompense,
At the time that their foot falters.
Yea, their day of disaster is near,
And destiny rushes upon them.

³⁶For the LORD will vindicate His people
ˡ⁻And take revenge for⁻ˡ His servants,

---

ʰ⁻ʰ *Lit. "I said, I will reduce . . ."; meaning of Heb* 'aph'ehem *uncertain*
ⁱ *Here, apparently, Moses is the speaker; God resumes in v. 32*
ʲ⁻ʲ *I.e. as everyone must admit*   ᵏ *For Heb* pelilim *see Exod. 21.22; cf. Gen. 48.11*
ˡ⁻ˡ *Cf. Isa. 1.24. Others "and repent Himself concerning"*

When He sees that their might is gone,
And neither bond nor free is left.
³⁷He will say: Where are their gods,
The rock in whom they sought refuge,
³⁸Who ate the fat of their offerings
And drank their libation wine?
Let them rise up to your help,
And let them be a shield unto you!
³⁹See, then, that I, I am He;
There is no god beside Me.
I deal death and give life;
I wounded and I will heal:
None can deliver from My hand.
⁴⁰Lo, I raise My hand to heaven
And say: As I live forever,
⁴¹When I whet My flashing blade
And My hand lays hold on judgment,
Vengeance will I wreak on My foes,
Will I deal to those who reject Me.
⁴²I will make My arrows drunk with blood—
As My sword devours flesh—
Blood of the slain and the captive
From the long-haired enemy chiefs.

⁴³O nations, acclaim His people!
For He'll avenge the blood of His servants,
Wreak vengeance on His foes,
And cleanse the land of His people.ᵐ

⁴⁴Moses came, together with Hosea son of Nun, and recited all the words of this poem in the hearing of the people.

⁴⁵And when Moses finished reciting all these words to all Israel, ⁴⁶he said to them: Take to heart all the words with which I have warned you this day. Enjoin them upon your children,

---

ᵐ Cf. Num. 35.33 Meaning of Heb uncertain; Ugaritic 'udmᶜt "tears" suggests the rendering "And wipe away His people's tears." Cf. Isa. 25.8

that they may observe faithfully all the terms of this Teaching. ⁴⁷For this is not a trifling thing for you: it is your very life; through it you shall long endure on the land that you are to possess upon crossing the Jordan.

⁴⁸That very day the LORD spoke to Moses: ⁴⁹Ascend these heights of Abarim to Mount Nebo, which is in the land of Moab facing Jericho, and view the land of Canaan, which I am giving the Israelites as their holding. ⁵⁰You shall die on the mountain that you are about to ascend, and shall be gathered to your kin, as your brother Aaron died on Mount Hor and was gathered to his kin; ⁵¹for you both broke faith with Me among the Israelite people, at the waters of Meribath-kadesh in the wilderness of Zin, by failing to uphold My sanctity among the Israelite people. ⁵²You may view the land from a distance, but you shall not enter it—the land that I am giving to the Israelite people.

וזאת הברכה

**33** This is the blessing with which Moses, the man of God, bade the Israelites farewell before he died. ²He said:

The LORD came from Sinai;
He shone upon them from Seir;
He appeared from Mount Paran,
And approached from Ribeboth-kodesh,ᵃ
Lightning flashing at them from His right.ᵇ
³ ᶜLover, indeed, of the people,
Their hallowed are all in Your hand.
They followed in Your steps,
Accepting Your pronouncements,
⁴When Moses charged us with the Teaching
As the heritage of the congregation of Jacob.
⁵Then He became King in Jeshurun,
When the heads of the people assembled,
The tribes of Israel together.

---

ᵃ Cf. Meribath-kadesh, 32.51
ᵇ Meaning of Heb mimino 'eshdath uncertain, perhaps a place name
ᶜ The meaning of vv. 3–5 is uncertain. An alternative rendering, with v. 3 apostrophizing Moses, is: ³Then were, O lover of people, / All His worshipers in your care; / They followed your lead, / Accepted your precepts. / ⁴Moses charged us with the Teaching / As the heritage of the congregation of Jacob. / ⁵Thus was he king in Jeshurun . . .

⁶May Reuben live and not die,
Though few be his numbers.

⁷And this he said of Judah:
Hear, O LORD, the voice of Judah
And restore him to his people.
*ᵈ*·Though his own hands strive for him,·*ᵈ*
Help him against his foes.

⁸And of Levi he said:
Let Your Thummim and Urim
Be with Your faithful one,
Whom You tested at Massah,
Challenged at the waters of Meribah;
⁹Who said of his father and mother,
"I consider them not."
His brothers he disregarded,
Ignored his own children.
Your precepts alone they observed,
And kept Your covenant.
¹⁰They shall teach Your laws to Jacob
And Your instructions to Israel.
*ᵉ*·They shall offer You incense to savor·*ᵉ*
And whole-offerings on Your altar.
¹¹Bless, O LORD, his substance,
And favor his undertakings.
Smite the loins of his foes;
Let his enemies rise no more.

¹²Of Benjamin he said:
Beloved of the LORD,
He rests securely beside Him;
Ever does He protect him,
*ᶠ*·As he rests between His shoulders.·*ᶠ*

¹³And of Joseph he said:

---

ᵈ⁻ᵈ *Better (vocalizing* rab *with* pathaḥ) *"Make his hands strong for him." Cf.* rabbeh,
Judg. 9.29
ᵉ⁻ᵉ *Lit. "They shall place incense in Your nostril"*
ᶠ⁻ᶠ *Or "He dwells amid his slopes"*

Blessed of the LORD be his land
With the bounty of dew[g] from heaven,
And of the deep that couches below;
[14]With the bounteous yield of the sun,
And the bounteous crop of the moons;
[15]With the best from the ancient mountains,
And the bounty of hills immemorial;
[16]With the bounty of earth and its fullness,
And the favor of the Presence[h] in the Bush.
May these rest on the head of Joseph,
On the crown of the elect of his brothers.
[17]Like a firstling bull in his majesty,
He has horns like the horns of the wild-ox;
With them he gores the peoples,
The ends of the earth one and all.
These[i] are the myriads of Ephraim,
Those[j] are the thousands of Manasseh.

[18]And of Zebulun he said:

Rejoice, O Zebulun, on your journeys,
And Issachar, in your tents.
[19]They invite their kin to the mountain,
Where they offer sacrifices of success.
For they draw from the riches of the sea
And the hidden hoards of the sand.

[20]And of Gad he said:

Blessed be He who enlarges Gad!
Poised is he like a lion
To tear off arm and scalp.
[21] [k-]He chose for himself the best,
For there is the portion of the revered chieftain,
Where the heads of the people come.
He executed the LORD's judgments
And His decisions for Israel.[-k]

---

[g] *Targum Onkelos and two Hebrew manuscripts read: "With the bounty of heaven above"* (meʿal *for* miṭṭal, cf. Gen. 49.25)

[h] *Lit. "Dweller"; cf. Exod. 3.1 ff.*   [i] *I.e. the one horn*   [j] *I.e. the other horn*

[k-k] *Meaning of Heb uncertain; cf. vv. 3–5 (with note c) above, and* saphun *"esteemed" in post-biblical Heb*

<sup>22</sup>And of Dan he said:
Dan is a lion's whelp
That leaps forth from Bashan.

<sup>23</sup>And of Naphtali he said:
O Naphtali, sated with favor
And full of the LORD's blessing,
Take possession on the west and south.

<sup>24</sup>And of Asher he said:
Most blessed of sons be Asher;
May he be the favorite of his brothers,
May he dip his foot in oil.
<sup>25</sup> <sup>l</sup>May your doorbolts be iron and copper,
And your security last all your days.

<sup>26</sup>O Jeshurun, there is none like God,
Riding through the heavens to help you,
Through the skies in His majesty.
<sup>27</sup> <sup>l</sup>The ancient God is a refuge,
A support are the arms everlasting.
He drove out the enemy before you
By His command: Destroy!
<sup>28</sup>Thus Israel dwells in safety,
Untroubled is Jacob's abode,<sup>m</sup>
In a land of grain and wine,
Under heavens dripping dew.
<sup>29</sup>O happy Israel! Who is like you,
A people delivered by the LORD,
Your protecting Shield, your Sword triumphant!
Your enemies shall come cringing before you,
And you shall tread on their backs.

34 Moses went up from the steppes of Moab to Mount Nebo, to the summit of Pisgah, opposite Jericho, and the LORD showed

---

<sup>l</sup> *Meaning of Heb uncertain*
<sup>m</sup> *Others "fountain"*

him the whole land: Gilead as far as Dan; [2]all Naphtali; the land of Ephraim and Manasseh; the whole land of Judah as far as the Western[a] Sea; [3]the Negeb; and the Plain—the Valley of Jericho, the city of palm trees—as far as Zoar. [4]And the LORD said to him, "This is the land of which I swore to Abraham, Isaac, and Jacob, 'I will assign it to your offspring.' I have let you see it with your own eyes, but you shall not cross there."

[5]So Moses the servant of the LORD died there, in the land of Moab, at the command of the LORD. [6]He buried him in the valley in the land of Moab, near Beth-peor; and no one knows his burial place to this day. [7]Moses was a hundred and twenty years old when he died; his eyes were undimmed and his vigor unabated. [8]And the Israelites bewailed Moses in the steppes of Moab for thirty days.

The period of wailing and mourning for Moses came to an end. [9]Now Joshua son of Nun was filled with the spirit of wisdom because Moses had laid his hands upon him; and the Israelites heeded him, doing as the LORD had commanded Moses.

[10]Never again did there arise in Israel a prophet like Moses— whom the LORD singled out, face to face, [11]for the various signs and portents that the LORD sent him to display in the land of Egypt, against Pharaoh and all his courtiers and his whole country, [12]and for all the great might and awesome power that Moses displayed before all Israel.

חזק חזק ונתחזק

[a] *I.e. Mediterranean; cf. note at 11.24*

# NOTES

# NOTES

# NOTES